£XCLUDED VOICES

First Published in 2021

ISBN:9798713994280

Cover Design by Maria Hennings Hunt

Edited by Mandy Marsh and Maria Hennings Hunt

This book is dedicated to the many lives lost in the Excluded Community through the deliberate policy choices of the British government that failed to support 3 million people in any way, shape or form during the Coronavirus epidemic. We remember them in our hearts, as we who remain fight for the justice and parity we all deserve.

To the wonderful ExcludedUK community on Social Media and particularly our group founders, volunteers and support teams (past and present). I'm honoured to be a small part of this team who I'm proud to call my friends.

Table of Contents

Foreword by Tony Robinson OBE

Hardworking, enterprising, and proud taxpayers

There are 150 voices in this book. Together they tell a horror story. The voices are of the bewildered, heartbroken, betrayed, abandoned, resilient, anxious, hopeful, crushed, angry, inspiring, and despairing.

Each voice deserves to be heard as they represent 3 MILLION ExcludedUK that have received no meaningful income support from the Government since the first Lockdown. Their stories explain why many have taken their own lives, why hundreds say, "most days I want to take my own life", why thousands now live from hand to mouth in a very dark place and why hundreds of thousands need mental health support. All of these brave people need hope.

These hardworking, taxpayers are victims of this Government's perpetual disregard for 5.6 million micro-business owners, including 600,000+ new start-ups each year. They patronise and insult them by calling them 'deadweight', a fraud risk or non-viable.

All these enterprising self-employed people, freelancers, Limited Company directors, business owners and highly skilled employees have been earning their living the right way to survive and thrive. They meet all business and tax laws. The multitude of reasons they have been excluded is perverse, particularly in comparison with furloughed employees and those receiving self-employed Income Support. 'There but for fortune go you or me'.

Victims of discriminatory COVID-19 income support policies, rip-off living costs and a broken welfare system

Those Excluded are victims because merciless discrimination has made them feel 'worthless' or 'punished', yet it is not their fault that they had to stop trading and so have lost their customers and income.

They have all been failed by the welfare system, including the state pension. It is not just people with their own businesses that have been abandoned for spurious reasons like having an employed job, paying themselves from dividends and earning over £50,000. Many have spent the last three tax years as employees that are excluded. Many were not furloughed, many have had a new job terminated during the pandemic, and many are newly self-employed. Most of the voices in this book have not claimed 'benefits' before.

The inadequacy of the financial 'safety net' is as humiliating for them as when Michelle Dorrel, with her home-based nail bar, told Government Minister Amber Rudd on Question Time in 2015 "I voted for you" and you reneged on your promise on tax credits. History repeats itself with this Government. She spoke for hard-working millions of homeworkers who found it impossible to pay for broadband and feed herself and her children.

The claim system itself and the 'digital by default' eligibility rules has shocked and sickened the Excluded as much as it did Katie and Daniel Blake in the film *I, Daniel Blake* in 2016. The cruel reality for those who fall through the cracks of society was laid bare. Millions are now living in a dehumanising and debt-ridden world. Reliance on food banks is tragic. You will read how some have resorted to desperate measures including closing their long-standing businesses, selling valued possessions, homes and, even, their bodies.

You mean hope:

1. By reading their stories, believing them, and supporting their just fight for parity with furloughed employees and those in receipt of self-employed income support

2. By getting behind the major influencers, politicians, and media that Government may listen to. These include 300 MPs, with many like Bill Esterson, Caroline Lucas and Tracy Brabin that have been warriors for many years on behalf of those now Excluded. Thanks to Andy Burnham, Steve Rotherham and Sadiq Khan, all the metro mayors are supporting the ExcludedUK campaigns. Household names like Gina Miller, Martin Lewis and Piers Morgan are trying to influence change. Let them know you're behind them.

3. By acts of kindness to those Excluded, you can make the world of difference. It can be a chat or something more tangible like a purchase of food and drink or a donation to the ExcludedUK hardship fund or mental health support fund.

4. By empowering others to take urgent action. Write to your MP. If you are a member of a small business membership body, trade association, or trade union tell them to be relentless in pursuing justice and parity for ALL 3 million ExcludedUK.

5. By joining in with the 30,000 volunteers on the ExcludedUK Facebook group. Throughout this book, you'll see just how much the activities, the campaigns, the webinars, the banter, and the mutual support have kept the community and the four wonderful co-founders of ExcludedUK going. I loved the virtual choir video and hated the sleepout.

6. By giving this book to someone else, particularly someone in the media. The weekly, £multimillion Government propaganda machine can only be stalled by many more people becoming aware of their inhumane treatment of the 3 million.

Finally, thank you, Stephen

It is the greatest privilege of my lucky and long, enterprising life to have been asked by Stephen to write this foreword.

Stephen's own story is the last one in this book and it is the most bizarre, as his award-winning business, home and life have been destroyed because the Government has deemed he and his employees were too successful. He is surviving, in awful living conditions with mounting health problems, through huge courage and the friendship within the ExcludedUK community.

However cold, and hungry he is, he is relentless, day after day, in supporting the ExcludedUK cause. When I'm allowed to travel to London again, he will be the first person I want to meet. He's a hero and putting this book together is the work of a hero.

His award-winning tour business is based in London and many of the stories you will read liken what has happened to the 3 million Excluded to what is described in Dickens's London. One voice said, "We have been left to hang. Just like how London dealt with the plague, leaving the poor to die in the streets, is exactly how I feel."

The recurring question that is asked in most of these heart-breaking accounts is, "Why is the Government doing this to us?" I think Charles Dickens had the answer to that:

"Thus, cases of injustice, and oppression, and tyranny, and the most extravagant bigotry, are in constant occurrence among us every day.

It is the custom to trumpet forth much wonder and astonishment at the chief actors therein setting at defiance so completely the opinion of the world, but there is no greater fallacy; it is precisely because they do consult the opinion of their little world that such things take place at all, and strike the great world dumb with amazement."

Nicholas Nickelby, Charles Dickens.

Keep #rocking their little, unreal world. Thank you, Stephen, thank you ExcludedUK and all the wonderful contributors to this important book. #YouRock and #MicroBizMatters.

Tony Robinson OBE (not Sir Tony!)

The Micro Business Champion

Introduction

Most discriminations that we have in this world are relics of prejudices and biases centuries or even millennia old. Slowly but surely, these are being both eliminated legally and whittled away culturally and politically. We are fortunate to live in a land and a time where being treated negatively because of our sex, race, age, beliefs (if any) or any impairments, is increasingly legally and morally wrong.

In the spring of 2020 the world fell under the horrors of COVID-19, and life as we knew it came to an end – hopefully only temporarily so. The British Government announced what they would like to call an 'unprecedented' series of support packages when understandably, if belatedly, it was mandated that society had to hunker down. The announced support was very generous to many, though not world-beating or in any measure the best. I was nevertheless surprised that, for perhaps the first time ever in our history, human life was being elevated, at least in some way, above the economy and big business.

Billionaire Chancellor Rishi Sunak famously announced that "No one will be left behind… or without hope". And why would anyone be left behind? Who on earth would deliberately choose to abandon anyone in the worst health pandemic in the country for over a century?

And yet that is exactly what proceeded to happen. The Government decided to do something almost without parallel and initiate a new form of official discrimination. Three million people, possibly more, were told they were potentially criminals and fraudsters, or were simply too difficult to help.

In a time when it is rightfully abhorrent to discriminate against 3 million people due to their sex or race, religious beliefs or any other number of long-since taboo factors, the

Government went out of its way to discriminate against them solely because of their preferred, entirely legal method of earning a living. In some cases, including my own, they had been actively encouraged into this by the Government.

Imagine going through the entire pandemic with all the worries of ill health, death, and uncertainty for the future, not being able and often legally not allowed to work, but not receiving any government support whatsoever. And yet, repeatedly throughout 2020 and into 2021, the other groups that comprise the majority of society were helped time after time after time.

The Government, of course, initially denied that anyone was without help. They repeatedly fell back on their lies about 'unprecedented support' before finally admitting, in a small way, that not everyone received as much help as they may have wished. In truth, of course, millions have received no help whatsoever. Our Excluded 3 million band have long been seen as the backbone of the economy; we certainly aren't too difficult to tax, and yet we are not worthy of help. When Rishi was doing his best to increase the R-Rate with his 'Eat out to help out' campaign, he was using our taxes to give the Furloughed majority discounted meals out, often at restaurants and chains owned by multinational corporations with at best a dubious record of honesty when it comes to taxes. And all the while, the Excluded were increasingly being reduced to food banks, handouts and charity.

If such a series of events were to happen in a far-off country there would be widespread outrage and condemnation by government and opposition alike. There isn't anything much more depressing in life than seeing government ministers, time and again, lie and mislead in Parliament and on television; and it is hard to imagine Labour Leader Sir Keir Starmer being any less interested in us, in a way that would unimaginable if we were making the news overseas.

And so here we are in February 2021 after almost a year of wilful state abandonment. Some would say it's state persecution in a manner at least somewhat reminiscent of tyrannical regimes of the past. Whilst it may be pushing it to compare Boris Johnson, Rishi Sunak and Oliver Dowden with Hitler, Stalin and Pol Pot, the fact is these people do have blood on their hands through the documented suicides of those who were promised they would not be left behind or without hope. Whilst the dictators above had a tendency to eliminate intellectuals or those in professions, Boris has taken a simple apathetic approach of just leaving us to die. It was easier to help everyone in this country, but they actually

took the harder route and drew up categories of people they would exclude from help and discriminate against.

History is written by those who write it. Today we read, empathise with and admire the letters of WW1 soldiers, suffragettes and civil right activists, and wonder how on earth society could inflict such suffering and injustices on them. Perhaps one day in the not too distant future we will wonder how this society and this government could allow all of this to happen on their watch, in the third decade of the 21st century.

This book does not pretend to document the ins and outs of the political process or the disaster that is the Coronavirus epidemic. Instead it is simply a compendium of accounts from a fraction of the 3 million or so Excluded people from all walks of life. Abandoned, discriminated against, and some would say persecuted by their Government and largely forgotten by their country. You can judge for yourself whether we deserve this.

These are the stories of just some of the 3 million ExcludedUK without a voice, in their own words. May our needless suffering be remembered, those who looked on be ashamed, and those who inflicted it upon us be condemned.

Towards the end of January 2020, I thought up the concept of £xcluded Voices and I put out an invitation for members of the ExcludedUK to send me their experiences of being Excluded. 150 people had responded within a week or so. These are their stories in their own words.

1.

NAME: Rosie Doggett

OCCUPATION: Independent Marketing Procurement Consultant

REASON FOR EXCLUSION: Limited Company Director

I have been happily self-employed for 17 years, starting as an interim for companies like the Royal Mail Group. In common with 99% of such companies, they demand that their contractors are Limited Companies.

Over the years I've earned over £3m, averaging £200k pa, and have paid substantial amounts of corporation tax, personal tax, National Insurance and VAT. I won't work out that calculation as I suspect it would depress me further.

There are very few British brands with the kind of marketing budgets that I work on, and when Brexit hit it became apparent that my European clients were deciding to employ EU workers. So that put paid to 70% of my income. The final 30% of my income ceased when COVID hit, my main client being TUI. As they laid off 9,000 staff, it was only fair that highly paid consultants such as myself should also be let go.

As a result of these double hells, I have received no income since March 2020, and no prospect of any on the horizon. I am now interviewing for permanent jobs, but invariably am being vetted by people in their late twenties, who use the excuse 'too experienced' as the reason not to hire someone in their early 60s. My income expectations have dropped to one third of my pre-Brexit earnings.

Most people I know have received Universal Credit, SEISS, ARG or have been furloughed, and many of them have worked throughout. It is supremely unfair that Limited Company directors have received zero financial support. Why does Rishi Sunak detest Limited Companies when we have paid our dues, and then some? Answers on a post card please.

2.

NAME: Stephen Willis

OCCUPATION: Taxi Driver

REASON FOR EXCLUSION: Newly Self-Employed

In January 2019 my father's health was deteriorating and over the following year he was in and out of hospital several times. It was at this time that I re-evaluated my working life. I was at a low point, in a job where I felt unappreciated and worthless. It became clear that I needed flexibility to combine a job with caring for my father, and after speaking to friends I decided to become self-employed.

It took me until August 2019 to retrain and obtain all the qualifications and 'knowledge' for my taxi licence. I started work in September, and between then and March 2020 I realised I had made right decision and that self-employment gave me the flexibility I needed.

In January 2020 I took the plunge and bought a vehicle, rather than renting. As it was my first year of being self-employed, I sought insurance. I had 32 airport bookings between February and August 2020, and anticipated my earnings would be higher than my previous employment.

On 20th March Boris Johnson announced that the country would be going into Lockdown. I immediately received cancellations from customers, and this was when it hit home that my income would adversely be affected. I guess nobody knew how long the Lockdown would last.

Unfortunately my Dad had been readmitted to hospital in January 2020, and on 23rd March he lost his battle. For the next nine days I had to arrange his funeral under very stressful circumstances due to the pandemic.

I haven't been eligible for any grants available for the self-employed because I hadn't filed for self-assessment with HMRC, and I cannot claim any benefits because my wife is working – in this day and age, both parents need to work.

In May I applied for a Government-backed Bounce Back Loan. In June I decided I needed to return to work, though fares would be limited, and I offered discounts for key workers as a way to keep earning. Although some restrictions were eased during the next few weeks, my income wasn't where I forecasted it would be when deciding to buy a vehicle.

So far I have managed to keep my head above water, but for the last ten months my income has been about £11,000 and my expenses around £10,000. I believe that, without the pandemic, I would have achieved my forecast of £18,000 turnover (as opposed to £14,000 from employment). So basically I have lived off my Bounce Back Loan. If I was still employed, my personal bank balance would be significantly different.

After working since 1992, I am one disgruntled tax payer. I feel I have paid enough contributions to warrant some financial support, but I have been failed by this Government.

I am stuck between a rock and hard place, and have become more anxious and lost sleep. I am in debt for six years with the Bounce Back Loan and a business overdraft, and I will still have to pay higher taxes when the pandemic over, having received no financial support.

3.
NAME: Maria
OCCUPATION: Dance Teacher
REASON FOR EXCLUSION: 50/50 rule

My name is Maria.

In 1999 I gave up a successful writing career in newspaper publishing to open a dance school. I qualified as a Dance Teacher and started my own SE London based dance school – called Dance Generation – in 2000. I am passionate about dancing – beyond a performance art – as an everyday skill that helps people find confidence, challenges them to learn something new, and helps them make friends. Dance Generation is (was) a small – but successful – dance school and I have paid tax as a self-employed person for almost 20 years.

In 2016 I got divorced. In order to help me buy a house, I took a drawdown from my United Newspapers pension. This was entered into my 17/18 tax return as 'other income'. I even paid tax on it.

When the government put the country into Lockdown at the end of March 2020, all my dance classes were closed overnight. Bang! Gone! Initially, I was not worried financially as I believed wholly in Rishi Sunak when he said that "No one would be left behind." At that very moment I actually felt PROUD to be a UK tax payer! (How stupid I feel now!)

When the government announced the SEISS I duly logged onto the .gov website, put in my UTC and was completely devastated when the 'you are not eligible to claim' screen came up. I burst into tears. Questions. So many questions were in my head. Surely this must be a mistake? What was I going to do? How was I supposed to survive? Didn't the Gov say they would help? How could it be right that my whole business was closed due to their restrictions, but I was not going to get any support?

I rang my friend, Cathy, who is also my accountant, in panic.

“Cathy!” I wailed, “It says I am not eligible for the SEISS! What am I supposed to do?”

Cathy told me not to worry. It was almost certainly a mistake she said, she would look into it and get back to me. I wiped my tears and took a deep breath. Of course, I thought, it must be a mistake.

Half an hour later she phoned me back.

"I'm so sorry," she said, "But you don't qualify for the SEISS. The qualifying criteria states that more than 50% of your trading profits must come from self-employment. Your pension drawdown in 17/18 is counted as 'income', which means that your trading profits are under 50%."

Maria at Dance Generation.

"But that's not fair!" I sobbed, "That money went towards the house! I can prove it!"

"I'm afraid it doesn't matter what you did with the money," she said, "Under HMRC rules, you don't qualify for the SEISS."

She then told me that she too – as a Limited Company director paid in dividends – was also Excluded from the SEISS. So we told each other not to worry, arranged a Zoom call to reminisce over happier times and both joined ExcludedUK.

I did try to stay calm. Like any sensible, self-employed person, I had some savings – which were to cover me if I was ever sick or could not work – but then, like many others, I believed the Lockdown and restrictions would last just a few weeks, maybe a couple of months. But now it's almost a year! Who has savings that you can live on for a whole year?

I eventually applied for a Bounce Back Loan – which I got – but then, when things got tough enough to apply for Universal Credit, I found I didn't qualify for that either – because I had taken a Bounce Back Loan!

I also did not qualify for any business grants, as I do not own a studio – I just hire local church halls and community centres to hold my classes in. So, I lived off my savings, which are all but gone.

How is this FAIR? Why should I not get the same support as everyone else whose business was closed down? Just because I took a pension drawdown in 17/18?

Even if the Government wants to count this as 'income', then surely I should still get 80% of my less-than-50% SE profits from the dance school? Anything would be better than absolutely nothing. I don't want more than anyone else. I only want what is FAIR.

I am mostly angry. I do believe I have been discriminated against, but, you know what? I don't think it's about the money anymore. I am grieving for my whole business. A business that I spent 20 years building up. Virtually ruined by COVID and the subsequent restrictions – and it may never recover. It's like it's worthless. In the eyes of the Government, I, and my business, that brought joy and well-being to so many people, are demonstrably not worth supporting. It meant everything to me, but it means nothing to them.

I've no idea what the future holds. Whether the dance school will survive or even if I will still want to teach. This goes beyond being ExcludedUK. Sometimes I wonder if we will ever be able to go back to a world where children can hold hands, share sweets and play together again, and where adults can gather, without fear, to sing, laugh, dance, share food and hug people they love. I am not suicidal and I do not want to kill myself, but if this sanitised, socially distanced, lonely and fearful world is the future – then I look forward to death with considerable enthusiasm.

I don't want this account to leave you with feelings of sadness and hopelessness, as there is considerable joy in my life too. I am one of the volunteer team behind ExcludedUK – and through my work with them I have met so many incredible, selfless and amazing people. And ExcludedUK has given me the opportunity to reconnect with my writing and designing, which I lost touch with for a while as I was too busy running the dance school, so for that, I am eternally grateful.

All power to you my fellow ExcludedUK Warriors. There is light at the end of this tunnel. Even if we can't see it – it doesn't mean it's not there.
Onwards.

4.
NAME: Jane Leigh
OCCUPATION: Journalism/Table-tennis Coach/Family Tree Researcher
REASON FOR EXCLUSION: 50/50 rule

I've been a journalist since 1978, in magazines and newspapers. I went freelance in 1994, and have never stopped working. My tax-paying history stretches back to 1977 – HMRC have all my returns – and I've never claimed benefit but always contributed to the system.

Back in March 2020, I watched Boris Johnson telling us to "prepare to lose some of our loved ones" and thought this was looking serious. I listened to Rishi Sunak's speech on March 26th. He said: "To you, I say this: You have not been forgotten. We will not leave you behind. We are all in this together."

Then we got to the nitty-gritty. He added: "To make sure only the genuinely self-employed benefit, it will be available to people who make the majority of their income from self-employment; and to minimise fraud, only those who are already in self-employment . . . will be able to apply."

Now my situation is maybe not representative. My income has been dreadful for the last four years, partly due to the death of regional journalism and partly due to the fact that my partner got a full-time job in 2018 and we moved 200 miles to Cornwall at the end of that year.

That meant he's working (thank heaven) but I had to leave all my work and contacts (I'd reinvented myself as a table-tennis coach) and start up again. So I've not earned enough to pay tax for the last four years, and the fact that for just over two years I've received a small final salary pension means that I don't qualify (it makes up more than 50% of my income) for ANY government aid.

I didn't expect to get much and so I reinvented myself again, starting up as a family tree researcher as I can do that online from home. It's bringing in a very small irregular income.

What I find truly appalling is the inference that I don't qualify because I'm a fraud risk – it's deeply offensive that, after 43 years of work, I'm deemed to be a potential fraudster. You don't have to look far to see who are the real fraudsters in this country.

One other factor: I'm 65 so I'm one of the generation of 1950s-born women robbed of the State Pension we've paid for all our working lives. The government decided we didn't need it for six years but forgot to tell us, so I should finally get mine in November 2021, six years late. I never intended to retire at 60, but to be put in this position where I get no help in a pandemic and I still don't qualify for my State Pension means I've been penalised twice for no good reason. The result is to make me feel, in turn, alternately worthless and furious. It's no thanks to the government that I'm surviving. I've always been self-reliant and will continue to do my best to provide for myself but at 65 I need a bit of help now and again, and they've denied me any.

All in this together? Rubbish!

5.

NAME: Julie Headley

OCCUPATION: Dog Boarding & Day Care

REASON FOR EXCLUSION: Trading Profits over £50k

In 1990 I went self-employed as a freelance secretary, but business ended up being 95% dog services (homeboarding/day care/walking) and 5% secretarial. I worked 18 hours a day, seven days a week – hard work, but enjoyable, to see the dogs coming into homeboarding stressed, and working with them to settle them in, create a routine and give them security, and the reward being a wagging tail and the eye contact which tells me they have 'connected' with me and are happy. OK, so my house takes a pounding, everything is covered in dog hair, and the dust – just don't go there. Oh, and don't ask for a lift in my car – wear dark clothing and you'll come out covered in white hairs. A successful business, all cash income declared, all tax paid.

Then came 23rd March 2020, the first Lockdown – all bookings cancelled, blank pages in the diary.

In the last eight years I had only had one night without any client dogs in. From 23rd March there were no homeboarders/day care/dog walks. And no income. But the Government said they would help and provide support to businesses. So I waited. Schemes were rolled out but, due to set criteria, I was ineligible – my net profit for the last three years was just over £50k. I couldn't believe it, it was so unfair – PAYE individuals were receiving 80% of their salary up to a limit of £2,500 per month, no cap on their actual earnings; other self-employed businesses under the £50k profit cap received help up to a cap of £2,500 per month. I couldn't take it in. Why not use the cap of £2,500 per month?

For the next three months of Lockdown I painted, I gardened, I cooked, I read, and my savings started to dwindle – I felt so angry and isolated. Rishi Sunak's policy decision had cost me £s and lost me lbs (the latter I'm not so angry about!). Different loans/grants were given out for sectors, but these don't help individuals.

In June I was fortunate to be eligible for a Discretionary grant of £3,000. In July I saw a comment on Facebook regarding a group called ExcludedUK. I joined and the support was amazing, the relief to find people who, for whatever reason, had also been Excluded from Government schemes. But the group could also be depressing; people were struggling financially, emotionally, mentally – and it was hard getting the message over to the public that this was actually happening. Even MPs didn't understand the situation, couldn't grasp that for almost 3 million businesses there was NO help, despite what Sunak and Johnson said.

But ExcludedUK, working with other groups, started to get the message out, and MPs started to push the Government, Sadly, at the time of writing, the Government has still not offered any meaningful support to the 3 million Excluded.

6.

NAME: Ellie Appleton

OCCUPATION: Personal and Business Development Coach

REASON FOR EXCLUSION: Newly Self-Employed

I have become part of very select group. And when I say select, I mean vindictively selected, singled out, made prisoner of circumstance through no fault of my own by those who purport to govern. Because that is how it feels; trapped, like a prisoner in an alternative universe previously unknown to me.

Let's wind back a bit. In 2018-19 I worked part time; in April 2019 I registered fully self-employed. And like most newly self-employed during that first year I ploughed everything – my heart, soul and money – into my new business as a sole trader.

As a carer, I need to work to support two of us. And I'm old enough to have a basic state pension. Because of that and being older, I qualify for no additional benefits.

Then COVID hit. Everything collapsed – stopped in its tracks. I scoured every website, hung on every word about support, but nothing. Not a penny available. Not for me, not for others. In March 2020 I hoped it would be over in a few months, we could scrape through. How wrong I was. At first we struggled. Now we barely survive, two people on £175 week.

By autumn I truly wept, in private, and sold so much to feed us. I lost weight, and tried to emotionally support a partner with severe depressive episodes.

It breaks my heart to see what has been deliberately, avoidably, inflicted upon us. Worst, for the first time in my life, I CANNOT CHANGE THIS SITUATION!! I scream that silently in my head.

It is beyond my control, and we are beyond hope. No point talking about the lack of heat, lack of everything. It feels like we Excluded are talking to someone lacking in imagination or empathy, we are prisoners of what this government has created.

I feel I have failed. I have let the love of my life down by following my passion to work for myself at what I love. It's out of my control and honestly, I know not how much darker a place I can stand.

7.
NAME: Anna Hardy
OCCUPATION: Company Director, Hospitality
REASON FOR EXCLUSION: Limited Company Director

I am company director of a few small limited companies including a little hotel. All of my work is in the hospitality industry. I have been Excluded as I have not been on my payroll for some years now. I was diagnosed in August 2016 with acute myeloid leukaemia when my son was less than a year old. I had taken time off to have him and unfortunately became ill not long after my maternity leave finished. There was no point putting myself back on my payroll as I was honestly unable to work frequently and had to get a manager in to cover my own work. There was no point being self-employed either. I have intermittently been on and off my payroll between various chemo rounds and stem cell transplants, but it then just became easier to pay myself via dividends or let the business take care of bills rather than actually paying myself.

I registered as self-employed two years into my illness, but despite 17 calls and a complaint to HMRC I haven't managed to file my self-assessment for last year never mind this year, because for some reason they have stopped recognising my unique tax reference. Because of this, I have been left Excluded from all forms of support.

I have had a grant for my business and a Bounce Back Loan but I have myself had nothing. I have had to prop up my business, which has had nowhere near enough financial support, with what was left of my very limited savings. They have run out now.

Getting sick left me already feeling like a car crash; being Excluded on top of it has made me feel like I'm in a never ending pile up. Some days it's difficult to work out whether I should worry more about my treatment being cancelled or which bill I can't afford to pay.

Every day it feels like a never ending nightmare and I cannot believe it is happening. I have tried so hard to keep my head above water all throughout my illness, in the end what's killed me is an illness I haven't even had; it almost makes me laugh.

8.

NAME: Marilyn Bonnici

OCCUPATION: Agency Worker

REASON FOR EXCLUSION: Denied Furlough

I had been working on a single assignment for three and half years on a temporary contract via an agency when, as I was considered 'at risk' for health reasons, I had to self-isolate at home. I asked the organisation if I could work from home but was told they hadn't considered that. (Please note that at this point I had been offered a permanent contract which was being sorted out).

I later discovered that several other colleagues doing the same role were sent home with equipment to work from home that very afternoon!

My agency refused to furlough me saying they could not afford to pay my holiday pay as it would cost them £11million for this region alone (I'm not sure I believe this as they are a large organisation). I offered to pay the holiday pay as the difference was negligible but they said this was against HMRC regulations. They also asked the organisation that I had been working for to pay the holiday pay, but they refused. The agency furloughed their own office staff so I feel completely discriminated against. They admitted they did not have many in my situation as most of their contractors were on shorter term contracts, below two years, which did not oblige them to consider them for furloughing. (£11m really!!!!)

I asked them to put this and their reasons in writing as all communications had been by telephone, but alas, they never did. A few weeks later I received my P45, again with no communication whatsoever!

The government was wrong to make furlough at the employers' discretion. I do not qualify for Universal Credit as I have a small inheritance from my parents which I am currently living off, but this will be totally spent by the time I retire in August this year.

Being so close to retirement age it is unlikely that anyone would employ me, particularly as I need to self-isolate with my health issues and only working from home positions are suitable.

I emailed my MP, who merely passed my details on to the Treasury. Their standard reply was irrelevant to my situation as it was more suited to a young person with their working life ahead of them. They clearly had not read my circumstances and it was of no use to me whatever!

I feel as though I am invisible to the chancellor and have been cast aside as though I am of no worth. The chancellor in my case has been shortsighted, as when my inheritance has been spent (which was supposed to give me a top up to my state pension) I will need to be supported by benefits to sustain me instead.

I would say "thanks" but I have been given nothing to be grateful for!
NOT ONE PENNY!
NO PRACTICAL HELP!
NOTHING!

9.
NAME: Mollyanne T
OCCUPATION: Food Safety & Quality Consultant
REASON FOR EXCLUSION: Limited Company Director

I am a Limited Company Director, working with food manufacturing factories to improve their Quality Management Systems, and how that translates in to food safety and quality assurance. This involves lots of coaching, mentoring, training, and auditing. I am paid by a small PAYE and Dividends, which is perfectly legal and the most cost-saving way of paying myself. I am Excluded because 'it is too difficult' for HMRC to differentiate between dividends paid in lieu of salary and dividends paid to a shareholder. My company consists of me, just me. I am Director, worker, admin and cleaner.

I have over 25 years' experience working in the food manufacturing industry, within the Technical Department (food safety and quality technical, not computers!). In 2008, I became self-employed as a Sole Trader and three years later was 'forced' to move to Limited Company status to win contracts. There was a brief period of permanent employment as a Director for four years, then back to being a Ltd Co Director starting in January 2017.

Being Excluded has made me feel completely inadequate in the evaluation of both my personal and work life, and unimportant to the economic status. I know logically that it isn't my fault, but it has still knocked my confidence, because if our Government doesn't think my business is important enough to be supported, then is it? My trading profit has exceeded £50k each year, so obviously it must be an important and viable business!

I do not let people get close to me in my personal life, have few friends, and am an introvert with low self-confidence. (At work, I can put on a persona mask and become the confident in-control Manager/Director). I have learnt through the last 12 months, that I can share my fears, thoughts and insecurities with strangers who have become my 'Excluded friends'. I haven't met them, but hope to one day; so I can show them my thanks and grati tude. They were there for me at a time when people I really thought I could turn to have chosen to look the other way and not see my emotional need.

Looking to the future, I will continue the 'eyes wide open' view of politics and the people that lead this country that I have been forced to develop over the last 12 months. I'll always be a green, environmentally conscious voter … but I'll be following the injustices that happen and doing my small part to increase public awareness through Twitter or other social media platforms. Apart from that, I will try and recover my financial security and savings so that I can one day afford to retire with some money behind me.

I'd like to say 'put life before work', but my retirement savings have been decimated and I'll need to work very hard for at least five years to recover. The dreams of a lower level, lower income permanent role for the last ten years of my working life will be shelved …. Maybe the last two or three years will be manageable.

10.
NAME: John Phillips
OCCUPATION: Plumber & Refitter
REASON FOR EXCLUSION: 50/50 rule

I started Oakfield Plumbing some 15 years ago after a previous life mainly in IT. There has always been 'just me' whilst I've been self-employed and although my income has been (considerably) lower than what I earned in my IT life, I have thoroughly enjoyed working with/for many customers and providing them with the bathroom they had always promised themselves. I have been a member of Checkatrade for well over ten years and pride myself on my consistent 10/10 customer ratings I have received over that time.

I was quite shocked to be Excluded. Having paid all my taxes over my entire working life and never before having had to rely upon the state, I had hoped that the Chancellor's promise of not leaving anyone behind would have been honoured.

My wife and I moved to Wales a couple of years back and took a pension drawdown to allow us to become mortgage-free and renovate a property. If I'd read the Ts&Cs closely, I could have predicted that I'd be Excluded. But, despite having paid all my taxes on the drawdown of my own money (none of which is accessible as it's all tied up in 'bricks & mortar'), I was deemed ineligible.

To be fair, the Government has done a lot to assist those affected, but I found it particularly upsetting that a great many of the self-employed have been singled out for exclusion on somewhat spurious and inequitable grounds.

If the 50% rule had been applied to furloughed employees, I maybe could have understood. How many furloughed workers have taken pension drawdowns or have other forms of income (pensions etc) that would technically take them over the 50% rule? And yet they have not been Excluded.

Similarly with the £50k 'rule'. Whilst I was nowhere near falling into that category, there must be tens of thousands of furloughed workers who earn more than £50k, yet they are still eligible for furlough payments.

If you are going to impose rules, those rules should be applied across the board, not just to the self-employed.

It is very debilitating to be constantly told by the government that other forms of support have been available (Universal Credit? Yeah, right!). They have totally failed to even acknowledge the volume of us Excluded taxpayers – taxpayers who will certainly not be Excluded when the time of financial reckoning comes!

Overall, as a self-employed person, I feel that I've been both viewed and treated as a second-class citizen, not worthy of the same level of support and assistance as a 'traditional' employee.

And the saddest thing? There has been not a single concession or acknowledgement from the government on the matter. As every day that passes, I feel we are drifting further away from any parity being provided.

11.
NAME: Hayley Wallbank
OCCUPATION: Language Services
REASON FOR EXCLUSION: 50/50 rule

From my first French lesson, aged 11, foreign languages have fascinated and inspired me.

Following a degree in Engineering and German I took the traditional route of working for manufacturing businesses in international sales and marketing. I did this for over 25 years. I got to see a lot of the world – Japan, Russia, Middle East, North Africa and over 80% of Europe.

As well as experiencing new cultures and people, along the way I also refined my language skills in French, German and Russian, plus a smattering of basic Spanish and Italian.

In 2016, I decided to follow my true passion for languages and set up business offering in-house language training to businesses as well as GCSE tuition to students. There was a considerable cost attached to setting up such a venture, so I worked part-time employed and part time self-employed, on a 75/25% basis for the first three years.

By April 2019 my client base and company brand profile had grown to such an extent that I was able to leave employment and become 100% self-employed. It is an amazing feeling

Hayley of HW Language Services

to follow your dream and in the process help others to do the same. I absolutely love what I do and my clients give me such positive feedback, it is a real vocation for me.

When COVID 19 struck my business was affected in many ways. My corporate clients were no longer able to facilitate our in-company, group language lessons; school exams were cancelled leading to both tuition and exam invigilation losses; plus Lockdown ensued with nobody able to catch their breath in between working from home, home schooling and anxiety issues alongside lost incomes. Online lessons worked for a couple of clients but over 90% of contracts were cancelled or suspended. School exams for 2021 have now also been cancelled, so again that income stream is wiped out.

Despite having paid National Insurance and Tax all of my working life (ca. £350,000), when I applied for Universal Credit I was rejected due to the fact that my husband still has a job. I also did not qualify for SEISS because the proportion of my self-employment income on the specified date (March 2019) was only 25%, which fell below the 50% arbitrarily specified quota. By the same token, I did not qualify for any of the Discretionary Local Authority Business Grants because I do not pay business rates.

The business which I have spent almost five years building up may now disappear due to lack of funds. This makes me so sad and angry at the unfairness of such discriminatory policies instigated by this Government.

One positive, however, to come out of this negative tale, is joining the ExcludedUK online Facebook community. Twenty-seven thousand people facing their most testing times yet maintaining their dignity, empathy, kindness, compassion, generosity and commitment. Thank you Anneka Hicks, Aron Padley, Sonali Joshi, Rachel Flower and all the volunteers in the team.

12.
NAME: Anonymous
OCCUPATION: Singer
REASON FOR EXCLUSION: Newly Self-Employed

I'm a woman, 34 years old, a singer, based in London. I grew up in Italy and developed an interest for music early. My mother was a singer and I stepped into her footsteps. Our little village, and the lack of financial means, brought me to London to study singing professionally.

I graduated successfully in 2019 and started my own business which was booking gigs. I quickly became booked out and made such an income that I moved into my own flat in Central London. Life was promising. I hired musicians for some of the shows and felt good about giving fellow artists the opportunity to work.

COVID changed everything. Overnight, gigs were cancelled. I was sure there'd be some financial aid in place, no government would force businesses to close and leave them to rot. But was I mistaken! My bills kept rolling in, my rent was impossible to pay. I received some

Universal Credit (UC) but the judgemental lady on the phone advised me to move into a different borough, to shared accommodation. During a pandemic!

My mother got seriously ill and telling her my situation during her final years (that's how much the doctors gave her) would be unthinkable! Besides, my family has no money. The bills kept coming, my landlord kept pushing, and UC doesn't work for London. I didn't want to wake up in the morning anymore. I would be homeless in a matter of weeks. I called UC, my Council, Equity, but nobody understood being trapped with high living costs, facing an unbearable gap between my old life and the brief taste of what I accomplished, in a foreign country.
The pressures and the feeling that nobody would care about me, the Government obviously being the least of them, the isolation… I started to sell my body in order to not end up on the streets. How else am I supposed to get together £2,000 for rent alone, which is on the cheaper side in Central London!

I hated it, I cried myself to sleep every night, some men were okay, some physically hurt me, none of them respected me. I started to drink, showered for hours, avoided looking at myself in the mirror. I began to self-harm, thought death can't be worse than this. I thought about my family and what they might think, my ill mother.

I have no money to move back, I have no money to stay. I'm on an NHS suicide prevention programme. I stopped selling my body as it became unbearable, but now I'm facing homelessness once again. I don't know how and if I'm going to survive this.

My life had been promising, full of joy and laughter. London was my home. Now, my life looks much different, I'm not that person anymore. I hate my body, I hate myself, I don't even know if I can ever be happy again.

If it wasn't for the ExcludedUK organisation, I would have lost hope. Thanks to this group and our exchanges, I haven't at least lost my life yet.

13.
NAME: Carolina Garcia
OCCUPATION: Tour Operator, Little Scottish Treasures / Pequenos Tesoros en Escocia
REASON FOR EXCLUSION: Newly Self-Employed

I am a tour operator based in Dunfermline, Scotland. My tours operate in both English and Spanish and my market is tourists visiting Scotland. I work alongside my partner, he is a great story teller and wears his clan kilt. When the tours are in Spanish and I translate what he is saying, everybody appears to love our combination and the way we work together.

In September 2018 my passion and love for Scottish history, its magical land and lovely country side, became a means of earning a living. My business was doing really well and 2020 was promising to be the year for growth – the tourism sector in Scotland was blooming, and we had great ideas to implement in our tours. However, I have been Excluded from any help provided by the government as I classify as 'Newly Self-Employed'. The requirement was to submit at least three years of tax returns, but by March 2020, I had only submitted one.

Facing the new reality has not been easy, but I am glad for two things. The first one is that I was able to claim Universal Credit, and the second is that I have an amazing ability to make money last. But I have never relied on benefits, and living with so little, along with everything else, has been very challenging. I don't want to sound ungrateful and I know there are a lot of people who did not even classify for Universal Credit, but personally this has been an all time low.

When you work in the tourism sector, especially in Scotland, one of your early lessons is to learn to save money for winter, when tourism is almost nonexistent. We are now living through our second winter without business, and the reality and fear of losing what we have worked so hard to build is devastating. For me, the way the government has dealt with everything had been extremely unfair and has brought out a darker side of me.

Before the pandemic, I celebrated everyone's progress; but now, the way some people in our sector have repeatedly qualified for help, while others don't, has brought an unfair level of competition. I see it as making the rich richer and others left fighting ... well, almost begging for recognition. Seeing a friend buying drones and canoes for his tour business and thinking it is all down to this help, while I need to do Amazon deliveries in order to keep my personal and business finances afloat, creates feelings that otherwise I have never experienced.

We all have seen friends and even family members who have enjoyed the Lockdown because they were furloughed, while we are worried and stressed. Both groups of people have been living through a global pandemic, but I have financial anxieties on top of all this.

Today I have received another email from Business Gateway regarding more help in the tourism sector managed by Visit Scotland. I am not surprised now that I don't classify for this one either, it is like a game of expectation versus crashing reality that is not good for your self-esteem.

I have no idea what the future will bring. We are living uncertain times, but what I expected from the government was a fairer system for everyone. In the meantime I will continue fighting for me and my family and try to keep my company dream alive. I am going to start a master's degree at the university of Aberdeen which hopefully will be used in my future tours, because I do not know how to throw in the towel, even in my darkest days. I wish I knew when all of this will end, so I can once again have the control of my life and business in my own hands.

14.

NAME: Kate

OCCUPATION: Music Teacher/Landlady

REASON FOR EXCLUSION: Newly Self-Employed

For 35 years I worked as Head of Music in schools, earning over £40,000pa and paying tax. In 2018, aged 58, I was burnt out and got a job through a company working two days a week teaching piano and singing in schools. I earned £8,500 a year (PAYE), and had lodgers in from the theatre, which gave me £7,000 tax-free under the 'rent a room scheme'. I was so happy with my small income and relatively stress-free life. I danced, sang, swam and sailed.

Due to COVID I lost my job and rental income and have had no income or support. I can't even claim Universal Credit because I have some savings which were for my future.

Friends and family complain that they have slightly less money, or feel isolated because they aren't at work, or can't see their friends, but they are furloughed or have been given grants. Some haven't even lost any income, but still get grants. There is little understanding of how let-down, dejected, abandoned and worthless I feel, or what it is like to go from having an income and sense of achievement to having absolutely nothing.

15.

NAME: Alison Powell

OCCUPATION: Language Tutor

REASON FOR EXCLUSION: 50/50 rule

My situation is that the tax year 2018-19 was my last of being both part-time employed and self-employed. I am now purely a self-employed sole trader (language tuition in school clubs) employing one individual (I employed three before the pandemic), who I furloughed in March.

In 2018-19 I earned £10 more (yes £10!) from employment than from self-employment. As a result, I did not meet the criteria of having more than 50% of income from self-employment. I appealed but to no avail, in spite of the fact that I clearly stated on my 2018-19 tax return that my PAYE job had ceased on 24th Feb 2019. If the 2019-20 return was used, (which I submitted in April 2020 in hope of a change of eligibility criteria) I would have been eligible for all of the SEISS grants.

My employee benefitted from some employment from September to December 2020 as I had seen a partial restart of my business and I was claiming 80% of her lost hours. In 2021, as schools have again closed for at least six weeks, I once more have no income, but I will continue to furlough my employee so that she can pay her rent!

So, I personally have had nothing from the government, in spite of being a tax-payer for over 40 years! I don't know how long I can continue to maintain a business with no income. If my business fails, two people will be unemployed not one! I feel abandoned and cheated. I can't claim benefits as, thankfully, my husband is still working.

I obtained a small Bounce Back Loan but that is a debt, so my failing business is now in debt. My MP Bill Esterson has shown amazing support for his constituents and ExcludedUK, campaigning tirelessly for parity for all but, in spite of the support of over 300 MPs like him, the Chancellor refuses to listen or revisit his flawed policies.

The government will need small businesses like mine to aid recovery. I don't understand the rationale of leaving so many without support and allowing their previously viable businesses to fail for lack of the support given to others.

16.

NAME: Huw Davies

OCCUPATION: IT Project Manager

REASON FOR EXCLUSION: Limited Company Director

I am a 61 year old IT Project Manager living near Bristol and have worked and paid taxes for 42 years. My employment contract was terminated in April due to COVID-19. Since then, the lack of investment by companies in voice and data infrastructures means I have been unable to find work.

I manage my contracts through my own Limited Company, so I am the sole director and employee. I have complied with IR35 for the last seven years, paying my tax and National Insurance on time in the first week of April, and this has meant I am not eligible for furlough financial support from the government.

As I help care for my 90 year old mother, I feel taking a job where I am in contact with the general public, such as supermarkets or van driving, would be an unacceptable level of risk for her, so I scan agencies and job sites every day and have applied for nearly 70 suitable jobs since May 2020.

I can claim Universal Credit but this doesn't even cover my rent, so I am spending my retirement savings on bills, food and emergencies.

I am divorced and my three children have all grown up and left home, so I only have myself to look after, which is lucky – if I was unable to provide for my children it would be devastating.

I have been part of ExcludedUK since May, a group of people in similar situations to mine, but for many and varied reasons. I have participated in numerous campaigns, including helping to organise a mass sending of postcards to Rishi Sunak. I started using Twitter at the start of my exclusion and have joined in the many 'Twitter Bombs' the group have organised.

I have tried to help getting the message out to the general public and have been on BBC Radio Bristol, BBC Radio London *Drivetime* twice and BBC Radio 4 *Call You and Yours*. I have told my story in the Bristol Cable, BBC News Online, Somerset Live and iNews publications.

I also attended the Bristol City Gathering chaired by Marvyn Rees, the Bristol Mayor, where I was able to explain the ExcludedUK story to leaders of Bristol's many organisations. I will continue to tell our story at every opportunity.

The ExcludedUK group is massively important to nearly 30,000 of us. The Admin team do so much to help people, fight on our behalf and ensure people feel included. We have had many suicides over the last ten months, but I know there would have been many, many more without them.

Reading the Facebook stories and updates posted by group members is often heartbreaking and I have found myself in tears on numerous occasions. There are thousands of Excluded who are much worse off than me and I feel I am lucky in comparison to many.

This Government knows what they have done. They do not care about the lives and businesses devastated by their refusal to work with ExcludedUK to discuss and provide the financial support required for parity. All the while, wasting Billions of pounds fattening the wallets of their friends and hangers-on. It's abhorrent.

17.

NAME: Emma-Lee Cunningham

OCCUPATION: Hairdresser

REASON FOR EXCLUSION: Newly Self-Employed

I have been self-employed just under a year as a hairdresser in a local salon. I have received no grants or funding and am down on average £600 per week, and I'm the sole worker in my household.

Excluded

Imagine a world locked down with restriction
A voice so irrelevant, our views so conflicting
The years and the tears into your education you've put
To be crushed like an ant beneath the aristocracy's foot
To be chained inside four walls through no fault of your own
An invisible prison, viewing life through a phone
Where loved ones are unfamiliar through stress and despair
Where a system is in place that is vague and unfair
Self-employed tax payers falling through the net
Savings for a future dwindling, now spiralling into debt
Swallowing your pride to see what help you can get
To be brushed aside forgotten, wallowing in regret
While our children are home schooled: "Mummy, why are you upset"?
"Just a headache my darling" I cannot mourn yet
For the business I've grown through blood, tears and sweat
Falling through my fingers with anguish I'm met
A glimpse in the mirror-just a blurred silhouette
If this is democracy then pause, rewind, reset.

18.
NAME: Cheryl Jones
OCCUPATION: Pet Sitter/Dog Walker
REASON FOR EXCLUSION: 50/50 rule

I am a British Army veteran. I gave 22 years service in many campaigns , including Afghanistan, Iraq, Bosnia and Northern Ireland, often fearing that I would never survive to return home. Thankfully I did. When I left the Armed Forces ten years ago my pension was not enough to live on, and would not increase for 13 years, so I set myself up as pet sitter and dog walker to supplement my income.

On 20th March, Chancellor Rishi Sunak announced the packages that were to be put in place to support people's income. A few weeks later he announced that self-employed people were also going to be supported. We would have to wait until June for any payment, but he repeatedly said "we are in it together" and "no one will be left behind". I was so thankful to hear this news.

Cheryl Jones - Take A Lead Petsitter - Rotherham

When Lockdown began my business closed down overnight. Everyone was at home, holidays were cancelled, and no one needed my services.

I decided to serve the community. I worked as a Volunteer NHS Responder and am registered with the 'Rotherham Heroes'. I have been doing voluntary work with the Brinsworth Senior Support Group, which involves shopping, keeping lonely people company and distributing food parcels. I have played a huge part in this by collecting all the donations every week.

In May I applied for SEISS but was told I was not eligible. I kept trying, thinking there was a mistake. I asked HMRC for a review, and they confirmed that I was not eligible for any financial support. My Army pension averaged about 53% of my income for the three qualifying financial years, so I am Excluded under the 50/50 rule. I was shocked to learn that I am one of the estimated 3 million Excluded tax-payers who have 'fallen through the cracks' of all the financial systems introduced. So I have lost almost half of my income, through no fault of my own. If the figures were the other way round then I would be eligible, with a cap of £50,000 profits. Anything over this you would not be eligible for any financial help either.

I cannot get Universal Credit or Job Seekers Allowance because I have a pension and savings. Recently I found out I was not eligible for a local discretionary Grant, as I work from my house. This is because I paid off my mortgage two years ago; the criteria is that you have to pay at least £250 rent or mortgage. I am so glad I did pay my mortgage off otherwise I might have been looking at been repossessed.

I am devastated. I have cried uncontrollably many times as I feel worthless, let down and abandoned by my own Government in my hour of need. I have worked since I was 16 years old and have never been out of work, I have paid my taxes and National Insurance contributions. I served my Queen and Country, I have a Royal Warrant and a Long Service and Good Conduct Medal along with other medals, and the sacrifices I made to maintain our freedom now appear to be insignificant and disregarded. I am an enterprising and successful owner of a small business. It is disgraceful and humiliating that I now find myself punished because I have been a good citizen.

ExcludedUK is a collective platform for individuals and businesses entirely or largely Excluded from the Government COVID 19 support. This situation urgently needs to be rectified so that we have the parity of support that has been given to the rest of the population during this global crisis. ExcludedUK has kept me from going under and I urge anyone who has found themselves in the same or similar position to join, they offer lots of advice and help.

We are now in 2021 and my pet-sitting business is still on its knees. In late August a few doggies returned but nothing substantial. Holidays were still cancelled and workers were encouraged to stay at home. I really can't see work coming back in the near future, as Furlough has been extended till April 21. I have lost nearly £10,000 income since Lockdown, which will mean in Jan 2022 I will not be paying any tax as I won't have earned enough income. I am eating into my savings now, I am not sure how long these will last.

My mental health has been battered, I have never before experienced these daily anxiety levels, crying all the time. I don't understand what I have done wrong for the Government to disregard me and 3 million others. I would like to receive 80% of my self-employment, around £5-600 per month, like everyone else. The Government have already said this will not be backdated, so therefore I would like to see a compensation package for being Excluded in the first place. I have always strived for parity and equal opportunity.

19.

NAME: Lisa McKenzie

OCCUPATION: Complementary Therapist

REASON FOR EXCLUSION: 50/50 rule

In my pre-Excluded life I worked as a primary school teacher for 19 years, working my final ten years in a specialist provision for autistic children. Being a part of the teaching profession impacted significantly on my mental health, leading to a mental and emotional breakdown in 2017.

After a year off work whilst trying to recover, with the help of therapy and self-healing, I decided to leave the profession for the sake of myself and my family.

I took the huge, risky decision to return to college and re-train as a complementary therapist. With my mental health continuing to be unstable, I decided to set up my own small

business. This would enable me to work the hours I was able to manage without the overbearing pressures which I had previously experienced as a teacher. I launched my business at the end of November 2018 whilst still at college, adding more and more therapy treatments to my list of qualifications during my first year in business. This meant I was self-employed for only four months of the 2018-19 tax year.

As my confidence started to grow again, I also started teaching ballet classes at my sister's dance school. In my younger days I was a student at The Royal Ballet School, before anorexia ravaged my mind and body. Returning to ballet after all of those years was a challenge but also a significant personal achievement!

For the first time, my adult-life was starting to feel calm, settled and positive....

So far during the pandemic my business has been closed for seven months. As a single parent, thankfully I have received Universal Credit, but this does not cover my household bills and expenses. My parents have generously helped by offering me money from their pensions, which saddens me deeply.

Being a single parent for most of my 18-year-old daughter's life had already forced me to be financially independent. So being Excluded has caused my confidence to plummet and I feel like a complete failure. I do not know what the future holds with regards to my business. It is always in the back of my mind that I could return to teaching, but to the detriment of my mental health. The thought of that terrifies me, sending my anxieties spirally uncontrollably.

I have paid my taxes for 21 years. However, this was disregarded when the COVID financial support packages were handed out. I made a career change at one moment in time (which probably saved my life!) but I am now being penalised for that! How are people expected to survive without meaningful support? It is not just 3 million individuals who have been Excluded, but their children too. It is a national disgrace!

I joined ExcludedUK in the early days and although I haven't posted my story, I am actively involved in fighting for parity for us all. This community of strangers is like one I have never witnessed before. Such sympathy, understanding, empathy, kindness, loyalty, fierceness and relentlessness.... The list could go on! My mood has been lifted by being part of the fight for justice. On difficult days, the ExcludedUK community remind me that we will never give up that fight.

And what of the future? Firstly, I just want to be able to hug my parents again. I will cherish every special moment and focus on making memories. With regards to business, what will be will be. I will leave that up to the Universe xx

20.
NAME: Raychel McGuin
OCCUPATION: Events, Marketing, Communications
REASON FOR EXCLUSION: Newly Self-Employed

In my pre-Excluded life I quit my job on my 50th Birthday after almost a year of on-and-off sickness with various physical and mental health symptoms. This was caused by a narcissistic manager using my indicators of menopause to manipulate and gaslight me into thinking I was incapable.

Year one of being self-employed was steady but slow, mainly networking to get future bookings. Year two never happened. I had over £9,000 worth of contracts cancelled from March to early May, and very little since.

I am very lucky as my husband is able to work from home for a utilities company, so we are managing. It's more about the fact that I can no longer bring in an income and contribute to the home and outgoings. My husband is fine with it, but my mental health and confidence have been rocked. I feel worthless. We were hoping my husband could retire at 55, but we've had to use our savings to survive, so that's not going to happen.

After 35 years of paying PAYE tax, I feel cheated. The whole thing is unjust, when some people are getting paid to sit at home or do second jobs/set up home businesses. They are undercutting those of us in the industry who are fighting to keep our heads above water.

I could not have gotten through this without the support from the ExcludedUK community. I have made some great connections and there are some really positive collaborations in the pipeline.

For over 20 years I have been thinking of writing a book and an associated course project based on colour energy. With not having to work I have been putting effort into getting that up and running, but the stress of this whole situation has sapped my mojo and really knocked my confidence, so it is taking way longer than it should.

Below is an edited extract from my blog of November 2020:
It's not true we are all in the same boat in this pandemic, we are in the same storm, yes, but certainly not the same boat.

Some are feeling queasy due to the rocking of their huge luxurious cruise ship, but the cabins are warm and comfortable, the opulent food is restocked daily, there's entertainment and it won't last forever, chin chin, bottoms up.

Some are battening down the hatches on their trawlers, still out there catching their own fish, fighting to survive on the massive swells that are coming more frequently to threaten their survival.

Others are in little rowing boats, desperately hanging on to their loved ones, not even enough life jackets to go around, watching the bright lights of the cruise liner as it powers by to calmer waters.

And then there's the ones who have already been tipped into the water, frantically clinging to the flotsam and jetsam around them, not knowing if the next wave will be the one to tug them under to their fate, and often not even having the energy to care…

I listened to Mayors Andy Burnham (Manchester) and Steve Rotheram (Liverpool) at an online meeting, showing their support for ExcludedUK and ForgottenLtd.

We heard of a business with 200+ animals to feed who have had no support and are looking at the possibility of having to euthanise their animals, because they can no longer afford to feed them. Of a teenager who is self-harming and refusing to eat as they feel they are being a burden on a family in crisis. Of a young family who have had to sell their home and move in with the in-laws as they are in the Arts and see no likelihood of theatres reopening.

We saw the strong and defiant, who have the balls to stand up and tell their stories, crumble when they realise the futility of it all; I'm watching through my own tears as dozens of others grab a tissue, breaking with them, as they can totally empathise.

If you are not affected by any of this, I urge you, please don't just ignore it. Call the coastguard, light some beacons on the shore, bring warm blankets, mugs of tea and reassuring smiles, a virtual hug, anything to give us some hope.

It may be dark out there at the moment, the blackness of the ocean is overwhelming. But deep-down humans are kind, compassionate and they care. Let this be a reminder of what, or more crucially 'who' is important, and find once again that humility that makes us human.

21.

NAME: Allison Rapo

OCCUPATION: Driving Instructor/Dog Agility Trainer

REASON FOR EXCLUSION: Newly Self-Employed

In 2017 I had been working for ten years as an Environmental Scientist, with reasonable hours, a decent wage, and close to home, but I decided it was time for a change. I retrained as an independent driving instructor while still working, and purchased my own teaching car in February 2018. By the end of September 2019 I had left my job and was a fully qualified Driving Instructor.

During the first Lockdown I was allowed to teach care workers; however, I only had a few on my books and the income wasn't enough. In later Lockdowns I wasn't allowed to teach at all, so I had no income from my driving instructor work. I also teach dog agility lessons, but a similar thing happened there.

I've been rejected for SEISS because I haven't got three years' accounts. I was also rejected for Job Seekers and Universal Credit, because my husband works hard and earns too much money. Currently I'm waiting for my local council to reply about the ARG grant, though I have no hopes for a positive outcome. I don't have business premises or pay business rates.

However, I was eligible for a £6,000 Bounce Back Loan, interest-free for a year. The application process was painful and meant I had to open up a business account which was supposed to be free for a year. I've used about £1,000 from this account to cover car insurance, tax, maintenance etc. I think I'm supposed to be grateful, but when so many people were given furlough, extra Universal Credit and grants from the government, I'm cross. I haven't been in debt for years.

Currently, I've estimated a loss in earnings of approximately £13,000. I was going to help my daughter at university with this money, and put some towards my retirement and upgrades on my house. What's really sad is that I now feel I've paid my debt to society and then some. I've always been generous with voluntary work and charity donations. Well, I've paid my bit now, £13,000 and still counting. My answer to future requests for charity donations is, "I've already paid, go ask the unemployed who get given money for nothing, go ask the vulnerable, go ask the sick, go ask the elderly, they owe me big time, don't ask me." I never used to feel like this but now I'm really bitter.

Aly Rapo qualifying as a Driving Instructor.

No, I'm not hungry or in hardship; I own my house and a little bit of land, I have my lovely life with my husband and daughter, my dogs and my ponies. I have always worked, except for about four years when I had my daughter and my husband provided for his new family.

We had no other financial support, and to be fair we didn't need it. But no way have I ever been lucky or privileged or blessed. I am the last of five children, my husband is the last of four, and our parents worked hard for everything they had. What I am, is hard working, responsible and sensible and I've never received financial help from the government to get what I have.

My husband regularly works overtime and earns a good wage. He works in the aerospace industry and of course, nothing is flying. Recently his employers needed to make 150 people redundant and he was asked to move to a sister company to work, about 30 miles from home. He knuckled down, wore his mask, and learnt a new, very tedious skill, just to keep his job. He survived the redundancy lottery but it was traumatic watching his colleagues lose their jobs. Planes are still not flying though, and it's possible the factory may have to close.

When I worked as an Environmental Scientist my daughter had just started school. I couldn't always be there after school to collect her as I didn't finish my working day until 5pm. I gave up time with my family to work and pay into the very system that has now Excluded me. She went to university in September and I'm cross because I can't help her financially. Instead, I'm supporting people I've never met, I'll never meet and who will never repay me. I don't want your praise or thanks and please don't clap me, I want to work and earn! I want my £13,000 in lost earnings!

I've tried to find a job that will allow me to leave as soon as restrictions are lifted. I looked at being a delivery driver, but they want me to lift 23kg. I'm 55 and don't want to damage my body lifting. I looked at environmental science jobs, but have had no luck there either. I suspect I'm one of millions looking for a job.

I could say I've been dealt a really bad deal, but I wasn't even allowed to sit at the card table. I've worked hard at parenting, marriage and my job. I'm bitter and have horrid thoughts about the people I'm supposed to be giving everything up for. Do you blame me? And if anyone says "But you don't know how lucky you are" one more time!!

22.

NAME: Ryhad Laurentus

OCCUPATION: Live Events Industry

REASON FOR EXCLUSION: Newly Self-Employed

I'm 33, with a partner aged 35. I started self-employment in April 2019, encouraged by my previous employers, as a way of securing more flexible work in the live events industry as we seek to start a family. I spent two years saving in a PAYE job, then spent my first year's earnings and my savings on tooling, a van, and training to diversify my skills (plus fuel and expenses to get to the work, all around the country). I was without work from February until October, when I was lucky enough to find a 16-hour contract working night shifts at Argos, but it barely covers my living costs.

We are living with my parents, financially destroyed (savings gone and an increase on loan rates from 3% to 12%). My van is SORN and the work is slowly destroying my physical health and putting unnecessary strain on the relationship with my partner.

I don't see a way to progress in the short/medium term. Without the love and support of my family, we absolutely wouldn't have managed. To start our own family in our current situation is however impossible. After so many years working two jobs to get to where I am, I feel punished for trying to succeed.

23.

NAME: Jo Kenny

OCCUPATION: Glass Blower and Tutor

REASON FOR EXCLUSION: Numerous

Winding the clock back to January 2020, I'm excited for the future. I had been working part-time as a special-needs teacher while carefully building up a small nest egg to invest in my glass blowing and steadily increasing my glass tutoring self-employment. Finally I felt confident enough to put in my notice at school, freeing up time for the extra glass work, which was building steadily. School offered one day a week guaranteed supply, and extra days ad hoc. It could not have been a better time to take the plunge, or so I thought.

Jo making glass in Blackpool

Lockdown in March saw all my glassblowing work shut down overnight. Distressing, but I think I can get over this, the glass blowing will come back and I still have a small salary from school until Easter. I use my time building a web site.

Easter comes and goes with no prospect of glassblowing coming back, and now I have no wage from school either. What now? I fight to get a refund on a glass conference in Sweden that is now cancelled, the money will come in useful. I talked to school about putting me on furlough. They were sympathetic but not putting anyone on furlough; however they agree to pay me for the one day per week supply until the end of July as promised, so that's great. Hopefully by then things will be better but, as a back up, I will sign up to a teaching agency.

London is a prison to me now, as soon as Lockdown lifts I am going home to Yorkshire. At least I can work on the house there (I can't afford to get professionals in to do the work for me now anyway). The Agency is keen to get me on board, so I sold my car and bought a camper van so I can reach more glass studios when work starts up.

I look into government support – lots of sympathy, but I don't qualify for anything. Maybe Job Seekers Allowance? No such luck, not enough stamp paid. But how come? I have paid PAYE on school work and self-employed stamp for glassblowing? Very sympathetic but all I can have is my stamp paid.

Ok, no income at all for August but at least I am home and glass blowing is planned for September, and supply teaching should start too. Schools are reluctant to let supply teachers in, so I have only three days work between September and Xmas. One glass gig, then the studio shuts again. January 2021. I don't need sympathy, just wake me up when this is over, I've no energy left.

24.

NAME: Louise Schakley Van Zyl

OCCUPATION: Learning Development Manager

REASON FOR EXCLUSION: Limited Company Director

I'd like to educate Rishi Sunak on the actual facts. I'm a single mother, two small kids, and not entitled to support due to being Limited Company Director. Yet many people who were already on a higher income prior to COVID are getting grants and additional benefits, then have the nerve to complain about how or what is in free school and food parcels.

A Bounce Back Loan is an appropriate lending option. However, the 'easy' application promised by Government completely false. I'm a small business and my criteria are ideal, but accredited lenders are including stipulations that the loans are available to 'existing business customers'. New applicants are required to apply and agree to a business account before the loan can be processed.

I banked with none of the lenders, except Santander personal banking. Santander refused to even attempt to help because the account had business activity. Rishi has not considered how excluding business support impacts personal finances.

I feel I'm being punished due to a few dishonest directors' income. HMRC apparently lack the ability to prevent fraud. I can only hope my clients will pay their outstanding invoices or I get some other support. I'd be grateful for a Bounce Back Loan. Lenders who are not adhering to Terms & Conditions or who include stipulations not approved by Government should be held accountable!

25.

NAME: Sam Thacker

OCCUPATION: Driving Instructor

REASON FOR EXCLUSION: Newly Self-Employed

Being Excluded has been horrible. I am a newly self-employed driving instructor. I took a leap of faith for a chance to better myself and have time for my family rather than working long hours. No financial help from government at all, I was close to losing my house, everything me and my partner worked so hard for. It's made me feel that I have no faith in the powers-that-be and I have been at breaking point, stressing out beyond belief. I have had to start work, then stop, then start, then stop.

The ExcludedUK group has been the best support and it's not all financial, it's somebody to actually listen, somebody to ask you how you are. People are in similar boats and some are even worse. I have been through so many emotions mentally that how can the government turn around to us and say we have all been helped when in all honesty we have been left out to hang? Just like how London dealt with the plague, leaving the poor in the streets to rot, that's exactly how I feel.

People have had to break the rules to survive. If every single person was helped we would not be in a position where innocent people have died, as some had no choice but to go to work when no decent help was given. 3 million Excluded is not a huge number of people to help when the country is in so much debt already. To protect lives you have to help people survive.

26.
NAME: Lisa Lamb
OCCUPATION: Yoga Teacher
REASON FOR EXCLUSION: 50/50 rule

Being Excluded has left me feeling that my business and its contribution to society is not worthy. I feel utterly let down by this government and feel truly saddened that people like me have been repeatedly ignored despite our many, many pleas for help and parity.

I have been a fitness instructor for 25 years, working in local gyms. In 2012 I trained to become a yoga teacher to enable me to reach my goal of owning my own business. I started classes in my local community, hiring local halls as well as still teaching my fitness classes for local gyms as a paid employee.

My self-employment business grew and finally in 2019 I made the huge leap to go even more self-employed. I dropped most of my PAYE classes to grow my yoga community business. I worked very hard and built up to over 100 students a week. I did further training and had many more things planned for 2020.

Then in March 2020 my business, along with many others, was forced to close. My job is more than just a job, it's my passion and life's work. It might not mean much to this government but it means so much to me. It brings people together, getting fitter and healthier together. Life-long friendships are made in group exercise, we share our life's ups and downs together. To have that taken away was bad, really bad, but there was worse to come when I realised I was going to receive no financial help for the business that I had worked so hard to build up. To be Excluded financially was a cruel blow to take; the unfairness of it all makes me feel abandoned.

The ExcludedUK group has been a constant support to me since the beginning of the first Lockdown. Many times I have been in tears reading the heartbreaking stories of the other members, the misfortunes through absolutely no fault of their own. I have found that it's difficult for family and friends to really understand what it's been like to be cruelly treated so very different to everyone else.

I can only hope that I can rise above this crisis and be able to build my business back to what it was, and more, in the future. But I will never forget the way the Excluded have been left abandoned in all of this.

27.
NAME: Julie
OCCUPATION: Beauty Clinic/Training School
REASON FOR EXCLUSION: Limited Company Director

I started in 1992, firstly mobile, then taking premises within a hairdressers on the High Street. After a year, I took on my first employee, and another employee each of the following four years. I then expanded into my own premises, where I have been for 21 years. Until the pandemic, I traded very successfully, paying Corporation Tax and VAT for all 26 years. I thought I would comfortably retire in the next year or so (I am 70), having accumulated a pension and a profitable business for sale. I am very proud of my achievements and was looking forward to a well-deserved retirement.

But, then the pandemic hit, and I found that although my employees were helped, I, as the business owner, was to be without my monthly dividends taken as salary. I would still have to pay my own living expenses, my employees' National Insurance, pension and tax contributions, and the business running costs (rent, insurance, telephones etc). I had a couple of business grants, but to be honest, whilst grateful, it nowhere near covered my expenses. I used up all of my contingency money within the first few months and have since propped the business up from my pension. I can see my pension slowly diminishing, a fund that I worked so hard for. How can that be right?

I have seen self-employed people paid a percentage of their income whilst they have still been able to work. Construction and the like. How is that fair? I have always voted for the Conservative party and never thought that over 3 million tax-paying workers would be ignored in this way. This was a party that encouraged entrepreneurs, only to let them down when they needed them the most. My employees are grateful for the help, but there are very likely to be many businesses who simply won't make it without parity for business owners, and they will be forced to close. That seems crazy to me!

I have good and bad days. Good days where I feel energised and work on the business ready for when we can return but, unfortunately, many more bad days where I feel like I'm treading mud and can't see how I'm ever going to catch up.

The ExcludedUK group has helped keep hope alive, that someday the Conservative Party may do the right thing and help us stay in the businesses we have spent so many years building up and providing employment.

I don't know what the future holds, but I could never have imagined being in this situation at 70, fearful for my future.

28.

NAME: Natalie Berry

OCCUPATION: Driving Instructor

REASON FOR EXCLUSION: Newly Self-Employed

I decided to go self-employed and set up my own business in July 2019.

Before this I worked in schools all over North Wales as a full-time supply teacher. I worked in Primary, Secondary and Special Educational Needs schools. I also worked evenings as a tutor offering extra support to children from my local area.

The main reason for my change in career was the difficulty with the language barrier. I had attended college to learn Welsh for three years and I was even a runner up for Welsh Learner of the Year. However, I still always missed out on jobs due to not having Welsh as my first language. I then decided to do something about it and retrained as a driving instructor. This cost a lot of money and took a lot of time and effort. I decided to go independent and started Pass With Natalie. Since then I have worked harder than ever. I work 8am until 8pm 6 days a week. Plus, I am available 24/7 for extra support for my learners. I have made a real success of my business with lots of test passes and numerous reviews and recommendations.

Then came COVID-19. As a close-contact business, I was forced to close and I was warned there would be fines if anybody was caught working. I followed every rule and didn't leave the house at all, didn't see family or friends, and waited patiently for the government to allow me to work again. The whole time we are in Lockdown I still have all my expenses to pay, both personal (rent, bills, food) and business (car payments, learner insurance, accounting bills). In 2020 my business was forced to close for 22 weeks. I have not worked at all yet in 2021, and still received no help from the government because I have not been established long enough to qualify for any support.

I am still very frightened as there seems no light at the end of the tunnel and my savings will only last so long. My anxiety has massively increased, I am constantly worried, I don't sleep anymore. I feel completely abandoned and I feel like I don't matter. All my hard work has been made a mockery of. Nobody understands as ALL of my friends are able to work from home. Most people believe the government are helping everyone. I am fed up of seeing people who are still working, working from home or furloughed, ignoring rules and doing whatever they like. Meanwhile, I am following every rule and trying to keep everyone safe. My Mum and my sister have both had COVID and were both very unwell, and not being able to see them or help them was heartbreaking.

I have never been in debt, I always live within my means which has meant I have savings. Savings I have earned by working long and hard hours in hope of making memories, going on holidays and a deposit for our first house. By the end of Lockdown I will have nothing.

The government has left me with nothing but worry and anxiety.

29.

NAME: Eleanor Gaywood

OCCUPATION: Dance and Fitness Instructor

REASON FOR EXCLUSION: 50/50 rule

Before Lockdown my company, Shimmy School, had just completed a community production which sold out the theatre on both nights; our classes and numbers had increased and diversified; we were training up new teachers and professional dancers, and had more than tripled earnings from the year before.

Since becoming Excluded I feel invisible, voiceless, not worthy, not a part of the UK. I have lost my identity and been incredibly stressed which has affected my pregnancy. I sold my house to survive the pandemic.

One positive is that I have been able to make an online version of shimmy school which has kept most of my students in touch and active, and has reached further afield geographically. The slower pace of life meant I could focus on my personal life and I am now about to have my first baby!

Eleanor performing through her company Shimmy School

As for the future, I have looked at what I really want and am even more driven than ever, I have applied to university to do a masters degree in my field. However, I cannot financially survive another year with no support.

30.

NAME: Jeanette

OCCUPATION: Freelance Hairdresser and Barber

REASON FOR EXCLUSION: 50/50 rule

I left school a very eager teenager, I couldn't wait to start earning my own money! Yes that's right ..... idiot now, I know.

I started as an office Junior in the local foam factory, basic admin but it got me started. I stayed here for a couple of years, always eager to learn and wanting more. So I quit and jumped straight into a role in Purchase ledger at another local company.

It felt great! I was doing well and earning well also, especially for an 18 year old. I was just getting settled when we learned they would be relocating to High Wycombe .... My role would be redundant!

Being young, I took this in my stride, more jobs where that came from!? I found a temporary job at a Landrover spares based in Tansley, great! Immediate start.

I worked here for six weeks until I received a call asking if I would like to go and work for my old company, but in a different department. Why not? They were a great company to work for, so back I went. Sadly this only lasted a further three years, until they relocated the rest of the company to High Wycombe and Stoke.

As one door closes another one opens, that was always my motto!

I got a job within weeks working for Tarmac, another great company. I worked on the Weighbridge for ten years before rumours started that we were to be made redundant. This really was a sad day as we all knew each other and worked like a small family. We all looked out for each other, very hard to find these days.

Sadly I was made redundant in 2013. I was just 33, but now my feelings had changed. I was married with a mortgage, so my income was far more important than just earning.

I decided I was not going to take this anymore and from now on I would have control over when and how much I worked. I was going to re-educate myself and go self-employed. Everyone thought I was joking, of course. I tolerated the jokes and the insults of "Don't you think you're too old to go to college!?" This just made me more eager to do this.

I made sure I had a job when I signed up for college, I was going to support myself all the way. No one would be able to say "I told you so". There would be no excuses for me to quit. I studied Ladies Hair Level 2, twice a week in the evening, and go from college to my night job as a carer. I worked waking nights throughout my training and went on to set up as a mobile stylist. This was extremely exhausting. I was on a Zero Hour contract, sometimes going well above 50 hours due to staff shortages. By night I was holding hands with people taking their last breaths and by day I was making them feel refreshed and beautiful.

I did this for five years whilst continuing to gain my qualifications, all the time being criticised that it would come to nothing.

In 2018 I had to make changes again as my mother needed me. She had been ill for a long time and I knew we were reaching End of Life. I quit my care job and worked in the local pub all weekend, followed by working freelance in the local Barber shop. This gave me the chance to be there when I was needed, the reason most people choose self-employment.

March 23rd 2020, and the shop closed. We reopened July 4th 2020, after 14 weeks with NO support. This was because my husband worked and I had savings over £16K. These savings were to build me my own salon.

On return to the shop I decided I was going to earn as much as I could to put away ready for Lockdown 2 – my gut feeling said this would happen, and so it did, 5th November until

2nd December. Still no support from the government. Along came Lockdown 3, January 4th 2021, with no guidance on when we can return? Still no support.

It's not worth crying as it won't change anything, I feel empty and let down. I have worked all my life and paid tax. No time out to have children. My husband has been a key worker throughout, paying taxes.

I don't have a fancy car, I don't spend money on my holidays abroad, and I save. Being brought up by a single mum who never claimed off the state, 'benefits' was a dirty word in my mum's house. She had three jobs and four children, and never claimed.

My question still stands: you have all my records from my pay-slips and my self assessment in which I have to include this income. I put all my money into the bank to pay bills, which is traceable. Where exactly is the fraud? Some of us are honest working class citizens which is more than can be said for our MPs with their rather large expenses. I probably don't claim for all my expenses as I should, my fault I know but surely that would tell you I'm not greedy!

#NO MONEY SINCE MARCH
#STILL STANDING
#WON'T GIVE UP
#BORN A STRONG WOMEN
#I'M WORTH SO MUCH MORE, RISHI

When COVID is over me and the 3 million will REMEMBER! And NO Rishi you are not putting my taxes up to pay for those who had the privilege of furlough. Why should we? My husband also works. Why should he pay?

Stop the furlough, you watch how quickly people will adhere to rules of the Lockdown and COVID would be sorted.

31.

NAME: Jo Bishop

OCCUPATION: Photographer

REASON FOR EXCLUSION: Newly Self-Employed

I have worked since leaving school in 1998. I joined the Police force and worked as a response officer for 12 years. Whilst working for GMP I began my photography business. I became pregnant in 2016 and closed the business down as I didn't know if I would be able to continue after I'd had my daughter.

In 2019 I reinstated my business by taking out a personal loan and building a summerhouse studio at home. I decided to take the leap to leave the police in the

November of that same year. My business was thriving and I was able to fit it around my husband's work until, three months later, COVID hit.

I was unable to get the profit percentage due to having no returns.
I was unable to get any grants as my studio was at home.
I was unable to get Universal Credit due to my husband's wage – yet his wage does not cover both our combined bills.

My savings have gone.

We are on our 2nd mortgage holiday and my husband had to take a loan out to cover my bills. This has now gone and we have little to nothing coming in. I have stopped all direct debits that I can't see as essential, such as my dentist plan & pet insurance amongst others.

I have seen other photographers gloat on social media that they keep being sent grants that they don't even need, yet I am having to go heavily into debt to get by.

I cannot take a small job in the interim due to how my husband's shifts work and our daughter is only three so she is not in nursery full time.

I have no idea how much worse It has to get before things pick up. We are broken. I have been a public servant for 12 years, but bad timing and lack of support has ruined me. My story may not be the worst, but it's mine and life is a massive struggle financially and mentally now.

32.
NAME: Helen
OCCUPATION: PhiBrows Microblading Artist
REASON FOR EXCLUSION: All of them

My name is Helen, and I am 54 years old. My company is called Take a Brow (you guessed it, I do brows). I am from Liverpool where the brow industry is huge – ever heard of the Scouse brow?

I was a primary school teacher for 20 years, teaching Reception children. I loved my job and thought I would teach till retirement. Unfortunately, I had a spate of ill health and I lost my hearing completely in one ear.

After three years off work and seven operations, I returned to school. It quickly hit me that I was no longer the confident, capable teacher I once was. I just could not cope with single-sided hearing in a noisy Reception class of 30 children, with undistinguishable sounds coming at me from all angles.

After a year of struggling, going to work with a feeling of dread, coming home tearful and exhausted, I was literally paid off by an unsympathetic new head teacher who saw me as dead wood. So, what did I do? I used my £18,000 dead wood money to retrain, open my own business and brow training academy, and life was good again. I delivered training in brow mapping, henna brows and brow lamination, and had a wonderful growing clientele. I set up my successful business without borrowing or going into any debt, and I felt happy after four years of struggling with my health and making the huge decision to leave my career.

Then in March 2020 national Lockdown happened. The beauty business was closed for a total of five and half months. Scary times but Rishi Sunak kept saying he was going to support us, we were all in this together, and it was going to be ok.

I rent my studio and little training area in my sister's beauty shop. That meant I was Excluded from the Business Grant. No worries, I thought, I will apply for the SEISS – but no, I do PAYE so I'm somehow not self-employed. I queried this with HMRC and a very nice lady rang me to tell me "you're not classed as self-employed, we don't know what you earn so you're not eligible". Hold on, I pay £40 a week PAYE as this is what HMRC told me to do after my first tax return, so how do you not know what I earn and how am I classed as not self-employed?

I am also a new business (started September 2018) and whilst building my clientele I was working two days a week as a supply teacher until I was confident to go alone, so the 50-50 rule also applies. Confused? Yes me too!

The next option was furlough, but again I am not eligible as I am the company director. I employ a lovely girl who is at college and training in the beauty industry; thankfully I was able to furlough her through each of the three Lockdowns we have endured.

As for Universal Credit, I am not eligible as my husband works. He does not earn enough to support us both, we've always both worked. And the struggles began.

Ten months on I had no other choice than to take out a £10,000 Bounce Back Loan to keep my business afloat. I was so proud that I initially set up my business without any debt or loans. I am confident that when we're open and this terrible pandemic is over we will bounce back, because brows are big business, especially in Liverpool.

The worst thing is my dear Mum gifted me £5,000 to live on, pay my rent and help me through Christmas to buy presents for my three children and two grandchildren. I applied for a Discretionary grant from Liverpool City Council and was awarded £2,500. I could have cried when the money came through. I cried because I had finally been given some support, and I cried because I had to practically beg for this money and it made me feel like a failure, a scrounger. I gave the money to my son who is a single parent; he lost his job the week before the March Lockdown so he was not eligible for furlough and has been living on Universal Credit and the kindness of family and friends. After all, as Rishi keeps saying, we are all in this together. I am lucky. I have got a roof over my head, food on the table, a few close friends and my family.

ExcludedUK has opened my eyes to the many others who are suffering so much more than myself. Businesses lost, homes lost, relying on food banks. The kindness from this group, brought together because of the utter incompetence of this Government, has brought me to tears.

People have died and others have been saved. Suicide. I read the threads and cry. I want to put my arms around the ExcludedUK community. I want to thank everyone; I want to meet our community and hug and hug. There are heroes who help and inspire others in the ExcludedUK community for no other reason than pure kindness, compassion, and common goals.

I have felt ridiculously small being Excluded. I have always worked, contributed to society, paid my taxes and I am a good person, I do not deserve to be treated like some sort of criminal of society.

When this is all over I will strive to build my business again. I will employ more people; I will contribute to the economy that Excluded me, but I will not be not heard. Twitter is my best friend now. How I love a twitter bomb @RishiSunak @BorisJohnson.

33.

NAME: Steffani Benton-Martyn

OCCUPATION: Singing Teacher

REASON FOR EXCLUSION: 50/50 rule

I have wanted to sing professionally and teach singing since I was a teenager, and in 2019 I achieved that dream, blissfully unaware that within months, my world would change.

When the schools first locked down in March 2020, it knocked out the vast majority of my income. I transferred a small handful of students online, but this is unfortunately nowhere near the amount I need to live on. So many people assume that being self-employed has made me eligible for help, but no. Until October 2019 I supported the growth of my business with PAYE work, before I was finally able to go fully self-employed. The PAYE work covered over 50% of my income, which has Excluded me from any current support. Even my local council help has only been for those with physical premises and business rates.

Steff Benton-Martyn.

Photo by Rebecca Andrews-Smith Photography.

Honestly, it is down to mostly human kindness (and the organisation "Help Musicians") that my husband and I have survived. Friends and family have helped, for which I will be forever grateful but the ExcludedUK group, too, has been an infinite source of help and support. We are getting by on just my husband's wage but it is a world of very basic living and scraping money together: a far cry from the career I thought I had in 2019. I feel a tremendous loss of identity, I miss performing to an audience, and I miss my students. I feel heartbroken.

After the COVID-19 pandemic has been taken care of, we will as a nation, I'm sure, have to address the resulting mental health crisis. So many are struggling, more so than I. Something has to give.

34.
NAME: Fiona (& husband)
OCCUPATION: Training and Consultancy Business
REASON FOR EXCLUSION: Limited Company Directors

My husband runs a face-to-face training and consultancy business which advises charities on how to raise money from trusts and reviews their fundraising strategies. He has no office, works from home, and has no staff, but a small network of freelance consultants. I work for a small charity part-time and my income doesn't even cover the mortgage. Prior to COVID he had been doing well, although nowhere near the income of £200,000 that my MP suggested most people who run a Limited Company earn – what a joke, our car is 16 years old.

In March 2020 COVID hit and all the training courses had to be cancelled. Many charities furloughed their staff so there was no consultancy either. Overnight, our income plummeted.

Every time a new scheme was announced we thought we would receive some support, and to find out we were not eligible was devastating. We took the Bounce Back Loan and didn't pay the tax bill, which has kept us afloat, but we have so many bills, and a family of four daughters all of whom we support in some way, including one at University whose accommodation we pay. My husband has managed to put the courses on Zoom and remodel the business, so we are grateful to have some income, as I know some people are in a far worse situation. But we have had to take a mortgage holiday for the first time, the credit cards are maxed out, and the bank is charging 40% interest on the overdraft.

Suffice to say it has put a severe strain on our relationship and we are desperate now, wondering how long this is going to go on for. It has been awful to write to our MP several times and be told that we should be living off savings! What savings? Also to hear of a friend who has received £1million from the government when we have received not a single penny. I can't believe the injustice and the unfairness of this, when we have paid our taxes and contributed to the economy, we truly have been cruelly and wilfully Excluded.

35.
NAME: Fiona & Chris Hughes
OCCUPATION: Creative Clothing Solutions
REASON FOR EXCLUSION: Limited Company Directors

We established our company (sportswear, workwear and uniforms) in 2001, and it is our life. When you begin a business, you put your heart and soul into it. There are no sick days, no holidays, no social events and no money, and many sacrifices are made. One week's holiday a year and not five weeks like when we were employees in previous careers! You can't afford to be away for any longer as it's your passion and dedication that you meet deadlines and maintain the reputation you have built up over many years.

Our company is our baby. It's personal. You put others first – suppliers, employees and landlords – and sometimes don't take a wage when times are hard. That's what you do when it's your own business. You are the beating heart, the last thing to give out when you need to meet your customers needs. We survived the recession by making personal sacrifices. We moved our business online, had pop-up shops in schools, and a home office. This flexibility allowed us to have a work/life balance and support our daughter.

That week in March 2020, I was in bed with suspected COVID. I listened and hung on to every work of Rishi Sunak's speech. I was relieved that they would be providing a safety net to help us get through. "We are in it together". I knew the Tories believed in small businesses and entrepreneurs – of course they would help.

Little did I know how those words would haunt me. I would continue to hang on to every word that man would say, like an addict waiting for a fix. We were desperate. Schemes were announced and then each time the realisation hit – we were not entitled to support. A door would close and when we went to the next step, the door would slam in our faces again. Endless begging calls to Council Tax offices, energy providers, mortgage companies. Our integrity and self esteem were shattered. Slowly we realised we were being left out in the cold.

My husband is older, 71, so between us we have paid into the system for over 85 years, never asking for a single penny. Months passed; mortgage breaks ended and still, every time it's raised, Rishi says they cannot help everyone how they would like. Would like?! The knot in my stomach churning. Anger brewing. So they know about us?! Why are we being left out? Surely it's a mistake and they will realise and put this right? Surely they cannot make up rules that would exclude us when we have done nothing wrong? What utter ignorance and disbelief that we, as Ltd Company Directors are in fact not 'self-employed'.

Online trolls suggest that we have not paid taxes or have even done something illegal; there is talk of fraud risks. We are offended and hurt, our integrity in tatters. Friends and family are silent, as if we have committed a crime. MPs, celebrities and even the Treasury Committee call for solutions, gathering momentum, but they are ignored.

In some ways, we consider ourselves lucky – we have worked all hours to generate enough money to pay our bills, to survive. Debts are mounting but we are still here, and so many are not. We are simply exhausted, physically and emotionally.

The most unforgivable experience is to be told “stay at home”. But that was never an option, we have not received the support that would enable us to stay at home. My at-risk, 71 year old husband has been forced to continue to work. He has a heart condition, and he has a 12 year old daughter. She has been terrified – “Dad, they say over 70s must stay at home!"

I have been terrified too. The hurt and exclusion that this government has caused is simply unforgiveable. We need to be heard for those that could not see a way through. We will continue until we are heard.

36.

NAME: Steph

OCCUPATION: Printmaking Teacher

REASON FOR EXCLUSION: Newly Self-Employed

I began the first three years of my business tentatively whilst also being in employment. I made very little profit in those years as I was buying materials and equipment, and it was supplementary to my employed income.

By year four (2019/20) it was clear that I could make enough money to make it a full-time job. I was on target to make £14,000 by the end of March 2020 – then COVID restrictions put a stop to my teaching overnight. I don’t have room in the studio to give the required social distancing, and the need for expensive equipment means online teaching is almost impossible.

The SEISS calculation does not take into account my more substantial self-employed earnings from 2019/20 or any from my previous employment. It is based only on the first three years self-employed income when my business was part-time, and my profits for those three years were £0, £3,000, and £6,000. This means the TOTAL sum of government support I have received for a year of lost earnings is less than £400. I had to use this to pay my 2019/20 tax return.

It would be so easy to see that I have never been able to survive on 0, £3000 or £6000 a year because I have employment records to show my earnings for those years.

The only reason I can eat and pay my mortgage is because of savings and the support of my partner and family. I am not eligible for any other scheme because my partner's work is not affected.

I feel hurt and enraged by the suggestion I spend my hard-earned savings to survive, whilst others are receiving support which is not means-tested. I have never felt such injustice in my life. I find it hard to explain how bewildering and belittling this feels. My business was doing really well and this has been utterly unacknowledged. I paid for a therapist to help me deal with it all because the depression was overtaking me every day.

I feel like all my hard work and cautious building of the business has been utterly undermined. While my business has shrunk, others who have had government support have been able to begin and grow new businesses as they find themselves with both time and money.

I have had to adapt my business without any money to support the changes. I began to sell print kits which went really well, until a combination of Brexit and COVID meant that I couldn't get a supply of the materials I needed. I had to take time away from my business to find a job in a shop to pay the bills. Then this job ended because of the further increased restrictions.

I have no choice but to spend my savings now. I am focusing my energy on selling my own artwork rather than teaching. I'm looking forward to this new venture but have a mountain to climb...

37.

NAME: Janice Hugh

OCCUPATION: Complementary Healthcare Practitioner/Teacher

REASON FOR EXCLUSION: 50/50 rule

In 2003 I was advised by a physiotherapist that to continue as a full-time PA would result in permanent disability due to RSI in my neck and shoulders. To enable me to work without resorting to sickness or disability benefits, I decided to retrain in complementary healthcare – principally reflexology, but adding therapies year on year, as and when I could afford it.

In June 2004 I took the plunge and became totally self-employed with my own practice. It was a micro-business; just me, no rateable premises, no employees. My client base ranged from babies to my own grandmother, who was 100 years old. I specialised in pre-conception and maternity work, becoming qualified to provide reflexology during labour. My additional therapies also proved popular and included Indian Head Massage, Spinal Touch Back Therapy, Hot Stone Massage, and several other therapies. These enabled me to secure an income and yet diversify my time and energies without compromising my health.

In December 2014, aged 64, I took my deferred State Pension and carried on with my micro-business, paying my taxes and all other dues. The only additional income I have is a small private annuity which, together with my State Pension, gives me a grand total income of approximately £910 per month.

I do not have the luxury of a substantial private pension, hence I had no intention of giving up my complementary healthcare practice as it was something I really enjoyed, it supplemented my Pension, and I was able to balance my health needs with my work.

In the first weeks of 2015 my Mum was formally diagnosed with Alzheimer's Condition. As she rapidly deteriorated, I found myself supporting my parents to the detriment of my business. I do not regret helping my parents for one second, but the drop in self-employed income was to have a far-reaching effect which at the time did not occur to me.

Fast forward to 2020 and we all know what happened... Being a close-contact, non-essential business, I followed the rules and closed my practice. My clients being in the vulnerable range, I closed before the official date. And waited, reassured by Rishi Sunak's infamous words, "We will do whatever it takes....."

How foolish was I to believe him?

By July 2020, with no business income, I mothballed my website and suspended my professional membership and insurance to reduce costs, in the hope that I might resume my practice before long. It hasn't happened.

Having a State Pension renders me totally without any financial help, no SEISS, no Grant from the UK Government, no discretionary grant or help from the Welsh Government or my local authority, because in each situation my main 'crime' is that my self-employed income was less than 50% of my total income.

I feel that, as a micro-business, I don't warrant any value to the authorities, and yet they knew where to find me for voluntary National Insurance contributions and tax. I veer from feeling very angry to feeling discarded, of no value, too little to count.

I was 70 in December 2020, and although I had planned to carry on with my complementary healthcare practice, that is now in doubt.

38.

NAME: Dominique

OCCUPATION: Dog Walking & Facilities

REASON FOR EXCLUSION: Newly Self-Employed

I am the business owner of a company that revolves around dogs. In January 2020, I resigned from my full-time job as a police officer to pursue my business full-time. I had been juggling both jobs, but wanted to take some time away from the police to fully discover my ever growing business and do something for myself and my happiness. I loved being a police officer, but the joy of running my own successful business was a feeling like no other. So I took the plunge.

The business grew rapidly. The demand for dog walking was insane and I outsourced work to over ten freelance staff. I expanded to having two 'bark parks' available for private hire, regular weekend playdate events for dogs, a doggy swimming pool, and more. My ambitions and vision for the business were huge.

Then came COVID. I remember watching the news a mere two months after I resigned from my job. I burst into tears, completely overwhelmed. Overnight I literally lost 90% of my clients. Panic set in, how are we going to pay our bills, how are we going to eat? My partner reassured me; he was still working in emergency services, so we had one salary. News announcements promised that NO ONE would be left behind, and that we all needed to close up shop. As schemes were launched, and I tried to apply but got rejected, I honestly didn't mind. I remember saying that the government has so much to think about, and they will get round to us. I have paid my taxes my entire life. I have been told to shut down my business, of course we will get help.

That help never came.

Because I am "too new in business", I am not eligible for any grants. Because my partner works, I am not eligible for Universal Credit. What they don't take into consideration is that our outgoings outweigh my partner's income. If we could survive on one salary, believe me lots of us would stay at home in general. Most couples BOTH work full-time because the cost of living dictates that we have to. Why should I not receive help because I have a partner? Why am I not my own person in our Benefit system's eyes? Why does it only take rent into consideration? What about vehicles/food/pets, and god forbid if we had children?

I have seen lots of hurtful comments online; one that stuck with me was "If you had contributed anything to our society, you would be eligible for support". I spent four years serving our society, being punched, spat at, dealing with dead bodies, suicide, the worst parts of humanity, and I am looked at as someone who "hasn't contributed to society". It makes me sick with sadness that this is what people think of us. Whilst I am no longer a police officer, I paid monthly taxes my entire working life, and ultimately our support packages are being based on our taxes. HMRC has records of ALL the tax we have paid, so it shouldn't matter if I have paid my tax under an employer or as self-employed. I have paid into a system I am now being Excluded from, whilst others around me say they are the richest they have ever been.

Dominique serving as a Police Officer before starting her own business & quickly becoming Excluded.

I have finally received my first slice of meaningful help from my council. But it wasn't without a fight and, averaged over the ten months of zero support, it only equates to £200 per month. No one can live on that sort of money.

The government and most of society argues "We can't help everyone." I dispute this. You can and you have to. Absolutely no one should be Excluded because of a deadly virus and a global pandemic. If one person gets support, then everyone should. You CANNOT tell people they cannot work or trade, but also not support them. Especially when they have contributed in taxes.

I feel totally discredited, punished for being self-employed, and I don't feel as though I am a member of our society.

I have stood outside Number 10 on countless occasions, protecting the people inside from harm, having bottles thrown at me and colleagues, because protests have turned violent, on our government's door. Not because I am a Conservative, but because as a police officer I took an oath to protect life, ANY LIFE, from harm. And now the government, whose role is to look after EVERYONE in our society, has totally turned its back on me, and many others.

A very sad state of affairs.

39.
NAME: Tracey Harper-Holbrook
OCCUPATION: Yoga Teacher
REASON FOR EXCLUSION: Newly Self-Employed

In my old life I was a Quantity Surveyor. Never really chose it, just fell into it, and in the past few years I really struggled as I was suffering from depression after my dad died, and was treated really badly at work. I should have been signed off with depression, but as my depression is triggered by being alone for too long I knew this would be a big mistake. I am divorced and no kids, just me and my little rescue cat.

I was studying to be a yoga teacher and hoped to move onto this in a few years. Then my yoga teacher decided to move abroad and asked me to take over her classes and clients as a going concern. I wasn't ready, but was so unhappy in general that I grabbed it.

I became self-employed in January 2019. The first year was really hard but then my confidence grew and I started to get my own students. In autumn I started teaching children in after-school yoga clubs. Then I started going into care homes and teaching chair yoga, which was just lovely. So I have taught from age 4 up to 83.

Then Lockdown – March 2020. I went into a total tailspin and immediately thought I would lose my business or/and my house. I was lucky enough to be able to claim Universal Credit right from the start; however, as I had £11k savings it was reduced, until about October when my savings had dwindled to allow me to claim the full amount.

I bought some equipment and started online classes, so not only am I able to make some money but I am able to connect with people online every day. Without this connection my depression would have overwhelmed me long ago. However, I could no longer teach at schools or care homes and so I am teaching to greatly reduced numbers.

I have had six months mortgage holiday and some credit card holidays. As well as using a lot of my savings I have also run up a large credit card debt of around £30K. The Universal Credit doesn't even pay my mortgage never mind food and other bills, but with that and working and a mortgage holiday, I can break even month by month. With the mortgage holiday finishing I will now be dipping into savings once more.

I received £1,000 ARG grant from my Council in December; however, this counts as earnings so I didn't get Universal Credit that month, and suddenly the grant is worth £409 less. This month I have been extremely lucky and received a second ARG grant of £4000.

My friends and family try to understand but really don't. My sister said the grant is like free money and then my mum says, oh brilliant you are ok then. That is four months money. To take me up to April 2021.

I am applying for a Bounce Back Loan, but things are very confusing – this is now the third time I have applied. Luckily someone from the bank is hand-holding me through the process, which is so complicated and time consuming.

Mostly I am ok. I did have a mini melt-down about everything last week. Part of it was the relief of getting £4K grant and just relaxing slightly, then I was ill with minor asthma for a couple of days and had to cancel some classes, so that's more loss of money. I do wake up every single morning with a feeling of dread about the future.

ExcludedUK really help me not feel alone. The hardest thing has been knowing what is available and when, and the only way I knew about the ARG grants is through this group. I love that there is mental health assistance for people. I did an online karaoke over Christmas and it was a brilliant laugh – really grateful for this group. I'm also keeping connected with my students daily online.

Even when I am able to go back to 'normal', which I did briefly between Lockdowns, there are many people who still can't afford to come or who are frightened of getting ill so won't come to class. If I have a handful of people in face-to-face classes I still have to pay for hiring the halls, which means I won't make any more money than teaching online. I figure I will be teaching to small numbers for at least the rest of this year, until people feel safe enough to get back to normal. I just want to get back to being self-sufficient once more.

40.

NAME: Hellen

OCCUPATION: Online Retailer

REASON FOR EXCLUSION: Newly Self-Employed

I have always worked where I can help, be it Wills & Probate, NHS, Hotels or Music Venues. I changed from contract work to a temping agency in October 2019 to gain new experience on the latest computer skills in preparation for becoming a Limited Company. I registered the business in December 2020 along with VAT, Corporation Tax and a Business Bank Account. I aimed to put my temp agency wages into the business to get it started.

On March 28th 2020 the temp agency terminated my work due to COVID and refused me furlough. I had to wait eight weeks for a Universal Credit payment of £28. I have been on £409 a month since and have slipped through every other net. I was really excited about the business – I'd purchased a new laptop and stationery, but needed (and was on course to get, before COVID) an accountant, insurances and a good printer to do this. I tried my local Council but was declined an ARG as I wasn't 'up and running'. No SEISS for being a Company Director either. How to start?

I will do this, as I have the enthusiasm, the will to succeed in online retail, and hope that the Government will come through for me, but what am I classed as? You can see I've paid taxes. Will I slip through the TIGS net too?

ExcludedUK has been a life-line, to know I'm not alone and that so many others are in the same predicament. Could you survive on £409 a month? Me neither. 'Debt' – such a small word, which has created the biggest hole. I don't want to be a victim, I want to run a successful business. Give us this help – others have been helped two-fold. ExcludedUK is full of dynamic, interesting, encouraging entrepreneurs who can really get the economy rolling.

41.

NAME: Emma Sheldrake

OCCUPATION: Groom & Rider

REASON FOR EXCLUSION: 50/50 rule

I was a self-employed groom and rider for a year but the following year one of the people I was working for asked me if I would go full-time employed. This was more money, with paid holidays and a pension etc, so I took that chance as it was more stable and a guaranteed income. However, the yard changed a lot while I was there, from eventers to Polo ponies which is not what I have trained for, so I decided to go back to freelancing until I could find a full-time role in the discipline I love –dressage. So I am Excluded under the 50/50 rule as my employed earnings were higher than my self-employed earnings in 2018/2019.

In March, after government advice to stay at home, I informed my two main clients that I did not think I should continue to visit. In hindsight I should have kept working, as looking after animals is essential. However, one client had 86-year-old parents and the other was going through Chemo, plus I was driving 50 minutes to get there which I did not think wise. I felt I was letting them down, but did what the government suggested.

They obviously had to do the horses themselves or get someone else to do them, so by the time Lockdown was lifted they no longer needed me.

I was not eligible for SEISS. I was not eligible for Universal Credit as I had savings and my husband was still working. I was not eligible for new Job Seekers Allowance as I had not paid enough Class 1 National Insurance and had not been employed for the last two years. I therefore lived off my savings. This was redundancy money from my previous job at a travel company which I intended to use for getting my own property to run my own business. I repeatedly advertised my services and got literally no interest – unheard of, but I think people were at home doing their own horses. Competitions were not happening, so people did not need professional grooms and people could not afford it.

In July my husband got made redundant after 21 years at the same travel company. In October I got some work locally but it was only about £50 a week, so not enough to live on. I applied for several jobs doing anything and everything but was unsuccessful – I had been too long out of an office job to be appealing. I even filled in an application to be an Iceland delivery driver that was like the Spanish inquisition, and never heard back from them. I applied for a job with my dog's vet which I did not get, but four weeks later they called me and offered me a different job. It's awful money but I am getting out of the house and getting some money in. I needed that as I was getting depressed being at home.

My dog has also needed several vet visits which have cost thousands of pounds, which I cannot afford but I want him to be comfortable.

I feel hugely let down by the government. I have worked and paid taxes since 1994 and have pretty much never claimed any help – perhaps a few weeks Jobseekers when I was 18. The rules are ridiculous, not thought through and have too many loopholes. The government has not listened or taken action. It is disgusting how so many people have been left with nothing and no help, yet others have worked throughout and have also claimed SEISS. They have had extensions built, bought cars, got a puppy, redecorated etc – there is something so wrong about that! I feel the government has literally ignored us and should be held accountable.

I can't think about the future that right now. I need to be busy and to work, so I will stay at the vets as they need to keep operating. After that I would ideally do what I love, either working with horses, or an office job with a decent wage so I can get my own horse. I have voted Conservative all my life but I am pretty sure my vote won't go that way the next time.

42.

NAME: Anita Mandl

OCCUPATION: Independent Tour Operator

REASON FOR EXCLUSION: All of them

I have been travelling all my life and I still do not know where I am going. From an early age I knew I had to travel. I sold ice cream on the beach in the South of France as a student then worked as a tour guide taking groups to India and other parts of Asia and South America. I loved every minute. I followed my dreams and set up my own travel company in 2014 and have gone from strength to strength, running and escorting small group tours all over the world.

Travel is in my blood. I love sharing fantastic destinations with my clients and get such a buzz when they have the time of their lives. My ethos is to provide the best travel experience and I always take good care of my clients. Working so much in India and being half-Indian, I realised that I wished to help the poor children in India. I provide some schools with equipment, uniforms and support for teachers.

Anita of Amtravelworld on an Indian Tuktuk

I put my clients before monetary gain, but I was nevertheless making a good living before the pandemic. Since Lockdown began I have not only had no business, I have also had to refund all my clients who had paid for trips for the summer and autumn of 2020. I refunded money I had not got back myself and did the right thing by each and every client. The right thing is what we all should do in life so we can hold our heads up high. I was so proud of my business, it defines me and is more than a mere means to an end. The pandemic is painful enough, but to have no support and be brushed off by our government as if I do not count, getting zero support, hurts even more, especially when £300 billion has been paid out to others. I have survived on my savings and handouts from my family.

My inspirations have always been my Father, Mahatma Gandhi, Martin Luther King and Nelson Mandela. My favourite Gandhi quote is "Live as if you are going to die tomorrow. Learn as if you are going to live forever." I suppose an apt Gandhi quote now would be "There is enough in this world for every man's need but not every man's greed", as I look at our chancellor Rishi Sunak with his billions, not caring about the ones who have been so impacted by the virus but received zero support. He definitely has not done the right thing.

The ExcludedUK group has also been an inspiration and a massive positive in my life, and I cannot thank the admins and members of this group enough.

I am trying to be resilient and positive, and I'm thankful that I have so many great clients who are eager to travel with me again. Not one to sit on my laurels, I started writing a book and hope to finish it in March 2021. *I was Born to Travel* or maybe *My Lifelong Gap Year.* I still live in hope.

43.

NAME: Susie Reynolds

OCCUPATION: Specialist Educational Assessor/Holiday Lets

REASON FOR EXCLUSION: 50/50 rule, Newly Self-Employed

When, in mid-March 2020, I drove home from a week's work in another county, little did I know that it was to be the last week of face-to-face work I would have for over ten months;

little did I know that the evil that is COVID-19 was lurking and was about to change my life so devastatingly.

First came the collapse of all of my booked assessment work because educational institutions were closed. Suddenly I had only my small occupational pension to cover my bills, and I found myself using some of my small savings just to stay afloat and eat. But the consolation was that it was only going to be for a short time as the Chancellor announced, that "we are all in it together" and that "no one will be left behind".

My other micro-business was a rustic lodge situated on a beautiful park in North Norfolk. In its second year of trading, I had lots of bookings spread across the year, many from returning guests who loved it so much they couldn't wait to come back. As soon as the first Lockdown was imposed the park shut and all holidays were cancelled. Despite the many refunds made it was going to be okay, as the Chancellor said there would be business grants to help businesses stay afloat.

A few weeks later I began to apply for the schemes made available and the doors began slamming in my face. The SEISS scheme shut me out as I set up my assessment business in 2018 and so, in the first year, I did not quite have 50% earnings from that work but had slightly more from a one-day-a-week PAYE role (with my employer refusing to furlough me). The Universal Credit and Jobseekers' Allowance doors were also slammed, as I owned a share in the holiday let.

In the following weeks and months I found the lodge Excluded from the Small Business Grant (no Business Rates account number), the Discretionary Grant (twice!) for the same reason, and the latest Additional Restrictions Grant as we "do not provide guests with a cooked breakfast".

My assessment business is home-based, so has failed to access the DG (three times) and ARG as my local council won't acknowledge anyone without a Business Rates account number either.

So, ten months have passed without any government support, my savings have gone and I have had to sell my share in the holiday lodge that was my dream and my passion, just to live. The anger and desperation run deep and I am left wanting answers. Why are the 37 years of tax paid into the system unworthy of me receiving help at a time of national crisis? Where is my equality with other taxpayers? I deserve an answer – we all do!

44.

NAME: Kate Wharton

OCCUPATION: Psychologist

REASON FOR EXCLUSION: Limited Company Director

I started my business in 1999 with great excitement and pride, and I have been privileged to work across the globe with some incredible people, all in the service of making work a better place.

I have put my heart and soul into my business and into supporting myself and my family. My husband (also Excluded) has poured his blood, sweat and tears into his business. We have employed others, worked diligently for long hours and made sacrifices, allowing us to bring up two much longed-for children and live in the countryside.

As a psychologist, my role is to encourage others to view themselves with optimism and inspire their confidence. My clients have entrusted me with their hopes and dreams, heartbreaks and fears, and I have put my energy into helping them enhance their contribution to their work and in turn create a positive force for good.

Being Excluded has been shocking – the word doesn't do justice to the feelings of torment, betrayal, alienation and destruction. Those first upsetting days in March, watching the pandemic sweeping across the globe, seeing Italy's doctors in trauma and then our country in the grip of an emergency, was haunting enough as a backdrop. I was reassured that "no one would be left behind". I felt safe at home with my family.

I'll never forget the fear when it dawned on me that we were not worthy of financial support to help us through the worst of this crisis. Despite the incredible support others were relieved to receive, and the congratulatory government narrative, I and millions of others appeared to be forgotten.

I didn't realise then that it was deliberate government policy, but as the replies to my desperate emails to my MP began to make clear, I was a fraud-risk, a tax-dodger, not viable, and my family didn't matter. I hunched over tutorials learning to deliver work online, interrupted regularly by my children and trying to cope with intermittent broadband. I turned to friends for empathy. You've had years of tax benefits, they asserted; get a loan, they advised; use your tax savings, they urged; the government can't help everyone, they pacified; get a job, said one! The government line was being swallowed.

For us, work doesn't appear out of nowhere. It takes months to develop business and longer to deliver and get paid for projects. This is a long-term setback that will impact us for years to come. I volunteered, counselling NHS workers in terrible emotional states. I gradually started delivering paid work, online, interspersed with looking after my children while they are at home. Frazzled but surviving!

I have been inspired by other incredible people in ExcludedUK and ForgottenLtd, and those who have listened and understood the Excluded. These are strangers, many in more desperate straits than me – I will fight hard for them. Being Excluded during a pandemic has changed 3 million people forever and highlighted some despicable attitudes towards those in need. I won't let this go – my campaigning days are only just beginning.

45.
NAME: Kelley Costigan
OCCUPATION: Actress/Sports & Remedial Massage Therapist
REASON FOR EXCLUSION: 50/50 rule

I have been an actress for the better part of 40 years, turning professional a good 30 years ago. As the business is precarious, I have taken other jobs over time and at one point was working a full-time as a management secretary and taking acting work short-term. When I was made redundant from this job, I took the money and trained as a sports and remedial massage therapist so that I could work for myself between acting jobs. When I first qualified, I had a part-time job as well, which I left in August 2018. From then on, I worked for myself scraping a living on my acting and sports massage therapy earnings. I had to borrow money sometimes from my partner to pay bills, but was just about getting by.

In November 2019, I needed surgery to fix a torn tendon and was off work for 13 weeks (without any pay whatsoever). By mid-February 2020 I had just resumed seeing my therapy clients again when the pandemic hit and we were in Lockdown. Both the entertainment industry and close contact sports massage were unable to operate, so I had no means of earning and I had used my savings while recovering from surgery.

At first I had faith that our government would look after all of us – isn't that what they promised? I waited (as I was told to) for the letter from HMRC telling me what I would be getting from SEISS. No letter came. I went onto the government website and checked. I was deemed ineligible, but not given an explanation. I contacted my union (Equity) to see if they could help. It took a while, but we learned that it was because I didn't earn enough money in the last couple of years to merit help now. I was upset, angry, and confused. How could the government say they would help EVERYONE but leave me, and millions of others, out?

I was let down at every subsequent release of SEISS, for the same reason. How did I survive? I applied for every arts funding and union aid I could find. I was given a small grant by Equity during the first Lockdown, but am not allowed to apply for any more. I can't apply for Universal Credit, or any other government aid, because they take my partner's income into consideration. I have never understood why, when they tax me as an individual, they then deem any benefits to be based upon not only my income, but that of anyone I live with. This is highly unfair. Their reason, I suppose, would be to stop fraudsters. Well, they need to revamp the tax system as it is totally unfair, in my opinion. My partner does not make enough money to keep us both.

I have borrowed from family and friends, putting out pleas on social media, and many kind people – many I have never met – have sent me money, because there are good people out there despite the evidence of our government.

Most days I want to take my life as I feel I am a burden to others. If I cannot support myself, why should anyone else feel I am worth the bother? I have eaten out-of-date food. I have tried to find work but I do not do well on online applications as most are multiple choice and do not allow you to expand upon your reason for your answer. If you don't get through the online application, you don't get an interview with a human being.

I am tired of the uncertainty of no income, of being poor. I grew up in a family of eight children on a school teacher's pay and I know deprivation –my parents sacrificed much so that we could have a better life, but I am poorer than they ever were. I have a post-graduate degree (MPhil in English), a BTEC Level 5 in Sports and Remedial Massage, and have many other skills, but still I am marginalised and Excluded.

46.
NAME: Lu
OCCUPATION: Trainer and Educator in Primary Healthcare
REASON FOR EXCLUSION: 50/50 rule

I have spent over 30 years as a nurse in hospitals and then general practice. It became evident to me that general practice in-service training was quite scarce; where it did exist, it was not of a particularly high standard, nor was it always relevant to general practice teams but rather was focused on hospital staff.
As I have a teaching qualification, enjoy training, developing and passing on my knowledge, and by all accounts am good at it, I decided to take early retirement with reduced pension and set up a business doing just that in 2013.

Having a modest pension I've only ever sought to generate enough self-employed income to bring my total earnings back to the level I earned as a PAYE employee, and my self-employed profits have always been 42-56% of my total income.

Lu getting help & support on the Excluded website.

Pre-COVID, I developed training packages, bespoke to a customer's requirements, which I would then deliver to GPs, pharmacists, nurses, health care support workers etc. My work comes predominantly from the NHS. As COVID 19 took hold in March, training and education for healthcare workers became a non-priority; they were too busy or too tired, and groups were impossible. My work and self-employed income simply stopped.

The first Lockdown ended and the NHS began to return to a new normal, but it was clear that training events with delegates seated in a conference room would not be re-starting. I have had to adapt my business model to encompass digital presentations

and remote learning. This comes with its own limitations; the revenues generated are simply not there and my self-employed income looks like it will be down on the previous tax year by some 60%. I was ineligible for SEISS due to my 2018/19 self-employed earnings being only 46% of my total income and my 3-year average was 47%.

Ironically, if I'd charged the NHS more for my work and not been so altruistic, then I'd have been eligible. If my 2019/20 tax return profit which I submitted in June was accepted then my 53% self-employed income would have made me eligible.

I can't currently get grants because I work from home or customer property. I can't get Job Seekers because I don't pay Class 1 National Insurance, and I can't get Universal Credit because I have a modest pension and savings for our old age, something that the government said was the right thing to do.

And please don't get me started on why income from a pension scheme which you have paid into is used against you under the 50/50 rule. Paid over 40 years of taxes, never claimed anything, self-employed for seven years, all returns submitted on time.

I know it's cliched, but I am one of the fortunate ones. I am now getting some work coming in, I have my pension and this, along with my husband's pension, covers the bills. We have worked hard, done the right thing all our lives, like everybody in this group. We made sacrifices along the way to be able to succeed – and for what? To be cast aside by a discriminatory policy decision as if we don't matter. Well, we do. Every single one of us matters and we are not giving up until this wrong is righted and this gross injustice is seen for what it is, Blatant Discrimination.

47.

NAME: Giovanni & Emma

OCCUPATION: Approved Driving Instruction

REASON FOR EXCLUSION: 50/50 rule

Giovanni is exceptionally good at his job and loves it. He's been building up his business from scratch for around 15 years, having previously been in the food industry. He became incredibly successful, always having a full diary and a waiting list from recommendations. I am a PAYE part-time Swimming Teacher, so Giovanni is the main earner in our household but he was finally looking ahead to cutting back on weekend hours and a 5-10 year retirement plan.

After Boris Johnson's initial Lockdown speech we heard Rishi Sunak explain more about furlough and promise how the self-employed would be looked after. Giovanni hadn't had a day off sick since recovering from bowel cancer and chemo five years previously; he didn't claim any benefits, it just made him even more focused on paying off as much on the house as he could. In 2018/19 he decided to cash in a dormant personal pension he'd paid into 20 years ago, and put it towards the mortgage to make up for the lost income whilst he was ill. The tax on the pension was paid directly to HMRC before receiving the balance. With this he felt more secure about making sure our family was in a good position if he were to have any recurring health problems.

As he'd been self-employed for many years and all his tax returns paid and up to date, we believed the SEISS would cover us, similar to how furlough worked. Eighty percent of his salary wouldn't have been the maximum £2500 p/m, and my own income had plummeted as my furlough was based on 80% of basic hours, not any extra private lessons. Still, we felt confident we'd get by.

He applied for the SEISS and waited for a reply; the longer it took the more agitated he got, feeling increasingly pessimistic. Bills were still coming in, including all the overhead costs on his driving school business. How would we survive, how long would it last? We were genuinely shocked when we discovered he didn't qualify on a 50/50 rule. He was told that his "income through other employment" was higher than that of his self-employment. We just couldn't understand how a pension was considered other employment so we contacted HMRC to see if there were any errors. We were told it was accurate but we could file an appeal. It was not granted, so again we queried it... we got nowhere

I contacted our MP for East Surrey; given that she had worked in the treasury I felt hopeful she could make sense of this for us. If I, being on furlough, had been in receipt of the same pension it wouldn't have precluded me from getting anything. So what's the difference? We have never received a proper answer to this question.

The days turned into weeks and the weeks, months. Thank goodness for outdoor space and sunshine!

We found ExcludedUK and people who understood, whereas friends didn't. They seemed to think, well, you must have lots of money if you don't qualify for support. They didn't realise the financial impact we were suffering with both our incomes hit. They didn't understand we'd rather be out working, as they seemed to see working as a punishment. Likes from posts stopped, paying into the system didn't seem enough.

G was able to make back some lost income by working long hours and weekends. Not long after, our daughter lost her job as the company were unable to go back to their office; another income down. I went back to work but on fewer hours. Our son left for University, and fortunately our daughter got bank work for the NHS.

In October, when furlough was due to end, my hours were permanently cut. That evening the next Lockdown was announced and furlough extended, but it was too late for me. Discovering that the next round of SEISS had the same requirement as the first was gut wrenching, we just didn't know how we'd manage and why they didn't want to help.

Now we are locked down for the third time and our savings have been used up. We find ourselves in the position of applying for Universal Credit, something we never thought we would have to do. We're yet to find out if we will get anything or how much. Our jobs don't look like they'll be resuming anytime soon, so what choice is there? At this later stage of life we didn't think we'd ever feel so useless and unvalued by our government. We're left feeling worthless and frustrated. It's relentless but we stay together and strong. One way or another we put one foot in front of the other and try to carry on. Just for how much longer?

48.

NAME: Caroline

OCCUPATION: Hairdresser & Landlady

REASON FOR EXCLUSION: 50/50 rule

I have worked hard since I was 16 years old, paid all my taxes and never claimed a penny. I am not rich and have no pension, which is why I took a risk in 1997 and bought a buy-to-let as my pension. Tax relief has been taken away and if you put up capital gains I am in a very scary situation. The UK pay the lowest state pension in Europe so I need every penny I can for my retirement.

I lost approximately 30% of my 25-year business after Brexit as many people left the UK. Then since COVID, many clients have left London, and being a hairdresser I have hardly worked and my business is now decimated.

In one tax year out of the three years needed to claim support, I earned 4% less than what I receive from my rental property, and so I got nothing. I now have to live off my savings.

I do not feel like a citizen but a burden, where the government is taking and taking. They rich are getting richer and I AM TRYING TO SURVIVE. This is how I feel I am being valued; no value whatsoever. People are being furloughed that own one or more buy–to-let properties, yet they are still being paid. Many people are ripping the system off, yet I am being honest. Where is my government in a situation that is not my fault? You have not given me a single penny since March 2020. Just a loan that I have to pay back. No help with my council tax or mortgage, nothing. Many have some savings, some small, some large, yet they do not need to use their savings to pay their heating bills and buy food like I do.

I am disgusted and embarrassed to be British. Helping people like me, in the grand scheme of what money you have already paid out, is pennies. I will end up suffering with tax rises and yet I have received zero support from my Chancellor.

49.

NAME: Jo

OCCUPATION: Driving Instructor

REASON FOR EXCLUSION: Newly Self-Employed

In 2009 my husband and I set up our own business, a high ropes adventure park. The same year my husband was admitted to hospital with pain caused by nerve damage following a traumatic amputation in the 1980s. By 2011 it became clear he was never going to get better and he was retired on ill health grounds aged 45.

I ran the business for ten years but it was harder than any of us could have imagined! I was a director of my own company but fully salaried. In 2019 we had a contract break point with our business partners. In the intervening years, my Mum had cancer and three lots of surgery and my Dad was given a terminal diagnosis. We talked it over and decided I should negotiate my exit from our business. I didn't make huge amounts of money but was able to leave clear of debt.

I became a Driving Instructor and set up my own business in April 2019 after 34 years of PAYE (since leaving school at 16!). It gave me the flexibility to care for my family in a way no employer could have done.

I structured a lean business that provides me with all the income I need. I bought my own car, I pay into a pension, I have accident and illness insurance that covers my mortgage if I am not able to work – but I hadn't banked on COVID and being told I couldn't work for eight months of the 2020/21 financial year.

As a newly self-employed business I was ineligible for SEISS. As a married woman, with my husband's Pension, we were refused Universal Credit. No Bounce Back Loans, and refused ARG by my local councils for Rounds 1 & 2.

I have done nothing wrong but have been utterly abandoned by the Treasury. They know to the penny how much I have earned and paid in tax since leaving school, but apparently I'm a fraud risk. They know enough to tax me but not to support me!

Thankfully, because of my husband's pension and my adult children stepping up to help out, we have survived better than a lot of people. My heart goes out to those who are not as fortunate as us.

50.

NAME: Heather Booker

OCCUPATION: Complementary Therapist/Clinic Owner

REASON FOR EXCLUSION: 50/50 rule

I began as a complementary therapist in 1999 with dreams of being in a position to help people. Having grown my business to a full-time, busy practice, the time came to open my own clinic and provide a space for other therapists to work from. I opened The Serenity Centre in early 2009 and soon had a busy multi-disciplinary clinic offering a range of treatments, with a family of lovely, independent therapists. Life was looking good if a little busy then, as is the way, I was soon reminded of the importance of self-care when I slipped on a mossy rock walking in The Lake District.

It became apparent that I'd done more than merely bruised my spine when the pain worsened and I ended up unable to work, sit, stand or walk. Ten months later, following spinal surgery and rehab, I was gratefully back working again, although my days of 13 hours treating clients were now in the past.

After an adjustment and some grieving, all settled down. And then COVID struck, a mere 17 months after my return to work. The Clinic and my personal practice were legally required to shut. As health and wellbeing practitioners, we felt bereft at being unable to help our clients when it seemed so desperately needed. Bills still needed paying, as did rent and other overheads, with very little income apart from the odd phone call or distant Reiki session. The relief when we were told that we would all be helped was immense. I'd just moved into a new house as Lockdown hit; our furniture and most of our belongings were stranded in storage, and we lived in a house with a bag full of other bits. And a substantially larger mortgage!

The shock when I discovered that after years of paying taxes I was Excluded because of a 50/50 rule was simply awful. The surgery and the time off work had tipped my clinic rental earnings to just over 50% of my total income, and the Government deem this non-trading income. I battled with the fact that I couldn't work, feeling utterly worthless and betrayed. I felt a complete failure not being able to help my clients with more than a phone call, and having outgoings at home that I just had no way of contributing to.

Colleagues simply couldn't understand how I was exempt from help. Many friends saw a new house and thought things were fine. The one bit of help I did get came in the form of the rateable grant which all went on overheads at the clinic.

Utterly betrayed by the promises of help which never came, and the continual lies and avoidances, I watched as my healthy bank account drained away. I heard again and again that we were fraud risks. I have an accountant, I pay my taxes, I had already had almost a year off work with no sick pay, and here I was again with no income, the same outgoings and being told I was fraudulent.

I had no choice in the end but to close my clinic. One of the worst moments was telling my colleagues they would have nowhere to come back to when we could begin work again. The costs needed to change things at the clinic to meet industry standards in this new world were just too high. It would take thousands, and I no longer had thousands to spend. If I'd received the full SEISS I should have been entitled to, the outcome would have been different.

It has been an inspiration to meet a whole new community of awesome people who have been Excluded. My husband has been a rock not only financially but also emotionally, listening to me tearing my hair out or trying to explain how utterly lost and useless I felt. I'm fortunate to have the gift of a grant to start a new business. I have a new outlook on life, a renewed sense of purpose, a new life balance, friendships and understandings.

51.

NAME: Donna Kirkland

OCCUPATION: Beauty Therapy & Sales

REASON FOR EXCLUSION: Limited Company Director

From leaving school I have always worked. I never had children as I always put my career first. I started as a Saturday girl in a hairdressers and then went to college for three years to learn beauty therapy. I had a work placement in a beauty salon for a week and totally fell in love with the profession.

I worked in beauty salons and did teacher training at night school so I could teach beauty therapy. I worked as a beauty therapist at Centre Parks then got the dream job of working on the QE2, travelling around the world with the beauty therapy company Steiner – I was a Steiner girl and so proud of myself.

Aged about 22 I moved to selling beauty anti-ageing machines. I quickly made my name as a good sales person because I have such a passion for my job and I worked successfully at all the beauty exhibitions around the UK. I was headhunted by a British company that leads the beauty industry and I decided I would go self-employed to be with them.

I have worked for them for over 25 years, initially as a sole trader and about 20 years ago as a Limited Company director. My accountant recommended I do this because my monthly earnings vary so much. I was selling lots of machines so my earnings were very good.

I absolutely love my job and where it takes me. I earn a substantial commission for each machine I sell. They are high-end machines selling from £15,000-£25,000 plus VAT. The company were unheard-of when I first started selling for them and now are the biggest anti ageing company in the UK, selling celebrity-and result-driven machines.

In December 2019 I got married in the Seychelles and was looking forward to 2020 being a holidaying, successful first married year together.

My husband is also in sales (doors and windows) and is Excluded because he was newly self-employed in February 2019. Fortunately for him, construction was allowed back to work quite quickly early in 2020 and he has been very busy because people are at home and doing home improvements.

For me it's a totally different story because close contact work was not allowed by the government. I have a home office which I used one day a week to confirm all of my meetings and to follow up and organise training for the salons that I sell to. This means that I don't qualify for the grants as I don't have business rates. As I am a Limited Company director I am Excluded because my accountant suggested that I paid myself in dividends.

I do get a very small furlough from the PAYE that my accountant files for me each month. I tried for Universal Credit but I didn't qualify because my husband works although he doesn't share his wages with me (such a Dickensian rule I think).

It has now been almost a year that I haven't been able to work and it has taken a huge toll on me. Having been totally self-sufficient all of these years and having a very successful business, it has had a catastrophic effect on my confidence, self worth and belief, and my mental health.

I have used up all of my savings. I have had to live off a Bounce Back Loan which I really didn't want to take out. If this carries on for much longer I will close my business; I cannot sell machines to salons that aren't allowed to open.

I did pay my corporation tax last year and my VAT quarters, as I still have overheads and expenses. I am awaiting my corporation tax bill at the end of March from my accountant, because I did work from June 2019 until February 2020. My last invoice to the company I sell to was February 2019.

I do wonder what Rishi Sunak will do when there is no corporation tax coming his way next year. So many of us have been unable to work so either there'll be no tax to pay or the companies will have closed.

It has been a very strange first year of married life. It has put quite a strain on us as I have gone from a very confident go-getter, very passionate about my job travelling 30,000 miles a year to suddenly becoming a Cinderella-like person cleaning, cooking, and gardening.

Every day is the same. My husband goes to work, I get up, get showered and start cleaning and tidying and preparing the meals for the day...... every day. He comes home, we have dinner, we watch a little bit of TV and we go to bed and then the new day starts again.

My spark has gone. I have had very dark thoughts. I have watched Parliament TV constantly. I follow social media and ExcludedUK and ForgottenLtd.

Back in September 2019 I did attend a meeting in London with ForgottenLtd. We met with MPs to put forward our stories for Rishi Sunak to watch. It gave me a sense of purpose; I felt like I was contributing something that would turn it around, and that he would listen and understand. We need parity and funding and grants, just like any others who couldn't work but got compensated for being at home.

I have felt so distressed hearing of many friends getting the grants, getting the self-employed income support scheme, buying hot tubs, having holidays last summer, while still working and really enjoying themselves. Whilst I've had nothing.

I still remember the feeling of stepping into the unknown of owning my own business, going from being employed with a company car, a very good basic, very good commission, pension and healthcare etc. I remember how totally proud I felt to stand on my own two feet knowing I would be successful – and I was. My family were so proud. I was busier than ever once I had taken that huge step to go self-employed.

I don't know what I will face if I can eventually go back as a lot of salons are closed, and a lot of salons won't be able to afford the machines that I sell or have the credit ratings to be able to get the machines on a lease.

There is also now a secondhand market for the machines that I have sold, because salons have closed and are selling off their assets. So the fear is now that I will spend time and money demonstrating the machines to salon owners, only for them to buy them off the Internet.

The positives.... finding ExcludedUK and ForgottenLtd and speaking to people that I have never met who have been so much more compassionate than the friends I have on my Instagram and Facebook pages, it's quite unbelievable!

I could post something about a snowy morning and get so many comments and likes, whereas if I post something about being Excluded it will barely get any likes at all. It seems that as long as the majority are okay, they really don't care about anyone but themselves.

I have learnt not to be so giving to the people who don't really care about me as an individual; this sadly includes my brother, who still says that Limited Company directors are a tax dodgers and doesn't want to understand because he's quite happily furloughed.

With my husband being at work every day I have spent so much more time with my wonderful mother and this is time I know I would never would have had if it wasn't for the pandemic. This, then, is my silver lining. Spending time with her has kept me on the straight and narrow and has made me realise how devastated she would be if I wasn't here. My father was also a Limited Company director and he was very proud that I followed in his footsteps and had my own business. Mum and Dad were together from being 16 and now mum is 76; after losing my Dad, she is the biggest positive in my life.

I am so happy to have my Internet family of ExcludedUK and ForgottenLtd as it's here where I feel safe and happy and can talk about feelings and try to keep positive for other people when they are having down days as we are all in this together. It's a group that none of us would've wanted to be in but we find ourselves here and we all support each other.

52.

NAME: Matt Brown

OCCUPATION: Events Timing Provider

REASON FOR EXCLUSION: Newly Self-Employed

Back in the long distant, carefree days of 2019 I was working in the sports events industry, employed by two companies in two different roles. Both were run by the same people; one company put on their own events where I worked as an event organiser, and the other company provided electronic timing services to other event organisers. Alongside this I worked on a few events that I had been personally involved in from previous years, using my leave to be able to attend them.

As time went on, it became more and more difficult to balance these additional events with my work commitments, and so I began looking into the possibility of launching my own business as a timing provider. Towards the back end of the season it all came to a head with my employer as I was being expected to do far too much work in my own time for his benefit, and so I made the jump.

The rest of 2019 was spent mostly getting things in place ready for 2020 and working a small handful of jobs. I expected to be in a good place for a busy main season, with bookings coming in, and I was developing a good reputation within the industry. And then we got to mid-March and everything went out the window. Races postponed or cancelled. From August onwards I managed to cover a few smaller races that went ahead, working with the organisers to put in place strong COVID secure measures, but there was nowhere near enough work to be profitable.

Every support scheme that came along Excluded me. Throughout this entire pandemic the only support I have received from the government has been a rebate of the tax I paid whilst employed in 2019, as the amount I spent on setting up the business took me back below the personal allowance. I have applied for grants from Dorset council and heard nothing back in response, despite them being one of the organisations that has actively prevented events that I was due to work on.

As we go into 2021, a year that I had pinned my hopes on, already the first quarter has been wiped out, with little hope of much, if any, work going ahead in the second quarter. Events that were due this spring have been pushed back into the autumn; whilst I am grateful that hopefully that will mean some work then, it also prevents me from being able to book in any new work on those dates. Additionally, I had quoted for some events in 2021 that need additional equipment, which I would have purchased with my expected earnings for 2020 but which now look out of reach.

However, throughout the entire situation, I have been extremely fortunate to have had the support of my partner, Karen, my family, and a group of friends who have on multiple occasions left me in tears with their unprompted offers of help that they can ill afford themselves.

Regardless of how things go, my business will endure. And I will remember the complete lack of support the government provided. But more importantly I will remember those who were there to help.

53.

NAME: Sarah Davies

OCCUPATION: Professional Development Consultant

REASON FOR EXCLUSION: Limited Company Director

My name is Sarah Davies and I have worked for over 40 years. I started my Consultancy business about ten years ago and I work from home.

Previously, I was previously employed in the Education sector for about 26 years. I had two successful headships and then worked regionally for three and a half years supporting the 'Every Child Matters' agenda and transformational change in schools.

A general election, and new government approach, meant that the job finished overnight in April 2010. Independent work seemed a logical step after that. I started my business to specialise in developing public sector leadership and workforce employability skills. I have always been motivated to help people improve their life chances through support and training, whatever their age, and I realised I really enjoyed the variety of consultancy work. I had a successful, viable business until the start of the pandemic. As education has been hit very hard, work stopped overnight.

As I often work with education colleagues, my income is variable around school term dates. I don't earn a lot, but enough to get by. I was encouraged to become a Limited Company to protect assets and be paid by dividends; in the public sector, it can also be requirement to be considered for work.

Being Excluded was a massive shock as I had always considered myself to be self-employed. I'd paid tax into the system since 1976 and I'd never needed help before. As I heard Rishi Sunak's "We will leave no-one behind" speech I was hugely relieved, but on checking with my accountant if that included me, and finding the answer was NO, I panicked. That feeling's not gone away nearly a year later.

Until circumstances change dramatically, and schools and universities get back to a 'new normal', my current situation will continue. I have tried to adapt to work online since April 2020, but it takes time to establish and recognise that the context we are all working in has changed.

I feel completely abandoned and ignored by government but thankfully I have amazing friends and family who have provided support, both practically and emotionally. What this time has taught me is that people who really care about you step up, and I will be forever grateful. But it's not right that my family have had to help me out with money so that I don't lose what I have worked for all my life. I have added to the nation's tax pot for over 40 years and have never before asked for help. I can prove my position and yet I am still deemed a fraud risk, which both angers and saddens me.

I have learnt too that the kindness of strangers is amazing. The ExcludedUK community, a random group of people that quickly became a team and force of nature, have been there in the darkest of times. There is such care and compassion and strength in numbers, and those bonds will be unbreakable going forward! I hope I have given something back too in my own way.

I can say emphatically I don't look at the future in the same way anymore. I won't take for granted some of the things I did pre-COVID. I will put life before work, I will travel when I can, and I will embrace life, family and friends even more. I will never forget how I have been helped and those who helped me, and how its shown me that, despite the utter awfulness of it all, I am a tough old bird!

54.
NAME: Hazel
OCCUPATION: Childminder
REASON FOR EXCLUSION: Newly Self-Employed

I spent the first 27 years of my career working in food safety. It was a career I loved although at times it could be incredibly stressful. Unfortunately ill health struck quite suddenly in the summer of 2018. I tried to work between hospital visits but it was becoming more stressful as I was aware of the impact my absence was having on my team. I left my role in January 2019.

My daughter had struggled with anxiety in her last couple of years at school which put paid to her initial dreams of going to Uni to study art and design. She started a job working with disabled children but it didn't work out as she lacked the confidence. Clearly we needed to find something that worked for both of us. Child minding seemed like the obvious answer as we had space in the house to convert to a dedicated area.

We spent the rest of 2019 working on the house and doing all the required training. Our longer term plan was child minding at home for 2-3 years then open a children's nursery somewhere local. At that point I would take a step back and just have a supporting admin role.

By early March 2020 we were ready to submit our application to Ofsted. Three weeks later the world was paused! Ten months on, our registration process is no further forward as I was advised by my consultant to reduce my contact with anyone outside my immediate family. Part of my condition means I have to take steroids daily.

My daughter has started a small graphic design business which thankfully is earning enough to keep her going. I was able to claim Job Seekers Allowance for 26 weeks but that has long since stopped.

I do know that we are very lucky as my partner's job has been unaffected by the pandemic. We have taken advantage of mortgage payment holidays and Santander have been really good by giving us further 'tailored help'. This will cost us more in the long run but we'll deal with that when the time comes.

We are doing ok as a family but every day it breaks my heart to see and hear about others who are really struggling. I have tried to help as many as I can, as I cannot just sit back and see people struggle to feed themselves, their children and their animals. It makes me so angry that people have been put in this position. Our government has blood on their hands. The longer the situation goes on the worse it gets.

It now feels like sheer arrogance is preventing them from doing the right thing – an admission they got it wrong. I've learned so much these last ten months. Strangers on your phone can have 100 times more empathy than your own extended family. I never realised the heart-stopping fear you can feel when you see a message posted late at night by a stranger who is on the edge and ready to give up. Then the enormous relief when one of the ExcludedUK admin posts to say they have literally pulled someone back from the brink. All of this entirely preventable. I pray for parity in 2021.

55.

NAME: Kate

OCCUPATION: Equine Stud & Horse-drawn Carriages

REASON FOR EXCLUSION: 50/50 rule

It all started with Humphrey, an 18hand part-bred Cleveland Bay. I bought him as a hack for a then member of staff at the yard and, after a life time with horses, my interest in Cleveland Bays was born.

The breed is critically endangered despite the support of HM the Queen and the Royal Mews. I set out to do what I could to raise the profile of this talented breed. To a horseman, they are all things to all men; they ride, they drive, they pull, they plough, they take your goods to market, they take your soldiers to war. The Queen and the then Crown Equerry, Sir John Millar, were delighted to support our work for the breed.

This was the early 1970s. To enable the project to go forward I moved to more land, and Pembridge Stud was born. Soon we were producing pure and part-bred Cleveland Bays. We sold them all over the world and raised the profile of the breed in competition.

The years rolled by and, not getting any younger, I resolved to semi-retire and fulfil an ambition to move to Pembrokeshire. The 'lad' who had been with the horses ever since we began came too and is still with them today; John is a well known figure in the horseworld and a gifted horseman.

Well, so here we were in Pembrokeshire in 2001, right in the middle of the Foot and Mouth Pandemic. It was a hard start to my semi-retirement. By the way that is a misnomer! I swear I am working as long hours now as I was when I was farming!

We realised some ten years ago that my pension was not going to be enough to support our work and so a small offshoot was formed – Carriages in the Park, a horse drawn carriage company doing weddings and tourist rides. Yes the hours were long, so much for retirement! But it was all so very rewarding.

Well, we all know what happened in March 2020. Suddenly everything that we had worked a lifetime for was at risk.

I know how much people loved the horses in Tenby and at the Stud, but unless they have horses themselves, they have no idea of the work and costs involved, nor the hours of dedication behind the scenes.

I remember going to our MPs and Welsh Parliament members and asking for help for the animals. I finally got an email from Ken Skates suggesting that I should approach my sponsors or local charities. Failing that, Crowdfund. In other words, beg.

Pembridge Stud and Carriages in the Park Pembrokeshire

There was obviously either no comprehension or care for the fact that horses who would normally be earning their keep and ours had suddenly became a full financial liability. Well, not to be daunted, I tentatively Crowdfunded and was humbled by the caring messages and donations from around the globe. If nothing else, it showed that the work we had done tirelessly for the Cleveland Bays had not gone unnoticed and was appreciated.

There was a ray of hope with the SEISS scheme but hopes were soon dashed here too. Apparently my pensions ruled me out.

I am frustrated that at every turn we fell through the cracks. Like farms, we don't pay rates, and despite dutifully filing annually and on time, nothing was available to me. At 76 I would not have been a likely candidate for any of the loans, so we have fallen back on our 'winter safety net'. When the horses are not operating out of season, we run Hackney carriages. This has always ensured we could do the horses well. Now even this eludes us. Due to the Lockdown there has been no real taxi income since the autumn.

I hear stories of drivers out all day for £10; I know how this feels. After doing the horses you sit on an empty rank in an empty town, hoping for a fare. I have been fortunate to receive a small grant for the taxi from the County Council, but this will not cover this extended, apparently endless Lockdown. I count my blessings. I am not cold and I am not hungry, but I grieve for many that are.

I am also fortunate to have the love of my animals. I can hug them and they are a comfort to me, and I really don't know what I would do without the dogs too!

Despite the grief for a way of life and life's work gone, I can ride to the beach with the wind running through my hair, it's free and 'They can't take this away from me!'

I have given a lifetime to the preservation of the Cleveland Bays and feel completely abandoned in what I have achieved. ExcludedUK has been tremendous support. Just reading of others' issues has helped me to keep perspective on mine and has been uplifting.

56.

NAME: Steph

OCCUPATION: Allied Health Professional

REASON FOR EXCLUSION:

I am an Allied Health Professional, a Diagnostic Ultrasound practitioner. After nearly four decades in the NHS, I worked independently through my own company till 2017 when Tax legislation stopped us working in the NHS . I continue to work in the NHS through an agency.

On 23rd March I was told my scheduled lists for the following week were cancelled due to COVID 19. No pay from that date. No explanation. No correspondence.

What happened over the following months was worrying both for patients and staff. In essence, my income instantly took a 50% drop. Some departments managed better than others and the other hospital I work for kept me working.

In the early weeks, I tried every route available to access information and return to work. The work gradually returned – but now the hospitals are filled to capacity with COVID patients. Routine work is again delayed or cancelled.

I am paid PAYE by the Trust, confirmed by HMRC. HR personnel laughed at me when I asked about furlough. I felt worthless. I have never ever been out of work or needed to claim benefits. I have contacted my MP four times. His initial response was "I can't believe we overlooked this". Sadly, he only repeated what I had already investigated.

Attached to his email was a letter from the CEO of the Trust. It was disappointing and condescending, putting me in my place as an agency worker. She suggested I sign up on the bank – but she also reminded me it would be far less pay.

I am waiting for the latest reply from my MP. He told me that I should have been furloughed and explained why. It was before Christmas that my case would be raised directly with the Health Secretary as a matter of urgency.

I wrote again on 7th & 8th of January. I received another response last week informing me that Mr Garnier had contacted the Health Secretary's office directly and is awaiting a response .

I have picked up a little extra work over the months but I am unable to fill the gaping hole in my finances that a 50% pay cut has left over the last ten months.

I am approaching retirement and have had to put my house on the market. My plans have been devastated. I am now training to support the vaccination programme. I have 50 years full National Insurance contributions.

I have been Excluded and refused without reason or explanation. I love my work, I love my patients and I feel they have been let down. It is heartwarming to hear of all the fantastic work these groups have been doing all these months.

We were promised we would be supported. The disparity and unfairness is beyond belief. Hard working, genuine, dedicated people just ignored, judged and abandoned. We deserve clear and valid explanations. Thank you so much just for listening. My heart goes out to everybody. Good luck to everyone.

57.
NAME: Isobel Rutter
OCCUPATION: Tour Operator
REASON FOR EXCLUSION: Limited Company Director

I have worked diligently, long hours and days, for the best part of 20 years, building up a successful business, only to see it decimated by the pandemic. As there is no longer a market for my product, there was no revenue to the business in 2020, therefore no income. There is nothing in the order book for 2021, so this year is likely to be an action replay of 2020.

I have previous experience of being Excluded by the UK Government, you'd think I'd be used to it by now. My darling husband died in 2001 and I found myself sitting in the DHSS office in Glasgow, completely pole-axed by his sudden death and struggling financially, only to be told that I wasn't eligible for a Widow's Pension. Why? Because at age 44 years and three months, I was nine months too young to qualify. I had to be 45+ when my husband died to meet the criteria. Make sense of that one if you can – yes I was a widow, but not enough of a widow to qualify for help.

The realisation soon dawned that I was on my own and no one was going to help me but me myself. I set up my tour operator business, specialising in arranging accommodation and trips to the UK by foreign schools and colleges and, although in the beginning my accountant said I'd make more money "walking the streets picking up loose change", I have built it up to be a fine and well-regarded business, with my name trusted and respected all over the world.

I typically earn around £25k-30k per annum, but as I am paid by dividend I am ineligible for government support. I do not meet the criteria for grants because I work from a home office, and to date I have not found monetary support from any source. For one reason or another I have always fallen between the many cracks.

I have been able to furlough myself for the inadequate sum of £575 a month, which nowhere near covers my ongoing business and living costs. At the same time, I must stand by and watch associates – who are sole trader status – receiving £2.5k a month. In some cases they have furloughed their spouse into the bargain! These people are doing exactly the same job in exactly the same business sector, but they are supported by the UK government and I am not.

I am a law-abiding UK citizen, I have always paid my taxes in full and on time, making the same contribution to the UK treasury as everyone else, but when the time comes that I need help coming the other way, the proverbial door has been slammed shut in my face. My heart breaks for those who have received NOT ONE PENNY of assistance since the pandemic hit. I am regularly reduced to uncontrollable sobbing reading the stories from ExcludedUK. The poverty, anguish and suffering inflicted upon so many is a direct consequence of the inequity and injustice of the heartless Rishi Sunak and the Conservative Government. This gross unfairness is an absolute shame and disgrace, and I think we deserve much more consideration and respect.

I am not asking for any more than anyone else, I just want what's fair. I quote the famous words from a well-known movie featuring Meg Ryan: "I'll have what she's having."

The irony is not lost that I am writing this on 25th January, birthday of our great Scottish bard Robert Burns. He will doubtless be birling in his grave to know that 250 years after his death "Man's inhumanity to Man" is alive and well and continuing to thrive in these Great British Isles.

58.
NAME: Liz
OCCUPATION: Property Management
REASON FOR EXCLUSION: Limited Company Director

I am the sole Limited Company director of a business accommodating tourists and mainly overseas students.

I've always said that my business found me rather than me pursuing it. I never thought of it as a calling. My studies and PhD are actually in foreign languages, so nothing to do with property, but that's another story (and a life I haven't lived for a long time). Property and me jogged along quite happily together, making the best of it for 15 years.

COVID came as a shock but I was optimistic I could work round it. That changed as soon as Donald Trump announced travel restrictions between the US and Europe. The cancellations came in faster than my inbox could cope. A year's worth of business, and all the work that had gone into getting it, cascaded through my fingers. All gone. Wiped out in a deluge, not a trickle.

My world caved in. Within a few days, I went from being a bright prosperous solo Mum, working hard to provide for me and my young daughter, to a frazzled shell managing the chaos of the fallout, with home-schooling landing at my feet for good measure.

While I was at my wits' end, Rishi uttered those words: "To all those at home right now, anxious about the days ahead, I say this: you will not face this alone". The relief was immense. I welled up. For the first (and last) time in my life, I felt gratitude to the Tories. We were going to be OK.

The lie was soon outed and the hope was short-lived. My daughter and I have received no support. Eighty percent of my business has gone.

The misery of the restrictions, and coping with all the practicalities of that as a solo mum, have been overwhelming. At times the isolation is unbearable. How to cope with friends – and good friends at that – who, without the slightest nod to my loss, tell me that they've actually done quite nicely out of COVID. The parents on furlough, home-schooling without needing to pummel at their inbox to keep going. And the guilt! Why is it my livelihood that has disappeared? How could I deserve anything when I built my daughter's and my future on something as whimsical as expecting people to stream into Gatwick and Heathrow! What a fool!

ExcludedUK and ForgottenLtd have been essential. What a gang to be part of but, oh, what a gang! The strength and resilience of so many people carries me through.

I will keep going. In a new form. Not the old me. I've joked often enough that my business is like a phoenix. Whenever I've tried to knock it on the head over the years, it's risen up and wouldn't let me. Now I need that to be true again. I believe we will rise from these flames.

59.

NAME: Judith

OCCUPATION: Sole Trader

REASON FOR EXCLUSION: Limited Company Director

I sit here thinking, “How did things come to this?”

I've been a UK taxpayer for over 30 years. As an employee for 16 years, I worked my way up to management level with a multinational corporate. Then, I had the drive and ambition to go it alone, on a sales and marketing consultancy basis, to see if I really was as good as I believed I'd become. And, yes, thankfully it seemed I was! So, I was a self-employed sole trader for a further ten years.

In 2016 my key client threw a curveball. They decided to only deal with freelancers with Limited Company status. I wasn't happy with this request, it incurred additional red tape and accountancy requirements. I earned a comfortable £30-40K salary, a true one-woman-band freelancer. But I didn't have much choice if I wanted to retain their business, so I had to yield.

Fast forward four years to April 2020. Like most other small businesses in my field, I lost my entire client base within a couple of months. I remember the weight lifting from my shoulders when I heard Chancellor Rishi Sunak announce the criteria of the SEISS. I ticked every box. Result! Until a couple of days later, when I saw something on social media about Ltd Company Directors being Excluded from support. And the rest, as they say, is history. I've not done a full month's worth of chargeable work since February 2020.

I see furloughed people taking up new hobbies, going on long country walks getting themselves fitter than they've ever been, doing volunteer work. Being paid up to £2,500 to do it.

I see self-employed people, my peer group, my collaborators and competitors, people who do pretty much the same as I do. Being paid up to £2,500 to do it.

I see self-employed people who've been completely entitled to claim SEISS, even though their businesses haven't been affected by the pandemic. Re-furbishing their homes. Buying new cars. Looking forward to booking holidays of a lifetime. Being paid up to £2,500 to do it.

I have the option to claim a princely £575 per month if I close my business down. Not even an option to take the pittance on offer, and top it up with any work I can pick up – which would be tax-generating work. If there's sense and logic in this, I've yet to understand it.

But, you know what? I say fair play to all those people. Those genuinely entitled to Coronavirus Job Retention Scheme and SEISS deserve it. Those who don't deserve SEISS… Well, I hate the game, not the players. I despise the sheer injustice, that this inept and entitled government think they have the right to decide which taxpayers to support. And which to ignore, shun, deride. For no reason.

Sometimes I have to try to forget about the situation to prevent myself imploding with rage at this disgraceful, disgusting discrimination. The feeling of powerlessness to change it is as bad as the situation itself. I battle on as best I can, earning approx. a third of what I did throughout the past 14 years of working for myself. It's not enough. As a result, my savings, which were meant to be pension fund money, continue to dwindle. How will this eventually pan out? What will become of me, after having a great career and paying my dues?

I grew up under the spectre of the Thatcher regime in the 1980s. I don't agree with many of her policies and principles. But, without her, many of the ExcludedUK group like me would never have had the opportunity to set up businesses. She believed in free enterprise, and the opportunity to reach personal potential, regardless of background, so long as you have what it takes.

The Tories have lost their self-proclaimed mantle as 'the party of business' forever due to this travesty. Thatcher will be turning in her grave. I hope she is.

60.

NAME: Jane Wallis

OCCUPATION: Reflexologist

REASON FOR EXCLUSION: 50/50 rule, Newly Self-Employed

Four years ago I was a time-served, high tax-bracket 'career woman' in the software industry, who had reached a point in her life where she wanted something different.

I decided to train to become a clinical reflexologist. I had a legacy from my lovely mum to keep me going, plus I worked a day a week in a fabric shop and took in curtain work. In November 2018 I set up as a sole trader, based at home. The uptake was steady but slow, and I was still working at the fabric shop to top up. Set-up costs and overheads meant another zero tax year.

Tax year 2018/19 modest income, no profit, little tax paid.

Happy? Very. Pats on back for changing direction and setting up a business helping other people to be their best selves.

In Spring 2019 I moved house to a place that would accommodate a treatment room, but which also needed modernisation. While the work was being done I rented a room in an Osteopath's clinic, and business really picked up. No more fabric shop. Content? Oh yes! All of this meant I started to believe in myself, and my clients were truly benefiting from their treatments. There was not much profit yet due to the rent, but this would do me nicely until I can get my pension in six years time (WASPI? – that's a whole other story!!).

In 2019-20 I was self-employed, had little profit, and no tax to pay. Who knew that on the horizon was a virus that was going to change all of our lives?

The massive impact upon the reflexology community was that we were closed down because we were categorised with massage parlours and hairdressers. Allow me to briefly explain how we do reflexology. We work with the body's own energy and access it through reflex points. The whole body is reflected upon the soles of our feet, and by gently working the reflex points, we can help the body to correct the imbalances in the flow of energy, which themselves cause disease. At the very least, clients leave our treatment room relaxed and feeling better than when they entered, and some leave without the symptoms, aches and pains that they came with. As most of our clients are at least 5ft tall and we are working on their feet, we are two, socially-distanced metres away from their faces.

Our professional associations have lobbied hard to have our classification changed so that, along with osteopaths, physiotherapists and other complementary therapies, we could continue to work and support our clients. But this hasn't been possible, and now, ten months on and in third Lockdown, we are still not allowed to work. As the majority of us are self-employed, we are now without income. And those of us who are new start-ups are Excluded from Government support.

What distresses me most is seeing the harrowing reports from Intensive Care Units, that show the stress and anxiety in the NHS staff who are working beyond their tolerance levels. We could be helping those very people who are saving lives – but we are not allowed.

How do I feel? Discarded, without value. Extinguished. Like an ant stamped upon by a Minister's boot.

61.
NAME: Sue
OCCUPATION: Therapeutic Counsellor/Clinical Hypnotherapist
REASON FOR EXCLUSION:

When the original Lockdown was announced in March 2020, the first thing that came to mind was sheer panic, shock and overwhelming fear – not for finances, but purely from a health perspective.

In the weeks prior to this it was clear that the world was experiencing a deadly virus. I had already spoken to my adult children – who are all single and live separately an hour's drive away from me – and said that, should a Lockdown be announced, I would come and collect them all so that they can move in with me. I hadn't anticipated their rejection but quickly appreciated that their "Thanks, but no thanks Mum" response was no reflection on how they felt about me! It was their confirmation telling me not to worry and that they would be ok.

Number One worry was safely ticked off the list. I remember sitting on the sofa next to my husband, a frontline working doctor, and feeling huge relief as Rishi Sunak reassured me that "no one will be left behind" in terms of financial support throughout this "unprecedented" crisis. My heart swelled with pride and reassurance, and I swear I felt the might of the government's comforting metaphorical arms enveloping my whole being as I took in those words with tears streaming down my face – as my husband watched on quietly, unresponsive and composed; God knows what he was really thinking. No doubt his clinical focus was on work the following day – although I'm sure he really had no inkling as to what was really in store for him and his magnificent colleagues over the next few months.

So now the reality of my personal financial situation came to the fore. I'm a 58-year-old therapeutic counsellor/clinical hypnotherapist who had worked in the NHS for 25 years until entering private practice on 1st January 2020. I was so proud. I'd worked and studied so hard for this, changing careers from Leadership/Management to a more direct healthcare role in the mental health sector (my passion).

Whilst I'm a doctor's wife, I'm also financially independent. I've no savings of my own as my adult children, from a previous relationship, have always been a priority for me. We've come as a 'package' for many years, so marriage to my present husband does not, quite rightly, afford me any advantages in that respect and being self sufficient has always been the main driver for my ambitions – family first; always.

So, self-employed – tick. Running a business from premises – tick. Bingo! Let's submit that application for a business grant and SEISS – other colleagues have. Well "not so fast" the system told me. You have premises but you're not yet on the Business Rates Register (on 11th March) and you've not been self-employed long enough – no tax submissions for 2018-19, only 2019-20. And no Universal Credit, because of my husband's income. So in the 21st century, as a woman I'm still defined by my husband!

Words I used in my emails to my Doncaster Council included "invisible, desperate, dismissed, unimportant, unfair, ineligible, unjust, hopeless ….".

I am one of the lucky ones though – after months of begging and fighting, I was given a discretionary grant. But SEISS still eludes me. Further grants have eluded me since then. I am VIABLE but my workload has decreased for obvious reasons. I give my business another two months before I hang up my therapist couch. A Bounce Back Loan to help me get through is a LOAN – it's not a solution. Thank God for the ExcludedUK community. Dark days have never been so dark. Their strength has been a genuine metaphoric arm around my shoulders.

62.

NAME: Louise Kenrick

OCCUPATION: Events Organiser

REASON FOR EXCLUSION: Newly Self-Employed

I have paid taxes via PAYE for 30 years and the last ten were in the higher tax bracket, all without complaint. Within the live events sector, there has always been great potential for innovation and growth. It's a sector that openly encourages entrepreneurship and I embraced this by becoming self-employed in 2019 as I did not want to restrict myself to one employer or be restricted in my ability to drive value for my clients.

Being self-employed allowed me the freedom to grow and offer my 20-plus years of expertise leading account management and client services. In a thriving sector placing significant importance in a client-facing environment, trust and effective communication cannot be underestimated.

I have literally gone from 100% income to zero overnight. The event sector was one of the first to be locked down and will be the last to recover, and I fear for my future.

Rishi Sunak's words in his broadcast in March 2020 were "You have not been forgotten. We will not leave you behind. We are all in this together." I cried when I heard this. I then had hope and trust that the Government would not fail me. After all, had I not paid tax all my working life? Have I not paid into the system and never had to claim a benefit in my life?

Almost one year later, and the events sector remains ravaged with no clear timeframe for recovery. I continue to apply for jobs in an ever-diminishing job market. To date, over 80 positions applied for and the vast majority do not even register your submission. My mental and physical health has been ravaged. I find myself with increasing physical pain as the stresses take their toll. Black days are increasing as my bank balance reduces. The tax money I had set aside is now non-existent. Receiving no meaningful support, I have had no choice but to use this to pay my bills and keep a roof over my head.

How much longer can I survive? Rishi, my very existence is being diminished by you. If it wasn't for ExcludedUK giving me strength and hope, I would be lost.

63.
NAME: Tracy
OCCUPATION: Barber
REASON FOR EXCLUSION: Newly Self-Employed

I've worked hard all my life, starting at a herb farm when I was 13. Always PAYE, until about ten years ago. I was a single mum to three boys for about 15 years, and although I quite often worked six days a week, and some evenings, we had fun and fairly good life. Never rich, but able to afford a few camping trips, and school trips.

Two years ago my world ended. My son Oliver took his own life, he was 23 and an identical twin. He was so loved by everyone, over 1,500 people at his funeral. My life was in absolute tatters.

I immediately stopped my self-employment, not knowing if I could ever face working again. I'm a barber, and just couldn't face the banality, the falseness and shallow talk. My son had died.

I eventually went back to work in December 2019, despite absolutely hating it, and looking for other employment.

Then Lockdown happened. Despite having a work history of over 30 years, taxes paid on time and National Insurance paid, I discovered I wasn't entitled to anything. I tried to claim Universal Credit, but my son had moved out just before Lockdown, and we live in a council house so I couldn't include housing costs.

We had savings of around £3,000, all gone. My husband is still working, but on a low wage. I'm not allowed to work because it's a close contact industry.

To top the whole year off, my other twin had a life-changing car accident in early December.

Useless, worthless, pointless, lonely, isolated and sometimes hopeless and desolate. My mental health has been affected, and I'm under a psychiatrist for trauma and PTSD. I have panic attacks and anxiety, made 100% worse by being Excluded.

The ExcludedUK community have been amazing, I'm so thankful for everyone. I'm not giving up, and I'm stronger than ever.

Thank you ExcludedUK.

64.

NAME: Marian

OCCUPATION: Cat Sitter

REASON FOR EXCLUSION: 50/50 rule

My name is Marian. I am Excluded.

I am retired, on a small private pension, waiting for my state pension. I earn a very small amount – about £2,000 per year – from looking after people's cats when they go away from home.

In the 2020/21 tax year I will have earned £200. For myself, this is not a bad situation. My self-employed earnings were to be spent on luxuries – clothes, day trips, eating out and treats.

I am Excluded under the 50/50 rule – perhaps fairly, because my pension is continuing and, with my husband, we can afford our household bills.

So I am not looking for any support for myself. I would not make a claim, even if it was possible. BUT – I have heard and sympathise with the stories of the people who have been Excluded. I was an accountant, so I understand about directors of limited companies. I have worked for 44 years, so I have been in many employment and self-employment situations over that time. I have changed jobs many times.

I was once faced with an employer demanding that I pay back an overpayment of salary going back five years, whilst also immediately giving me a substantial pay cut. I had just relocated with that employer, at my own expense, and I had more financial commitments than my new reduced income. Thankfully, I was able to turn to my Trade Union for help and representation during that awful time, and my case was heard.

Where is the representation for the ExcludedUK? This is such a diverse group of people. Perhaps, if it was a few thousand people, we could rely on families and friends and charities to help them out. But this group has so many members, and often whole families are affected.

What I cannot fathom is how anyone is expected to adjust to zero income overnight. Even all the best debt advice in the world has no solution if people have no income at all.

As a pensioner, I support this group in tiny small ways. Perhaps a word of encouragement at three o'clock in the morning, or a small gift here or there to encourage the group's fundraising. I also now volunteer at the local food bank – giving my time to deliver emergency food to families. My heart is broken that this service is needed.

So why is the government of our country not hearing the cry of these people? It might be 'complicated' to provide some help. So put some human beings onto the task rather than relying on computer algorithms that keep saying 'no'. Give some hope so that they can pay for their basic survival until they can go back to earning again.

65.
NAME: Juliet
OCCUPATION: Cook
REASON FOR EXCLUSION: Refused furlough

After 27 years working in the same job in the Midlands my partner was offered a fantastic new job in Devon. I had been working as a private cook and for eight years we were never able to have days off together unless we took holiday. Finally, we could have a better work/ life balance.

Before we moved I started applying for roles and was put on the books of an agency providing dinner parties in holiday homes.

We left our jobs on the 28th February 2020 and my partner started his new job on the 2nd March. My first job was to be at the end of March.

We then went into Lockdown. All my work was cancelled and there was no chance of me applying for jobs. I was advised to go back to my previous employer and ask if they would be willing to furlough me. They said no.

I managed to get Job Seekers Allowance of £148.70 a fortnight from May to October. Since then I have received no government financial help. I was refused Universal Credit. If I had been furloughed I would have received around £1,600 per month. Having found some part-time work in November, I have now lost my work again due to Lockdown, and once again don't qualify for furlough.

My partner has had to support me through all of this even though we are not married. I have paid tax and National Insurance for 40 years and never claimed for anything before. Why have the government compensated others but not me? They have all the records of my payments. This is not parity.

Having worked hard and supported myself since the age of 16 it is totally humiliating having to live off the kindness of others. I have used up all my savings and my partner's savings, and am grateful that I have someone to help as the government has totally let me down. However, there are so many others far worse off than me, so I do feel really lucky.

Having voted Conservative all my life, my vote will never go to them again. In the future I intend to earn just enough to live on, working in a voluntary role helping others to make up my time, with as little going to the government as possible.

66.
NAME: Jon Mank
OCCUPATION: Wedding Photographer
REASON FOR EXCLUSION: Limited Company Director

So, it's almost a year since Mr Sunak said "We are all in this together". If only that were true!

My exclusion is due to being a Director of my own wedding photography company – the government call me the Director, but actually I'm a photographer. It's a business I'm proud of, having set it up whilst working as an employed Estate Agent. It took a few years of working two jobs to get to the point of being able to take the full leap of faith into being my own boss and working a way that suits me and my family.

James Mank aged 13.
His home-made video made national news.

I don't earn £200k+ but I earn a good enough amount to support myself and my family. I've never ever not worked, and I consider myself hardworking, honest and a decent bloke. I was brought up to work hard, pay tax and have never claimed a benefit in my life. I'd rather be contributing to the system than needing help from it. We all pay our taxes to help those that can't.

So when I realised that I, as a Director, was Excluded, it hurt really badly. Why anyone would be Excluded was alien to me, just unfathomable and, to be blunt, disgraceful. As a full tax payer, paying my corporation tax, PAYE tax and National Insurance, it's an utter insult to be considered a fraud risk. I truly cannot fathom it out, HMRC has all my tax records.

Why should others get support, and especially those that don't need it, yet I and others are getting zero? I am using my savings to pay the bills and feed my children.

Wouldn't it be fairer that everyone got something? that everyone got something? NO ONE should have been left behind.

Mentally and emotionally this has been the hardest time of my life. It's the contempt shown by Mr Sunak and the feeling that we are not worthy. I KNOW I am. No one eserves this, it's cruel and just plain and simple wrong.

Why will Mr Sunak not even meet ExcludedUK? That to me is hard to understand. He's a new Chancellor, a young Chancellor, a rich Chancellor, who simply does not understand what it is like to not have the wealth to survive a pandemic. Why are we expected to survive without support unlike those being supported, why are they more worthy than me, just why?

67.

NAME: Rachael Hattersley

OCCUPATION: Holiday Home Owner

REASON FOR EXCLUSION: Residential-based business

In 2018 we came to Scotland to follow our dream. Drumwhill is the most idyllic place, and as soon as we found it we knew that we had come home. It's our home, our business and our life.

Our aim was to create our business and living from our home and to do so in a way that is deeply sustainable and respectful of the planet, nature and ourselves. To no longer go out to work. To integrate it and bring it all together in to one place. We would invite others to share it with us by coming here on holiday, either on retreat or to have different nature, wellbeing and outdoors experiences with workshops and activities.

Drumwhill is perfect for it. It has a 3-bedroom self-contained bungalow for renting, a large communal space for workshops, and two spare bedrooms in the house which can be used when we have slightly larger retreats. It is also situated in glorious and forgotten Galloway with the most magical and magnificent surroundings of woods, rivers, lochs and hills. Most of all, it is my home. Perfect, or so it seemed.

And we started! We spoke to Business Gateway about the set up to make sure we had got it right. We renovated the bungalow, and in 2019 we offered a couple of retreats and rented out the bungalow a little. In 2020 we were all ready to go, we had built our website www.drumwhill.com, registered with Visit Scotland, implemented a booking system and signed up with booking providers … and then boom, COVID happened.

At first I felt sure we would be supported. I recall the highs and lows of "Oh yes there is a grant…" – oh no, it's only for people who are on business (non-domestic) rates, not for those of us who are residential and pay council tax. I rang Business Gateway to make sure were set up right and they said yes. And then there would be another grant and another, and the same thing would occur – the optimism, then the deflation of being left out again. I was even desperate enough to apply for one that was for self-catering properties, though we didn't meet the business rate criteria. I thought, perhaps no one knows I am here, and when they do they will wish to help and sort this mess out. But no, just a curt decline.

Rachel and Matt Hattersley at Drumwhill

I wrote to Nicola Sturgeon and my MP, asking that we include everyone in our support packages, saying a society where we leave just one person out is no society at all. I believe in that strongly. And I rode my own shockwave of despair, anger and then deep, deep grief for a society that wasn't what I thought it was, that I had supported all my life and that didn't support me.

And yet people sent money, wrote cheques and made sure we were OK. In July 2020 we were allowed to open again for four months, which was such a gift. I feel truly blessed to be here; it only makes my conviction to live and to create my business and a world where we all care for each other a deeper and more heartfelt thing.

68.

NAME: Sue Attwood

OCCUPATION: Walking Holidays Provider

REASON FOR EXCLUSION: 50/50 rule

I am a recently self-employed sole-trader running a small company that organises women's walking holidays around the UK. I have always enjoyed maps and exploring new walking areas, and these holidays originally started as an unpaid venture with a few friends. I then realised that there are a lot of single women who appreciate the opportunities for small group walking holidays, where they can socialise with like-minded people. Solo holidays aren't much fun and can be difficult.

I was primary school teacher for about 30 years and when this journey began, I was burning the candle at both ends as I was also still teaching. Throughout 2017 I trained as a Walk Leader and First Aider and travelled widely in school holidays to research walking routes and find suitable group accommodation around the country. Although I invested heavily in terms of both time and money, the benefits were that not only would I hopefully create one of the small businesses that the government encourages, but that this would eventually also provide tourist income for accommodation businesses around the UK.

By April 2018, I was confident and well-equipped enough (and there was enough demand) to take the plunge to stop teaching and focus on running the walking holidays for a living. A scary step!

2019 finally reaped modest but sustainable earnings. By early 2020, and with more hard work and preparation under my belt, I was proud and excited at the prospect of earning a proper income at last, as twelve of the holidays for 2020 already had 85% of secure bookings. But as the realities of COVID government restrictions and Lockdowns evolved, all the bookings had to be cancelled.

My income disappeared overnight and stress levels soared. As I knew many people who were claiming furlough and grants for self-employment and even holiday homes, I naturally applied for the government SEISS. It was a considerable shock when this was quickly rejected – as was a subsequent appeal. I was told that this was because of the 50/50 rule. I thought it most unfair that the government were supporting so many others whilst abandoning approximately 3 million people in the self-employed sector.

Whilst looking for temporary employment I applied for Job Seekers Allowance but I did not qualify. Another blow. So, despite the fact I had paid full taxes and Class 1 National Insurance contributions for 30 years as a PAYE teacher, I could not receive SEISS or Job Seekers Allowance.

My applications for local authority grants were rejected because I do not pay business rates on premises. So, since March 2020 I have had no self-employed income and have had to live very sparingly on my hard-earned savings that had been carefully put away to draw on in retirement.

I have no words to describe the impact that being abandoned by the government has had on my mental health. My new business looks doomed to fail as it is now impossible to plan group holidays with any certainty, or consequently to take any bookings for 2021. It is impossible to keep new customers interested when you have nothing to offer them. This is especially cruel when you have worked so hard to build up a product and a customer base from scratch, but now have to let everyone down. Yes, people understand – but you are also soon forgotten.

There is a lot of competition out there. I have spent most of my life giving years of service and hard work to the classroom. I have also long been encouraged by the government that it is a good thing to branch out, be brave and be entrepreneurial.

I am facing a very uncertain future. I find the absence of any financial support from the government for people like me to be grossly unfair and completely soul-destroying.

69.

NAME: Anonymous

OCCUPATION: Events Organiser

REASON FOR EXCLUSION: Director Paid in Dividends

I am a director of a small Limited Company running events and have been a single mum for ten years. In this time I have financially supported myself and my children. I have a daughter in university and a son waiting to do GCSEs.

On 7th March 2020 I flew to Barcelona to manage one of my two biggest events of the year (the other took place in January). Because I have two guaranteed pieces of annual business, with the remainder of my work being ad hoc for agencies throughout the year, I pay myself in dividends and Annual PAYE, which is paid at the end of the tax year. 2020 was already confirmed.

On 14th March we shut down the job in Spain (one week early), packed up, ensured all delegates were on flights, and flew home.

On 23rd March we were due to go into Lockdown and the same day I unexpectedly received a shielding letter which meant that my daughter needed to move back to her rented flat and my son to his dad's. We also needed to attend my partner's father's funeral on 25th, so the process was mismanaged and, as a consequence, my son took this as a rejection and hasn't spoken to me since. My daughter has been in a damp flat where she can't get out of the contract and has to continue paying rent.

The thing I didn't think I would need to worry about was finance. "No one will be left behind," said Rishi Sunak. He talked about furlough, so I assumed I would be eligible for this and wondered how they would work out how my dividends would be calculated. It soon became clear that dividends would be not be counted but at least I had my furlough. Once the rules became clearer still, it seemed that Sunak had Excluded anyone on Annual PAYE who had paid themselves after 19th March although the tax year ends on 4th April. Why? I have paid tax like everyone else for the last 36 years.

Luckily (?) I was able to claim Job Seekers Allowance due to being shielded (£585 – hardly enough for my mortgage and my daughter's rent) but that only lasted three months. I then looked into Universal Credit but, oh no, I've got too much in savings. Yes, I'd been one of the sensible ones who had saved for a rainy day – whoever thought it would be a rainy year!! I've put the house on the market to no avail. My partner and I have split up because of the stress of him not understanding how I've felt with being Excluded by the government, and the situation with my kids. Ironically, we are still living together because we can't afford for him to move out.

Too many emotions through all of this, but I should not have to worry more than anyone else about finances. I have never once not paid into the system and have never once claimed anything. I have been made to feel worthless and totally and utterly Excluded!

70.

NAME: Lynn

OCCUPATION: Approved Driving Instructor

REASON FOR EXCLUSION: 50/50 rule

My name is Lynn. I served my Queen and country in the Royal Air Force for 22 years, serving in different parts of the world including the Falkland Islands and Germany. I am now receiving a small Armed Forces pension but it's not enough to live on and pay my business expenses. After leaving the RAF in 1998 I worked as a pre-school assistant for ten years to top up my pension and be able to live comfortably. I paid my taxes throughout that time.

In 2008 I decided to change direction and train to become a self-employed Approved Driving Instructor, and I worked part-time. I submitted a tax return annually and paid my tax on time.

Then Lockdown hit us. I wasn't unduly worried as, like a lot of people, I thought it would be dealt with quickly. Furlough was announced for PAYE, and when Rishi Sunak said there was to be SEISS for the self-employed I was relieved. Then I listened in despair as he listed the groups of people who were not going to benefit from it and I realised that I was one of those Excluded. My profit from my self-employment, over the last three years, is less than my pension, so I am eligible for nothing.

I tried claiming Universal Credit but as I had just above the limit in savings, I was not eligible. I took on a job as a delivery driver for a supermarket; the hours were unsociable, the work was hard, and lifting all the boxes became impossible as they were so heavy, so I left. I felt useless because I couldn't even do a basic job.

During this time my Mum and my brother-in-law passed away and I was devastated. After the first Lockdown I was lucky enough to be able to return to work for four months. Things were looking up, bills were paid, and there seemed to be a light at the end of the long dark tunnel. There was a new normal. Then we heard there was a 2nd Lockdown, and back to square one – four weeks of no work and no income. Then, back to work for four weeks, followed by Tier 4 and a 3rd Lockdown – no work and no income.

I've used up all my savings. They were supposed to be for my retirement and to pay my tax this month. I have applied for several other jobs, but there are so many people applying for them I don't stand much chance of getting one.

Every day that passes, something else happens to make me feel worse. Today I received more devastating news, my best friend of 36 years passed away, she had lung cancer and hadn't told me.

I'm heartbroken, and this just feels like the straw that breaks the camel's back. I know there are many Excluded people who are far worse off than me, so really I am one of the luckier ones, it just doesn't feel that way at the moment.

71.

NAME: Elaine Little

OCCUPATION: Food Sales and Catering

REASON FOR EXCLUSION: Newly Self-Employed

After 38 years working PAYE I felt it was the right time to go it alone. My father left me money when he passed away four years earlier. Not much (£15,000) – I spent some of it, but I got a little unit inside a gym where I would sell healthy-option foods. Catering is all I really know and I enjoy my work. I spent around £2,000 getting the unit right, then went off on a pre-booked holiday, though I couldn't wait to get back.

The day I got back was my Mum's birthday. I phoned her, and learned that she had been diagnosed with cancer the day before. Nothing could be done, she had six to eight weeks to live. I went straight over to Ireland and stayed until after her funeral, a total of five weeks.

My Mum was a pensioner on state benefits, not a penny to her name (my parents were divorced). I was informed that I had to pay for my Mum's funeral. I told them I had just become self-employed so I had no income coming in. It fell on deaf ears. £4,600 later, I'm back at home.

Feeling deflated about my Mum and the finances that had gone, I knew I was going to struggle. But I got there. I got regular customers and two catering contracts for local businesses. I thought, wow this is great. One contract started at the end of January 2020, the other was due to start at the end of March.

Then came the Lockdown. As I am inside a gym, I was locked down when they were. The first Lockdown was 14 weeks. After a month I applied for Universal Credit (UC) as I was running out of money fast. I have a mortgage and a car, but the car is SORN as I cannot afford to run it. It's there if I have to sell it to pay my mortgage, but it was the last thing my Dad bought me before he died. So, Universal Credit is £95 a week including the extra £20 COVID top-up the government are trying to take away now. I cannot get help for housing because I have worked bloody hard all my life. A single parent with three children, never been out of work, never claimed benefits.

I declined the offer to take a mortgage holiday because all I could think was that's extra money to pay back after the six months, and there was no certainty of what was going to be happening then. I live on my own and my outgoings are £580 a month before utilities & food.

I am totally disgusted at how I and the Excluded have been treated. I shop for yellow labels in shops at night, I wear three jumpers or double PJs, I have my curtains closed for warmth, I don't go out apart from night shopping. I've never felt anxious before but by God I can't begin to explain how I feel now. Just totally SHIT, USELESS, ABANDONED for doing absolutely the right thing and following the government's orders.

I've managed to work 18 weeks in 2020 and my savings are almost gone. The business will be gone if I'm unable to reopen before the end of February. But I promise you one thing, I will never until I take my last breath pay another penny to this government in tax. I am fully paid up on my National Insurance for my pension. I have a private pension I will be cashing in this March before they take that off me. I probably won't even make state pension age to claim it with all the stress/anxiety this government have put us through. If I do, it might be in the mental hospital, aptly EXCLUDED FROM SOCIETY.

72.

NAME: Karen Squance

OCCUPATION: Music Teacher

REASON FOR EXCLUSION: 50/50 rule

A successful, enthusiastic teacher, my world was shattered in 1986 when my daughter was diagnosed with overwhelming severe congenital heart problems.

My decision then not to work was considered a personal choice, so no help was given apart from child benefit. These conditions remained for the whole of her childhood, with 18 minor and three major open-heart surgeries. I was able to supplement a little by teaching piano privately at home.

Fast forward to 2003; she learnt to drive, and gained her first taste of independence. When she left for University, I was able to re enter the work world. I was employed by Somerset Music and paid voluntarily into the teachers' pension scheme.

However, my daughter's condition was deteriorating, and despite achieving an Honours BSc she was unable to take up a post of speech and language therapist as it was just too exhausting. In 2010 she decided that she would have another open-heart procedure with the hope of leading a fuller life. No longer a child, there were no free facilities for me to stay with her at the hospital in London. She had her surgery on April 13th 2010 and never left hospital. She died on August 25th 2010.

No one pays any bereavement or funeral expenses if your 'child' is over 16. The loss of earnings and costs and funeral expenses came to just under £20,000. For a year I could not pick myself up. I did receive some Employment Support Allowance for 6 months, but when I needed to extend this I saw my notes from the doctor who had recorded 'death of daughter' under 'minor illness' .....

In 2011 I returned to work. By now my 84-year-old father was starting to struggle, so I was trying to fit in visits each week which meant a 160 mile round trip. One day, starting out for school, I had to pull over, unable to continue. I deposited myself at the doctors. Thankfully a locum took pity on me and gave the immediate diagnosis of out-of-control diabetes. The doctor also said "something has to give, or you will". She suggested concentrating on private teaching rather than class work, and to only do it three days a week to allow time to visit Dad.

At the beginning of 2019 I was living two days a week in Cardiff with my Dad, and teaching the other three days in Somerset. I was not earning a King's ransom, but along with the small teacher's pension it was enough to have a good work/life balance. I was also pleased to be awarded a carer's allowance, backdated to January 2019. Unfortunately Dad soon needed full-time care so sadly was moved into a care home, and my carer's allowance was stopped in October 2019.

Then COVID hit. The trust informed us we were 'non-essential' and we were told not to come into school. Our government told us that "We are all in this together" and "Nobody will be left behind". We soon learned that if the money you received for looking after your elderly parent, which you no longer receive, combined with a small private pension, takes you over 50/50 of your self-employed income, then you will not be eligible for any SEISS payment. You won't be considered for Universal Credit because your husband 'earns' a state pension. You won't be worthy of Job Seekers Allowance or Employment Support Allowance because you haven't paid Class 1 National Insurance in the past two years, despite having 39 fully paid years under your belt. So you are worth nothing.

Forgive me if I don't see how we are quite "all in this together".

73.
NAME: M
OCCUPATION: Charity Membership Recruiter
REASON FOR EXCLUSION: Newly Self-Employed

I was a civil servant, PAYE, for 20 years. In 2018 I took voluntary redundancy; there was a move to cut staff and my current role had come to an end, so I decided to jump before I was pushed. The previous five years had been very stressful for a number of reasons, both in work and at home, and after over two decades of being a single parent to three children I was burnt out. I drew my works pension early, but as I had worked mostly part-time this is quite small.

For over a year I lived off my pension and redundancy money while wondering where to go next. As a stopgap, in September 2019 I became self-employed working under contract with an agency which recruits members to various national charities. This involves direct, face-to-face contact with the public in a variety of venues, from supermarkets to big exhibitions and shows. Payment is commission only, and I have to pay my own expenses. Winter is not the best time for this kind of work, and I was still learning, so I earned less than £3,000 before Lockdown. Normally summer would be much more lucrative with better venues and bigger audiences, so I was expecting to earn enough to see me through the leaner winter months without having to dig further into my savings. But that is impossible to prove to HMRC, of course.

When restrictions were eased I was able to work a little in Sept-Dec 2020, but I could only work outside, standing in increasingly cold temperatures, and I had to observe social distancing which makes it harder to engage with the public. The venues are booked by the agency, and they have found it difficult to plan ahead because of uncertainty and the limited number of places that are open. I found, too, that people were less willing to sign up to the charity because their finances were already stretched. I earned less than £1,000 before I had to stop working again.

I am Excluded because I don't have three years' accounts and my small pension would take me over the 50/50 rule. I wouldn't get Universal Credit because of my pension and redundancy pay. This latter was supposed to be a nest egg to help start a new business or see me into retirement, but it's rapidly been used up. There is little employment where I live even without a pandemic. Like other WASPI women, I spent most of my life expecting to retire at 60 (in 2021) and only learned comparatively recently, and by accident, that I will not receive my State Pension till I am 67.

The only silver lining from this horrific Exclusion by the government is that it's shown up how massively unfair the benefits system is, with its nonsensical, arbitrary rules and inequality. This is not just in times of a pandemic, but for thousands of people who have suffered cruelly ever since the 2008 economic crash. The refusal of the government to even meet with ExcludedUK, let alone deal with the injustices, shows that they have no understanding of the complexities of everyday life for most people. And it is short-sighted, because all these unfortunate people who have lost their businesses will end up costing the government – ie, taxpayers – more money in the long term. The sooner they are out, the better.

A few years ago PM Theresa May told us there was "no magic money tree" – and yet, miraculously, one has been found. The Government has pulled out funds, not just for supporting those eligible for SEISS and furlough, but for spending billions on contracts such as the inept Track and Trace. Where has that money come from? How are they intending to recoup it? I fear for what happens next if these people continue to govern.

74.

NAME: Paul & Sarah

OCCUPATION: Café Owners

REASON FOR EXCLUSION: New Starters

We are a husband and wife and have both worked as teachers for a combined total of 45 years. Following the loss of my father, we felt it was the right time to follow our long-held dream of opening up a café.

Using the remainder of our savings, we spent weeks refurbishing a premises. We traded for six weeks before we were closed down due to COVID.

Our accountant submitted our first wage (for March) at the end of the month, meaning we missed the cut off date for the Real Time Information (19th March). Due to this, we were not eligible for the furlough scheme, as we were in the 'New Starters' category.

We have five children. We had used all of our savings for the new business, and as well as our own household costs, our eldest daughter was in her final year of University, so we still had to pay for her student accommodation, despite her being sent home.

The financial and emotional implications of being Excluded have been devastating – all for simply choosing a change of career at the wrong time.

75.

NAME: Alex

OCCUPATION: Writer & Tutor

REASON FOR EXCLUSION: Complicated

As a self-employed person living alone, I have felt Excluded during England's response to COVID-19 in a number of ways.

Firstly, financially. Because I have some rental income from a second property, I did not qualify for compensation for loss of earnings from tutoring. My tuition business involved teaching up to 16 students a week face-to-face and had a focus on exam preparation: since in-person teaching was banned under the first Lockdown and has been followed by ongoing confusion about exams, it is no longer viable.

Secondly, as someone living alone in a flat, I have been acutely affected by the social isolation of Lockdown policies. Restrictions limiting time outdoors have deprived me of a vital way of maintaining my mental and physical health. Prior to March 2020 I was heavily involved in community and cultural life and so the lack of state support for theatre and performance venues during their prolonged closures made me wonder what would be left of the vibrant arts scene that had made up my life in London.

By the end of 2020, with no end in sight, I concluded that a decent life in England for the foreseeable future was not possible for someone in my position. Government policies seemed to be designed around a group of people with secure incomes, commodious accommodation and the presence of partners or loving family ('social capital').

Close friends with a large house outside London, their privately-educated teenager supported by live online teaching, tell me their lives haven't changed much; my former neighbours say they want restrictions to go on as long as possible so they can spend time at home with their young child. To meet my basic needs, however, I have to be able to work, see other people and spend time outdoors. A society outlawing these things for long periods is not one that is healthy or safe for me.

I am now living in Portugal where I have obtained residency. When I came here with one suitcase in December 2020, I intended to return in the spring to manage my two properties. I had hoped to return regularly to the UK with a view to keeping open the possibility of returning to live there in the future. However, at the time of writing, with costly, state-enforced hotel quarantine about to come into force, I have no idea when this will be possible. With talk of restrictions in England over next winter, I am now questioning the viability of even owning property in the UK.

76.
NAME: Ele
OCCUPATION: Boarding Kennels
REASON FOR EXCLUSION: Limited Company Director

I have run boarding kennels for 12 years. I set them up from scratch in 2007 and business was booming. Life was good. I was busy, saving and planning my retirement.

Then COVID hit.

I sat and watched that famous public announcement. I listened and made notes when Sunak said that no one would be left behind, and when Boris said their arms would be wrapped around everyone.

The schemes were rolled out quickly and efficiently and I was impressed. I have a large house and kennels on 16 acres, on a commercial lease. I am, therefore, committed to fixed costs of £2,600 per month, which increases depending on the number of dogs that are boarding. But I genuinely thought it would all be over by September and would affect my business for summer 2020 only.

I realised that I actually wasn't considered self-employed in this instance and my only option was to furlough myself and get £572 pcm. But then, I would not be allowed to work in the business. I furloughed my staff; some were on more than me and then, to add insult to injury, I was asked to pay 10% and 20% of their wages from MY SAVINGS! My staff are zero hours, so I didn't have to furlough them as it is the employer's choice to do this, but I believed that was the right thing to do, so I did it, but at a cost to me.

In total I had £572 to live off and pay £2,600 business costs. No one needs a calculator to work out that this wasn't a good proposition. Still, I genuinely thought it would all be over soon. I can do this to save the NHS, I thought, as I clapped on a Thursday evening.

But weeks turned into months and I went from being a successful, carefree business woman earning over £160K to counting every penny and not sleeping. Luckily for me, I had to shield due to long-term health problems, so, swallowing my pride, I applied for benefits for the first time in my life. I am in now in receipt of Employment Support Allowance. I get £300 pcm because I am ill, not because it is part of the Coronavirus Job Retention Scheme or SEISS. So glad I am ill.

I have always been a happy and positive person, but I found it crushing to be referred to as non-viable, not from what I had done, but from what the Government had done to me!

I discovered ExcludedUK, and quickly realised I wasn't alone, thank God! Whilst I was happy to join ExcludedUK to raise awareness, I found it harrowing and depressing to read of all the tragedies of others. My business was offered debt, whilst others were given furlough/grants. Why was there such a glaring lack of parity? That is what hurts the most.

I cannot believe that it's almost a year down the line, and it is like Groundhog Day.

I have tried to remain as positive as I can throughout this, but I am a different person now.

I am now more aware of the benefits system and its shortcomings.
I am in regular contact with my MP, even had a phone call from him.
I regularly tweet to share the cause and raise awareness.

I have done more to help others (members of ExcludedUK), a small gift of money, a supportive comment, a private message, and have found great comfort that small things can help others and in turn help me.

This has been a complete shit show. I am now poorer, have to work much longer until I can retire and, due to the stress, my health has suffered immeasurably. I feel depressed, crushed and passed over. I have been treated appallingly, but I will come out of this a better, stronger, nicer person, due to the collected group that is ExcludedUK.

I truly hope that we ALL get through this. I will never forget!

77.

NAME: Cheryl

OCCUPATION: Make-up Artist

REASON FOR EXCLUSION: Accountant Error

My position is a little niche – but here goes. I have been a Make-up Artist for the last 20 years and freelance for the last eight. I work almost exclusively for Hollyoaks and their company policy states that all freelancers need to take a 'break' during the year. It used to be three months but now it's just one.

For the last five years, I have saved hard and used that break to budget backpack, mainly round south-east Asia. This is always around January. While I am backpacking, I rely on my accountant to file my returns. I have paid my tax on time every year, but this year HMRC didn't issue any reminder as apparently they didn't have my (unchanged) address. My accountant therefore didn't file my return even though all the paperwork had been completed.

I returned to the UK on 1st March 2020 and went back to work, unaware that my tax return had not been filed.

I was 100% positive that SEISS would be given to me. However, on the eligibility checker I was deemed ineligible. After much investigation, when I discovered that my return had not been filed I tried to rectify the issue. I submitted my return and appealed. As far as I can tell the computer says "NO" on ALL appeals. I took my appeal as far as I could. I broached HMRC, solicitors and my accountant, but it was like banging my head against a brick wall.

I hadn't applied for Universal Credit (UC) as I was convinced that the SEISS would come through. There's no back-dating on UC. I finally managed to get £400 for the last 14 weeks. So between my £900 wages and £400 UC, I've had £1,300 total income since December to live on.

I am at a loss as to what to do. Make-up freelancers aren't being used at the moment and supermarkets don't want me. My CV is irrelevant to most available positions. I've emailed shops, bars, cinemas, friends, MPs, barbers, salons, etc. There's either excess furloughed staff waiting in the scenes or a national freeze on current recruitment. My other industry is Theatre – another closed sector.

I've been put on anti-depressants and am considering all my options. But I don't know what to do or where to turn to.

Many thanks for letting me release some of the frustration that surrounds me at the moment.

78.

NAME: Karen

OCCUPATION: Business Consultant & Holistic Practitioner/Teacher

REASON FOR EXCLUSION: 50/50 rule

I was Excluded for making more money in an employed role than I did in my sole trader business during the year 2018/2019. I was made redundant and I decided to focus full time on my own business.

Due to my work, I spent a lot of time traveling, but all that stopped, overnight, in March 2020 when the country was put into Lockdown.

I'm currently not allowed to do a huge chunk of my work. I struggle to pay my bills. Six months of deferred credit card and loan payments have helped, but I now have higher monthly re-payments because interest is added. My Bounce Back Loan has long gone and I'm not sure how that will be paid back. It's cost me at least £20k this year already.

I managed to get some consulting work when we came out of the first Lockdown, but how embarrassing it was at the time as I didn't have enough money to put fuel in my car to get to the job and pay for a B&B. My neighbour loaned me money for this, for which I'm eternally grateful, but mortified at the same time. Now I'm trying to work out how to pay that back along with all the other massive debts I've accrued this last year.

I'm frustrated and angry. What's hard to swallow is a Government that knows you exist but chooses to look the other way. That's deliberate, that's personal, and that's just cruel.

As a holistic teacher I hold space for others constantly, which is instinctive, it's just who I am. It's a vocation for me but I'm beginning to break now, and some days don't want to get out of bed.

Every day I shed tears. I'm trying to sell all that I can over the next few weeks so I can pay my rent and credit card bills for maybe a month or two more.

The members of the ExcludedUK group are incredible. I'm so grateful for each and every one of them and their support. I've been able to get out of my comfort zone, do things in my business I never thought I would, and there's been kindness from places I would not have expected.

I'm probably moving into one bedroom at my parents' house (with my cat). But I won't give up. And I look forward to the day I can meet with others in person again, see their smiles without the need for a mask, and hug them. That will be a very good day.

79.

NAME: L

OCCUPATION: Yoga Teacher

REASON FOR EXCLUSION: Newly Self-Employed

I have been employed in offices almost my entire adult life across both the public and private sectors. I left my last office role in January 2020 to build up my freelance Yoga teaching schedule which I started part-time in June 2019. Things got off to a great start and it felt wonderful to be doing so well, so quickly, for something I love doing.

But less than two months later, all the venues I taught at were forced to close for the first Lockdown in March 2020.

My only option was to try to switch to online teaching, but unfortunately the bulk of my students were from leisure centres so I did not have their contact details and could not let them know about my online classes.

It was difficult to get the online business going with only a small following. A few people attended here and there, but interest had really worn off by the end of last year and my attempts to run short courses/classes this year did not generate any interest at all.

It has been demoralising and heart-breaking. I'm grateful, however, that one private student who started with me in the first Lockdown, paying on a donation-basis, continued to stay with me when I had to up the costs to standard fees from October. But it is now the only income I have coming in and it barely covers groceries.

I had savings from a recent inheritance, so I was only eligible for the new Job Seekers Allowance scheme, which provided £44/wk based on previous NI contributions. I was not eligible for the local council grant (ARG) as they do not accept my home address as my business address, and will not take into account any business-related expenses that were paid annually outside of the Lockdown period. Nor will they accept the costs of rent/council tax/internet etc as being relevant, even though I have been forced to teach online from home after all the venues I was teaching at previously have been forced to close.

My savings are going down rapidly. I have to cover all my living expenses AND the running of my business and I feel like it's being wasted as this wasn't my choice or the plan I had for my business.

I feel frustrated that I'm having to make these sacrifices whilst others have been able to sit at home watching TV and still receive their salary. They haven't had to justify, explain or sift through documentation to prove themselves, and made to feel like they are just begging to be seen, heard, supported.

Being Excluded has left me feeling completely ignored by the Government and even friends and family don't really understand, or even think it's not really happening, because it's not happening to them.

It's repeatedly made me question the value of my business, even though I love what I do – helping others see the benefits practicing yoga can bring. The irony is not lost on me! Yoga is known to be excellent for health & wellbeing generally, especially during stressful times such as this!

I'm tired of hearing 'no' and having doors closed in my face. I've been applying for jobs but no success yet, even when I've ticked all the boxes.

To be honest, it leaves me feeling that even when we're able to travel freely again, I'd like to take my business and my savings and go live in another country and let them benefit from it. I've worked my entire adult life yet it means nothing now.

I am so glad I found the ExcludedUK group and can get useful tips, advice and motivation from the fantastic people there. Unlike my closest friends and loved ones, the group knows how this really feels and whilst it is really sad to see people in much worse situations, there are also many posts that unite, show continual strength, and a tremendous determination to be seen and heard, which is fantastic and uplifting. I don't feel so alone.

The whole pandemic situation and resulting fallout has made me think about the way I work, the kind of work I do and who I want to work with in future.

I feel a bit down-trodden, but also feel it's given me time to pause and really think about WHY I want to do this kind of work, which I might not have had the opportunity to do otherwise. I need to find more efficient ways of working and especially pandemic/ Lockdown-proof work!! Quite possibly in another country. ;)

80.
NAME: Shabana
OCCUPATION: Actress
REASON FOR EXCLUSION: Combined Self-employed/PAYE income 50/50

As an actress I was getting roughly 25 acting/voiceover/modelling jobs a year. Twenty-five percent of my work is from repeat clients. I had signed up to a new talent agent and was getting castings for big shows like Eastenders and Emmerdale.

2020 was on track to be my most successful year yet in my 20-year career as an actress.

At first, I didn't think the Lockdown would go on for so long and I was very happy to stay home to protect the NHS for the initial three weeks. There was no talk of furlough at that point. In fact, I had never actually heard of the word!

As the Government extended the Lockdown and increased the financial support offered to a lot of sectors I started to feel more and more under pressure.

I have been unable to find work during this time, and unfortunately being an actress means there are little transferable skills. With more and more people on furlough taking second jobs, it felt like an incredibly unfair system. Some people were financially doing better by not working or taking on second jobs whilst others were losing everything they had built. It seemed like anyone who was brave enough to risk it all to follow their dreams was being punished.

I don't think people realise that the constant worry of having no income and little ability to find employment is incredibly stressful. You have zero bandwidth to come up with creative ideas or find new ideas for businesses. There was also little understanding or empathy coming from people I knew, so I became more and more isolated. My world is now a smaller place filled with anxiety, fear and impending doom.

Shabana Hussain starring as Samia Shahid in the BBC documentary 'Murdered for love'

I found the ExcludedUK community at the end of 2020, and just to be part of a group of people who are also in the same situation has given me strength. I am still unable to process how many people three million are if we all stood outside together. But it makes me feel like I'm not alone and that every day a bunch of strangers are fighting on my behalf to get parity.

For the future, I'm hoping I can travel again and even though it's a 24/7 kind of job, I will try to find other things to spend my time on and I will take more time away from my career.

81.

NAME: Andrew

OCCUPATION: Freelance Consultant

REASON FOR EXCLUSION: 50/50 rule

I worked for 33 years as a police officer and then a further five years as a civilian police trainer and I receive a police pension. In the last tax year that 'other income' exceeded my taxable income by just £19.

I am also divorced, and as part of a lawfully binding solicitors' agreement, my ex-wife receives half of my police pension – once it has been paid to me. So in real terms my 'other income' was well below the amount of my taxable income, but HMRC are not interested, because the pension comes to me first.

I have been Excluded from any Government support and am not entitled to any benefits.

I have been working as a freelance consultant for over eight years, advising two of the major running event organisers in the country. The most high profile of these is the Manchester Marathon, which is now the fourth largest marathon in Europe. At a stroke, back in March 2020, all events were cancelled and I was out of work straight away. Now (end of January 2021) there is no certainty as to when I can get back to work.

I am hopeful that we may be able to run an event in October this year, but that is still a long way off from being a certainty. That will mean that I will have been out of my self-employed job for 18 months – with no Government support.

I have paid tax and National Insurance for 48 years. I feel totally betrayed by those in Government. Especially those who seem to be able to evade questions in parliament and lie about the circumstances that are impacting not just me, but 3 million others in similar circumstances. All I want is parity, not charity. There is a code of conduct for those in public office, which we see broken on a regular basis, and to which there appears to be no redress. I would have been thrown out of the police service for any such breach.

Andrew Peter Thompsett, having served for 33 years as a Police Officer, now works for himself through APT Enterprises and is Excluded.

I feel betrayed, let down, discriminated against, left without a voice. The Government rhetoric is such that the majority of people just do not understand. They believe everyone is supported. Even when I try to explain, I get the feeling that some think that it is my fault. I have cried on more than one occasion, worrying about how to support my family.

I had to bite the bullet and I now work 20 hours a week at B&Q. It's not what I want to be doing, but it was necessary. After months of jumping through hoops, I also got a Bounce

Back Loan and have just spent over half of it paying my tax bill. Anything the Government has offered has just been more debt. I am thankful that I am not as bad off as many.

I thank God every day that I am still here, for the support of my immediate family and the ExcludedUK group.

But I will not forget. I will never, ever vote Conservative again.

82.
NAME: Jo
OCCUPATION: Not Given
REASON FOR EXCLUSION: New Starter

I feel like I am a fraud, not because the Government tell me that I am, but because, incredibly, we are doing OK financially and in business at the moment – although still counted as Excluded.

I am sharing my story though, because it's not just the financial impact and loss, it's the change in friendships, in beliefs and the ongoing strain of no safety net. British citizens have been led to believe they have paid for a rainy day in this country. This is a false sense of security. We as a family are really only hanging on by a thread.

My husband was made redundant at the end of January 2020. He started a new business on 1st February 2020 manufacturing looms and cables, subcontracting for the company he had been made redundant from. He used his redundancy pay to start this.

February was a blur of activity, getting everything set up with manufacturing and organisation. Luckily, my husband already had a customer and work relationship.

I was working as a community mental health rehabilitation support worker, making home visits to people with a vast array of mental health conditions.

In early March, I had a meeting with my manager to request a top up to my PPE – I was running low on gloves and hand gel. The meeting never happened as my visit to the office to collect it was cancelled.

Maybe this isn't relevant to Excluded but it led to my decision that, with a pandemic in the country, I was putting my family at risk by continuing in this job. My husband was the main bread winner and provider and it seemed prudent to protect his health. Subsequently I have seen studies indicating jobs with the highest death rates from COVID during the pandemic so far, and see mine listed as one. (No surprises there)

I knew Lockdown was coming and I followed the news with increasing anxiety knowing that it was possible that we could lose everything overnight. I decided to put my own job on hold and immediately began to work like stink with my husband to get a pallet load of orders sent off and invoiced before the country was shut down. We got our first big order out just before the Prime Minister's Lockdown announcement, which meant we could invoice and get paid.

The next few months proved a steep learning curve for both of us. I had to learn how to be a manufacturing production operative/engineer alongside my husband.

Luckily, our 16 year old daughter got furloughed, so we had one very small wage coming in for food. We realised we would not be eligible for any financial help other than ones that would increase our debts and problems long term. I'm talking mortgage holidays and Bounce Back Loans. We decided to try and avoid these. Remarkably and unexpectedly, I received a few thousand pounds from mis-sold PPI from years ago. The timing couldn't have been any more like a miracle.

I still don't know how we survived the spring and summer but all three of us put our heads down and carried on. We worked out of the industrial unit and our sole mission was to avoid catching COVID and keep working to keep the business going. We even used a bucket to wee and poo in. I upset many friends who thought I was being extreme, who didn't seem to take in the enormity of the growing pandemic. We were also incredibly lucky in that after an initial few weeks of hiccups, we were able to carry on working as we support the transport sector and provide some army cables. The business would have ended before it began if we had been forced to close.

Every day is a rollercoaster, not knowing if today the company that we have our most business with will survive. Brexit is also a concern, as they are a French company, but we are picking up more customers.

Eleven months later my job is still on hold (at least I think it is – I haven't received my P45 and I got a *Happy Christmas* text from my employer!)

I am still no clearer about our future. We still have no reliable financial safety net if we become ill.

However, some friendships will never be repaired. There are friends who are experiencing a completely different Lockdown, who are making the most of time off to enjoy grants and furlough, exercise, indulge in life hobbies or start new ones, shop, build, cook, create for themselves with the increased funds and time they have.

We have friends who are secure in the knowledge that they will be paid if they are sick, so they don't worry so much about methods of preventing transmission and Government rules and advice. Friends who ignore Government advice but still believe there is support for everyone and no one is Excluded. 'Friends' who make snide comments, gas lighting our situation.

I found the ExcludedUK group on Facebook and joined. It was such a relief to finally find a community who understood the extreme stress, but it was also desperately sad and heartbreaking hearing so many people in impossible no-win situations. People left destitute, having had self-esteem and purpose ripped off of them so cruelly by this pandemic and a Government that left them out to dry financially and in poverty.

I spoke to my local MP John Penrose online, who offered no solutions or advice. I joined local council meetings to raise the Excluded issue. They did try to be helpful but the small amount of ARG that would be offered to us and the time, effort and loops we would have to negotiate meant we did not apply. We also did not qualify for the £500 isolation grant.

We felt that as we were surviving the money should go to others in more needy situations. I shared hashtags, links and information to try and help awareness. I feel privileged to have been able to donate small amounts, via the ExcludedUK COVID Fund, to people who have desperately needed funds immediately to live, and I've encouraged others to contribute.

I try to stay away from information about banks freezing and closing accounts and businesses, investigating them for fraud. We are just relieved and glad we didn't need to resort to that route even if we had been eligible. It certainly doesn't help the mental health to start believing conspiracies no matter how much evidence. In time the truth will out.

It's helped me personally to be able to share our good fortune of current financial survival with those who are hanging on by a thread. I am so proud of my husbands' determination and resilience.

Although we are in a much better business position a year down the line, we are taking one day at a time. We have talked about getting other jobs if needed and doing whatever it takes. Our motivation and energy reserves are low right now. Being newly self-employed at the start of a pandemic and reducing your family income isn't ideal, but we are still here as a family, with a home and business – I just don't quite know how.

83.
NAME: Ian
OCCUPATION: Driving Instructor
REASON FOR EXCLUSION: 50/50 (or bad timing as I prefer to call it)

From 1986 to June 2018 I had a PAYE career in retail. I paid full tax and National Insurance contributions, much of which was at the 40% mark for every year of that period.

This also included such things as company car, pension, and private health care taxes on top.

I was made redundant in June 2018. Approaching the age of 50, I knew that finding a job at that age was going to be challenging. I decided to future-proof myself and therefore I invested money from my redundancy payment into re-training to become a driving instructor.

Essentially, I took the gamble and I paid my own money out to ensure that I had a good sustainable income so as not to be a burden on the state and to enable me to work successfully up until retirement.

Tax Year 2018/19 was the cut-off point for the SEISS scheme but in that year it included salary from a well paid PAYE role that I had held for 14 years, plus the equivalent redundancy package, so by the time I filed that return, despite posting a small profit from my new self-employed career, I obviously earned more through PAYE.

Imagine your stereotypical working class Geordie lad who, despite leaving school at 16 with nothing in terms of qualifications, worked hard, paid his dues and forged a successful career for himself. He never once relied on anyone. He paid his bills. He had a good credit reference. His mortgage was ticking along nicely and he was absolutely a good solid British tax-paying, law-abiding citizen and then Boom! COVID-19 came along and

everything changed because he suddenly had his livelihood impacted severely whilst watching support being handed out almost everywhere.

I waited thinking my turn will come for help but instead I watched countless interviews from Boris and Sunak denying I even existed. At the same time I also watched and listened to stories of people who openly admitted they didn't need the financial support, but got it and continued to work, making even more money. It broke me – piece by piece, day by day.

The worst day of the lot was when an amazing friend of mine turned up unexpectedly at the door with a significant amount of shopping for us. That day broke me up in a big way and the big tough working class Geordie bloke cried and cried, and although I felt loved, I also felt I was a failure to myself, but most of all to my wife.

As I broke up piece by piece, my confidence took a hit and my self-esteem lessened. My mental health suffered as a result. Every day yet another rejection for help, and I am not going to say I wanted to kill myself but I cried and often did the sums and thought if I wasn't here, when everything is added together would my wife be OK financially?

There are times now, in January 2021 that I sit and think, why me? Was I not good enough for support? Why did my country disown me and others like me? I still don't know.

I have a good business, I will never give up despite now having £15k of debt that I neither wanted nor needed, but what I will do is remember who did this to me and ensure they never get my vote.

I also reflect on the fact that of the 3 million Excluded voices I am one of the lucky ones as I got to go back to work, when many didn't.

84.
NAME: Simon
OCCUPATION: Inbound Tour Operator
REASON FOR EXCLUSION: Sole Director Ltd Company

"Simon. We've made it to Brussels Airport! Flight availability was our concern. Thanks so much for planning everything and for being so flexible. Hope to see you again once sanity returns."

Annette and her two American pals had been half way through a WWI battlefield and chocolate/foodie tour of Brussels before their nerves got the better of them and they bailed. Missing out on Bruges, Antwerp and Amsterdam.

And with that, my last clients scarpered from Europe.

That was 12 March 2020, and my company has not seen a pound of revenue since.

From a record year in 2019 to a big fat zero for 2020. Quite surreal when you look at my company's figures.

My father was in the British Army. I was fortunate to experience some incredibly lucky and amazing postings of his. Which, following a BTEC at Bournemouth and working in Switzerland as a ski guide, was always going to lean me towards a vocation within the travel & tourism industry.

In May 2003 I stepped off the gravy train and into self-employment. Using my nous and experience gained over the previous decade, I picked up the telephone and made calls to the smaller U.S. and Canadian travel agents looking for a bespoke, English speaking person 'on the ground' on the other side of the pond. Cold-calling gives you two polar opposite reactions: 20 seconds before the recipient firmly says no but have a great day. Or 15 minutes with someone who is after just such a contact.

For everyone working within the inbound travel sector, we know our enemies well: terrorism, volcanoes and recessions. Fear, unable, cost. And we understand that, when working for yourself, it means no revenue for several months. We get it. We carry on.

But then a global pandemic arrives and shuts down our businesses.

I, like everyone else, cancelled 50% of bookings and pleaded on others to postpone. Importantly, the deposits are held with those hoteliers and suppliers contracted for that particular itinerary. In their eyes, they see Harrison Maxwell Ltd – my company – as 'existing'. More on that later.

You listen to the Chancellor stating, "No-one will be left behind". You look across the Irish Sea where their Government ensured that any adult unable to work received €350 per week, until support schemes were implemented. That's "wrapping your arms around people".

Soon became obvious though – I was facing a triple-whammy.

I'm a Sole Director of a Ltd Company. That's £480.00 per month = 19% furlough.

The temerity of working from a cabin at home means no fancy grants. Not one.

Inbound travel industry means no revenue since March 2020. And 2021 looks a washout as well, due to booking five to six months ahead.

New Zealand, Croatia, Greece and Germany are those countries that offered targeted support as they recognised one size doesn't fit all and that some industries will not just 'bounce back.' The UK Government unfathomably, despite our own industry segment being worth £28bn to the UK economy, decides to sit on their hands. Illogical.

April saw me searching for a job, any job. And I found one. As a seed-picking packer in a factory. After the rush there, I hopped across to Hermes, floundering around the narrow streets of Cambridgeshire like a wacky racer. Summer 2020 saw me in my third temp job, up-keeping pub gardens, and then painting and decorating the outside windows of a gorgeous property in Cambridge. I'm currently working as a building assistant, surrounded by electricians, plasterers and plumbers – all on SEISS and totally oblivious of my plight while I keep making their tea. All of them are enjoying a record year of income, while receiving SEISS.

When I returned home from my temp jobs, I found that I resembled a surreal version of Winston, George Orwell's character in 1984, in that everyone I had met or heard or watched whilst outside my home had been supported. The glazed look of anyone you informed of your Excluded situation, was contrary to what they had heard from their Government.

Hush, you're fine. This will blow over. I began to think maybe it was just me.

My own MP (Lucy Frazer) claims, “There’s no point in supporting those that won’t exist”. So through no fault of my own, I have been told by the Treasury that I am resource-intensive and admin-difficult. Basically, a deadweight. Not viable, and I don’t exist. Not one of these criticisms were laid at the door of those fortunate enough to land full furlough or SEISS.

And so, the mental health disintegration starts. You wake up and travel to your temp job, you see empty streets and think, "Where is everyone? Oh yes! At home on full furlough." Once at work, you experience the conversations with the SEISS chaps (never been busier), you return home and see a procession of sympathetic MPs asking the Treasury ministers, "Is this right to Exclude so many?" Only to have their questions sanctimoniously batted away. You find yourself retreating, all the while being bashed on the head.

Mental strain every single day, with worries. My 16yr old daughter asking my wife if Daddy is OK?

Early June, thankfully, saw me find ExcludedUK, a campaign group founded by four people who had never met each other, who had managed to get the word out about our discrimination.
I remember hazy summer evenings reading and writing to fellow Excluders and hearing even more horror stories. And yet, being in the same small boat meant you finally didn’t feel so alone.

But those Groundhog Day feelings of hope swiftly turned to frustration due to continued lack of recognition from our own Government. Why are tax-paying human beings, the population equivalent of Glasgow, Belfast, Liverpool, Nottingham, Birmingham and Cardiff, having to fight tooth and nail for parity of support? It's Unfathomable. Unforgivable. Unforgettable.

My father died on 30 September (Alzheimer's) and I hadn’t seen him since he went into a care home in April. Mum agrees that, being a lifelong Conservative voter, he would be apoplectic on seeing his son’s dream smashed through no fault of his own. Dad would have remembered Lord Tebbit’s "get on ya bike", and so I and 3 million others did just that.

Under the cloak of COVID, the same Party has become the enemy of small business and freelancers. The Great Excluded Scandal is what I call it on Twitter. I can only hope that when, at some time in the future the enquiry is held, the Millennials will look back with incredulity on why this decision was permitted to be made by a rookie Chancellor with an absence of any scrutiny and accountability.

With utterly no recognition by my own Government, it's fair to say that I feel abandoned.

COVID 19 said, "Hi" and our own Government said, "Bye."

85.
NAME: Nicky
OCCUPATION: Trauma & Anxiety Therapist
REASON FOR EXCLUSION: 50/50 rule

My name is Nicky. I'm 54, divorced, living on my own in Cumbria with a 23 year old daughter, who works in our local hospital.

I'm a trauma and anxiety therapist, supporting people (young and old) who have PTSD, CPTSD, trauma-related mental health issues, anxiety and serious life conditions. I also deliver therapy training in Reiki and EFT (tapping). My private practice – Nicky Forbes Therapies – has been established for over ten years, supporting the general public, but particularly members of our emergency services and medically discharged military veterans.

After the death of my Dad in 2007, I was passionate about using complementary therapy to support patients at end-of-life and their families. So I was delighted when, in 2015, I was accepted as initially the Reiki therapist and then the Complementary therapy lead in our local hospice for adults and children.

I took a significant drop in income to split my working week between three days at the hospice and the remainder in private practice.

I left the hospice at the beginning of April 2020 as I had been offered a voluntary opportunity to deliver trauma therapy in Kenya and India for a charity supporting young women affected by abuse and FGM.

Of course, due to COVID, the charity work is on hold. And, in spite of no salary from the hospice since April 2020, I have been Excluded from SEISS, because the salaried income was more than 50% (just) of my total income the previous year.

I have been able to deliver some online therapy sessions, and during the softening of restrictions in summer 2020 I was able to run a couple of weekend courses. However, my income is significantly reduced. I've not been eligible for SEISS, nor Universal Credit due to the small amount of savings I have from selling our marital home.

I have always gone the extra mile to help whoever I can in need of support. Up until last year, I also believed our Government and local councils did the same. However, in spite of all the letters, emails and providing evidence, no help has been offered. Instead, my Mum, who is in her seventies, and close friends have been incredibly kind.

As a mental health therapist, I am extremely concerned about the immediate impact we see with those suffering due to Lockdown. Plus the tsunami of mental health issues to be expected in the months and years to come.

The support, energy and determination demonstrated by the Excluded group on Facebook has restored my faith. It is the most cohesive, caring and courageous group. It's a group none of us wish to be in, yet we find ourselves in it and I'm proud of the love, camaraderie and sheer persistent commitment the admin team and all members show.

I've learnt and seen demonstrated what is really important in life: Honesty, care for others, being grateful for the small things in life. My 2020 gift was meeting a new man. He too is Excluded, as an outdoor instructor working with school aged children. However, with little money and plenty more time. we've explored the fells of Cumbria, scrambled up waterfalls and made do with what we have.

I'm hoping the tide will soon turn, that the public and the Government recognise we deserve parity, the same treatment as the rest of society. That is all we have ever asked for, to not be left behind – to not be Excluded. The Government has the ability to make good the errors of last year's decisions. I only hope it happens soon

86.

NAME: Jo

OCCUPATION: Teacher Trainer & Examiner

REASON FOR EXCLUSION: 50/50 rule

Let me start by describing me. I am not defined by a pandemic, by politics, by richness or poverty, sickness or health. I am just …me.

I am also a mother who has brought up two lovely children without any support (another story) and, for sure I am biased (she writes, smilingly). Also, I am humbled for being provided opportunities that so many others have been denied access to in the UK and around the world.

My roots are Northern; I am a mining village lass who was considered a bit outlandish at the time, during the strike of 1984, for going to do a BEd Hons degree to teach. Anyway, I qualified and became a teacher after four years, swiftly followed by the birth of my daughter. Let's fast forward – a lot!

I worked for 20 years full-time as a teacher in various schools, with minimal maternity leave as the wage earner in our family. There were many great (but some tough) times. For example, challenging children living in very difficult social and home contexts, often.

They pulled their punches, but I understood them and dealt with all that, doing my best for them – both educationally and compassionately – and modelling what is a positive and social way to act. I encountered the best and the worst of colleagues and managers; I dealt with these and grew because of them. I was ('scuse ma French) pretty much knackered all the time with the job, extra tuition, examinations to make extra cash for summer breaks. I feel guilt that I did not feel able to take the foot off the pedal to see and do more with my kids. A huge regret, but I still feel I had no choice. And perversely, all that extra effort led to Jo Newton teacher training in Mandalay 2017.

Jo Newton teacher training overseas

I became a Literacy Consultant working for Sheffield Local Authority in 2008. I was proud to have a different challenge working with adults, sharing my skills with teachers and supporting staff to raise attainment prospects for schools struggling with so many issues. I was sanguine when we were all made redundant by the Cameron/Clegg coalition and austerity measures; I would go it alone, embrace self-employment and 'back myself'. Our country encourages enterprise. Doesn't it?

It's hard working for yourself. Chasing every contract, being evaluated, chasing every invoice, chasing renewed contracts. Don't get me wrong. I did this for ten years. I embraced joy and opportunity too – so much positive feedback from sharing my knowledge with colleagues in south-east Asia and Bangladesh. How lucky am I, to feel that I can make some kind of difference to teacher knowledge and children's learning globally?

And then, after all my life as a taxpayer, I was left behind in March 2020. No furlough. No SEISS. I have supported our economy, our next generation, our educational standards and our moral compass.

WHY. WHY. WHY?? Rishi, can you hear me?

87.
NAME: Jacqueline
OCCUPATION: Beauty Therapist
REASON FOR EXCLUSION: Not in Profit

My name is Jacqueline. I am 40 years old and have worked ever since I was 15. I am from East Kilbride, South Lanarkshire.

After I left school, I went to college to do a three-year Beauty Therapy course. In my interview, I got asked, "Where do you see yourself in ten years time?" My answer was, "Having my own salon." On graduating from college I thankfully got a job straight away in the industry. And after 13 years of being employed, I decided 2014 was my time to go self-employed and I started in a local salon.

I loved it. The harder I worked, the more it rewarded me. I love my job, my clients, the laughs, and the relationships I build with my clients.

In 2018 I decided to open a salon of my own with another girl I knew. We made it work, even though there were plenty of obstacles in our way and it took over a year to get there! But in 2019 we finally opened and the shop has been a great success with a wonderful team and I was extremely happy with how my life was going. I was finally getting rewarded for all I'd ever wanted!

Then COVID struck. We got closed down. Then opened again. Then closed again.

I have slipped through the net of any type of help. The years they are looking at financially include the year we opened the salon.

In tax years 2016/17 and 2017/18, I was in profit. In 2018/19 the salon was opened, and I had a lot of outgoings for obvious reasons! Unfortunately, my outgoings for that year basically cancelled out my two years previous profits – making it look like I had earned nothing over the three-year period.

I handed in my 2019/2020 tax return ASAP in case I could appeal as I was back in profit as normal, but they were not interested in that year.

I owe hundreds to my gas and electricity company, over £1,000 to my council tax. With no money coming in, how am I meant to support my two children and myself and pay all my bills with zero help!?

Being in the house more means there is more gas and electricity being used, yet I have no income to pay for this.

This is the first time in my life I have been unable to support my family. My credit cards got maxed out in the first Lockdown, and I had to borrow from family to pay bills.

For the first time ever I feel like I'm failing as a parent. I am struggling mentally every single day. I was beginning to lower my dose of anti-depressants as I hate being on them but unfortunately this situation hasn't let me do this. I've tried applying for jobs so I have an income of some sorts coming in but not been successful so far.

I am a single parent with two daughters. One at college, the other just turned 13. The closure of the salon has had a horrible affect on us as a family. My eldest and myself both struggle with mental health issues. She is having to work from home for college and is mentally struggling with not getting out the house as she normally would for college. I worry about her daily, which in turn takes its toll along with everything else I worry about on a daily basis.

Something needs to be done and fast. Nearly 365 days with zero help from our Government is beyond a farce!

I'd like to see them all do a week in our lives, see it from our side and how it really is, the constant daily worry about paying bills, feeding your children, but unfortunately that'll never happen.

Thanks for reading.

88.
NAME: Karen's Husband
OCCUPATION: Gas Engineer
REASON FOR EXCLUSION: Limited Company Director

Where do I begin? It feels like forever that I have been feeling so down, so many tears, so much of future plans lost, because my husband is Excluded.

My husband has worked hard all his life, his only goal to take care of his children, and now since we met four years ago, to take care of me also.

He was an apprentice and trained as a Gas Engineer. Fifteen years ago he took the brave decision to set up his own Limited Company – a typical one man band. He did this so he could manage his own time and to raise his children, particularly important after his divorce.

He chose Limited as his income was unpredictable, and if anything happened he wanted to protect his house so his children would always have security.

He was and is successful. He kept his home and developed an excellent reputation.

I met this wonderful man four years ago and we have been married for 18 months now. He is a gentleman and a gentle man – a hard worker and a man of high scruples.

Then COVID came and we thought, as tax payers, we would be taken care of – how wrong we were!

During the first Lockdown I watched this strong, capable, determined human become broken, with feelings of worthlessness, and had to listen to him talking of "going to lie on a railway line." I don't think I will ever recover from that conversation.

Even though he could work, people were too scared to have him in their homes, and as I am also clinically extremely vulnerable, he really did not want to go to work.

We tried everything to survive. I applied for new Job Seekers Allowance, but I was not eligible as I have been out of work for two years renovating the house I bought before I met him, and then I looked after his Mum after his Dad died.

After exhausting everything else, we succumbed to a Bounce Back Loan to keep us afloat, and he took the pitiful sum of £560 a month furlough for a few months – that doesn't even cover our bills let alone our two mortgages.

We are now selling my house, which was my pension, and we have spent all our savings on trying to survive. Our plans for a secure future are gone. At 60 and 51 we are starting again.

Through the next two Lockdowns he has gone to work and we are literally scraping by. He is worried every day that he will bring COVID home to me – but we have no choice.

I know we are luckier than many. We won't lose our home, and this overwhelms me with guilt when I read the stories of others.

I was a strong, determined, high-earning woman and I am a shell of that person now. I am full of guilt and self-doubt and I blame myself because I feel I can't help him.

He carries on, but this has changed him forever. He feels vulnerable and so angry about this Government's disgraceful lack of morals and their seemingly deliberate ploy to destroy him.

We have lost our future, and financially we will never recover from this. In our hearts we carry the burden of everyone in this group that has taken their own life, those who could see no way forward, because that could have so easily have been us.

As I write, the tears are streaming down my face. How can we, as British citizens and taxpayers all our lives, mean NOTHING to this Government which has sworn to support us? Do we mean so little, they don't care about the helplessness, the suicides, the broken families?

If it was not for this group and the bravery, strength and compassion here – I dread to think were we would be.

Thank you.

89.
NAME: Ruth
OCCUPATION: Retail Worker
REASON FOR EXCLUSION: Denied Furlough

I was working in a local shop a couple of days a week. I'd been requested to replace a lady who had retired at the end of 2019. By March 2020, only weeks after needing me, my employer contacted me, not on my work day, to inform me that that my role was to be made redundant on a 'last in-first out' basis.

Looking back, this happened to be the same date that the Government's Coronavirus Job Retention Scheme (CJRS) was announced to employers. I believe the writing was already on the wall and that this was an opportunity for my employer to get rid of me, instead of having to bother putting me through for furlough monies.

When I learnt of the CJRS, and knew that I was HMRC eligible, I approached my employer to request to be furloughed. After several requests, my employer kept responding, no. His decision was final.

I asked my Conservative MP to clarify to my employer, my eligibility to be furloughed, but the response still came back no, with the following information:

In this respect the furloughed staff support scheme has been very helpful in enabling us to retain 17 out of 19 employees all of whom are on indefinite furloughed leave at this time, moreover we have also written to each of these 17 staff confirming that we will be "topping up" the Governments 80% support with a further 20% from ourselves for the months of April, May and June 2020.

In the case of Ruth and one other employee a 'Saturday girl' [not paid via HMRC, not eligible]), we decided not to include either position within the furloughed scheme as the losses in this part of our business are such that we will simply not be able to retain all of the employees once things gradually begin to return to some form of normality.

We are not willing to 'abuse the scheme' by furloughing staff we are already aware that we cannot and will not be able to provide continuous employment for and this would certainly be the case in this specific situation with regard to Ruth. In essence this is what Ruth repeatedly wants us to do, presumably with the mindset 'it's the Governments' money, why should you be worried when all you have to do is re-hire me and register me as furloughed'

I have had no income during Lockdown, no opportunity to work due to Lockdown, through no fault of my own.

My employer preferred to discredit my reputation than support me through the pandemic Lockdown, with the inclusion of such a slanderous and fictitious quote. Even after regular email requests to my MP, he concludes that CJRS is the responsibility of the employer and he can't force the employer.

90.

NAME: John

OCCUPATION: Contractor

REASON FOR EXCLUSION: Limited Company Director

My story starts February 2020. The company I was contracted to was already worried about Brexit and then COVID struck in China and caused them to stop production, and I was told that my contract would end at the end of February. I immediately signed on for Universal Credit (UC).

I soon found that UC caps rent payments and I also found that they work a month behind, so I started to borrow money from my Limited Company to pay the bills and for food. When Lockdown finally hit I had faith that we would be OK based on the Chancellor's statement of support.

The following month I discovered that because I had my last pay in March, my UC was £0. My partner managed to get a job, but unfortunately she earned enough to cancel out both April and May UC payments too.

Desperately, I cashed in a small pension so we could eat. This was a bad move. UC took this as 'income' too, so the June UC was also £0. And then my partner lost her job. We still had no support from the Government so that meant more borrowing from the company.

In July we received the princely sum of £47.49 from UC. To help us, a friend set up a payment to pay our council tax and we started selling some of our possessions. I even sold my big car for some cheap little one.

During August and September UC gave us £1040.72. We sold more items and borrowed more money from the company. I managed to get a Bounce Back Loan of £8k but I could see the company could not make its corporate tax payment.

My thoughts started to get even darker as I realised that the Government were not going to give us any support. Things now had started to get fraught with my partner. One night, in the middle of September, I found I had unconsciously taken a new blade from a box of knives and had been running it across my wrist. Luckily, it did not cut deep enough and people at ExcludedUK talked me back from the brink.

At the end of September, I got a job at Amazon and in October, because I was at Amazon, my UC payment was reduced to £963.31.

Still no support from the Government. And the company account was now at £25. My partner managed to get a new job (although it was 150 miles away), so the November UC was £0 since we both had wages. Borrowing from my bank hit its limits and after speaking to Chris in ExcludedUK, I made the decision to write to all the company creditors and say that the company was no longer viable.

In December, I had to talk to the bank and tell them I was now on debt management and could not pay my debts.

The accountants become very unfriendly when they realised I could not pay for their services and at the end of January, because of problems due to Brexit, Amazon ended my contract.

A few tentative jobs have appeared but things are moving slowly. Just to top things off, our landlord has decided to end renting so we have until mid July to move out. No idea where we will find the money to pay movers or make a deposit since we are now £39k in debt. Also, my partner has decided not to move with me.

So, I am sitting here wondering how I will survive February.

91.

NAME: Tina

OCCUPATION: Café Owner

REASON FOR EXCLUSION: Newly Self-Employed

I'm Portuguese, but I have been living in the UK for the last 19 years. I have always worked.

I am a single mum and in 2019, I decided to do something more about my future. I love cooking for everyone, so I put an application to open a Portuguese Café. Everything went well and I signed my contract on 17th ecember 2018 – my daughter's birthday.

After lots of hard work, I finally opened my Portuguese Tapas Cafe on 25th February 2020. I went part-time at my job at Center Parcs (to 18 hours a week), so that I still had some money to come in and my daughter was at the Café on my working days.

You know already that my life turned around 360 degrees completely, just three weeks and three days after I opened the Café, with the first Lockdown. I was devastated.

But I tried to be positive that I could make it. Just a few months and summer coming, so the Café could move on positively after Lockdown.

Being self-employed for first time I didn't know anything about rules and Government legality (still learning); even my accountant is busy and with problems herself.

Being granted furlough from Center Parcs (£695 monthly) has saved me a bit. My son still works, so he has been my lifeboat. Instead of planning his future, he is at the moment holding my life and all the rest of my bills at home because I barely pay my rent (£700 monthly) with my money.

My daughter finished her last year of college during Lockdown in June 2020, and after Christmas she decided to apply for a cleaner job at our GP medical center to earn a bit money because she can't find another job now.

I apply even to work on factories of production, and any agencies of work, but I'm restricted in not working Mondays and Fridays because of my furlough at Center Parcs, so it's really difficult. I felt lost so, so many times already, it's unbelievable.

I couldn't believe it when I saw the rules for the self-employed workers. I didn't have any records in 2018 or 2019 so I couldn't have any support at all, so many months without wages.

All 2020 with no income from my Café, a lot of initial investments, my little savings empty and the feeling of exploiting my son's money and future, knocked me down straightaway.

Lockdown after Lockdown, Café shut; when I opened in the summer, most customers stayed away because of the risk of the virus.

My landlady last November decided she wants the house (I've lived here nine years) and she gave me six months' notice. Now I'm counting down days and weeks to move out. I'm hunting houses basically.

I don't need to tell you that my earnings are against me for renting a new house since I'm just a part-timer at Center Parcs now, so I'm forcing my son to keep living with me so I can rent a place.

My life has been a completely nightmare. I can't describe to you how many nights of no sleep and crying, so much alone in the dark, so my son and daughter don't see me doing it. I'm supposed to be an example for them.

My Mum in Portugal has a pension of €350 to live on and I can't help her at all. My Dad died in 2018 so I feel so bad for not be able to take care of her like I did previously.

My heart, it's in pieces at the moment with so many things wrong, just because I decided to open a Cafe for my future. And I don't know what to expect from 2021 at all.

92.

NAME: Jennifer

OCCUPATION: Professional Singer

REASON FOR EXCLUSION: It's complicated!

I was a salaried HR Manager by day and self-employed professional singer evenings and weekends. Following a bad car accident I had several years off sick, whilst having lots of operations and procedures to put me back together again. I am not moaning, as I was clinically dead at the scene for four minutes before being defibrillated back to life (obviously – hence this account!)

This situation meant that, not only was I in a lot of pain physically, mentally I was all over the place as music is my first love, and the after-effects of the car accident meant I was unable to leap around a stage as I once did. I had to accept that my disabilities were such that I had to adapt, and I gave up being an HR manager and started doing smaller and shorter gigs in residential care homes and dementia care support groups.

In August 2017 I was rushed into Addenbrookes hospital for an emergency spine operation following going numb from the neck down and being unable to walk unaided.

I have been recovering since, whilst doing the occasional gentle sing-along for groups when I was physically and mentally able to do so.

When the pandemic hit I was unable to provide three years accounts to qualify for SEISS. As my husband earned too much, I was not eligible for Universal Credit.

This made me so cross as I have paid tax all my working life in the faith that if ever I needed support I would be looked after! Historically, I had already had a fight with the DWP following my car accident as they took me off Incapacity Benefit on Christmas Eve despite still being under the care of the hospital and unable to work.

In addition, as my injuries were due to a car accident, the first people to be paid out via insurance compensation were my legal team and then the DWP, so it was a glorified loan anyway!

Anyway, I felt let down by the system again, but at least I was financially secure with my husband's salary so I could think clearly.

I also have an auto-immune disorder, meaning that I have not left the house at all since 16th March 2020! And, as my husband is a key-worker, I had to move out of our home and have not lived with him since 16th March 2020. Fortunately, I was able to move in with my sister and niece.

I was feeling like I did not have a purpose until a fellow singing friend introduced me to ExcludedUK. As a singer, I felt compelled to get involved with the Virtual Choir and loved being part of the video that was broadcast on the side of a van in Westminster as part of the peaceful protest on 30th September 2020.

Aron Padley, one of the founders and directors of ExcludedUK, then invited me onto the team and I am now his PA, the team HR Manager, and work on various teams to keep the organisation ticking over.

It is the best thing I have done during the pandemic and it has kept me sane whilst being incarcerated. The volunteer team are amazing and the members are a fabulous family of support who make me so proud to be a part of.

I set up the COVID Support Fund before Christmas, following an emotional conversation with Aron, about how dreadful it was that we were talking to so many who would not be able to afford Christmas dinner, let alone any presents. Parents feeling that they had failed their children and children comforting their parents, was all so wrong.

So far, between 3rd December 2020 and 31st January 2021, we have raised over £30,000. This has been shared with over 250 families who are so grateful, not only for the money, but also that they were even thought of.

Working on the member welfare team as a mental health first aider, I have seen too many horror stories, especially from those who have attempted to take their own lives, or the 13 so far who have taken their lives, including my own dear friend who I had known for 20+ years.

The fact that the Government gloss over this and pay lip-service to how sorry they are whilst spouting they are "putting their arms around the nation" makes me sick to the stomach. I have talked members out of overdosing, hanging themselves, jumping off bridges etc, and will continue to do so until these people are cared for and their lives respected.

I get involved wherever I can to keep up morale and run the Tea & Chat group on Zoom every Saturday between 5-6pm, which is so popular, the regulars becoming good friends and keeping in contact with each other outside of the regular event.

There are so many positives I have taken out of this truly dreadful situation that we found ourselves in, through no fault of our own, mostly the altruism and compassion that the ExcludedUK family have shown each other.

I feel so much richer as a person for having been part of this amazing organisation, saving so many lives and finding lifelong friends who have lived a shared experience through the worst of times, and this has, for me, been the best aspect of the pandemic.

93.

NAME: Rachel

OCCUPATION: Company Director

REASON FOR EXCLUSION: Company Not in Profit

I started my small Campervan Hire Company in 2016. As a stay-at-home Mum, I needed a job which enabled me to continue to care for the needs of my four children and working from home was the perfect solution and so my home became my business base.

I had some savings, and with family investment I managed to purchase my first campervan without the need for a loan. Business was slow to start as I had no experience.

To my surprise, most customers were international. My first full trading year March 2017-October 2017, saw customers arrive from the USA, Middle-East and all over Europe. We did not make a profit the first year due to so much personal investment.

Between March 2018-October 2019 we traded at a steady rate, but still no profit made as we invested in a second campervan. My Dad had recently died of Alzheimers and we decided that a percentage of any profit would be donated for research into this cruel disease.

March 2020-October 2020 was to be our first year in profit, with two vehicles available and our booking calendar filling up nicely. Alas, we all know what happened: a virus from China caused a global pandemic and I had no option but to cancel all bookings and refund customers their money. I have made no money at all this year, but continued to have monthly outgoings, and there was no support package available from the Government to help us.

Our monthly outgoings were not huge, but it drained all we had. Insurances, on-going vehicle costs, security, website, IT and accountants' fees still needed paying. We could not be furloughed. We couldn't claim a Bounce Back Loan and because we are a home-based business, we were not eligible for a grant of any kind due to criteria set by my local council. I had no income but could not claim Universal Credit due to my husband's wage. I had nothing coming in and no savings left.

My husband was just about covering our expenses and the business, but we had to cut back on everything. We had a scaled-down Christmas, but the kids understood. We are both from working-class backgrounds and no strangers to living frugally, but we felt angry that there was no support for us, no parity.

That's when I heard about ExcludedUK. I saw a TV interview with a group member and was in tears hearing his story. I joined ExcludedUK and found comfort and security from a bunch of complete strangers. Support was available 24/7 from caring and knowledgeable volunteers.

My business is dead in the water. I can't trade due to the situation with COVID and there's no point trying to continue. In 2021 I will sell my vehicles, pay off my debts and have a clean sheet.

I am 48 years old, have paid taxes all my life and I feel let down and mistreated by this Government. Although it's too late for my business, I will fight to see justice for the three million people who have been discriminated against since March 2020. The Government and local county councils need to be held accountable for the bad decisions they have made and the lives they have ruined.

94.
NAME: Hayley
OCCUPATION: Vocalist – UK & International Tours
REASON FOR EXCLUSION: 50/50 rule

I work part-time for NHS in admin (currently working from home and shielding), I am studying to be a CBT Therapist (self-funded), and I am reluctantly home schooling my eight year old son!

The Day the Music Died.

14th March 2020-Pontefract
We waited in the wings to be announced onto the stage. Our nerves seemed even more intense tonight as everything had been so last minute. Frantic calls between the agent and the organisers of tonight's event, talks of cancellations, all due to some virus from China.

This deadly virus was quickly making its way around the world and had been likened to the Spanish Flu of 1918. This virus was so infectious the Government were advising that all businesses, unless essential, should close and people shouldn't mix. Media hype surely?

Anyway, eventually it was decided that tonight's event would go ahead as planned. So the PA was loaded into the van, costumes packed and we made our way onto the motorway and to tonight's venue: a luxury Hotel nestled in beautiful countryside just outside Pontefract, North Yorkshire.

It was a capacity crowd, a charity event. The room had been beautifully dressed by venue dressers. There was a photo booth which guests were enjoying at the back of the room, providing lots of giggles. During the evening there was to be a raffle with all proceeds going to the Charity, wonderful prizes donated by generous business owners.

Our play-on music was playing: one last check of our costumes and make up, we hug each other and step out onto stage. We are met by a sea of smiling faces, most of our audience dressed in 70's fancy dress and already getting into the party spirit. They are straight up onto the dance floor, singing and dancing along. It's a delightful night, the kind of night that reminds you exactly why you chose this job as a career. The reason we had worked for over 20 years in this field.

It isn't always this easy. The audience isn't always on your side from the start and there is so much work that goes on behind the scenes which the general public isn't privy to – but tonight, tonight was one of the good ones.

As our play-off music plays we exit the stage smiling, waving and taking in the applause. Once we are changed out of our costumes it's time to pack down the gear and load it into the van, ready for the journey home.

When we packed the gear into the van, when we said goodbye to the lovely and hardworking staff at the venue, the last few straggling audience members, and the organisers who had worked tirelessly to bring this event to life, who knew then that we were saying goodbye to our beloved industry?

That night the lights went out on our stage for months and months to come.

Hayley Arnold on tour

LOCKDOWN 23rd March 2020

We watched in disbelief as our Prime Minister Boris Johnson addressed the nation on our TV sets and officially put the entire country into Lockdown. The virus from China had become a pandemic, causing huge numbers of deaths and threatening to cripple our NHS. Schools would close and all 'non-essential' businesses – gyms, hairdressers, non essential shops, pubs, restaurants, theatres – all closed with immediate effect. People were told they must work from home and not mix with other people outside of their family unit.

Planes were grounded, the roads were abandoned. Our world as we had known it had stopped! With the belief that the Lockdown would be a relatively temporary measure, we remained hopeful that as long as people followed the rules, this craziness would be over in time for the summer. We looked forward to a busy summer season of festivals, weddings etc. Hopefully, we would be able to re-coup some of the loss of earnings we would inevitably face over the next few months. Yes, by the summer we would be back!

In the meantime, the Government announced rescue packages for its workforce. To protect the economy, they launched a number of schemes to protect workers and businesses. We waited with bated breath for the package that would cover us. However, when the Self-Employment package was eventually announced it came with strict criteria which would see over 3 million people Excluded from financial help. One of which is me.

Our summer season sadly never materialised, the country was back into Lockdown and we lost our busy Christmas season too. Panto season, Christmas party season – all cancelled!

And as for financial help… almost a year later we are still waiting. The 3 million Excluded! Three million people who have been told that their businesses are not viable for Government support.

We are now into 2021 and the Government has told us that this Lockdown will last until at least March. Who knows when our industry will be able to open, or ever be the same again? We have already lost so many of our beautiful theatres. Sadly, we have already seen many of the ExcludedUK group forced to close their businesses for good, and unsurprisingly the lack of support is having a detrimental effect on our mental health.

ExcludedUK continues to fight for the forgotten 3 million. They have given us a collective voice. They continue to support members mentally too. Each member has their own story… this one is mine. It's hard to remain hopeful, but even in the word hopeful, there is hope!

95.

NAME: Callum

OCCUPATION: Freelance PAYE Assistant TV Producer

REASON FOR EXCLUSION: Not able to be Furloughed

Feb 2020 was a month like any other – I was spending my days hard at work as I was heading towards the end of a contract on a mainstream TV dating show. As I was finishing up, the company decided they wanted me for an extra week to help with some finishing touches. I agreed, but only for four extra days as on the Friday I was going to an important meeting at the wedding venue where I was due to get married.

Never did I realise that important wedding meeting would cost me so much.

As COVID hit and support schemes got announced, I was delighted to hear of the furlough scheme and the company I worked for were absolutely up for helping.

However, it soon became apparent that I needed to have been contracted to work on that Friday – that one extra day – for the company to have legally been able to furlough me. That situation never changed. Ten months on.

While the TV industry is still 'going' as of January 2021, it has massively reduced the amount of new content and the size of the workforce, which has led to there being far too many superb candidates for any role. So many I know are unemployed, and I've been rejected from many jobs even outside the sector, including delivery driving!

I'm freelance PAYE. It's so easy to support us as our tax is done at source through HMRC. We also pay the highest bracket of tax due to the uncertain nature of our work. They could easily calculate 80% of three years earnings with just a few clicks of a button.

It's been gut wrenching throughout. My savings are depleting, my partner is working super hard to keep us going, and there's just a cloud of unfairness every day. It's horrendous seeing people who have really struggled sadly end their lives. It's hard to even have words for the situation and the injustice of what is happening to the Excluded community.

ExcludedUK are a Godsend. The team are amazing. Pushing the message out, getting the media on side, and helping mental health issues.

I would be gobsmacked if, after we get what we deserve, a documentary on the community isn't in the works. They deserve it, as nothing has been quite so heart-warming as seeing complete strangers rally together to help each other out and fight for parity.

My wedding's postponed. And we fight another day – every day.

96.
NAME: Sheena
OCCUPATION: Business Consultant
REASON FOR EXCLUSION: Limited Company Director

In 2010, after 32 years of working for big companies, I made the decision to go out on my own. I had gathered a lot of experience and wanted to work for companies, where they either needed an extra pair of hands or lacked the skills. In order to do that, I set up my own company as most companies won't hire on a contract basis if you are not a Limited Company Director.

When the pandemic hit, I was working in the airport industry and my contract was terminated due to COVID-19, despite having a further three months to complete. After four and a half months of being out of work, I am now working but during that time I discovered, that I was ineligible for any support at all.

I was eligible for a Bounce Back Loan but that is a loan and potential debt for the future if no work is forthcoming. At that time the market was looking grim and continues to do so.

I have followed the Government's response to this situation with growing disbelief. Initially, with everyone else, I thought the lack of support would be rectified. I watched the activity generated by ExcludedUK, resulting in an All-Party Parliamentary Group (APPG). I saw upwards of 280 cross-party MPs join the APPG in support. Over and over again the question regarding the lack of support was brought up in Parliament and sidestepped by the Government, whilst telling us how much they had given to everyone else.

The refusal of the Government to listen to anyone regarding this situation has left me feeling deeply concerned. These are taxpayers of many years, with viable businesses. I cannot understand why these people have been Excluded and continue to be so. I cannot understand why there has been no cap on furlough, no investigation into wasteful spending, continued payments made to the same recipients, often still working.

I used to think an MP was there to serve their constituents. I used to believe the Government supported everyone and spent the tax monies we pay, carefully, wisely and fairly.

I don't believe this any longer.

97.
NAME: Louise
OCCUPATION: Professional Childcare Provider
REASON FOR EXCLUSION: Trading profits over £50k

In my pre-Excluded life I was totally committed to my work but always had time for fun, family & friends. Partial to a gin and tonic – or three!

Monday to Friday were (mostly!) for work. As a childcare professional for 34 years and a proprietor of an Ofsted-registered before-and-after school club for the past 18 years, my life has revolved around children, be them my own or someone else's.

Before COVID, my company, The Play Pad, employed five staff and catered for 120 families with approximately 50 children per session. I had overall responsibility for running the entire show, from providing the hands-on care for the children, to shopping for provisions. I managed all of the accounts (including PAYE) and catered for all health and safety concerns including risk assessments. I interpreted Ofsted's forever changing guidance to write meaningful policies and procedures and implemented them within the setting. I led the team and together we successfully saw the provision develop and grow to meet the ever-changing landscape of working parents.

My motto in life has always been to 'work hard, play harder'. The weekends were mostly glorious even if the weather was rotten – entertaining friends and family, a few beers at the rugby club or a local pub, cosy nights in, dinner dates out, occasional weekends in Norfolk for cycling and walking.

We did festivals, live music, gigs, concerts, camping trips, theatre shows, sun holidays, ski holidays – everything was fuelled by life itself, the love and laughter of a shared experience and a desire to have a go and live in the moment, be it dancing embarrassingly or singing un-tunefully – both are done equally appallingly and fired by 'one too many'... the result being I'd want to eat chip-shop chips with mushy peas, ketchup and mayo!

Being Excluded has put me on a rollercoaster of emotions. There have been highs; the first time I received the money for the successful furlough of my staff; the relief when my application for a discretionary grant was accepted; the unbelievable emotional support from my adult children, my parents and my brother; the time my partner turned up unexpectedly after weeks of Lockdown; the uncontrollable laughter that came alongside the sheer disbelief that I was faced with losing everything I had worked so hard for over the past 18 years.

The lows were low. So low, it's scary to go back. I cried a lot. Over a 100 consecutive days of tears. The scariest day was when I called the Treasury Select Committee at Westminster. The receptionist got a policewoman to call me back as I had told him "the M1 is a five-minute walk away" – it still haunts me that I actually said that to another human being.

I never thought I could be so relentless. Emails to my MP, calling the Chancellor's office in North Allerton, communicating with the Chief Executive of my local council, being brave enough to speak on national TV about a situation that had affected me and so many others.

There's so much irony involved. The desire to pursue every avenue was driven by Boris Johnson himself – at the very beginning of the pandemic he urged his citizens to "do the right thing". The Chancellor (who shall not be named) promised that "no one will be left behind" ... bring it on #Relentless #Wearenotgoingaway #ExcludedUK

I've learnt so much from being in this group, the group no one wanted to be a part of – but quite possibly, the group no one now wants to leave. The camaraderie, the drive, the passion, the honesty, the resilience, the tears, the sheer ability of us to bare all publicly and continue the never-ending, relentless fight of ExcludedUK – you have all given me so much, 'thank you' will never be enough.

Going forwards, I do not know. I am managing with one day at a time. My business might survive. Once the Government called it a 'vital' service; now it is spiralling out of my control.

P.S. I've always wanted to be an 'extra' in a film – open to offers!

98.
NAME: Christina
OCCUPATION: Coaching & Mentoring/Alternative Education
REASON FOR EXCLUSION: 50/50 rule

I run the www.thek9project.co.uk, an alternative education, coaching and mentoring service. I work with vulnerable folk, kids in care, those with special educational needs or mental health difficulties, and I work alongside previously abandoned and homeless awesome dogs to create great outcomes for children, young people and adults.

Honestly, as an older woman I feel completely abandoned. I have worked as much as I am able since I was 14. Always and always paid tax – lots of it!

For many years, I worked for a local authority and accrued a modest Pension which I had to take at 60, after working a reduced workload when I was caring for my dad who had dementia and complex health needs.

As my state pension age kept getting pushed back I needed to work, so I set up the K9 Project in 2008, realising a dream of working with young people alongside dogs. It's a special kind of magic. It would never make me rich, but my working life was full of joy, achievement and adventure.

Chris Kent runs the K9 project

I had a book published chronicling my journey, and the stories of the dogs and the young people. A few years later, my dad had died and my mum moved in with me. Unfortunately, in the years the Government counted to qualify for the SEISS, I had reduced my workload again to look after my Mum.

My world shrank as I struggled to care for her, but still provide K9 project services and earn some money. But my earnings were now less than my pension. 50/50! One strike and you're out!

The pandemic stopped me working, my mum died, and then the body blow of being Excluded.

I'm no angel or hero but I have always done my best for my family and my business, valued highly by the people I support. I've won lots of awards but wont brag. And then basically, because I stay home to care for my dying mum, and don't earn much, I get penalised.

I feel disgusted with this Government. Worthless. Devalued. Ignored. Bereft. Sad. Hopeless. Defiant. Depressed. Wondering why me? Trying not to get envious when others seem to be doing so well.

The impact has been mostly debt. Lots of debt – for the first time ever. I'm trying to cope with all these additional feelings on top of grieving for the loss of my beautiful mum. I'm trying to reinvent my business. Not wanting to let the Government beat me. At the same time I want to give up, I'm so tired.

BUT – I'm relentless . I'm going to keep fighting for parity for myself and my Excluded compatriots. I'm going to shout from the rooftops about the injustice.

And I'm going to keep moving forward.

99.

NAME: Carolyn

OCCUPATION: Stunt Woman/Aerial Circus Performer/Gardener/Sports Therapist

REASON FOR EXCLUSION: 50/50 rule

Since my mid twenties I have worked as a stunt woman, performing in shows and films around the world. As competition in the stunt world is fierce, I took on a 'normal' part-time job to supplement my income.

For the past few years I have combined being a self-employed stunt woman/aerial circus performer/gardener with employment as a First Aid trainer for the commercial division of a college.

I also took on work at a firm that head-hunted me to help them with their accounts department, as in my early twenties I had qualified as an Accounting Technician. Due to a set of incredibly bizarre circumstances, this firm cut off my work at the very end of 2018 when my car was written off. However, they refused to issue my P45, saying I wasn't employed there, even though I clearly was. Around the same time, the structure of staff at the college changed and I, along with a male First Aid trainer, found myself being managed out.

At the beginning of 2019, a friend asked me if I would consider joining his sports therapy business. Though still very fit and capable, at the age of 43, I considered this a sensible, grown-up way to supplement my income, and I duly commenced training to achieve a Level Five Advanced Diploma in Sports Therapy & Rehabilitation.

At the end of February 2020, I taught a First Aid course and was told shortly afterwards that the new management was not obliged to offer me any more work at the college. In March 2020, the firm that had refused to issue my P45 finally did so, settling the matter out of court – this was a firm of solicitors, would you believe!

When Lockdown was announced all my aerial circus gigs were postponed indefinitely or cancelled. I have had no work from the college, and no offer of financial help. When I applied for the SEISS, I was told I am not eligible because my employment income exceeded my self-employment income for the qualifying period, yet I am no longer employed by the legal firm, and my employment from the college is nil.

On the upside, during the first part of Lockdown I finished my sports therapy qualification. This means I can now Not Work as a sports therapist alongside Not Working as a stunt woman or aerial performer. Thank goodness for gardening! From June 2020 to date, I have managed to earn a little over £3,000. It is hugely unfortunate that my career choices have landed me in this predicament, but I remain optimistic.

I have found far more kindness from strangers than I have within my own family. Oh, and that's another thing. At the end of March last year, I was on the verge of moving so I could join the sports therapy business. When that had to close, my friend advised me to wait for the time being. For the past 12 months I have been living with my septuagenarian parents, and my 43 year old, never-left-home brother. All three are very set in their ways, each believing they only speak facts; my opinion counts for nothing. I ought to have made a stand sooner but I did not expect to be here this long.

My patience and resolve have been tested to the limits during this time. Though it is physically not as drastic, mentally and emotionally, I feel like a prisoner of this war because of the situation with my family, and the limitations that Lockdowns put on my ability to break free.

While I wait, I'm studying contortion – an additional skill to add to my repertoire, and one it is possible to train for in the house (prison). I have always been a survivor, adapting to situations and rising to challenges. Now I'm aiming to become as flexible in body as I am in mind. I am resilient.

100.

NAME: Ester

OCCUPATION: Wildlife Camerawoman

REASON FOR EXCLUSION: Newly Self-Employed

During my masters degree I decided I wanted to be a wildlife camerawoman. On a whim I moved down to Bristol as that's where you needed to be, but little did I know how hard that uphill struggle against the rife gender bias would be. After getting too jaded I took a break, worked in Canada with grizzly bears, and finally came back for one last attempt. And it finally worked! After a year of bashing my head against the walls that the industry had around it, I finally broke through and got my first job. I was finally breaking through – much slower than my white middle class male counterparts, but I registered as a sole trader in 2019.

My last shoot was in December 2019. I used that money to see me through the typical winter lull in January and February. I had three, three-week shoots lined up from the end of March 2020, the most I'd ever had. I was finally getting the right experiences.

Lockdown happened a week before I was due to leave for that first shoot. With no savings, and no work in sight (as international travel played a big role), throughout 2020 I didn't get paid for a single day's work. I had to live off of Universal Credit, which barely covered my rent, and I went on the emotional rollercoaster ride of trying to get a Bounce Back Loan (four months in, they said no, then they finally said yes). A hard drive failed, meaning I lost all my work from 2019, and my friend of six years kicked me out of my house forcing me to live on my own in an expensive flat. The only relative I was able to see the whole year was my father and that was only once.

I lost my mother in 2005, when I was 17. It was an eventful year as her death was such a sad event that still haunts me to this day, but I finished school and went to university in a foreign country – negativity counterbalanced with lots of positivity and opportunities for growth. No year will be as bad for me as that year, but 2020 comes in a close second, losing my career, my income and my mental health without what felt like a single positive (there was only one single positive). I have never felt quite so low in my entire life, even after I lost my mother. Things went really dark and I felt like I was walking around with a coat that weighed 100 kgs on my shoulders.

My world, which used to be so big, became very, very small. I didn't even recognise myself in the mirror.

I've always wanted to diversify and now more than ever. I will learn to keep a bigger stash of savings in the bank. I will make more time to see my family, because you never know when you can't anymore. And I will be more confident about trying to seek connection and community.

101.
NAME: Maisy
OCCUPATION: Interpreter & Voice-over Artist
REASON FOR EXCLUSION: 50/50 rule

Before the pandemic, I was full of hope and excited about the opportunities I saw on the horizon. I enjoy my work and the variety of it immensely. Over the last couple of years I have also been developing my own physical theatrical work in my spare time, on top of teaching circus skills to adults and kids and performing aerial acts in festivals.

Throughout my self-employment I saved where I could, and over the last couple of years I spent a significant amount of my savings in professional development and upgrading the equipment that I use for work. But my self-employed income tends to fluctuate, so I let out my home as a way to ensure financial stability and I rent a room somewhere else.

I was not eligible to receive the SEISS due to the 50% rule. And because I don't live in my own home I am not eligible for Universal Credit either. My tenant is facing economic hardship as well, so that added to the uncertainty.

When my Dad passed away in a care home with the virus very early on during the pandemic, I spent the first month or two feeling completely distraught and in disbelief, whilst I tried my best to help my mum deal with my Dad's will.

By August 2020 I knew I had to give up my room, as keeping it became untenable. I am very fortunate that my boyfriend, who I had only known a few months before the start of the pandemic, let me stay with him, but it's been hard for me mentally as I have always been self-sufficient.

This third Lockdown has caused me to be very depressed. I can't understand why there are so many of us Excluded from any financial help and left to fend for ourselves for the last 11 months. For the billions of pounds this Government wasted on an ineffective Track and Trace system, and for all the grants we never benefited from, please can they not make us pay them through taxation.

My dad's death has brought me and my siblings closer and my boyfriend is a good, generous guy. I learn day by day to be a better version of myself and focus on the NOW. Also, it is wonderful to come across people from the ExcludedUK Community who are kind and supportive to one another.

I will remain optimistic and fight my own demons. Whatever turns out – I will be OK.

102.
NAME: Suzie
OCCUPATION: Laundry Services Company
REASON FOR EXCLUSION: New Starter & 50/50 rule

My new business was a laundry service for holiday let premises in North Norfolk. In January 2020 I told my employer I would cut my hours to just the bare minimum – six hours a week – so I could concentrate on my new business as it was getting busier and I was struggling to juggle the two.

When we were told to at stay home to protect lives, that meant that people couldn't go on holiday, so that meant no dirty laundry to wash, which meant I had no work.

My husband had recently started working for a new construction firm on quite a good wage, so he said, "Don't worry, my wage will cover us".

But a week later, I saw him being dropped off early from work – where was his work van? Why was he home early?

He walked in the house and I asked if he was OK. Has your work been put into Lockdown too? He didn't say anything, just waved his arms in a cut-throat motion. He had been laid off.

What were we going to do?

After a restless night, we got on the phone to anyone that could offer a job to either of us. We were applying for absolutely everything and applying for Universal Credit (UC) in the meantime.

We currently live in a two-up, two-down house, in North Norfolk. We have a boy, eight, and a girl, six, sharing a small bedroom with bunk beds. After trying for around a year to find an affordable home with more space, to no avail (North Norfolk is quite the hot spot for second homes – hence my business!), we decided the best option would be to make our existing home bigger. So, a few months prior to the pandemic, we applied to borrow more money on our mortgage to enable us to build an extension on our home.

Due to the mortgage money sitting in our account waiting to be paid to a builder, we were told we had too much in 'savings' to claim UC! I still had six hours work with my employer, but we basically have both incomes gone, no UC – oh but we do have all these 'savings'!

The SEISS was announced and I was Excluded due to being a new starter and my previous income was predominantly through employment.

Roll on a few months to June 2020 and people can travel again! My business absolutely boomed, I was working 12 hour days and exhausted, but I loved it because I could help to pay off some of the debt we had created through the first Lockdown – but it was short lived. We found ourselves in the Tier system, which cut my work load down, and then eventually we were in a full Lockdown again.

No furlough because I'm needed to do those six hours a week for my employer, no SEISS because I'm still a new starter, no UC because we still have a bit of the mortgage money to build the kids a new bedroom.

When and if I manage to start again, and be as busy as I was in June, my business will be hugely successful. I will be an asset to the tax system. I bet they will want me to be included then!

103.
NAME: Nicki
OCCUPATION: Newborn Photographer
REASON FOR EXCLUSION: New Starter

I've always had a passion for photography even though I was a primary teacher for 11 years. When I had my daughter in 2017, things changed at my school and although I absolutely loved teaching, I knew I couldn't spend all my time planning and marking in the evenings and at weekends as I had my daughter. So in September 2018 I decided to train in newborn photography and follow my dream of setting up my own photography business.

The first six months of my business (to the end of the tax year 2018/2019) I didn't make a lot of money because of the investment in my camera, lenses, training, lighting, backdrops and props.

I'm the sort of person that puts 200% into anything I do – I have to be the best of whatever I do, and I was getting busy and building my client base. I was pleased with how my business was growing, and I had many returning clients and amazing reviews and recommendations.

In September 2019, I gave birth to my second child, and during my maternity leave I used my savings for the development of my business. I converted my garage into a studio so that I could have a permanent place to work ready for April 2020 when I would return from my maternity leave. I had lots of newborns and cake smashes booked in for when I could reopen.

I was so excited for 2020! It was going to be my best year yet.

But along came COVID. My business was forced to close before I could even re-open. The bookings I had, I had to refund. My council gave me no support in terms of grants because my business was a business at home: I had no rates to pay. I couldn't claim SEISS because of my teaching career, even though I hadn't taught for nearly two years. I couldn't claim Universal Credit as fortunately my husband was still working.

As my photography involves close contact with newborns, I was closed for some time. Luckily my clients understood and I am so grateful for their continued support.

104.
NAME: Anne
OCCUPATION: Not Given
REASON FOR EXCLUSION: Filed tax return late/Newly Self-Employed

I went newly self-employed in March 2019, such good timing! And I have been Excluded because I did not file a self-employed tax return in time!

I have paid tax & NI for 47 years and I think it is very petty of the Government to Exclude me. Why could they not use my previous employment P60s to grant me support?

I complained. In response I received an email stating that I could not be identified and could be part of an organised criminal gang or indeed fraudulent!

Really? I have a driving licence, a marriage certificate, a passport, a birth certificate, a mortgage, car finance, a bank account, credit cards etc. etc. So why can I not be identified? Oh! And a reminder from HMRC that my tax return is due by the 31st January. How did they manage that when I cannot be identified?

Whilst I am on my soap box, I am also Excluded from my pension. Having been told years ago I have enough in my pension pot, I still had to pay National Insurance to support the Government – fair enough – but now when the chips are down, can they not support me?

105.
NAME: Vanessa
OCCUPATION: Yoga Teacher/Landlady
REASON FOR EXCLUSION: 50/50 rule

I am a yoga teacher but because this does not generate enough income, I also rent out my home whenever necessary. I also support my adult son, who suffers from anxiety, and we run yoga retreats together. Since I was diagnosed with glaucoma I could no longer work in the way I used to, so I changed my lifestyle. I earn very little and spend very little.

During the first Lockdown, when the guests and students cancelled, I was sure I would be furloughed. I remember HMRC telling me that I was Excluded, and the confusion and worry I felt.

Why would I be Excluded just because my yoga teaching income was a little less than my rental income?

I was told to claim Universal Credit (UC), which I applied for five times, but I was not eligible because I own a third of a property abroad which I am unable to sell or access.

I was told to apply for Personal Independence Payment because I have glaucoma. I went through another humiliating interview, only to be told I was not eligible. My son was told to go through this ordeal as well and was also found ineligible. It was very distressing.

I panicked. As soon as Lockdown lifted, I moved into temporary accommodation and rented out my home for August and September.

It is very hard work, preparing the house for guests every weekend. I am told by HMRC that this is unearned income. I can tell you, I earned every penny of it! My hands were hurting because of all the cleaning and gardening, but I ignored this. I was not sleeping or eating enough and I could not relax.

During the second Lockdown when the guests and students cancelled, I renovated a caravan to move into so I could try and pay off my debts. I was now using the credit card for essential items and selling belongings. My hands lost their power while I was working on the caravan. I ignored this again, because I was frightened, I just kept on working. I was signed off work by my GP but still could not get UC.

During the third Lockdown, when guests cancelled again, I asked my father for help. He refused and suggested I sell my home. It took so much strength to ask for help, and the only people I would accept it from were the Government and my estranged Father. They both refused.

Then I was diagnosed with a rare hand disease (from so much manual labour) and told to have the operation privately. I couldn't cope with the debt, the Exclusion, the reaction from my Father, the hand disease, the glaucoma, being unable to support my son, the pandemic, the lack of community and ability to work... but by now I had found ExcludedUK. I found my voice and was able to find help and solidarity. I eventually received a £500 grant, the only help I had had for ten months.

The impact of being Excluded has been devastating. It made a very hard year quite unbearable. I felt humiliated, and mostly terrified of losing my home. It is disgraceful that so many were Excluded and many, many others have suffered so much more than me.

I write this thinking of those who took their lives. I write this for them and their families. I am so very thankful to the admins of ExcludedUK who helped me gain perspective and were there for me when there was no one else.

I pray we will all be helped soon and justice will prevail.

106.
NAME: Maxine
OCCUPATION: Market Trader
REASON FOR EXCLUSION: 50/50 rule

My name is Maxine and I've been a self-employed market trader for 20 years. My stall consists of two lines: souvenirs & various smoking accessories. I was the sole bread winner for the family throughout that time as my husband gave up work through ill health and became a house husband. He is now retired on a small private pension.

Three years ago, my business took a bit of a downturn as I'd had some competition come into the market and general trade wasn't as good as past years. So I decided to take MY private pension as a one off lump sum. This pension was from a previous job I had done for 17 years at Cadbury Schweppes.

So I paid the £4.6k tax, reduced my mortgage and had a little left over in the bank to upgrade my car.

Fast forward to March 2020 when we were told to stay at home and the Government said, "we won't leave anyone behind". To be honest, when I heard this I was secretly looking forward to spending some time at home with my husband, finishing a few small jobs in the house and have a much needed rest.

After a few weeks with numerous frantic calls to the accountant, it finally sank in what this 50% rule meant. Zero income for the foreseeable! To say I was gobsmacked was an

understatement. I opened up for a few months after the first Lockdown, but people were scared to come out and trade was awful. It was demoralising to say the least.
I managed to get three small ARG grants, which I've kept aside for the rent on the stall. But I have no personal money, nor wages at all for myself. We are surviving on my husband's £115 a week private pension. We are not entitled to Universal Credit as we had some savings that were quickly reducing – but that was money we'd saved for my retirement. Money we'd planned to help our daughter get a deposit for her first house!

Maxine's Market Stall

Family friends don't understand at all. They can't believe that the pension drawdown YEARS before all this could do this! They are bored of me bringing it up.

In October I said I can't go through another Lockdown with no income. I got a job in my local Asda. I did four shifts there and I caught COVID. I got no sick pay. I had to finish at

Asda. I was really bad for four weeks and I aggravated an old injury from years before – plantar fasciitis!

In ten weeks I went from being an outgoing, happy, sociable person, to a quiet withdrawn lazier-by-the-day, unfit, miserable person with my feet up all the time.

I really don't know whether I'll go back to work, or if the market will even open again. So much uncertainty now.

Was it all worth it? All this working hard for a living, to end up with nothing?

107.
NAME: Catherine
OCCUPATION: Corporate Events Organiser
REASON FOR EXCLUSION: PAYE Agency worker

For the last 11 years, I have occasionally been working as a Limited Company freelancer but mainly as a PAYE freelancer through agencies, depending on the contract. I worked in corporate events for 16 years until April 2020 when my last contract ended.

The agency I was working for at the time was not able to furlough me as my contract was always due to end in April and did not end because of COVID. If these Lockdowns hadn't taken place, I would have gone on to find another role and carry on as I had for the last 11 years, working full time in corporate events. Many of my roles have been in the public sector and several of the organisations would be considered fundamental for the wellbeing of the general public.

I know many people who have been furloughed or received self-employment grants, but despite paying all my taxes and working almost solidly since I was 18 years old, I have received nothing. No support or recognition from the Government. It feels very unfair to be Excluded and rejected by my own Government, when I consider myself to be a respected, contributing member of society.

My partner also works in events, so he has not been able to work throughout this time either. We are having to sell our house in London as there is no income and it doesn't seem like there will be for a long time. We have both worked so hard to be able to live here, and to have it taken away from us is devastating. We are not ready to leave London and would not have left so soon if we had some support from the Government to pay our bills.

Neither of us has been able to work for the last nine months. It is comforting in a strange way to see there are others like me. This has brought a lot of people together and it does give you hope that there are lots of kind humans out there. But it is also deeply upsetting to see how many people are unnecessarily struggling so much because they have been Excluded like me.

108.
NAME: Anonymous
REASON FOR EXCLUSION: Limited Company Director

I started my business up a few years ago and have literally shed blood, sweat and tears building it up, working all the hours God sends. My partner, prior to setting up the business, was a sole trader and at clients' request we formed a Limited Company. Business was going really well and we were set to have our best year to date.

Then along came the pandemic.

Being Excluded has made me feel penalised for doing the right thing. I operate from home to balance being a mother and working all hours. It keeps overheads down, but of course invariably results in better profit margins, meaning more tax paid. Since trading as a Ltd Co. we have contributed more in corporation tax alone than in our combined tax contributions with my husband as a sole trader and myself working PAYE in another industry. Yet this made us ineligible for Government grants?

I've always ensured all our liabilities were met, and I've paid all the sub-contractors meticulously on time, gaining trust and a reputable reputation.

Everyone around us in our industry is getting SEISS grants. They are being helped when either their trade has not been affected or they have gone off and claimed Universal Credit whilst working cash in hand – yet we are the fraud risk? Rishi Sunak is so out of touch with reality! I have seen huge sums of money thrown at people who don't need it and who continue to do very well out of the pandemic at the expense of the public purse.

I also experienced domestic violence for the first time during this pandemic. My partner's stress, anger and hurt was sadly directed at me. Another bloody awful situation for me to deal with. Hurt and anger does not cover it.

My mental health was at an all-time low when I found ExcludedUK. The group is amazing and literally a lifeline to so many. I have been so inspired and motivated to help us have a voice. We are the hard-working tax payers not the fraud risk we are labelled by an out-of-touch chancellor.

I've read stories on the group's Facebook page of people's struggles, and seen people on the edge. I've witnessed strangers' kindness and compassion to bring them back where they belong, in a place where they are appreciated and cared for. I will not let this Government take everything I've worked so hard to build, I will spend my future building it back up. And I'll instill in my children what I already practice in life but ExcludedUK reinforces.

Be kind and help others!

109.

NAME: Lisa

OCCUPATION: Travel Consultant

REASON FOR EXCLUSION: Limited Company Director

I have run my small travel consultancy business for nearly 20 years, providing sales and marketing services to luxury hotels in Asia wanting to promote themselves to the UK market. I have paid taxes throughout this period and employed up to six staff at any one time – thus providing jobs.

As we work with hotels overseas, our contracts were cut as of last January, and by March all contracts stopped.

We have had no income since then. Whilst the furlough has been great for my staff, there has been no support for the business itself, other than a Bounce Back Loan, which I have to pay back. I get nothing personally as a Limited Company director.

I have been almost a year with no income – instead I have had to live off my savings. There is no excuse. HMRC can see what taxes I pay every year. I have worked damn hard over the years, often in excess of 12 hours a day and this is how I am supported?

I cannot claim Job Seekers Allowance or Universal Credit because I have limited savings, yet people who choose not to work continue to take state benefits and want more. Where is the logic in this! The system sucks!

One of my staff has got furlough and is working full time in another job – so double income. I find it utterly disgusting that this is possible when the company owner has nothing. It is starving the hand that feeds the baby. What is the point of offering furlough if there may not be a business to go back to? Surely the Government priority should be to support small businesses to survive so that they can help the economy to grow again?

Also, what about the businesses that have received SEISS but have not stopped working for one day – instead, spending their grant on new bathrooms, cars, hot tubs etc – when others have not received a penny! Where is the fairness in this? I always believed the Conservatives encouraged entrepreneurial spirit and have always been a supporter, but sadly this last year has proved that in fact they don't. The Government needs small businesses to help aid the post COVID recovery – so why is there no support for us?

Ten months on and we have still been forgotten – there is no excuse.

The travel industry was the first to be hit and is likely to be the last industry to come back. So, not a penny of income since March 2020.

110.
NAME: Debbie
OCCUPATION: Candle Maker
REASON FOR EXCLUSION: Not in Profit

My name is Debbie. I was a civil servant for 13 years until I was made redundant. My husband is blind and works part self-employed and part PAYE as a piano tuner.

After being made redundant, it became clear I needed to take over more with child care as my husband's eyes had got worse, so I worked part-time for the local council and the local school – both short term contracts. In 2012, just as I planned to go back to full time work, my daughter starting having issues and was diagnosed with scoliosis (a twisted spine) which became very serious, very quickly. She had surgery to put a metal ladder around it, and post-surgery it became obvious there was another issue. In 2014 she was diagnosed with POTS, which is a condition that affects blood flow. I had to work around numerous appointments, including getting phone calls to be in London the next day. Who would employ me?

I decided to turn my hobby into a business. Many, many people were making jewelry, so I tried different crafts, ending up with beeswax candles. Each time I get going, my daughter has a 'crash' and I have to drop everything to care for her. I'm not allowed carer's allowance because I don't have to give her 24 hour care.

My business had been in the red until a couple of years ago when I made a very, very small profit. In 2020 I had arranged to do craft fairs, local pop-up shops, my website, a room for the garden to work in, as well as collaborations, and I was looking at starting my therapy business too. I had a room to rent on an ad hoc basis in a local Pilates studio. But all this is gone now.

I have tax returns but no profit on them and cannot PROVE I would have made money. Therefore, I am unable to claim any help at all unless I close my business under my council's rules. I would have cracked if it hadn't have been for my business. I feel worthless and ignored. My daughter isn't working so we support her too, and although my husband was able to get furlough for his part-time PAYE job, it's very little income

I know many are worse off but I'm so worried that if my husband's company stop his furlough, we will be in debt and lost.

Thank you for speaking for us.

111.
NAME: Audrey
OCCUPATION: Company Director
REASON FOR EXCLUSION: Limited Company Director

Mr Johnson, Mr Sunak – I need help, I am EXCLUDED. I need financial support like you have given others but you left me out – due to your assumption I am fraudster, I am a risk, and that I earn 200k?!

I am an honest, law-abiding, middle-aged, disabled woman, trying to hang onto some semblance of sanity, putting on a brave face for my family and staff who – in reality – is a crumpled mess of worry and panic waiting for you two to wake up and see what you are doing to people like me.

I am broken.

I am second generation of a small Limited Company, we are 49 years old this year, born 1972, and we have survived many changes and many difficult times. That it may not be here for a third generation, after all of our hard work, through no fault of our own, is heart-breaking.

What did I do? What was so wrong?

We have been a Limited Company for a long, long time, a system not invented by me or my Dad who came before me; we have paid lots of tax for all of these years, we created jobs, they paid taxes, we contributed – for what!?

I am supposed to be shielding as I am immuno-suppressed, in the 'highly vulnerable' category. But I can't afford to shield. I am at work, manning three phone lines, three PCs, taking deliveries, post, day-to-day maintenance, trying to find us scraps of work. I don't want to be here, I worry about my health, but so many people rely on me. I don't want to die a horrible death, but I have been put in this position by the Government that was supposed to take care of me during this pandemic, supported by money from a tax system I paid into! I have been denied support as I am paid by PAYE and dividend. You said no one will be left behind!

All my staff are furloughed. I am not. If I furlough myself, by Government guidelines, I can't work on or in my business. How does that work then Mr. Sunak? I would love to know. My employees are supported by you financially which I am grateful for. They need me to process their furlough payments and their pension contributions, their National Insurance. They need some sense of security from me; some have been here with the company for 40 years, and we are an ageing staff, where do they get jobs if I go bust?

SEISS claimants can work on their business, work somewhere else, earn and claim up to £2,500 a month. All I want is the same, just the same opportunity, that would have meant the world to me, to us. So much less worry. All I want is parity.

As for me, I feel sick every day, full of dread, constant headaches, I can't switch off the worry. I can't plan a future, I can't sleep, I wake up panicking unable to breathe often in the night, and stress is a trigger point for my health issues, so this situation does not help at all.

I know my family are worried about me, they don't want me to come to work, but what alternative do I have? I can't afford to pay staff to come in. You put me in this situation Johnson and Sunak.

My partner and I have spent nothing this last year. We have lived frugally as best we can. Basics only. We were helped by my son using his house deposit money when we needed it, and that's gone. We couldn't get Universal Credit, we tried: my partner has a minimum wage term-time job as a teacher's assistant so somehow we earned too much! So all we had was his small wage. It didn't cover the bills, never mind food. So where do I go now? Mortgage the house to support the business? Sell the car? I can't live any more frugally. I want to work! I want my staff to be in work but to do that you need to help me.

Soon please.

112.
NAME: Charlotte
OCCUPATION: Kitchen, Bathroom, Bedroom Designer
REASON FOR EXCLUSION: Newly Self-Employed

I was taken on as an employee at my current workplace as I wasn't comfortable with going self-employed: at the age of 22, I didn't know much about it as I had always been employed.

It was coming up to almost a year at my employment when I got asked if I now wanted to go self-employed. After discussing it with the other designers in the company who were self-employed, and seeing how much more I could potentially earn, it did seem a great opportunity. So in March 2019, I took the plunge. At the same time my boyfriend and I decided to get a rental flat together. For the rest of that year I was earning good money.

When COVID hit in March 2020, our showrooms closed and all installations stopped. Originally I did not feel worried, I thought this would only be short term. When I realized that this was a serious matter and was going to be longer than I had anticipated, in April I started looking for help. Seeing friends and family on 80% wages while I was receiving nothing didn't seem right.

I applied for Universal Credit but since they class my boyfriend and me as one, and he is an essential worker who did not stop working through the Lockdown, I was entitled to £0 because of his pay.

My partner and I were baffled how his wage has anything to do with my own situation. I have my own bills and wanted to cover my share of the rent, house bills, and food shopping. I remember him telling the lady on the phone that, fair enough if he was a millionaire, but with him having an average wage, how is this OK that I receive nothing?

When I was told I was unsuccessful, the woman mentioned that since I was employed during the 2018 and 2019 tax year it may be worth putting in a claim for New Style Jobseeker's Allowance (JSA) as this does not take into account my partner's income. I filled out the forms online and had my telephone interview. To my surprise and shock, I was successful, and at the start of May I received my weekly amount. Although these payments didn't even cover my share of the rent, I was thankful I was receiving some money and was finally able to contribute.

When I was able to go back to work in July 2020, we had an influx of customers wanting to do home improvements. I was busy working again and trying hard to make up for losing out on a pay and the JSA stopped.

My partner and my parents have been a big help throughout 2020 and now 2021. My boyfriend has supported me financially and his wages have kept us out of debt. This could really have broken us apart, which it nearly did last year. It has caused a few arguments and my mental health took a dip. I count myself lucky that he has stuck by me, but feel deeply upset and guilty that I have been using his money; he shouldn't have been the one to step in and help me but the Government should have.

My parents would get online shopping sent to our flat and were always there to listen to me and distract me from my troubles. If it wasn't for my boyfriend and my parents helping me, I could have been homeless. It is such a scary thought to think what could have happened to me if I didn't have the support around me.

When the Lockdown was announced for the 26th of December, I was again hopeful it would only be short term. But now, having no pay for over a month and not sure when we will be able to go back to work, I find myself back in the same situation as I was last year.

The Government still has no help for us. I am still trying to remain positive that the Government will issue help for the 3 million people Excluded from the current support schemes.

113.
NAME: Kate
OCCUPATION: VIP Manager
REASON FOR EXCLUSION: Newly Self-Employed

My name is Kate. In 1991 I moved to Manchester to study – and stayed, through a passion for late nights, meeting people, music and alcohol. A part-time bar job in a basement venue led to me forming a Limited Company at 25 and becoming half-owner of the Roadhouse, one of Manchester's finest live music venues.

Easy call – I'd been managing the business for several years, and knew that it was a sound prospect. Also I couldn't have imagined living any other way. Confucius apparently said "*Choose a job that you love and you will never have to work another day in your life*". I think this holds true for the majority of music industry veterans, indeed most small business owners – many of whom are also Excluded.

Sadly, after 22 years, the club closed in 2015 and I pin-balled around the restaurant world, quietly resenting being an employee. Then I helped deliver the VIP package to Billy Joel fans at Old Trafford. And loved it. Take That and Spice Girls followed and gave me the

wherewithal to become self-employed as a VIP manager – a joyful return to the world of showbiz. 2019 was a good first year; I made £20k, which is enough.

My estimated total earnings for the current tax year are £6.5k – the baseline is £12k. My parents have helped me out, which I am both grateful for and embarrassed by. I live with my partner who is working from home, so I have no access to Universal Credit.

In September 2020 I joined a local restaurant team, and have since been furloughed with them. There are no savings or assets to sell, and no pension either. But I am child- and debt-free, thankfully.

I'm living well, within my means. Cooking good food, sleep, exercise and books are my days now. Self-acceptance and growth are my job. Having the time and inclination to do both is a gift, as is the realisation that I don't need any more stuff. I consider myself a fortunate member of this group.

I have mourned the loss of my business already. Weirdly, knowing it wouldn't have survived this brings a long overdue peace of mind. I am on the other side. It's massively shit being discriminated against, but then I am white, able-bodied, and cis – rarely on the losing side.

This experience should kindle empathy and solidarity with all groups seeking parity. ExcludedUK has given us reassurance, consensus and hope. We will carry on, do better, differently, with humility and resilience. Our 3 million votes might bring about real change.

See you on the other side, whatever the outcome of this ExcludedUK campaign.

114.

NAME: Chris

OCCUPATION: Driving Instructor

REASON FOR EXCLUSION: 50/50 rule

I'm Chris. In January 2019, I became self-employed (sole trader) as a driving instructor after leaving my previous employed job as a car sales executive.

Due to the timing of becoming self-employed, I was of course Excluded. Well over 50% of my income for the 2018-19 financial year was from my employed role, and so I slipped through the gaps for any support from the Government, other than a measly sum total of £180 to cover me in the first Lockdown. I was forced to take a Bounce Back Loan of £9,750 to survive, and took a couple of month's mortgage holiday.

Between Lockdowns (when I was allowed to give driving lessons) my business still suffered due to the amount of pupils having to self-isolate at short notice.

The second Lockdown in November again resulted in no income (or support). This Lockown saw me using all of the small savings that I had, in order to keep my head above water.

My first year in business was already lean in income, due to start-up costs and training etc, so I am now in a position whereby I just don't know how I will pay my bills next month, or thereafter, simply because the Government, in particular, Rishi Sunak, chooses to consciously turn his back on us – that is, until we have collectively made the effort to force him to turn around and face us very soon. All we ask for is parity and fairness as the tax-paying 'included' have had.

A couple of nights ago I was in contact with one of our members (an instructor) who was having suicidal thoughts, but thankfully is feeling less so.

Why has it come to this? I have volunteered as a Police Special Constable in my area for the past 16 years, and so I'd like to think I give something back to the community (and the Government).

Why is it that they can be so inhumane and reluctant to support us in this crisis?

115.

NAME: Jane

OCCUPATION: Florist

REASON FOR EXCLUSION: 50/50 rule

After my NHS career ended, floristry became my lifeline. I have a small business as a Wedding and Event Florist and I enjoy the creativity, working with people, and I love being a small part of their most important day.

My husband works with me, alongside his part time self-employed role with the RHS. Both of us are Excluded from SEISS due to our pensions and the 50/50 rule.

My business developed after training, from a longstanding hobby. By March 2020 it had grown to 40 weddings/events a year. We grow a high proportion of the flowers and foliage, and the business is based at our rural home. We have minimal advertising, the business having developed by word of mouth.

We had enough bookings not to need to use social media and our future was full of plans.

The closure of venues in March 2020 put us 'on hold' and we have not been able to restart. I am continually moving bookings forward and dealing with stressed couples. Keeping the website and my ancient IT system are ongoing expenses, along with insurance.

Throughout childhood the need to save for a rainy day was instilled in me, alongside the will to be self-reliant and honest. So, in better times we put money into savings to top up our pensions in later life. We are living on these savings now. Our finances have taken a hit, which will affect our future.

We do not have children but a good network of extended family and friends, but everyone assumes we have had the same help as other self-employed. When I hear of others getting their SEISS payments, I stay quiet – it's just too much to discuss without getting upset. Knowing some are still open and able to work while receiving a sizeable financial top up is hard to understand. An application for ARG has been made.

I have paid tax and National Insurance all my life and have never claimed benefits of any kind. We took a mortgage holiday but decided not to apply for a Bounce Back Loan as we didn't want debt beyond our mortgage.

Joining ExcludedUK has been a lifeline and helped me to just keep going, knowing I am not alone in the struggle to understand what the Government is doing to people. I can often only check in on comments or add a word of support when someone is feeling low, but I am always humbled by other members' stories and their resilience.

The values of ExcludedUK are entrenched in kindness, supporting and caring for each other and fighting for all regardless of why we are Excluded. A group of people who might never have met have been united, and it is a mistake to ignore the message of parity for all when voiced so eloquently by our leaders. The members who have been strong enough to be filmed or speak out in the press are truly awesome people.

For me and for my husband, I feel humiliated, devalued, betrayed and discriminated against. After a lifetime of work and contribution to our society, Exclusion feels wrong on every level. It feels as if the 'safety net', 'lifeboat' or any other preparation we had made to cope with a crisis has been stolen from us.

There are so many in the group whose lives are tougher than ours, but like me, they are keeping going simply because of ExcludedUK.

Thank you all.

116.

NAME: Dani

OCCUPATION: Travel Consultant

REASON FOR EXCLUSION: Limited Company Director

I have been in the travel/concierge industry for over 20 years and I began my career overseas as a holiday rep for a renowned tour operator before moving back to the UK. After several fantastic seasons abroad, I joined a top London concierge company and there my passion for luxury travel ignited. I started my own travel business in 2016.

My business was absolutely thriving pre-COVID, with referrals from happy clients and lots of luxury holidays being booked for HNW (High Net Worth) clients, including footballers, hedge funders etc... I was travelling the world and being paid for it, all in the name of research of course! I was living the dream. Being my own boss, loving life and working from home, fortunate to be able to take my daughter to school and pick her up every day, life was SO good!

Since March 2020, my mental health has really taken a battering. I feel like I don't matter to the UK Government and I am worthless. I have dutifully paid tax for the last 25 years so why, in my time of need, have I been left to rot?

I don't understand why my business isn't worth saving, yet someone else doing exactly the same as me, but paying their taxes in a different way, is given grants for thousands whilst I get nothing.

I feel sad and bereft, like I am grieving a business that I worked so hard to build up. Why hasn't there been industry sector-specific help? The travel industry is on its knees, yet the Government turns a blind eye and it breaks my heart, not just for myself, but for everyone in our industry that is losing their businesses through no fault of their own.

My husband was unemployed for six months at the start of the pandemic and Excluded from any financial help (also Ltd Co. director). Thankfully he managed to land a contract and this has helped us keep a roof over our heads and food on our table (if it was up to

Fishy & Bojo we would survive on air pie and windy pudding!). Otherwise, we would have lost our house like many others sadly have.

I have heard of saving for a rainy day but who saves for a tsunami?! It really upsets me when I see people who have been given grants and also able to carry on working, who are having extensions done, new kitchens and buying cars etc... I don't begrudge anyone their grants, but all help should be equally distributed and there should be no discrimination.

Back in November I saw a post on the ExcludedUK Facebook page from a company looking for members of ExcludedUK to do some part-time paid work. Up until that point I had been holding out hope for support and also that the travel industry would make a comeback. But then I realised that I couldn't just sit waiting for things to change, so I got in touch with a lovely guy called Steve from the Geeves Mastermind Club and he introduced me to Garrick who runs HK UK Support (a business assisting people with their move from Hong Kong to the UK). I have since joined their team on a part-time basis as a relocations manager, and I absolutely love it. Long-term I can see me assisting the HK UK clients with concierge and travel requirements; in the meantime, the relocation role keeps my brain active and gives me some much-needed pay.

As my husband can work remotely, for our own sanity and mental health we are looking at relocating overseas somewhere sunny, possibly the Caribbean, so that our daughter can be free to swim and play without restriction.

Quite frankly, I have lost all faith in this country and our Government and just don't want to be here anymore. If we can rent out our house we will be gone in the next few months, which can't come quickly enough as far as I am concerned.

I keep the faith that travel will come back and when it does my business will once again thrive. Until then, I count my blessings that we are all healthy.

117.

NAME: The Carmichael Family

OCCUPATION: Sound Engineer/Tour Manager

REASON FOR EXCLUSION: Trading Profits over £50k

Before COVID this family of five were doing OK.

My husband brought in a steady income as a self-employed Sound Engineer/Tour Manager, but when COVID hit, things went downhill pretty quickly. A full year of planned touring work was cancelled, and by the end of March it was very clear that he wouldn't be working again any time soon.

It was with a mixture of disbelief and panic that we realised that his loss of income would not be supported as his net profits were a fraction over the £50k cut off.

We had to adapt quickly to survive. We both found work quickly but there's not a lot of choice around so it's mostly at minimum wage. We are not eligible for Universal Credit and as we have three young children to care for now at 'home school', we are somewhat limited as to how many hours we can put in. Which to choose? Caring for our children or providing for our children? We're trying to get the right balance.

Our current income is not enough to cover our mortgage and bills, it's a fraction of what we would normally earn. We've just applied for our second mortgage holiday (ironically so that we can start paying our January tax bill).

We have no savings. Over the past ten months we have sold possessions that we did not want to sell. Every day we make difficult choices as to how we spend what little we have. We hear about others who are going bankrupt and some who are feeling suicidal. How many of the Excluded will be dealing with the financial aftermath of this situation, for years to come?

Rishi Sunak says that the majority of people earning over £50k were actually earning £200k. We were definitely not, and the majority of people were not. This is a great example of how to skew statistics though, Rishi!

We look to the future and see that it is very likely that 2021 will be another full year of no 'normal' work and income. Mass gatherings, festivals and concerts seem a very long way away. How can any family be expected to survive and keep paying their bills without their normal income, for a whole year? Maybe two?

Overnight, your income disappears completely, with no warning, with no time to prepare? Imagine that. What are we supposed to do?

But not everyone has been Excluded like us. Most people whose income has been affected have (quite rightly) been given adequate support, generous support even, regardless of their level of income. The Government promised to support everyone. So why not us? Where did we go wrong? Why should I have to work evenings and weekends stacking shelves in a supermarket whilst other mums, who got furloughed or supported through the SEISS scheme, get to stay at home, safely, and put their little ones to bed? Why should this family have to put all our future plans on hold and accept money from our pensioner parents to help us buy food?

We are totally exhausted; there's an all-consuming, constant anxiety to deal with, on top of all the COVID worry. It's hard to keep it together in front of the kids. I think about the disparity of the situation all the time, and I think about all the others who have been Excluded like us, especially those who are in a much worse position than us. I think about the people who have claimed financial support when they haven't really needed it. And I wonder how any of it can be right when hard working people who have paid their taxes can continue to be Excluded from all support for no good reason.

118.

NAME: Judi

OCCUPATION: Translator

REASON FOR EXCLUSION: 50/50 rule

When Rishi Sunak appeared on TV on 26th March 2020, peeping over his podium and uttering those now-infamous words, "You have not been forgotten. We will not leave you behind. We are all in this together," he was lying.

Purely and simply lying.

I believe he already knew, through the studies he'd done in the design of his rapid COVID-response policies working with special experts, dedicated departments, statisticians and Government agencies, that many, many people would be ineligible for any support.

My heart sank when I heard that to receive help you had to be, 'majority self-employed'. I receive a modest Widow's pension that is slightly more than my self-employed income as a translator. This means I wasn't eligible for anything.

My work comes from Spanish agencies and is mainly for UK tourists in Spain, so suddenly, owing to Spanish Lockdowns and COVID travel and tourism bans, I had no self-employed income. I do realize that I'm luckier than some who have received nothing at all this whole time, but my pension doesn't even cover my rent. It's tough and scary, and I never, ever thought I'd be in this position at 60 after being a self-employed translator for 20 years.

Something that really irked me right from the start, though, was why a woman in a PAYE job who receives slightly more Widow's pension than her PAYE salary (i.e. similar to my case) was entitled to 80% furlough, whereas I was not. It's just pure discrimination – and that really, really hurts.

By rolling out his furlough and SEISS schemes at such pace, he acknowledged that people could not survive without any income, even for a short period of time. Yet here we are, over 3 million taxpayers, ten months later, destitute, despairing and dispirited… but certainly not out.

It just seems so cruel that he was fully aware that the ultimate safety net, Universal Credit (UC), wouldn't be available to Excluded people if they had an earning partner or savings, and even if they could access it, how do you survive on around £80 week when you have pre-existing financial commitments?

ExcludedUK was formed shortly after Sunak's 'debut' and it has been a life-saver for many, finding solace being part of a community of people in the same situation. I am so grateful for it and for the hard work and tenacity of The Team. The stories and pleas shared are just heart-breaking – of people living in cars, eating plain rice, not putting the heating on (like me), losing their homes, livelihoods and even loved ones to suicide. Sunak's 'deliberate policy decisions' have been the final, sad straw that has broken the camel's back for many.

Having always intentionally lived within my means, I am now several thousand pounds in debt and unable to access UC. I am having to borrow from family and friends. I can't just move out of my rented flat to something smaller as, like many, I'm stuck in a contract, plus, which landlord would take on a non-earner anyway?

There have been many dark days when I've just wondered, "what's the point", which is not how I usually am. But a while ago I decided to put that darkness back into its box, lock it as best I could, and fight to gain parity for all Excluded with their taxpaying peers.

This exclusion and utter discrimination of such a huge swathe of British small businesspeople and others will go down in history as a national scandal.

I have a perfectly viable job and all I needed was a bridge to the other side of COVID, as was given to my working peers. As Chancellor, the overriding motive behind any of Sunak's policy decisions should be to protect the wellbeing of each and every UK citizen equally, and most especially during a pandemic.

Sunak has spectacularly failed to do this, but paradoxically, in trying to airbrush us out of existence, he has brought about the creation of a group that is so strong, committed and caring for one another that it will relentlessly continue to fight against him for the parity we all deserve. ExcludedUK.

119.
NAME: Tess
OCCUPATION: Sound Engineer
REASON FOR EXCLUSION: Newly Self-Employed/PAYE

My name is Tess. I am a fully qualified sound engineer, who worked in the West End Theatre sector.

As of the 16th March 2020 I have been unemployed as the theatre sector is classed as 'mass gatherings'. I feel like this sector has been hit very hard, as we were one of the first industries to be hit by the pandemic and I also feel like we will be one of the last to reopen.

I remember back in early 2020, I was eagerly watching the daily Coronavirus updates in the hope that there would be some form of support given to me, as my daily work had just disappeared within a matter of hours.

I will never forget is Rishi Sunak's statement, "No-one will be left behind" which filled me with optimism; it soon faded as new support schemes were put into place and I found that I wasn't eligible, due to the nature of my work. I am usually PAYE, but when the pandemic hit, I was newly self-employed as my contract on the show that I was working on at the time was only a short contract. I was unable to be furloughed as my contract was essentially terminated on the 16th March 2020. I was unable to claim for the SEISS, as I was newly self-employed as of February 2020.

I applied for Universal Credit, which I was denied as I had savings. I felt this was totally unacceptable especially in these, "unprecedented times". I even wrote to my MP several times in regards to this matter, but was met with the same response – which was basically listing all the other support schemes on offer that I wasn't eligible for.

One of my criticisms of the savings been taken into account, was that I know I am probably regarded as being lucky because I have savings, but why should I now rely on these in order to survive? You always hear that people seem to live off the benefit system these days, and I could guarantee that they will still be able to claim these benefits, but their circumstances have not drastically changed, whereas I am been punished further by the fact I have decided to save my own money.

Upon further research, I found that I could claim the New Style Job Seekers Allowance, I claimed this from the end of March to mid September 2020.

I continued to watch the daily updates and kept an eye on the news as I was still optimistic that something else must be available, but I am still waiting for this support.

So many people seemed to be complaining about not been able to survive on 80% of their wage, which infuriated me even more, as at least these people had already had some form of support from this pandemic.

The final blow to the year was due to the work I did manage to complete in the 2019/20 tax year as self-employed. I now owe HMRC money! I am expected to carry on as if all is normal, but it's just yet another expense that I have to pay, as well as my ongoing mortgage payments, utility bills and everyday living expenses.

I would like to point out that I am aware these are very difficult circumstances for everyone, but perhaps everyone should be included.

Sorry for ranting but felt like my situation needed to be heard in order to prove a point that we do exist.

120.

NAME: Sarah

OCCUPATION: After School Club Owner

REASON FOR EXCLUSION: 50/50 rule

I am an ex-teacher who opened up a breakfast and after school club called Acorns in September 2018, for primary school children.

When I opened my business, I was also working in a nursery part-time as this was something I could do alongside running the club. Obviously, with it being new, I wasn't making a lot of money to start with. For this reason I'm Excluded. On my tax return for 2018/19 I was earning more in employment.

I received a small discretionary grant and got a Bounce Back Loan. This by no means made up for my loss of earnings and I was told the grant was only to cover ongoing costs.

I'm in a lot of debt already and things are getting worse. I've now got the Bounce Back Loan to pay, a £3,000 tax bill and another £900 to be paid for tax in July. I've two children and no income. How is this fair? My staff are furloughed, which is great for them, however I can't see why I have been left out of any Government help.

I'm lucky to have a husband who is earning money as his teaching job is secure; however, this is not enough and we are not entitled to Universal Credit.

I hope in the future I can keep my business open to provide a service for the parents, as they desperately need it. It has been decided by the Academy where I run the club that I currently can't open due to the bubble issue, so I have been unable to work since the beginning of January.

We are, to be frank, losing money at a vast rate and I really hope we are included soon.

121.

NAME: Louisa

OCCUPATION: Supply Teacher

REASON FOR EXCLUSION: Denied Furlough

I am used to working four days a week, pretty much the whole of term time, but since March last year I have worked for only ten weeks in schools! Being a supply teacher, and with school closures, my work has rapidly declined.

I am a single parent of two school-aged children and I own my own home, so my income is crucial.

I received ten weeks of furlough (80% of my average wage) last year and the other months I was out of work. I have lived off a few tax credits and savings I obtained from re-mortgaging my house.

When the school closed during the third Lockdown, I was told I would not be furloughed as my umbrella company who pay me cannot afford the National Insurance and pension contributions they now have to make under the new scheme. My agency who book my work say it is down to my payroll provider. I am stuck!

This has meant that I have only had ten weeks' wages plus ten weeks' furlough in nearly a year! I am now at the stage where I have all my bills to pay next month and not enough income. I fear for this month as I will not have enough money to feed my children. I have been a teacher for 15 years and have only been on supply for three. I have worked since I was 16!

The stress and worry of this situation has led to depression, relapse of an old eating disorder, alcohol abuse and general lack of self care. I continue to fight this so I can be there for my children, but they will have seen some suffering I am sure.

It looks like this month (as I have no wages) and due to reaching maximum benefits entitlement, I will be using a food bank for the first time. I have no other option.

To be in this situation, after all I have paid into society for the future of this country, is soul destroying. I feel like I will not proceed in this profession any longer if the Government cannot look after their teachers (permanent or supply).

I am a broken woman, mother and teacher!

122.
NAME: Nital
OCCUPATION: Graphic Designer
REASON FOR EXCLUSION: Denied Furlough

Having studied Graphic Design at university I worked for a few different companies before working for the same one for 17 years.

In 2019 we moved home, and I decided it was time for a change, so I started searching for new jobs.

I was offered a Graphic Design job for a beauty company which I accepted. A short while after I started my new role, the pandemic hit and I got made redundant. I contacted my old company (as per Government advice) to ask if they would take me back or furlough me. My old company of 17 years refused, even though the Government was advising companies to take people back, to furlough them, to help them, to do something.

I am so annoyed at the lack of ethics and accountability of these types of companies as well as the Government.

I have been without a full-time job since the end of March 2020. I was only entitled to a few months of Job Seekers Allowance, despite the fact that I had been working, both part-time and full-time jobs, all my life – ever since my first paper round at 13 years of age! I took some temp jobs, and have been applying for jobs, trying to get freelance work and doing things to improve my skills.

This is the longest time in my life I have been without a proper job and it has hit me hard. My self-confidence, self-worth and the confidence in my abilities has been affected so badly. There have been so many days with endless flows of tears.

In October, we found out my mum has terminal cancer and there is nothing they can do for her. So, in between applying for jobs, I am making memories in the home with her. I can honestly say the last 11 months have been some of the worst in my life.

The Government should have put something in place for all the new starters like me, instead of encouraging companies to furlough them. They should have made it a legal requirement. Alternatively, they could have created a separate scheme for all the new starters. We work hard, we pay taxes, follow the law, are kind, do voluntary work – yet this is how we are treated by our very own Government.

This is the same Government that promised, "You have not been forgotten. We will not leave you behind. We are all in this together."

Well, they lied and have done what they said they would not do. I am beyond angry and upset about the situation and genuinely believe there is no help coming for people like me. My MP has not responded to anything and she simply doesn't care. We are now seriously considering moving abroad soon to a country that cares about its people.

123.
NAME: Kate (& Sophie aged ten)
OCCUPATION: Piano Tutor
REASON FOR EXCLUSION: 50/50 rule

A bit about me....
I am a self-employed piano tutor who usually teaches in three local schools, in students' homes and from my home. I have tried to teach online but numbers have dwindled more and more as students and parents tire of 'online everything'. I am not allowed to use the

school premises to teach at this time. And I am clinically extremely vulnerable. I am down to four students from 32.

In 2017 I moved house because my landlord sold our home. I had to start all over again, so to keep our heads above water I got a second job working for a music shop. I was working 21 hours a week there, whilst working so hard to rebuild my business too. I am a single mum of two and it was tough, but I did it.

In March 2019 I left the music shop to tutor full time. I am Excluded because I earned more at the music shop those years. But, I don't understand why they can't look at my tax return for 2019/20! The one I filed last May. That year was my best and 2020 should have been even better.

Here is my story about my daughter Sophie's Santa wish.
Last weekend we put up our tree. We sang carols with Bublé as we hung up the baubles and Sophie giggled at my silly dancing.

But, inside I was scared, screaming, crying.

That evening I noticed my daughter had left a note for Santa beneath the tree. It stayed sealed in my bedside drawer for 4 days. I was unable to open it knowing this year I could not afford whatever she wished for.

Today I plucked up the courage. It was not what I expected. Sophie was reaching out to me. Tears rolled off my cheeks onto her sweet words.

I thought I was putting on a brave face. I did not realise she could see through my fake smiles to my fear and sadness each morning. It is heartbreaking that she feels my pain. She worries with me. She is just ten years old.

Am I failing to protect her this way?

Excluded, we have been left to struggle.

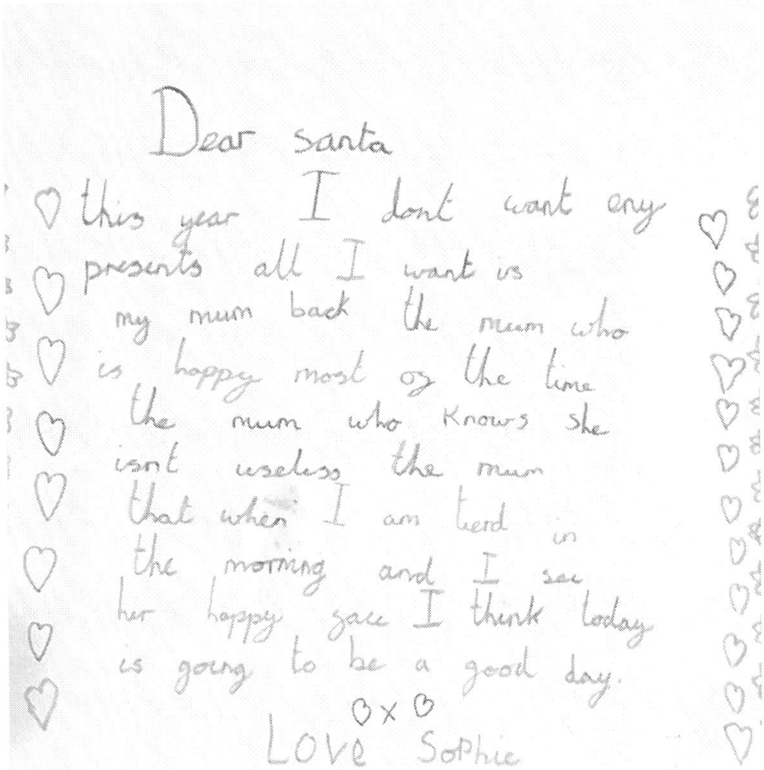

Dear Santa
this year I dont want eny presents all I want is my mum back the mum who is happy most of the time the mum who Knows she isnt useless the mum that when I am tierd in the morning and I see her happy face I think today is going to be a good day.
OxO
Love Sophie

Sophie's letter to Santa

Although I am grateful for the tax credits we receive, they do not last to the end of each month. Bills are bouncing, overdrafts and cards all maxed-out, my rent in arrears. I am desperate to get back to work full time, but know it will not be easy to scrape up the remains of my business once I am able to. The business I worked so hard to build, whilst single-handedly caring for my children.

I've always been passionate and motivated but this year, I'm increasingly anxious and exhausted. Hopeless. This pandemic has shattered my business and now my mental health.

As clinically extremely vulnerable, I hang my hopes on that vaccine, unsure how we will manage till then.

I cannot sleep. The only reason I get up each day, the only reason to live, is I have to keep going, keep smiling, keep trying for Sophie.

I have to keep willing her Christmas wish will come true.

Please someone out there give me the strength to do this for her.

Thank you ExcludedUK for trying to highlight the gaps in support for so many families.

124.
NAME: Diane
OCCUPATION: Pet Services/Dog Boarding/Day Care/Walking
REASON FOR EXCLUSION: 50/50 rule

After being made redundant from my compliance job in the motor trade in August 2017, I accepted a part-time manager's role at our local vets. The following July I opened my first business: administration and support for small start-up businesses, running in tandem to my work at the vets.

In December 2018 I left the vets, and opened my second business – dog home boarding and pet services which operated alongside my admin work.

I was able to run both businesses from home, allowing me to spend time caring for my husband, who has numerous health issues. In my first year I had two days off out of the 365 – not a complaint, just a fact. I was finally doing the job that I had yearned for and only having two days off didn't concern me because I loved it. It never felt like work. No more Monday morning blues!

I have always been a very cautious person, sort of borderline risk-averse. It took me a long time to have the courage to become self-employed and back in March 2020 I initially thought, "This will be ok – no way will they leave us to fend for ourselves".

I'm glad I didn't know then how long this would last as I doubt I would have coped. The early days were filled with panic, then I tried to 'go with the flow'. My husband is older than me and has been quite ill in recent years, so I try not to burden him with the worry of our situation – turns out though that he sees me stressing and worries even more! He feels bad, ironically, as he is the reason I can't claim Universal Credit, because he receives a state pension.

I hate that my own identity has been ripped away. Like a lot of people, not just women, our sense of self has been denied to us and we have become one half of something that means nothing to the Government other than a reason not to provide help.

I'm happy to be 'Mrs Keavey', but have always worked and earned my own money for 38 years. But the worst thing is being ignored. Being made to feel that no matter what the issue is or how bad the situation, the people running the country do not even feel it worthy to acknowledge our existence.

The ExcludedUK Group has been a sanctuary and from it I have made new friends and new business acquaintances. My family and close friends continue to provide us with support which means the world to us. I created Team Susie (my labradoodle and Boss of our pet business) for the Three Million Miles campaign, and 23 of my friends joined up, and my brother even enlisted his Jog Scotland team. We currently have accumulated 40K miles and I feel that every one of those miles shows support for our cause.

As for the future, at the moment, I have no idea. I've had to close my admin business so it's all on the pet services. I need to take care of my husband, which is my number one priority, but also strengthen the bonds developed through Lockdown with extended family, close friends and neighbours.

125.

NAME: Donna

OCCUPATION: Podiatrist/Chiropodist

REASON FOR EXCLUSION: Trading Profits over £50k

I am a busy podiatrist/chiropodist, having been in private practice for 20 years, and previously in the NHS. My work involves treating patients either in clinics, their own homes or care homes. I have worked since the age of 16, supported myself through college, and worked hard all my life paying taxes.

In March 2020 patients started to cancel before Lockdown as fear about the Coronavirus took hold and people started to shield. Then Lockdown hit and I had to stop work and cancel everything; we were only allowed to see 'emergencies'. I saw two patients in the whole of April 2020.

At some point in June, we were advised we could see patients again; however, the care homes were largely still locked down, or hesitant to have me visit, despite getting tested beforehand. My visits were slow to return; and my clinic was shut longer as the treatment room I rent was within a sports park, and they were shut.

Work is still very hit and miss, as many of my patients are in the 'at risk/vulnerable' groups. Despite being Excluded for being over the £50k mark for the previous three years, my 2019/20 year end salary was below £50K and my 2020/21 year end is likely to be 50% less.

I live alone. During the first Lockdown, I was very anxious about the virus myself as I have autoimmune conditions, and I didn't know whether I could be more at risk. I was very lonely as all my usual activities were off. I used to do a lot of dancing, connecting with people, and all of a sudden I was grounded. I worried about everything. Then, when I heard the self-employed would be getting help, I waited patiently; only to hear there would be no help for me.

I have lost a lot of sleep over the last year, and despite the initial flurry of friends and acquaintances showing concern, it all went quiet. I think people didn't know what to say, or couldn't put themselves in my shoes and consider how they would feel.

I felt abandoned by the Government. Initially I thought, OK, it's three months, just take one day at a time, but unfortunately we are almost a year on and things are still challenging.

I realise I have been more fortunate than some, but still feel that I have completely lost out, having to use up hard earned savings, whilst others have been helped. I want parity.

This situation seems to rumble on in Britain, whilst other countries have largely eradicated or controlled the virus. I try to live in hope, but it's been very difficult. I've joined various online therapy/support groups and gone walking whenever I can.

126.
NAME: David McKie
OCCUPATION: Consultant Director, Construction
REASON FOR EXCLUSION: Limited Company Director

My name is David McKie. I am based in the North East and I am a Consultant Director for TSSS Ltd and work predominantly in the Construction Industry. I was Excluded due to being annual PAYE, and also because I was required to operate and market my business after losing a major contract due to COVID. I was asked to become a Limited Company Director by my Clients as this aligned to the requirements of the industry and government regulations. I am also registered from home and have received no grants from the government or my local authority as I do not meet the requirements of their policies.

I have been part of Excluded UK from the beginning, and part of a wide family and community fighting for parity with other taxpayers. I will continue to support the group and look forward to seeing what the future holds. I have learnt many lessons and connected with many other people and businesses.

127.

NAME: Kelly

OCCUPATION: Massage Therapist

REASON FOR EXCLUSION: 50/50 rule

After 20 years of doing admin work, seven years ago I started as a massage therapist. I loved my new career. I was part time self-employed offering treatments in well-being at holistic day centres. Around the same time I got a part-time job in a hotel spa. I worked at both jobs and trained in other therapies.

Being Excluded has made me feel lost and useless and like I have lost my independence. I feel trapped and stuck on a benefits system I was working hard to avoid. Friends don't understand my struggle and why I don't want to give up what is left of my business. Most of my family don't know that I'm Excluded and I can't face them and what they may think of me.

I'm torn and hurt. My relationship is suffering as I'm so scared that I am going to lose everything, my home, my business, my car. I've worked hard for my house and the things I have, I don't want to lose them. I feel like I just want to go away and never come back.

Being part of the Excluded community is comforting as I know I'm not alone. Hearing how others feel, and how they too are in the same place as me, gives me faith that the fight to show the Government is worth going through the shit-show we are going through now.

I intend on keeping my business. It may take a few years to get back to where I was but I will keep going, to show the Government and others that being self-employed and doing a job I love will make me happy and I will not lose my independence.

Being part of a 3 million strong group is giving me the strength to continue.

128.

NAME: Sangita

OCCUPATION: Healthcare Provider

REASON FOR EXCLUSION: Director Paid in Dividends

My name is Sangita. For 16 years I was employed by my local authority on temporary contracts. During that time the Labour Government were in power and there was a massive focus on regeneration. I worked on a wide cross-section of projects including stimulating the local economy redevelopment of disused shops and sites, employment initiatives, community development etc – each project was on a time-limited employment basis.

When the Tories came into power, regeneration grants stopped so I had reinvent myself. I took an admin role in the NHS, and due to my tenacity I managed to prove my worth and was asked to deliver a small, freelance, part-time project.

Due to the success of this commission I managed to secure a 13 month contract working for the NHS in East London. I formed my Limited Company at the request of the Trust, in 2013.

Every year since then I have seen a steady growth in my turnover. I have literally gone wherever work has taken me. I have been up at 4am to be in East London for 7.30am, working 15 hour days to fulfill contracts. My business continuity didn't come by chance, it was through sheer hard work and sacrifice.

My company specialises in Continuing Healthcare; providing service redesign; clearing backlog; assessing patients with long-term conditions whose health care needs are not met by universally commissioned services; making efficiencies in operating budgets etc. To say the contracts are demanding is an understatement.

When the Government announced the first Lockdown, continuing healthcare, as with many other pathways such as cancer, was put on hold. The nurses were deployed to the frontline and the immediate priority was COVID-19. All other commissioning stopped and therefore my contracts from the NHS stopped.

As a small Limited Company, I am required to do all aspects of business delivery – finding contracts, health and safety, risk management, operational delivery, admin, book keeping. I probably do the work of three people to run my business. I take a basic salary and when I have surplus, I then reward myself with dividends.

As a direct result of this I have been prevented from accessing the same support as a self-employed person. My accountant has just finalised my accounts for 2019/20 – I drew £79,500, the highest that I have ever been able to draw, and my tax for 2019/20 is £12,200 and advanced self assessment tax is £4,400. During the COVID period I have received furlough payments of approximately £509 per month.

Mr Sunak. I would like to ask you how anyone in this country is supposed to live on £509 per month for over ten months – that's £16 a day! And how, in this climate of 'start-stop' is anyone supposed do any kind of business planning? I'd be grateful to hear your suggestions on how £509 pays a mortgage, gas, electric, water, TV licence, council tax, etc, and buys food.

I'd like to ask you how you reconcile the inequality in support. You say that it is not possible to permit grants to limited companies as there is a fraud risk – again something I'm struggling to understand. The system has my self assessments, it had my quarterly VAT submissions, it has my annual accounts, my bank details, my credit file – is there anything the system doesn't know about me?

Mr Sunak. I'd like to ask you, if my taxes are good enough for Her Majesty's Treasury, then why am I not entitled to the same support as every other tax payer?

Lastly, I'd like to ask you Mr Sunak, if YOUR livelihood was taken away from you through no fault of your own, say by a National Pandemic, would you be able to survive on £509 per month? And by this I mean would you be able to pay all of the basic things listed above. I realize that you are fortunate enough to be a millionaire, but could you park that for a moment and place yourself in the position of a hard-working small company director?

You would earn a great deal of respect if you listened and understood the plight of small businesses. Small businesses matter and are vital to this country's economy! I can say for certain that for the last seven years my taxes have contributed to this country's economy.

I mentioned my background in Regeneration. Cities, towns and deprived neighbourhoods were bought back to life by the Labour Government, but it honestly feels like this Government is breaking something that will need fixing later on through targeted interventions.

I have a few very simple business principles. First, I don't break something that's working, that's counterproductive. Second, that it's never too late to make positive change and take people on your journey; and third, no one does anything on their own – I can't deliver projects without a team and likewise you, Mr Sunak, will not be fixing this country's economy on your own.

129.
NAME: Una
OCCUPATION: Dog Day Care
REASON FOR EXCLUSION: 50/50 rule

I have been a UK taxpayer and financially independent since I was 16 years old. I am married with two children and I am also the main carer for my 83 year old mum who lives with us.

In 2016 I retired from my last job with a pension. I decided to show my kids that you can achieve anything you want if you put your mind to it, so I set up my dog-walking company, and with the help of my family we made it a great success.

Two years later I expanded the business by renting an industrial unit and setting up day care for dogs. The set-up costs were high but I knew I would recoup them in time.

Within 18 months I had doubled my takings and started to use the unit at night for training classes, which again was bringing in additional income.

The last payment for my company van was due in June 2021. I did not take a wage from the business, choosing instead to put the spare money towards clearing the set-up costs. Everything was on track for the company to be debt-free by 2022.

In March 2020 COVID hit. I had to close the business and use some of my own money to pay my staff their March wages before I was able to furlough them.

I did not qualify for furlough as I had not been taking a wage. My pension meant I did not qualify for Universal Credit, and I did not qualify for SEISS because of the 50/50 rule, as I made a loss in 2018/19 due to the set-up costs.

My daughter was due to start as Cabin Crew with BA in April 2020 and that job fell through, so I had to financially support her until she got a new job.

My business was closed from March till August 2020. I received the initial £10k premises grant from the Local Council, however my rent alone is just under £1k a month, and I still had van payments, electricity, insurance, staff tax and pension contributions to pay.

I reopened at the end of August for two days a week, beginning to gradually build the business back up to opening five days a week

In November 2020 our area was placed into Tier 4 and the local council stated that all non-essential businesses had to close, but pet shops, vets and agricultural premises could open for animals. I closed the business for the three-week period and applied for the temporary closure grant. Seven weeks after closing, and during the second Tier 4 closure, I was informed I did not qualify for the temporary closure grant and should have remained open. By this time the Council had updated their site to include a whole host of animal businesses which could remain open in Tier4.

I was forced to take out a Bounce Back Loan to keep the business going and I reopened the business in January 2021. Still on reduced days and trying to build the business back up for the third time, but my heart is not in it as I feel I have let everyone down including myself.

Instead of showing my kids you can achieve whatever you want I feel I should have said "Why bother?"

Rather than reduce the set-up costs, I have taken on more debt. When my van payments stop in June, I will start paying the same monthly amount for my Bounce Back Loan for the next five years. This will equate to the cost of a new van – only I will have nothing to show at the end of it.

For the first time ever I am not financially independent. My pension is paying the business costs whilst I am relying on my husband to pay all the household bills and financially support our children.

Thankfully, I have a very supportive husband; had I not, then through no fault of my own I would have been placed in vulnerable position had I needed to flee domestic abuse.

130.
NAME: Rahima
OCCUPATION: NHS Worker
REASON FOR EXCLUSION: PAYE/Taxed at Source

I was permanent NHS staff until Dec 2019 and thereafter PAYE; however, my tax was paid at source. Due to my care responsibilities to my mother, who has numerous health conditions such as damaged lungs, failing heart and diabetes, and is prone to infections and pneumonia, I could not leave her and go out to work during the pandemic. I required flexible working hours and remote work.

I had no choice but to protect my mother from COVID-19. However, whilst others were offered remote work, this was not made available to me.

Having contributed towards our taxation system since aged 18, I was under a false impression that this would provide some sort of security, something for us to fall back on, especially during a national pandemic. I was, however, very mistaken. With a ten-year civil servant background and 15 years' service in the NHS, I worked crazy hours supporting a Government that now refers to us as 'unviable'.

Being Excluded has made me feel extremely let down and abandoned by our current Government.

Being part of ExcludedUK has helped me keep grounded, as there are many in more dire situations than me. I had saved up a little money to redecorate my home in the summer of 2020. However, my savings have dwindled away since early March 2020.

ExcludedUK is a community that's available 24-hours for a chat or whenever someone was feeling low or wanted to share their small successes. For some, managing a short walk was a personal triumph. Not being able to support your own family, bring food to the table or even give a small gift to a child was heart-breaking for us to hear, but somehow we pulled together and arranged to give, take or swap what we could to help one another. A COVID support fundraiser helped to share the monies raised to help the less fortunate ExcludedUK members.

Since the initial Lockdown in March 2020, my mother's general wellbeing and mental cognitive health has gone downhill. She now requires constant care. Looking after her will make it much harder to go out to work and work the crazy shifts that I am accustomed to.

Many people around me worked from home and luckily had an income. I don't think they understand what it's been like for us Excluded and they aren't supportive of our situation.

Many think we have not been paying our tax and are fraudsters, no thanks to Rishi Sunak who repeatedly implied this about us.

The failure of our Government to support its citizens has made me more determined to succeed without their help. We, the Excluded, are finding ways to diversify and pick ourselves up again.

We will always be readily available for the Excluded that were relentless for parity and equality in welfare support.

131.
NAME: Barney
OCCUPATION: Music/Arts/Event Management
REASON FOR EXCLUSION: Newly Self-Employed

For 17 years I'd poured my heart and soul into running a lovely Arts Centre in Aldershot. I'd promoted shows for everyone from a whole range of people including Katherine Ryan, Foals, Nadine Shah, James Acaster, Biffy Clyro, Nish Kumar, Miriam Margoyles, The Unthanks and Songhoy Blues, as well as working on countless community projects and a ton of workshops and classes.

I absolutely loved it there but it was time to go, so I pulled all my courage together and became self-employed under the banner Kick Arts UK, doing a mixture of artist management, tour booking, music business lecturing and consultancy.

I also set up a literature festival called 'Illuminate' with the help of friends and family. My brilliant friend Lorna helped me with all of it. I was working with world class artists, but by its nature it would take a while to come to fruition as a lot of the time payment follows the activity.

Looking back, I was actually in a pretty fragile place even before the pandemic. I missed my friends at the Arts Centre and was under pressure to make a go of my new business.

When the pandemic hit, I plunged into an abyss. The literature festival had to be postponed a full year, two recording sessions were cancelled, three tours were cut short or cancelled altogether, two funding bids were put on ice – we were sunk.

Barney Jeavons before the postponed Illuminate Literature Festival

My wife Emma's boss was great and let her know she would be furloughed, but her wage was nowhere near enough for us to live on. There was still no help for the self-employed at this point, and I was terrified for my daughters (thank goodness now in their late teens and early 20s – I have no idea how we'd have coped if we were still home-educating them). Eventually they both got furlough too. But it soon became clear there was no help for me.

After a heart-stopping time, I plucked up the courage to reach out to friends with a crowdfunder. I was so full of shame and embarrassment I couldn't even bring myself to set it up, my friend Laura kindly did the nuts and bolts for me. To my eternal relief my friends rallied round and we were quickly gifted over £4,000. It was a lifesaver, not only in financial terms, but I also felt loved and supported – and that we wouldn't die.

This was the turning point for me. I pushed on. Arts Council England gave me an emergency grant of £2,500. Two of the projects I was working on reconfigured what they were doing and included me in their funding bids. I was offered a repeat contract to do some music business lecturing in the autumn (with the most amazing students). I worked as one of the regional co-ordinators for Music Venue Trust – initially for three months and then for six as the scale of the pandemic became apparent. That involved helping over 90 music venues to survive, and stay sane, while it looked like their industry had been forgotten.

As the Government lurched from one quick fix to another I was dragged along with them, like a child's doll tethered to a runaway bull.

How we all kept going I'll never know. It was emotionally very tough. But we looked after each other and we did it. My friends quietly checked in on me. Everyone I worked with was on my team. Having Emma and the girls around me during the various Lockdowns was a significant silver lining, I love them so much.

I also started giving 1-2-1 arts consultations and discovered I had a talent for it and actually knew far more than I gave myself credit for. Another thing that came out of all this is that I know I am not alone. I saw horrendous stories in the ExcludedUK Facebook group where people's family and friends had been incredibly unsupportive and hurtful, but mine were wonderful. Even the people who suggested ditching everything I'd worked on and get a job in a supermarket only said it out of love (I asked everywhere and did apply by the way, just didn't get selected).

At the end of the year I slept out in the rain with Excluded to help raise money and awareness for the homeless, the people who work in events and my fellow people Excluded from Government help.

I raised far more than I ever dreamed I would and it felt amazing simply to reach the end of the year, and even more so to be in a position to help others. I am grateful I've struggled through this far.

A year ago the future was big and scary. I felt very bleak and alone without my Arts Centre family. Going through this hell has been incredibly hard but also helped me realize that I can get through almost anything with the help of my family and friends. I learned to reach out, and made more friends. I know I have been lucky – far luckier than many others – and I passionately hope that as a society we'll learn from this and make the choice to look after those less fortunate than ourselves.

132.
NAME: Diane
OCCUPATION: Childminder
REASON FOR EXCLUSION: Newly Self-Employed

My name is Diane. I turned 39 in December...yes...another Lockdown birthday. I've been married for almost ten years and have two children.

When my son was three, we realised that he was struggling with his social and emotional skills. Very early on we knew that he needed extra support. I was pregnant with my daughter when my son started school in Sept 2016. We thought he'd love it there. We thought he would embrace after-school clubs and breakfast clubs, and that my ten-year property asset management career would continue. How wrong we were.

The transition from nursery to school was not easy. He refused school clubs. He refused to go to a child-minder. So, whilst pregnant with my daughter and also whilst on maternity leave following her birth, I made the decision to re-train as a childminder. I became a self-employed Ofsted-registered childminder in August 2017 and gave up my property career.

As a new childminder, I also made the decision to supplement my income by working in a local pub. I've worked in lots of bars and pubs. So for a year, between June 2018 and June 2019 I did some bar work as well as child-minding. All the while, my son was still struggling, and despite waiting lists, hospital appointments, paediatricians etc, we still had no formal diagnosis of what we suspected. Autism.

When schools shut in March 2020, the change in routine affected my son's behaviour massively. So much so, that he often said, "I want to die", which is the worst thing you can hear as a parent. He was having meltdown after meltdown, struggling to process his own emotions and feelings, destroying his bedroom and our possessions and being physically aggressive to me.

At that point I knew that I could no longer continue to childmind. I could not give my son the time, love and attention he needed with other children around, and neither could I keep other people's children safe with his emotional turmoil. It was just an impossible situation.

We got a letter from hospital, for a 'phone call assessment'. Yes, only my son would reach the top of the waiting list for assessment at the start of a pandemic! And lo and behold, after one hour on the phone, they need to see him face to face to diagnose formally. But – they can't see him face to face because of COVID. Just great.

With no income since March 20, I applied for Universal Credit. Rejected. I applied for the new Job Seekers Allowance. Rejected.

My husband works full time and basically my childminding never made enough to pay tax, plus I worked in the pub for a year earning more income, so I was Excluded from the SEISS. I couldn't even try for a Bounce Back Loan as I had no childminding business to bounce back to. No grants, as my business folded due to my own choice, though the way things were going, if I hadn't closed it down then somebody else would have due to my sons behaviour. Harsh but true.

So now my new pub is closed due to the pandemic. I'm furloughed on 80% of my five hour pay on minimum wage. My son is again being home-schooled and hating life. The face-to-face assessment became a video call just last week – and it's ten MONTHS since he reached the top of the waiting list. We finally have his diagnosis of ASD. But now what? All the support groups are closed. We don't know where to turn.

I've gone from having everything to having nothing. I've never felt so worthless in all my life.

I'm thankful my husband has worked all year to keep us afloat. Without him, there is no question we would be homeless right now.

There are times when I go for walks and just carry on walking – not wanting to come home as I just feel so empty. All of my working life is in tatters. How did it come to this? My children keep me going. I get up every morning to be there for them. But who is there for us?

Here is a poem I wrote on 22nd October 2020:

Oh Manchester Oh Manchester

Oh Manchester Oh Manchester
Oh Manchester we're in Tier three

Oh Rishi Sunak, I've not had a penny
Oh Manchester we're in Tier three

7 months without a penny. #beyondajoke ExcludedUK

And on the 9th October 2020 I wrote this poem

2020 I am done

4 years ago feels like centuries
When I worked in Property Development
Pregnant with my daughter
With a son going through torment

I had 2 jobs at the time
Also working at a pub
But something had to change
In order to be there for my loves

Without an 'official' diagnosis
A spectrum overwhelmed
Autism/ADHD/additional needs
And all I could do was pretend

Pretend that everything was great
Smiling when I could
When inside I knew
I had to make a change for the good.

So I retrained as a childminder
So I could be there for my own
And help the others in my care
Flourish with the love and attention shown

But then almost three years went by
And COVID-19 struck
Kids at home, school closed
Childminders to shut

Lockdown began in a flash
Emotions everywhere

Wondering how to pay the bills
With Boris' schemes I despair

Oh I'm not entitled
I earnt too much from the pub!
So all my work feels worthless
I'm drowning in mud

Sinking even further
And yet another kick
Yes my husband works
So no I can't have benefits!

Whilst my son is out of routine
Struggling to process
My home is being trashed daily
My life is in a mess

Months go by with not a penny
But life cannot just stop
Food to eat, home to keep
State of mind lowering drop by drop.

And then when life resumed slightly
And the pubs reopened
I got a little weekend job
The curse of 2020 broken

Five hours a week though
Is not survivable
I feel hopeless when
Once I felt indestructible

Yet now another spanner
As it looks like another hospitality closure
Because according to Boris and his chums
That's the reason there is so much COVID-19 exposure

So here I am
Thoughts laid bare
Where on Earth do I go from here

2020 please just stop
2020 I've had enough
Boris please just give me a break
2020 how much more do we have to take

2020 I am done

133.
NAME: Amanda
OCCUPATION: Braunton Girl Friday
REASON FOR EXCLUSION: Newly Starter

I have worked ever since leaving school and I have 42 years PAYE on record, over 30 years in NHS/Private healthcare and over 20 years as a registered nurse, my latter years in management.

I've never been afraid of hard work. In December 2018 I decided I was ready for a new challenge so I started my Girl Friday business. It was a tough year, but hard work paid off and by the 31st Dec 2019 the following year was fully booked. Things looked so good I was considering taking on someone to work with me. I was on the cusp of having the life I dreamt of. Living in a beautiful part of the world, I had amazing clients and I was my own boss... life was sweet.

Then COVID-19 hit.

The first Lockdown was hard, I was scared, I had little money left, but then I heard them say, "We'll leave no one behind" and I rather stupidly believed them.

Ten months on – I've lost all trust in the Government. Heating is now a luxury. My children have helped support me, something I am grateful for, but inside I feel it's wrong – I should be the one helping them!

I find myself constantly embarrassed and humiliated by the position I am now in. I have been able to claim Universal Credit, but it doesn't even cover my rent.

I am in debt. Debt I can't ever see myself getting out of or even living long enough to pay off! I applied for a Bounce Back Loan last year, but I hold out no hope. With the debt mounting, credit score falling and bank accounts constantly empty I can't see I fit the criteria anymore.

I didn't need much, but it would have stopped this downward spiral. I was advised to shield during the first Lockdown, but this time I have had to take work where I can as I can't afford to stay home. It's a risk, but if I die at least my debts will be paid off.

I feel as if I am drowning in debt and despair whilst the Government chose to ignore us.

I am blessed; my friends and family are my rock. I have met so many lovely people in the ExcludedUK Community, they are kind and inspirational, and with them I realize I am not alone, that this situation I find myself in is not my fault, I didn't do this. I've found hope. I even had a lovely 86-year old client send me £50 at the beginning of the first Lockdown, because she was worried about me!

This has been done to me, done to all of us that are Excluded.

I left school believing I'd retire at 60. That's not going to happen now. I'll have to wait until I'm 67 for my state pension. I am now re-training, and moving forward I will need to work two jobs to clear my debts.

I'm tired now. I've worked hard all my life, but without parity my future is looking bleak. At this time of life I just wanted to enjoy my family time and not be scared of my mounting debts.

134.
NAME: Kerry
OCCUPATION: Park Worker
REASON FOR EXCLUSION: Denied Furlough

A meeting on Monday 23rd March 2020 changed my life.

All of the permanent members of staff had been asked to attend a meeting. Our general manager informed us that due to Government directives regarding COVID-19, our place of work was to close. Everyone not able to work was to be placed on the Furlough Scheme. Then came the words that still haunt me, "Kerry, I will speak to you afterwards".

I had worked at the park for six and half years. Permanent, fixed, weekly hours. I loved my job. I know I was very good at my job. Staff loved me, customers loved me. I was loyal, hardworking, always went above and beyond what was expected, and was agony aunt to many.

To be told I was not being furloughed as I was on a zero hour contract and that was that, was, to put it mildly, utterly devastating. They were leaving me with nothing. I remember breaking down outside. I was aware colleagues were watching. No one could come hug me or console me. We are not allowed to touch due to COVID.

We are now ten months on. I am still so angry with my employers! Ten months of no financial support from the Government. Ten months of existing rather than living. I still can't get my head around the fact they chose to abandon me. Chose to leave me financially, emotionally and professionally unsupported.

Days after the meeting, it was confirmed by the Government that zero hour staff could be furloughed. I emailed my employers the good news. They could help me now. Only to receive a rather 'unpleasant' reply. They would not be putting me or any other zero hour staff on furlough. They had other priorities and me and my son were not one of them. Denied Furlough. Excluded twice, firstly by my employers and now, secondly by the Government.

I collected my son from Uni. Having him at home probably kept me alive. I am a lone parent, no partner. My son has been my rock and my motivation to try and be strong.

I went into a very dark place. The feelings of abandonment and rejection brought up thoughts from my past. My moods switched erratically from anger, devastation, terror, numbness, disbelief, hopelessness, bitterness. It didn't matter we were not allowed out, or to see people. I didn't want to see people. Friends sent lovely messages and we were given amazing food parcels and shown kindness I will never forget. But no one could really understand how I had been made to feel.

I found ExcludedUK, a group of others who, due to no fault of their own, had also, 'slipped through the cracks' of financial support from our Government. I didn't feel so alone anymore.

As a group we are fighting for acknowledgement and parity of support. The admin team blow my mind with their relentless work, passion, commitment to the cause. The group, though, is doing far more than campaigning. It has set up numerous events etc – I have sung with them, cried with them, enjoyed yoga sessions and found a new mental distraction drawing mandalas! There are sadly a lot of group members struggling mentally as well as financially, and the team have set up a much accessed and valued mental health support network.

This group should never, ever have been needed, but thank goodness it was set up by truly inspirational people. It has been a lifeline to many.

135.
NAME: Laura
OCCUPATION: Performing Arts Professional
REASON FOR EXCLUSION: 50/50 rule

WE STAND TOGETHER

"We stand together", "You're not alone,"
encouraging words, but lies are cheap,
but we believed, we closed our doors,
locked up our lives, our faith did leap.

But once we were bound to stay away,
the tales told grew quickly rotten.
The price we paid to our great nation
was too complex, we were soon forgotten.

Stories of the Excluded spread,
so many lives affected deeply.
Our family grew to work as one
to fight these unjust rules completely.

You see, our treasury could not predict
how strangers would connect, stand strong.
A group with ambition and dedication,
Together, we belong, to right the wrong.

136.

NAME: Sharon

OCCUPATION: Children's Entertainer/Actor/Tutor

REASON FOR EXCLUSION: 50/50 rule

My name is Sharon. I'm a children's entertainer, freelance actor and tutor.

For over 20 years I have worked a PAYE job, 40% of my time, as a zero contract/casual music researcher. Due to a company take over, I was laid off on 31st March 2020. My P45 was backdated to 28th February 2020 so they didn't have to furlough me.

I also worked 40% of the time as a self-employed children's entertainer and actor. Lockdown meant I immediately lost all work for the foreseeable future. The places I work normally were all closed down, from nightclubs and pubs to theatres and community centres.

I've only been self-employed for two and a half years so I fell through the gap there, and I am not able to get SEISS or other business support, like ARGs etc, because of the 50/50 rule. No profit to date, nor do I pay business rates on my studio premises, just commercial rent, which is £259/month.

I only just about cover costs to stay afloat. Any money I made was reinvested into developing the business after paying living costs.

I did get some Universal Credit, which only helps to just about put food on the table and cover some bills. It doesn't pay my mortgage. This has now ended even though I'm technically now unemployed again.

The last 20% of my earnings was from freelance work as a community artist and project-based workshop facilitator – which has died off too. As an artist I applied for emergency grants and was lucky to get a small one, which would have been invested in diversifying my work but this has only filled the money hole to survive. I have moved in with my elderly dad to help him, who, in return, is paying my mortgage for me out of his paltry pension, what he calls his, 'living will' for me.

I've been applying for jobs, but I feel I'd be taking away from others while all I want to do is carry on working in the entertainment industry, bringing giggles to children's faces and acting the fool making adults laugh. However, I don't want to be the laughing stock of those who have been lucky enough to get some support from the Governments, 'one size solution fits all solution'.

I managed to get work in another part-time, zero hours, minimum wage job, in childcare, but after two months I've now been laid off again with closure of schools in early 2021. My new 'career' hangs in the balance.

The job search continues, possibly in vaccination centres as a temporary solution. In the meantime, I'm gaining more skills, exploring new online courses, and recently was granted a loan towards buying new equipment for a new venture in my music career.

ExcludedUK has been there for me since April 2020. Heartfelt thanks to the founding team, the volunteer admin team who work endlessly round the clock, raising funds, saving lives, fighting for parity, promoting our multifaceted cause and hosting free events.

You're my new family. And gratitude to new friends who I hope can meet up with soon to celebrate our achievements.

We are not going way!

137.

NAME: Jodee

OCCUPATION: Children's Retro Toy Buyer/Seller

REASON FOR EXCLUSION: 50/50 rule

My story is a little bit different from most. I moved to Britain in 2009 because I found my lobster. Me and my lobster got married in 2011 we had a gorgeous boy, who is now nine. In 2013 I got Swine Flu. It took its toll on me and I ended up in a coma for five weeks.

The long-term effects of that are that I now have to deal with and manage my PTSD every day. Our little boy was born with Autism which means that he requires more time from his mum and his dad to help him navigate a world that is not designed to accommodate his needs. So this is what motivated the birth of my business – it's all retro baby.

I started out buying nostalgic toys and selling them on eBay. I registered myself as self-employed and ran with it because it gave me flexibility and I could have a flexible work/life balance that would allow me to always be available for Seth. As time went on, profitability grew as I adapted and changed the business model.

When Seth was eight, we fell pregnant again and had a little girl. I had a difficult pregnancy and needed to have two emergency operations while 20 weeks pregnant in 2019. This was still a profitable year, however. It was down a little bit on 2018 but still a very healthy profit. I felt invincible and accomplished, and proud that I could provide for my family in all aspects of life. I hit the jackpot.

Then 2020 came along. It turned my business from challenging but profitable, to complete devastation. The devastation didn't come from my business collapsing – that can be rebuilt. The devastation comes from being completely shaken and disorientated by trying to solve the puzzle that was effectively unsolvable.

Initially, I stepped up to the challenge of trying to adapt while home-schooling and meeting Seth's needs, but it become apparent a tsunami was coming and I couldn't stop it. I feel like I missed the boat every time the lifeline was thrown out. I could not obtain a Bounce

Back Loan because I run my business as a sole trader using my personal bank account. I was Excluded by the 50-50 rule for the self-employed. I was shaken but not stirred and I still carried on trying to find a solution.

When it occurred to me that my Visa for discretionary leave was running out in February 2021 and the reality was that I could not afford the fees attached to renewing the visa, I hit my lowest point. The thought of having to leave my family if I returned to Australia has been overwhelming, but the heaviest burden of all to carry has been accepting that none of this was my doing. I bounced back after a life-threatening coma, I bounced back after needing to have two operations while 20 weeks pregnant, and I continued while having the challenges of Seth and a new baby to juggle to make my business successful. But I couldn't beat COVID. I felt like I had failed.

It's taking me a long time to accept this is not me failing. I am resilient and I am viable. I've proven this over and over again in my life. What scares me is not how to rebuild by business – I have walked that path so I know the way. What scares me is the Government's role in my life! I feel like I've been in a glass box screaming and no one can hear. Nothing I've faced in my life has caused the same devastation that the inadequate policies the Government continue to rollout!

We as a family have never accessed public funding of any kind and I took pride in being financially independent. I truly hope the foundations of my core beliefs of value and fairness for all can be restored. I now feel like the Government has gone past the point of bring fairness in to play and is now just a token. My fear is that the damage their in-action has caused has left a scar that will run deep for a long time for far too many.

2020 will be remembered for me as the year that broke my heart.

138.

NAME: J

OCCUPATION: Logistics

REASON FOR EXCLUSION: Part PAYE/Self-employed

Seven months of hell.

When I first heard about this virus that was spreading so quickly, I was terrified. I believed the hype about people dropping down dead in the streets of China and I very much supported a Lockdown.

My husband wasn't told to stop working until the end of March and I thought that was too late. We finally got locked down, and at first it was a little exciting to be at home with my family, no work and a promise of "No one will be left behind, we are all in this together."

Oh how quickly that changed!

I set up my business in 2017. I had worked in the Transport & Logistics sector for over 20 years. I had a lot of contacts and spent three years building up my business. Anyone who has tried to set up their own business knows it isn't easy, so I had to work PAYE as well to make sure I had enough income to survive.

I got married on New Years' Eve 2019 and on the first day back in January I secured a new contract which was going to be able to provide me with a full-time wage just from self-employment. I was over the moon! I handed my notice in at my PAYE job in February, just before the Lockdown, but sadly, it was one working day too early to be able to claim furlough. That was kick in the teeth number one.

When Rishi Sunak announced that the self-employed would be able to apply for a grant, I thought to myself "OK, but why do I get one and furloughed people still get paid every month? Surely my stomach will get just as hungry as theirs?" I am 41 now and have paid into the tax system ALL of my life!

Luckily for me, I earned a couple of quid over the 50/50 rule so I had a staggering £580 in May, which covered me from March to August and then in August had another £500.

I was emailing my council every few weeks asking, "How can this be happening to me? How can you just leave someone rot?" And there was Rishi, still coming on the TV, patting himself on the back boasting how, "unprecedented" his support packages were!!!

I applied for Universal Credit and Job Seekers Allowance, and got signed off by my doctor that I was unfit to work, but even that couldn't get me any financial support. Not a penny was coming into my bank, no earnings. We went through our savings, tax bill and wedding money and when that ran out – I was left with nothing.

I have never cried so much in my life, every day was a sheer struggle.

Then, when we thought things couldn't get any worse my husband lost his job as his company buckled under the Lockdown restrictions. We still haven't recovered from this even though we are now managing, unlike some who still haven't had a penny in financial support.

I ask anyone reading these stories to just please, think about how you would cope if you were left for almost 12 months with zero income.

139.
NAME: Marg
OCCUPATION: Driving Instructor
REASON FOR EXCLUSION: 50/50 rule

My name is Marg. I am 68 years old and live and work in North Warwickshire. I have been a self-employed driving instructor for the past nine years following 40 plus years as an employee.

I am Excluded from any Government help under the 50/50 rule. My state pension is more than the net profit from my driving school business, mainly due to the fact that my Franchise with one of the largest driving schools costs approximately £10,000 pa.

During the first Lockdown the driving school waived the franchise fees, which was a big help, and when we were allowed to return to work in July I was able to defer payments for the next eight weeks (thereby racking up debt). Work was intermittent between July and October, with many pupils cancelling due to positive COVID tests or self-isolating.

When the November Lockdown came, I was able to defer franchise payments once again – but by the end of November, I owed the driving school more than £2,000.

We are now in Lockdown number three and again the driving school want full franchise fees (deferred but still a debt) for a car that is unable to earn a penny.

My only income is my state pension which is less than the cost of the car! I live alone, so I have no other income coming into the household and I am too old to qualify for Universal Credit.

Unfortunately, in October my contract with the driving school was discontinued and I had to sign up to a new contract which ties me in for 12 months; there is no way out of this without paying the full fees, plus repaying the debt I have incurred, and continue to incur, until I can get back to work.

I had intended retiring at the end of this year but now see no way of doing this as I will have to continue working to pay back the debts.

I have managed to survive the past ten months using savings, credit cards, Bounce Back Loan etc. But, I feel totally let down by a Government that continues to ignore the 3 million taxpayers in similar situations.

I have contributed to the system for 50 years and paid more than a £100,000 in tax and National Insurance during my working life. I have never claimed a penny, so to be ignored and Excluded from any financial support for such a long period is soul-destroying.

I love my job, but the uncertainty of not knowing how much longer this situation will continue, worrying about how I will repay my debts and how many more years I will need to work, is now taking its toll on my mental health.

My plan to retire at the end of this year is definitely scuppered.

140.
NAME: Raini (Lorraine)
OCCUPATION: Pet Care
REASON FOR EXCLUSION: 50/50 rule

My story really begins before the year 2020.

In 2000, I trained to teach children with special needs, using sign language and patience (that I never knew I had!). I loved my work and never missed a single day in 12 years – through sickness or even when, sadly, my much loved Dad passed away from cancer. My devotion and loyalty to each and every one of those children was what defined me. It made me the best person I could be.

Then in 2017, I had a stroke. The next year flew by, with hospital visits and getting my health and strength back. By the end of 2018, I knew that although physically I had recovered, my brain had not. I was left struggling constantly with exhaustion and brain fog. I also quickly realised that I could no longer cope with the shouts of "Miss, Miss, Miss" all day long. So I made the difficult decision to leave.

In Dec 2018, instead of going down the benefit route, I decided to start my own Dog Walking and Pet Care Service called 'Paws Pampered Pets'. My love and passion for animals came from my labradoodle, Seren, who is my absolute world. I spent December setting up advertising, websites and Facebook business accounts. I walked miles, posting 4,500 cards through letterboxes in icy conditions, around all the local housing developments, feeling optimistic if I heard a 'woof' or saw a cat-flap fitted, as they hopefully could be my future clients!

The business very quickly became successful. Within ten months, two employees joined the team, who loved animals as much as I did. All was going along so well.

Another happy customer at Paws Pampered Pets

Then March 2020 COVID hit! Our world was shattered – within hours of the Prime Minister's 'Stay At Home' statement, the cancellations came flooding in.

Suddenly, our diary that was full of bookings, right through until February 2021, was empty! Clients working from home, all travel cancelled – our Dog Walking and home visits were no longer required.

Not realising how long we as a business, would be affected by the virus, I was at least relieved that I received a small private pension which would hopefully see me through financially. When the Government began releasing details of all the support packages, I naively thought I would be included. However, as my business was new, my start-up costly and therefore profits low, I was Excluded from the SEISS scheme due to the 50/50 rule.

I was expected to live on £75 a week. That's when reality hit! Bills, food, essentials and, sadly, high monthly vet's charges all to be paid for – but how and with what???

The Government I've paid taxes to for over 30 years had abandoned me, at the one time that I asked for help.

Over the last ten months, I've had every emotion possible. I've had highs and very bad lows, struggling more than I ever thought possible.

I've had my credit cards declined in shops, no money in my purse and, humiliatingly, had to ask for help from people including my lovely 85-year old disabled Mum, who lives with me. I've sold my work van, jewelry and other assets and even shut down my website. I'm desperately trying to save money whilst keeping the business afloat.

I've always been a positive person, constantly looking for the silver linings. I even have the saying, *'Life isn't about waiting for the storm to pass, it's about learning to dance in the rain'* on my wall. I want to be that woman again! That's who I used to be, not the someone who I don't recognise and don't particularly like anymore.

I look to the future now totally differently. I'm resigned to what will be, will be, and there isn't anything really that I can do to change it. I don't know if Paws Pampered Pets will be here in a year's time.

All I know is that I will be. I won't be the person I used to be again, I will be stronger and more resilient and I will get through this.

My Dad, when I was little, always told me I could be anyone or do anything I wanted. That, "I could fly." Hence the small butterfly tattoo on my wrist. So yes, my future will be brighter again and hopefully anything is possible and I will learn to fly again…

141.
NAME: Deborah
OCCUPATION: Freelance Costumer
REASON FOR EXCLUSION: 50/50 rule

My name is Deborah and I work in Costume for Film, TV and Theatre, and as a freelancer I take on a variety of jobs throughout the year for different companies. I am fully self-employed but some of the companies I work for insist I pay my tax through PAYE (not my choice).

During the years looked at for SEISS, I paid just over 50% of my tax through Multiple Short Term PAYE contracts , the rest through my UTC.

So – I paid FULL tax for over 35 years but received ZERO SEISS, ZERO furlough and I was not eligible for Grants as do not have business premises.

I have lived off my savings since March, but have been lucky enough to have had 11 weeks work which put some money in the bank, and I have recently started another three month contract.

Others are not so fortunate, and reading their stories makes me determined to keep fighting for parity for me and them.

Shame on this Government.

Thanks for all your work ExcludedUK.

142.
NAME: Claire
OCCUPATION: Event Management
REASON FOR EXCLUSION: Limited Company Director

I'm the sole director of a Limited Company and pre-pandemic I was travelling Business Class around the world with my luxury automotive clients, delivering prestigious invitation-only events to UHNWIs (Ultra High Net Worth Individuals).

I was super-organised, hardworking, very sociable, and never without a manicure! Today I'm sat in loungewear, hair scraped back into a bun, no makeup and broken nails. I've lost my mojo and my purpose; I feel depleted and my spark has gone.

When taking the leap to go freelance in 2017, my clients demanded I operate as a Limited Company. Business boomed and the diary was fully booked into 2020.

Then the pandemic hit and all contracts were cancelled in March. The live events industry was the first to be closed and we'll no doubt be the last to return. I've sacrificed so much in my personal life, working crazy hours to build my career then, just like that, it's gone, with no idea if and when it will return. It's completely devastating.

It's not as easy as, 'just get another job' during a pandemic, so the stress and anxiety of not knowing when I'll be earning again has been unbearable at times. I live alone so my mortgage and bills are solely my responsibility; I have no one sharing this burden. Yet I feel like I'm one of the 'lucky' ones without dependents and with savings to live off. I feel frustrated with the Government and it feels so unjust that other taxpayers had their income supported and so their savings remain untouched. I've always paid into, not taken out from, the Public Purse, yet in my time of need I've been abandoned.

Despite incredibly supportive family and friends, I have felt isolated. Still having their jobs means they can't fully relate to what I'm going through. Finding ExcludedUK was a godsend. The understanding, empathy, kindness, sincerity, generosity, and support from the group restored my faith in humanity amidst this storm. It is such a relief to speak to people who relate to all of the emotions I have been experiencing.

I used to burn myself out, all to have a successful career and savings, at the expense of me-time. The past year, I've been given time; time to slow down, to take better care of myself, and to enjoy and connect with nature.

My focus for the future will be to live a happy life doing things I love with the people I love, as that's what I think is most important. I hope that, once life returns to some kind of 'normal', ExcludedUK will remain a supportive community for each other. I'm looking forward to the day we get to meet in person and celebrate the relentless pursuit for parity of support together.

143.
NAME: Bev
OCCUPATION: Massage Therapist
REASON FOR EXCLUSION: Changed from Limited Company to Sole Trader

A tribute to Mum and Dad.

I view myself as a positive realist. I was raised during the 1960s in Bolton, an industrial town. I'm proud of my heritage.

I'm thankful for the way my parents created a home and nurtured me, ensuring I was safe. I was nourished emotionally, mentally and physically. I can never remember being hungry. This is the foundation on which I flourished.

How well I remember that yellow Formica table round which we sat each evening. We laughed, we made decisions, we discussed, and importantly I was encouraged to make my own decisions. It is this foundation that is supporting me through this time.

I left home at 18 to launch my professional career. Initially I was employed by a major PLC. I had a high profile job, a good salary, received brilliant training, and had a whole range of experiences in the 13 plus years I worked for them.

Since 1989, I have been either a director of a Limited Company or a sole trader. I have supported myself throughout and I've strived to gain degree-level qualifications. I have paid tax of many kinds every year since 1975, including corporation tax and personal tax.

Then, without invitation, along came COVID-19. As a full time massage therapist my business closed and my income disappeared overnight.

Initially it seemed good; I was living in the Cornish countryside, I love outdoor exercise and the weather was glorious. I was ignorant to the implications that because I had ceased trading as a Limited Company in December 2019, to become a sole trader on 1st January 2020, I had become Excluded.

I miss my clients, my work and my hugs. Synchronicity or Coincidence? On pure impulse I sold my house in 2018 and moved into rented. In February 2020 my inheritance dropped into my account. Mum and Dad, even though no longer here, still had their arms wrapped firmly around me.

My car died on the A30 on my way home to Cornwall after I had spent Mothers Day with my daughters. It was Lockdown eve. I had been looking at new cars just that day. I placed an offer on a flat in Gloucestershire the week before actual Lockdown.

I worked such long hours supporting myself and my desired lifestyle. I was buried deep in my perceived understanding of the world. I'm having time to catch up with the real world now. I may never go back to paid work but what I do feel is that I, and people like me, can utilise our new-found time and voices to challenge and question authority and not to assume that everything is being done in our best interest.

Watch out world! We are a community of hard working citizens, entrepreneurs, and innovators who have supported ourselves and made a significant contribution to the economy and we have been Excluded.

I feel like I have been personally insulted too. I am not a fraud. I have never abused the tax system. I recognise and am thankful daily that had it not been for my parent's vision and planning, that I would not be able to do this. I am thankful that we hugged to the end of their lives and were able to say goodbye.

They wanted me to thrive in all aspects of my life. I did before and I shall again.

144.
NAME: Lisa
OCCUPATION: Swim School Owner
REASON FOR EXCLUSION: Ltd Company Director

Hello, I'm Lisa, a small, private swim school owner, Mum of two amazing daughters, long term partner to Dave, the most wonderful man ever and the father of my children.

I'd just like you to know a little about my family before I explain the devastating impact of being Excluded.

In 2010 I started my swim school with the emphasis that they would be top quality lessons taught on a 3:1 ratio, so kids would progress properly, learning water safety skills as a priority. Within two years the number of kids taught at the swim school grew to 300. I knew every kid's ability and every parent's first name, it was like a huge family and I loved it.

Over the years Dave and the girls also qualified as swim teachers to help out. I was so extremely proud of our swim school, seeing the kids' water skills and confidence grow was priceless. However, life is life and sometimes the water gets rough, very rough.

In 2010, our eldest daughter Elle had to undergo brain surgery to treat hydrocephalus. Elle was originally diagnosed with scoliosis but after an MRI scan at Alder Hey children's hospital, water on the brain was also detected. The same year, Dave lost both his parents – his Mum to cancer within two weeks of diagnosis and his Dad six months later. The funeral was held the same day Elle was admitted hospital.

In 2015, Elle had to undergo eight-hour spinal surgery to correct a pronounced curvature in her spine. And then in 2018, our youngest daughter Leah starts to have mental health struggles and is self-harming, largely due to pressures at school and poor self-image.

Fast forward to January 2020, and I'm struggling with depression. Most days I have a huge black cloud looming over me. What keeps me going is the thought of my two beautiful daughters having no Mum. I know only too well how it feels to lose a parent, my Dad died when I was 15 due to alcoholism. I've had to remain strong for many years but the buried pain and grief is rearing its ugly head. Some days I can't bring myself to work or reply to messages, it's too hard. Luckily my partner and two girls are able to teach in my place, dodging questions from customers, "Where's Lisa?" The parents don't know I'm poorly, I feel like a complete failure.

As January comes to an end, I become conscious of a big shift in the news. Wuhan has been entirely locked down. Elle is also working in a busy city restaurant so I plead with her to be extra careful whilst serving customers and to wash her hands constantly. She, as many other youngsters her age did, felt I was overreacting.

Beginning of March, a global pandemic is clearly apparent and I'm extremely nervous. With no protective procedures enforced yet, I'm scared for my staff, the kids and their families. On Wednesday 11th March, I decide to close the swim school. I know in my heart that money is not a justifiable reason to remain operating whilst people's health is at risk.

Mid March. My eldest daughter is told to remain off work for the weekend due to a dry cough and an overwhelming sense of tiredness. She then proceeds to lose her sense of taste and smell which strikes us as unusual (anosmia was not on the list of COVID symptoms at this point).

On the 23rd March Lockdown finally happens and I'm proud of myself for halting the lessons early and the majority of parents are very supportive of my decision.

Soon enough though, parents start to ask about fees, refunds etc. I'm convinced the Government will help businesses that have been forced to close. Rishi Sunak states no one has been forgotten and I cry with relief as he states the self-employed with profits under £50,000 a year are eligible and that certainly applies to me. However, the elation is short lived. When I call HMRC, they tell me I'm only entitled to £575 per month furlough as a Limited Company Director, meaning my income will be £30k short over a 12 month period. I'm also ineligible for grants as I don't have any premises (we hire school pools). Immediately I call Dave in complete panic, feeling confused, scared, enraged, upset, overwhelmed. I have a panic attack and fight to breathe, I don't know what we're going to do. The dark cloud has become even darker.

I then begin to hear of acquaintances who are working, but simultaneously claiming SEISS of £2,500. They're doing home renovations and planning holidays. Enraged, frustrated and distraught, I feel a huge sense of worthlessness settle. Why haven't we been treated equally?

Dave says to me, "Imagine rations being distributed this way in WW2, giving people five rations but then giving some people one ration or no rations at all!"

I cry most days as I simply can't stand the injustice of it all. The news becomes an endless stream of heartache, imagery of people dying from COVID, struggling to breath, mental health spiralling and now suicides due to being Excluded from financial help, it's all too much.

I do my best to hide the tears from my family some days, as I know I have to stay strong. I don't want my girls to worry about their Mum, but the sense of being completely left to rot by this Government takes its toll. I'm so upset for everyone Excluded, the heartbreaking stories are neverending. I'm struggling, really struggling.

The second Lockdown in November is announced, the swim school has been open six weeks since March. Shortly after, I reach a new low; I've drunk far too much alcohol and my mind isn't my own. I wander in to the main road outside my house, standing in front of cars wanting them to hit me.

I want this Government to know how it feels. How could they be so cruel and unfair to so many hardworking families throughout a global pandemic? To people who've worked for most of their life and paid their taxes?

I have just one question to this Government, why have you done this to us – just why?

145.
NAME: Steve
OCCUPATION: Coach Driver
REASON FOR EXCLUSION: 50/50 rule

I have been doing coach driving most of my life on and off. Two and a half years ago I was asked to cover a school run for a local firm. At the time I was doing a local bus run part-time and after the school run one became two and so on, the coach operator asked me to go full time. Having worked in the industry before, and for my own selfish reasons, that was a deffo 'no', as your life becomes theirs, so I said I would go self-employed. This meant I could say no to jobs and pick my own. This lasted about six months and then the transport manager had a word with me and said HMRC are clamping down on self-employed drivers and said the best thing you can do is start a Limited Company.
I started in April 2019, and by July I had four other companies I was working for, doing local stuff like football trips etc. One company, Peter Carol, specialised in high class travel and another from Sheffield did tours of the UK and the Continent. I had a really good year.

Then COVID struck and coach travel dried up over night.

Steve parked outside Derby FC

I did do some work in November 2020 for a couple of weeks, taking nurses to hospital, but that's been cancelled now. I have just been able to furlough myself, which is a help but only pays some bills. That's about it. If the schools open I will hopefully be doing runs – but that's only five hours a day.

146.
NAME: Lisa
OCCUPATION: Freelance Salon Supplier
REASON FOR EXCLUSION: 50/50 rule

Having had various PAYE job roles, with no gaps might I add, and a gleaming 30+ year history of paying Tax and National Insurance, I made the decision to transition to become self-employed, full time, as a freelance agent in the trade hair & barber supply industry in December 2018.

I'm a people-person and utilise those skills to offer salons the support they need, providing them with innovative new products and then enjoying watching their businesses flourish.

When COVID Lockdown hit in March 2020, I'd already paid my first 2018/19 self-employment tax bill. As it was only four months of trading from the year prior, it was slightly lower income overall than I was used to. Momentum quickly grew through 2019 and I remain in the same job today, but it's been hard to stay positive this year after not receiving any help whatsoever from any scheme this Government made so readily and easily available to others. I feel discriminated against, abandoned and forgotten.

I have to admit, I was relieved when Rishi Sunak announced the SEISS support scheme as I obviously couldn't supply trade business during closures. However, I soon learnt that due to my non-earning profits being lower than my PAYE for the year 2018/19, I didn't qualify for SEISS. It's called the 50/50 rule.

I was shocked and worried and so I appealed to HMRC, thinking they must have made a mistake! But was informed I couldn't get any financial help, even though my 2019-20 self-assessment was about to be submitted. I asked if this more current record could be used, but I was told no.

It was then suggested by the Government that SEISS is too open to fraud and on occasions we were referred to as 'fraudsters' – a term I vigourously dispute being applicable to me. I was, and in fact still am, shocked by this. They have all my records, I pay on time, I use an accountant, why on earth can't they help me?

I wrote to my local MP, Fabian Hamilton. Twice. But never received any reply. I'd have been grateful for any advice or support. I've tagged him in tweets, but again no replies. He is clearly not interested in my fight for parity. He won't ever get my vote.

What I'm still struggling with today is that my self-employed business during 2019 was great, I was regularly earning more income than I was used to, and month on month there was clear growth. I can't comprehend why this couldn't be used to 'assess my circumstances'.

Due to my income being reduced during Lockdown, I've had to rely on other people for financial support to help pay personal bills, household bills and food purchases. This goes against my very independent nature of being a self-supporting person. It's been a year from hell, and whilst I'm thankful I have people to lean on, not everyone does.

Tragically a family member and a close friend both found this to be all too much and in July of 2020 they took their own lives. This Government has blood on their hands, and I'm not sure I can ever forgive them.

I'm personally Excluded from not just SEISS, but all support packages – the Bounce Back Loan, benefits and grants. I have no premises, I don't have a business bank account as it's not needed for a freelance position, and as a freelancer I'm considered a home worker. I didn't even qualify for the local discretionary grants either. The local councils were all awarded extra funding to offer grants to those previously Excluded BUT each council had their own criteria and Leeds decided not to help 'homeworkers', so again I'm Excluded from any support.

My last resort was Universal Credit, but due to my husband having some recent inheritance savings over their threshold, money that is NOT mine, and me having 'tax savings', I didn't qualify for that either.

Ironically, just last week I was reminded to pay my tax bill on time – after a year of reduced income from no fault of my own, and having had no financial support whatsoever from any scheme.

I hope Rishi Sunak and Boris Johnson reconsider financial support for the Excluded and apologise for their ignorance in that "No one will be left behind" quote!

147.

NAME: Shauna & Jordan

OCCUPATION: Self-employed Electrician

REASON FOR EXCLUSION: 50/50 rule

When the news broke that the country would basically be shutting down and that there would be support packages, we thought we'd be ok. My partner Jordan is a self-employed electrician, he finished his apprenticeship in August 2018 and became fully self-employed during that month. This is the one and only reason, that he didn't qualify for the SEISS scheme.

He had earned more that tax year while being an apprentice than he did for the remainder of the tax year being fully self-employed. This means that the SEISS scheme classes him as having 'two incomes', which in no way reflects his financial situation now, three years later.

All we could think about was, "they'll change their mind", "they've got to include us, surely", "they'll announce support for us in the next update". These things never happened. I was seven months pregnant when the country went into Lockdown, and we faced having our newborn with no financial support from the Government whatsoever, not even qualifying for Universal Credit as we had savings put away for our newborn, and I'm a part-time student with the Open University alongside my full-time job. This left us with a joint income of £600 a month, which was my maternity allowance, down from a joint income of £4,300.

The £600 allowance barely covered our mortgage and council tax, let alone anything else. I remember crying on the phone to HRMC, nine months pregnant, because we were so worried that this would go on and on and our savings would just be depleted.

We are blessed with an amazing family who have continued to help us financially in a way that we'll never be able to pay back or thank them for, and I dread to think of our situation if we weren't so lucky. We used to have faith in our Government. We've studied, worked, been entrepreneurs, paid our taxes, saved and saved to get money behind us to secure a future for us and our baby.

Being a part of the ExcludedUK group has made things so much easier, despite losing £18,000 of our income since March. There are amazing people making us feel like we aren't alone, and we thank them all. We now have an absolutely fantastic baby boy, Jack, who is eight months old, and amazingly beat COVID-19 at six months old. He makes us smile and laugh every day.

148.

NAME: Paula

OCCUPATION: Community Outreach Tutor

REASON FOR EXCLUSION: Denied Furlough

It is a fundamental human right to be able to work and earn a living. We were told to stop working and stay home. The majority of the population was compensated but 3 million others are still waiting.....

I'm Paula. Single parent to teenage twin boys. I worked in a school as a teaching assistant and forest school teacher for over eight years in a primary school. The job was great as I was able to work around being a full-time mum of my boys and not worry about weekends, holidays etc.

In February 2020 I decided I would make the move and change my job – still working in education, but for an agency. Working as an Outreach Mentor/Tutor to children who cannot access education, the move was an exciting one where I could work fewer hours for the same money. I was looking forward to bettering myself.

I left my job in the primary school on Wednesday 18th March. The following Monday, the UK was put into Lockdown due to COVID and my new job was put on hold.

At first I thought everything will be OK, this will only last a couple of weeks. Then Rishi Sunak announced his furlough scheme and how people like me, who were between jobs, could go back to our old employers and ask them to furlough us. I thought that's brilliant, because I worked in a school and surely a school cannot deny me furlough? So I contacted my school who got back to me to say that they cannot furlough me – as they are a publicly funded school, they cannot access the furlough system. They also couldn't take me back because someone had already taken my place there.

I wasn't happy with this and was sure something was wrong, so I contacted my local MP Fiona Bruce. Fiona wrote back to me with correspondence from my local council. The school was right. The Government's guidelines on furlough wouldn't permit them to furlough me.

Following this, I found out I wasn't eligible for Job Seekers Allowance because I did have a job – it was just on hold. I couldn't collect Universal Credit because, as a single parent on a low income, I already received Tax Credits and Working Tax Credits. Even though my tax credits didn't cover my outgoings, this was my income for the next four months of Lockdown until things started to ease.

It is now over ten months since this all began. I am still working for the agency but my work is sporadic. Since March 2020, up until the end of January 2021, I have worked less than 200 hours for the agency. I am very grateful that I have my boyfriend and family who have helped us through this terrible time, but my mental health has taken a beating. It isn't easy writing this but it needs to be said, we have been left behind, but we are not going away. We will fight for justice.

149.

NAME: Rosie

OCCUPATION: Accounts/Bookkeeper

REASON FOR EXCLUSION: 50/50 rule

I am Rosie – a divorced mother of five, grandmother of five. I am 67 and I live in the West Midlands. I have been an accounts technician and bookkeeper for eleven years.

I just want to share that I feel belittled and overlooked completely as an Excluded sole trader. It feels like I am in a bad dream and I am like a sort of Alice in Wonderland who has fallen down a black hole. I have been waiting in expectation for months to have someone rescue me and give me a hand back up, and yes, even an apology for not noticing me down there.

The first two quarters I would not have claimed the SEISS grant – I had sufficient work that had piled up that would keep me going and that I could still bill for. But by September, I could see my income was going to drop right off because, as a book-keeper, the companies I recorded transactions for had had no transactions! A beauty clinic, a dentist, a private physiotherapist. All forced to discontinue or minimise trading.

I was denied help because I receive a State Pension, plus another small personal pension of less than £200 a month. So it was the 50/50 rule. I have never understood why the pension gross figures were assessed against the net profit figures of my bookkeeping business. Or why there could not be a sliding scale.

Try living on this small amount with five kids and five grandkids and the demands of life. I still have to pay my membership subscriptions of my certified body under which I am licenced, my professional indemnity and my ICO fees.

I am also a carer, but this has been split in two in terms of income I can expect, due to only being there for essential work.

At 67, I would have liked to be able to retire gracefully but I will always have to continue to work to make ends meet. Fortunately, I LOVE my work and my clients. I have been self-employed for 11 years. And I would very much hope my clients will come back when COVID is defeated.

I have watched people in ExcludedUK desperately trying to hang on to their businesses and even the roofs over their heads. I have watched people struggling with not just losing family members to COVID but dealing with loneliness, lack of self esteem and being Excluded on top of it.

There are 28,000 people on the ExcludedUK Facebook Group who support each other and who are kind and caring. (Not to forget the rest of the three million) They have done nothing wrong, are not committing any fraud, have paid taxes for years and just need to be given a hand at this time and parity with how the rest of the British workforce have been treated.

The Government have turned a deaf ear and a blind eye to the cries of many ordinary citizens of England, Scotland, Northern Ireland, and Wales and even to the likes of Mayors, MPs, Martin Lewis, leaders of other Political Parties, countless interviews on TV and a full day of peoples' stories on the BBC and they still do NOTHING – they don't even give an answer.

It's like being at a horrific Mad Hatters Tea Party (to go back to the Alice in Wonderland analogy) where NOTHING makes any sense. The treasury and chancellor are asleep at the table and too many people are wearing hats they do not deserve!

150.
NAME: Leigh Hodgkinson
OCCUPATION: Children's Author / Illustrator
REASON FOR EXCLUSION: 50% Rule

I am a children's author/illustrator and children's tv series creator.

I have been self-employed and paid tax and national insurance for all of the 20 years of my working life.

I am excluded from SEISS due to the 50% rule. This is because the one and only PAYE job I have ever had (lasting only 2 years) was the very time that HMRC judged for support eligibility. For that time, my PAYE income was 0.4% over 50%- so I got (and still get) nothing. The ridiculousness of it was that my PAYE job finished a year before the pandemic even hit us in March 2020, so their out-of-date information that was used to determine my fate hasn't actually been relevant since March 2019.

Leigh Hodgkinson showing what it feels to be Excluded.

151.
NAME: Stephen
OCCUPATION: Private Guided Tours/Ye Olde England Tours
REASON FOR EXCLUSION: Trading profits over £50k

I created Ye Olde England Tours in 2013 after a series of redundancies in the previous few years. I'd rather work hard and earn my own living than take the easy way out and live a life on benefits.

I haven't taken a day off in seven years. I worked every single day, even Christmas Days and often 18 hour days at that. I liked my job. I've won several awards and I have a huge array of clients from around the world as well as notable figures and government institutions in the UK.

Over the years I built up Ye Olde England Tours and employed nine people on a freelance basis. I always tried to hire people that might not easily find employment elsewhere. I have an old fashioned outlook of using my position to help people just as much as the old fashioned work ethic. Knowing I was doing OK in life, I overpaid my taxes to do more for the NHS than just clap for it. What good did I get from that?

On the 6th February 2020 I was pushed under a tube train whilst giving a tour. I worked another four and a half hours in agony with a hairline fracture in my leg. That was to be my last full day's work of 2020. Here we are on 19th February 2021 and I've not worked since or had any help at all.

Rishi promised no-one would be left behind or without hope and yet I am the very definition of being left behind and without hope.

He knows it too, as he has ignored several letters from me and I've been on Sky News, on many radio stations and in national newspaper features. It's hard not to come to the conclusion that he and his Government just don't care, because it would be so very, very easy for them to prove they do care.

Stephen giving a special Sherlock charity tour for BBC Comic Relief with two rather special guests.

Along with some other issues, I also have chronic asthma – so I have in effect spent the entire year shielding on my own. If I speak for more than 15 or 20 minutes, I go hoarse from spending weeks upon weeks and month after month waiting for this hell to finish in my often freezing and leaking home, a broken car and eating food bank food.
I have been abandoned by the state and repeatedly discriminated against. Whilst understandably no effort is too great to save the lives of virus victims, my life doesn't seem to matter one bit.

As everyone else was paid to stay at home and later paid to eat out, and as idiots crammed onto beaches and jumped off cliffs, or rioted in London and so dragged out the whole pandemic, I remained at home; alone, unsupported, and in effect left to die. Even worse, the Government closed down my industry and actually made it illegal for me to do my job.

Of course, it is very understandable why it did so, but it is also inconceivably wrong that I would not be supported or compensated in any way. Even Russia paid people to stay at home. Rishi tells us we are unviable, but my tours have been rated the number one authentic London experience by Viator (Trip Advisor). I've even done tours on behalf of the Government and civil service.

My Lockdown project resulted in my writing a number one best-selling book, *Secret Gardens of the City of London.* I have a BA Honors Degree, a Masters Degree, and can speak multiple languages. I don't need to retrain. I am already the best at what I do, which is more than can be said for our pound-shop Churchill impersonator in #10 Downing Street or the billionaire who lives next door.

Yet, being Excluded has given me the chance to help or inspire countless others, not just here but around the world, and through ExcludedUK I have met the most wonderful, hardworking and inspirational people and formed new friendships and contacts that will last a life-time, a sort of wartime camaraderie so to speak.

Normally when I am out and about in London I help homeless people, not just at Christmas time, but every day. I assist struggling police making arrests until backup arrives. I go out of my way to help everyone but now, after over 30 years of paying tax and being the very model of a good citizen, the one time I need help – not special help, but just the same help as everyone else has received – I get nothing.

I won't ever explain to a tourist about democracy; it being a hollow sham.

I won't ever put anyone else before myself nor do my bit for a country that sees me as a firmly second class citizen albeit not yet forced to sew a Star of David on my coat.

I won't ever try and better myself more than I have to, or go without holidays, or get up extra early to squeeze in more work.

I won't ever forget the food, clothes and donations from around the world just as I won't ever forget those closer to home that did nothing.

Most of all I won't ever, ever forgive those who left me to die alone and in poverty for over a year. I hope they rot in hell.

About Excluded UK

The following information is taken from the Excluded website to assist those reading this in 2021 who may be Excluded and for those in the media and would like to know more.

ExcludedUK is a grassroots, volunteer-run, not-for-profit organisation working towards bringing about an end to the Exclusions in the UK Government's COVID-19 financial support measures across all employment statuses, circumstances, professions and industries. These Exclusions have led to significant disparities within the support offered, resulting in unfairness, injustice, discrimination and severe hardship for those affected.

ExcludedUK was established on the founding principles of inclusivity, collaboration, resilience, empowerment, transparency and integrity. As such, these principles lie at the heart of our vision and strategy. ExcludedUK was registered as a Community Interest Company on 30 May 2020, with the clear purpose of working for community benefit at large as a longer-term sustainable organisation. We chose to set up as a CIC, aware that the Government may not be willing to provide a quick and easy fix for those Excluded from support, despite all our calls for urgency. Therefore, we were all too aware that there may well be work to do in the longer term, not least to offer ongoing guidance to those who have thus far gone several months without meaningful support and on little to no incomes. We wished to have a legal status and to put in place good governance, while remaining a not-for-profit organisation.

COVID-19 and the ensuing Lockdown presented the most unforeseen challenges to many individuals and businesses across the UK. While Government support packages have provided much needed support for many, there remain some three million taxpayers – 10% of the UK workforce, who find themselves Excluded from meaningful support, leaving large cracks within these measures.

From new starters, those in between jobs or due to start new jobs after 19 March, those denied furlough, the newly self-employed and new businesses, those earning less than 50% of their income from self-employment, +£50k trading profits, those on maternity, parental or adoption leave, those on PAYE freelance short-term contracts, small Limited Company owner-directors and businesses ineligible for grants, and a whole range of personal circumstances affecting eligibility through no fault of their own… The list goes on.

Livelihoods are at stake, businesses risk folding or may have folded already. Many individuals have been on extremely low to no income since March.

ExcludedUK Aims and objectives
As an organisation, we aim to play a crucial role in facilitating support and assistance on multiple levels, both for now and into the future. The wider effects of the pandemic may be far-reaching and long-lasting and we intend to continue our efforts to provide ongoing broader help and support.

Our key objectives are to raise awareness by engaging with national and local press and media, lobbying for support and communicating the concerns of those Excluded and wider messaging around the issues they face to relevant parliamentary bodies and MPs, while maintaining dialogue with them as well as with industry bodies. ExcludedUK equally exists to offer wider support – signposting towards resources on mental health, counselling and well-being, business guidance and networking, debt advice, upskilling and training, as well as fundraising in order to seek to provide such support. Most importantly, our hope is that our efforts can help propel affected individuals and businesses forward in the face of adversity resulting from COVID-19 and being Excluded from Government support, while equally working together in seeking to help each other emerge from this crisis.

We Are ExcludedUK and we exist to:

- raise awareness of the three million UK taxpayers Excluded from UK Government COVID-19 support
- lobby for support and communicate the concerns of those Excluded and wider messaging around the issues they face to relevant parliamentary bodies, MPs and industry bodies, while maintaining dialogue with them as well as with industry bodies

- conduct research and data analysis to inform our advocacy, through publications and reports
- provide a support mechanism those affected, facilitating advice and support where possible
- signpost affected individuals and businesses to resources on mental health, counselling and well-being, business guidance and networking, debt advice, upskilling and training
- provide and a safe space for discussion, to share stories and concerns, through a community forum and private Facebook group
- fundraise in order to seek to provide support

ExcludedUK is working towards bringing an end to exclusions in UK Government COVID-19 support for:

- Newly self-employed
- Those earning less than 50% income from self-employment
- Self-employed with +£50k trading profits
- PAYE freelancers
- New starters
- Those made redundant before 19 Mar
- Those denied furlough
- Directors paid PAYE Annually
- Directors paid in Dividends
- Directors of Companies not in Profit
- New Businesses
- Businesses ineligible for Business Grants
- Those in maternity/parental/adoption leave
- Those whose personal circumstances have affected entitlement to support eg. pensions, bereavement allowance, carer's allowance, students

ExcludedUK aims to provide as much support as possible through a community forum, while our hugely supportive community group can be found at:
www.Facebook.com/groups/ExcludedUK
www.excludeduk.org

Statement from ExcludedUK by Rachel Flower, a founding member.

The stories you have read in this book are the true and human reality behind the statistics. When we came together under the ExcludedUK campaign in May 2020 we had no idea of the uphill mountain that lay ahead. We naively thought that we would shine a helpful light on the problem, be part of the solution, and pull together in the wake of the Covid-19 pandemic to quickly get people onto an equal footing to weather the storm. The words of the Chancellor March 2020 were clear: 'You will not face this alone. We want to look back on this time and remember how, in the face of a generation-defining moment, we undertook a collective national effort - and we stood together. It's on all of us.'

https://www.gov.uk/government/speeches/the-chancellor-rishi-sunak-provides-an-updated-statement-on-coronavirus

This was swiftly followed by a further announcement : 'To you, I say this: You have not been forgotten. We will not let you behind. We are all in this together.'

https://www.gov.uk/government/speeches/chancellor-outlines-new-coronavirus-support-measures-for-the-self-employed

It was on these words and this promise that hard working British people stayed home, to protect the NHS and to save lives. They did their civic duty. It was several months later once the small print of the support schemes were published and people began to apply and find themselves ineligible and rejected on spurious, arbitrary grounds ... that the messaging changed.

On the 29th May 2020 the Chancellor said 'But I do want to acknowledge that we haven't been able to support everyone in the exact way they would want.

I understand some people have felt frustrated. But you were not and have not been forgotten. Even if you don't qualify for the furlough or self-employment schemes, we've provided a wide range of support…from discounted loans, to tax cuts, mortgage holidays and enhanced welfare.'

https://www.gov.uk/government/speeches/chancellors-statement-on-coronavirus-covid-19-29-may-2020

Since that time ExcludedUK has continued to raise its collective voice for justice. We have called for parity between taxpayers and asked that attempts be made to fairly close the gaps in the support schemes so that people should not be unnecessarily disadvantaged. For us all to stand shoulder to shoulder as a nation, we need to know that people will be treated fairly and equitably and given a chance to weather the storm. We have never asked for anything more than fair access to support for all. In particular we have raised concerns about the division in society caused by unequal access to the schemes, and the impact on mental health and well-being upon those who have been left out in the cold without any justification. People who have paid their taxes in full over decades of work and yet in their hour of need were left unable to claim even basic living expenses. These same people will be required to continue paying into the tax system in the years ahead, a system and a democracy that has failed them.

We are proud that we have raised our collective voices against this injustice. It has been heartbreaking to see so many people, households and families falling into debt and hardship especially when it could have been so avoided by addressing policy issues early on in the process. There has been overwhelming evidence that these people were excluded through no fault of their own, with the Treasury sub committee and the National Audit Office together with organisations such as Standard Life and Resolution Foundation providing data and evidence to back up our own findings.

Through it all, we have seen within the ExcludedUK community incredible kindness, support for each other, compassion, solidarity and that has restored my faith in humanity. I do believe that good comes out of adversity and that the affected people can rise again, leaning on each other to recover despite the terrible despair and frustration of being cast aside by the government that they expected to do the right thing. This story is not over. We will continue to fight for justice but we will also continue to champion and support those excluded to ensure that they find ways to recover from the devastation and harsh treatment they have endured. I would like to thank the team of volunteers at ExcludedUK who have come together and shown incredible resilience and compassion and of course to each and every member of the community who has stood strong in the face of adversity. Thank you to Stephen for publishing this collection of stories so that the voices of the people can be captured in history forever and their voices will not be lost. These stories matter just like every person within our society matters. That is the root of equality and inclusivity and that is why we created ExcludedUK.

It's on all of us.

Glossary

APPG – All Party Parliamentary Group. A cross-party group of MPs seeking to address the stark short-comings in government support.

ARG – Additional Restrictions Grant. Discretionary grants which the Excluded can apply for since November2020. Each council sets its own conditions and payment limits.

Bounce Back Loan – A government initiative to help small businesses, but crucially this is a loan and not a grant or non-repayable payment.

CJRS – Coronavirus Job Retention Scheme

ESA – Employment Support Allowance. A state benefit which is aimed at people with health and disabilities which inhibit their ability to work. Often pays less even than Universal Credit.

Furlough – A government support scheme which the majority of the working population were able to take advantage of. Essentially being paid to stay at home with up top 80% of a salary being paid by the state and the balance by the employer.

Gaps in Support – a catchall term to reference those unable to benefit from state support.

HMRC – Her Majesty's Revenues & Customs.

JSA – Job Seekers Allowance, a form of state benefit for those seeking employment.

SEISS – Self-Employment Income Support Scheme. A government grant scheme to which many Excluded members are in illegible in whole or in part.

UC – Universal Credit. Another supposed safety net but many are unable to receive this, particularly if they have savings.

Index List of Contributors to £xcluded Voices

59	Jeanette	Hairdresser and Barber
62	Jo Bishop	Photographer
63	Helen	PhiBrows Microblading Artist
65	Steffani Benton-Martyn	Singing Teacher
67	Fiona and Husband	Training and Consultancy Business
68	Fiona and Chris Hughes	Creative Clothing Solutions
70	Steph	Printmaking Teacher
72	Janice Hugh	Complementary Healthcare Practitioner and Teacher
73	Dominique	Dog Walking and Facilities
76	Tracey Harper-Holbrook	Yoga Teacher
79	Hellen	Online Retailer
80	Emma Sheldrake	Groom and Rider
81	Anita Mandl	Independent Tour Operator
83	Susie Reynolds	Specialist Educational Assessor; Holiday Lets
85	Kate Wharton	Psychologist
86	Kelley Costigan	Actress; Sports & Remedial Massage Therapist
88	Lu	Trainer and Educator in Primary Healthcare
91	Giovanni and Emma	Driving Instructor
93	Caroline	Hairdresser; Landlady
94	Jo	Driving Instructor
95	Heather Booker	Complementary Therapist and Clinic Owner
97	Donna Kirkland	Beauty Therapy and Sales
101	Matt Brown	Events Timing Provider
102	Sarah Davies	Professional Development Consultant
104	Hazel	Childminder
106	Kate	Equine Stud and Horse-drawn Carriages
109	Steph	Allied Health Professional
110	Isobel Rutter	Tour Operator
112	Liz	Property Management
114	Judith	Sole Trader
116	Jane Wallis	Reflexologist
117	Sue	Therapeutic Counsellor/Clinical Hypnotherapist
119	Louise Kenrick	Events Organiser

120	Tracy	Barber
122	Marian	Cat Sitter
123	Juliet	Cook
124	Jon Mank	Wedding Photographer
127	Rachael Hattersley	Holiday Home Owner
129	Sue Attwood	Walking Holidays Provider
131	Anon	Events Organiser
132	Lynn	Approved Driving Instructor
134	Elaine Little	Food Sales and Catering
135	Karen Squance	Music Teacher
137	M	Charity Membership Recruiter
139	Paul and Sarah	Café Owners
140	Alex	Writer and Tutor
141	Ele	Boarding Kennels
143	Cheryl	Make-up Artist
144	Karen	Business Consultant; Holistic Practitioner/Teacher
146	L	Yoga Teacher
148	Shabana	Actress
150	Andrew	Freelance Consultant
152	Jo	Not Given
155	Ian	Driving Instructor
157	Simon	Inbound Tour Operator
161	Nicky	Trauma and Anxiety Therapist
163	Jo	Teacher Trainer and Examiner
165	Jacqueline	Beauty Therapist
167	Karen's husband	Gas Engineer
169	Ruth	Retail Worker
171	John	Contractor
173	Tina	Café Owner
175	Jennifer	Singer
177	Rachel	Company Director
179	Hayley	Vocalist
183	Callum	Assistant TV Producer

184	Sheena	Business Consultant
185	Louise	Childcare Provider
187	Christina	Coaching and Mentoring/Alternative Education
190	Carolyn	Stuntwoman; Circus Performer; Gardener; Sports Therapy
192	Ester	Wildlife Camerawoman
193	Maisy	Interpreter; Voice-over Artist
194	Suzie	Laundry Services Company
196	Nicki	Newborn Photographer
197	Anne	Not Given
198	Vanessa	Yoga Teacher
200	Maxine	Market Trader
202	Catherine	Corporate Events Organiser
203	Anonymous	Not Given
205	Lisa	Travel Consultant
206	Debbie	Candlemaker
207	Audrey	Company Director
209	Charlotte	Kitchen, Bathroom and Bedroom Designer
211	Kate	VIP Manager
213	Chris	Driving Instructor
214	Jane	Florist
216	Dani	Travel Consultant
218	Carmichael Family	Sound Engineer/Tour Manager
220	Judi	Translator
222	Tess	Sound Engineer
224	Sarah	After School Club Owner
225	Louisa	Supply Teacher
226	Nital	Graphic Designer
227	Kate (and Sophie)	Piano Tutor
230	Diane	Pet Services
232	Donna	Podiatrist/Chiropodist
233	David McKie	Consultant Director, Construction
234	Kelly	Massage Therapist

235	Sangita	Healthcare Provider
237	Una	Dog Day Care
239	Rahima	NHS Worker
241	Barney	Music/Arts/Event Management
244	Diane	Childminder
249	Amanda	Girl Friday
251	Kerry	Park Worker
253	Laura	Performing Arts Professional
254	Sharon	Children's Entertainer
256	Jodee	Retro Toy Dealer
258	J	Logistics
259	Marg	Driving Instructor
261	Raini	Pet Care
264	Deborah	Costumer
265	Claire	Events Management
266	Bev	Massage Therapist
268	Lisa	Swim School Owner
271	Steve	Coach Driver
272	Lisa	Salon Supplier
275	Shauna and Jordan	Electrician
276	Paula	Community Outreach Tutor
277	Rosie	Accounts/Bookkeeper
279	Leigh	Children’s Author / Illustrator
281	Stephen	Private Guided Tours

About The Author

Despite being described as non-viable by Rishi Sunak I have been writing a range of fiction and non-fiction books for 20 years as well as magazine articles relating to the environment and travel features in the Independent.

During the summer of 2020 I wrote Secret Gardens of the City of London which instantly became an Amazon best-seller and is based on Ye Olde England Tours Secret, Sacred Gardens of London Tour which has been rated by Tripadvisor as being the number one off-beat and local experience in the whole of London!

My books are available from book shops and in various online formats such as Kindle, iBooks and many others including Lest We Forget: A Concise Companion to the First World War by Lume Books of London, 101 Most Horrible Tortures in History and Straight From The Horse's Mouth - 100 Idioms, their Meanings and Origins.

I have a popular blog which regularly attracts over 100,000 readers with history, culture and travel related posts along with my own aimless musings and have spent much of the last year making appearances on TV, Radio and newspapers as well the obligatory Social Media as a tiny part of the wonderful #ExcludedUK in order to seek justice for the 3 million.

Prior to that, most of my time since 2013 has been spent creating, running and expanding Ye Olde England Tours. I was the first to offer private and totally bespoke door-to-door tours in London. 99% of them were original when I created them, it's easy to check that out too. I've never wanted a Blue Badge, I have multiple degrees in history and love showing people around as if they were family. Many of my tourists comment that they are glad they are on our tours and not with those self-important staid blue badge guides who are very particular over how long their tours last and where and what they will cover. Indeed during the Coronavirus I've been receiving lots of food parcels and donations from around the world from my new family!

These days there are various people who have tried to copy my ideas but they can't replicate the passion, good humour and knowledge or the dedication.... I've worked every single day from autumn 2013 to 2020. Ye Olde England Tours has hundreds of 5-star reviews on all the big and little sites. Bizarrely, I'm not at all money orientated which is maybe why I've become successful and I've worked with the Commonwealth War Graves on war related projects, BBC Comic Relief with our original and much imitated Sherlock Tour as well as television producers, celebrities, international and national leaders and best of all the general public from 0-94 years of age so far.

Check out our website at www.yeoldeenglandtours.co.uk or visit our listings on Trip Advisor, Viator, Get Your Guide, Expedia and others.

Failing that, why not try one of our growing number of virtual online tours? Whilst you do that, I'm going to try and write my own personal book about my experiences of Shielding and being Excluded for over a year.

Printed in Great Britain
by Amazon

57870700R00177

LOUIS EVELY

By the same author

Market Unlimited

God's Communicators

Michel Quoist – a biography

Bibles Across the World

LOUIS EVELY
Once a Priest

by

NEVILLE CRYER

MOWBRAY
LONDON & OXFORD

ISBN 0 264 66392 6

First published in 1980 by
A R Mowbray & Co Ltd
Saint Thomas House
Becket Street, Oxford OX1 1SJ

Typeset by Getset, Eynsham, Oxford
Printed in Great Britain by Billing and Sons Ltd
Guildford, London, Oxford, Worcester

Contents

1 *Meeting the Man*

It was in 1963 that I first became aware of a new theological writer called Louis Evely. I was browsing among the varied shelves of a large London bookshop. My eye was caught by a fairly tall volume with a most unusual title and a very modern black and green cover. The cover showed the Christ, suffering and bearing his cross, and the words that accompanied that picture were stark and gripping. The title was 'That Man is YOU'. I was drawn to pick up the book and look at its contents. After reading only three or four extracts I knew that this was a book that I ought to have and one that would serve me for much longer than its first reading. For a young priest in a parish that was no small matter when it came to buying books. I have that book on my shelves to this day, and it is still a book to which I regularly turn. Little did I think then that one day I would be writing about its author.

The book itself is a collection of profound meditations on various aspects of the life of Jesus. You pass with him through temptation and loneliness. You help him choose his disciples. You enter into the upper room of the first Eucharist. You stand at the door of the tomb of Lazarus and you discover with him the richness and also the cost of real prayer. The whole book is like a 'midrash', a subtle commentary on the Gospels, so that you are almost drawn to imagine at times that it is a form of scripture which you are reading. The insight, the immmediacy, the humanity of the whole work is unmistakable and that is what makes the title so apt. For the experience that the writer obviously sought and which he almost unconsciously conveys is that of making the reader enter personally into these experiences of another and then reflect on them for his own good. From looking at the one of whom Pontius Pilate said, 'Behold the man!' (Ecce Homo) the reader is helped to accept Louis Evely's own reminder — 'That Man is YOU'.

This is all the more remarkable when you realise that the work is not in origin an English production at all. It was written in 1955, published in Belgium in 1957, and what is now on my shelves is the first edition of a translation. It does not read like one and having read the original since I compliment the publishers of the English edition for so accurately capturing both the spirit and the style of what Louis himself wrote. What was most striking and fascinating about this English edition was the psalm-like or blank verse lay-out of the pages. With the irregular lengths and flowing succession of thoughts of each printed line the reader is carried along through what might otherwise be a series of hard, indigestible propositions about the life and death and resurrection of Christ. That that does not happen, that one can digest these immense truths about all humanity and still want to read more, and read it again and again, is a measure of the quality of the thinking and expressiveness of this Christian author. For me the reading of this book was as if I had met a completely new acquaintance and not just found a useful and stimulating book.

The freshness of the discovery still stays with me. These were, after all, pre-Vatican II days, and the fresh awareness of how biblical and how Christ-centred a Roman Catholic book and its priestly author could be came with a special shock at that time. I remember taking the book to the old Irish parish priest with whom, in those days, our first Anglican-Roman Catholic link at parish level was being established and asking him if he had come across this author before. He had not, but he was almost as fascinated as I was by the style and the liveliness of the presentation. We both recognised in it what we believed to be the heart of the matter — the divinity and the humanity of our blessed Lord.

There was soon a chance to test the effect of the work on another audience. I was preparing at the time for a mission weekend in a rural-cum-dormitory parish in the Medway valley in Kent. The vicar there had kindly offered me an opportunity to speak to all the various church groups or activities throughout the weekend and to use all the occasions for preaching on the Sunday. In what was, or had been, a fairly 'Catholic' parish this exposure at all levels to the facts of the Gospel was something unexpected and disturbing. The vicar was ready for that and had planned for it in our preparation. By Sunday lunchtime the feelings of one man, a lay-reader, bubbled over into speech. As we disrobed in the vestry he turned on me in some desperation — 'I do not know what you think you are doing', he said, 'but we want none of this Protestant rubbish here — and certainly no more from the evangelical book you have quoted from.' He had, of course, chosen to take his stand upon the one ground which could not carry him. When I showed him the book and he saw that it was produced by both a Roman Catholic publisher and a Roman Catholic author he was covered with embarrassment. He didn't apologise but he went away a very puzzled man.

There is no better book to use for introducing a newcomer to the subject of this biography, even though the last edition of it ceased some years ago and it may take a library a little while to find you one. Moreover, a library edition is likely to have lost the paper jacket which gives the reader, and gave me, the first glimpse of its author's appearance and something of his life story. Not much but something. Looking out from the inside flap of the back cover the reader meets a man in a familiar French soutane, somewhere in his early forties, clean-shaven, with a firm, rather pointed chin, a strong but not too pronounced nose, well-trimmed and slightly wavy black hair and striking, though friendly, eyes. Since this was the first book that one had seen bearing his name it was a shock to realise that he had already had many others published and that they had achieved the distinction of being translated into many languages, especially those of largely Roman Catholic countries. He was listed as a broadcaster in Belgium and elsewhere and as being a native of Brussels, born in 1910.

That was as much as any reader could then learn and it wasn't much. What was clear was that the publishers were not selling this book on Louis Evely's name, but on its contents. They were convinced, and they were right to assume, that what would introduce their English-speaking public to Louis Evely fastest was not his own achievements but the way in which he had so deeply and perceptively met the Man of all men, Jesus Christ. That, as I now know, was what Louis Evely was himself eager to convey to his readers. In one sense he, the author, did not matter at all — what mattered was that people should have the chance to meet the one who made Louis Evely, who still makes Louis Evely, the man he is. If anyone wants to meet this author and thinker, who nowadays no longer wears a soutane and who is happily married, then he will first need to encounter the one Person who has never changed for him — our Lord Jesus Christ. Of him and from him Louis would be the first to claim — 'If I am anything it is because That Man is ME'.

To meet Louis today is to meet the same man in a later edition. Let us meet him in Brussels in the middle of 1978. The occasion is something very much less common in Belgium than in Britain or the United States — it is a school reunion. It is not a regular or established gathering and it is not very large. In a country, however, that is nothing like as familiar with Old Boys' associations and ties, or Phi Beta Kappa pins and sodalities, to find any pupils actually wanting to meet up with their old schoolteacher is quite the exception, especially when it is almost thirty years afterwards. There is another distinctive slant to this particular gathering. It is that half of those present are there with their wives, and this includes their former teacher. Since the teacher was once a Roman Catholic Priest that adds some flavour to the meeting, not forgetting that all these were pupils at a Catholic college and most of those present are still believing, if not practising, members of that church. Surprisingly, it is the wives who were most anxious for this meeting to take place and who are as eager as anyone to meet again, or for the first time, a man who has obviously had a profound effect on the lives of their husbands.

We gather first of all in the bar of the Hotel Metropole in the Place de Brouckère, at the very heart of Brussels. The principal guests, Louis and his wife, have not yet arrived, but there are apéritifs all round and a first chance for a visitor from Great Britain to get to know something about these old scholars of 'Père' Evely. They are all men in their early or middle forties. One is a jeweller called Jean. He and his well-dressed wife are the quieter members of the group but were the first to arrive and obviously take a lively interest in all that happens. Their car puts everyone else's in the shade but this is not to be an occasion for comparing how well Louis' boys have got on in the world. Like another, Robert, whose wife is working and could not get away, Jean and his wife are still devout Catholics and Robert's family all belong to the church. Robert is now the manager of a heating installations firm in the suburbs and like the others is putting to practical use those groundings in Commerce which they received under Louis' direction in the post-war years.

Another Jean, a textile firm manager, is one of the most talkative of the party, and certainly one who shows his great affection for Louis. Though a believing Catholic who goes to church on the great festivals he is by no means a regular churchgoer even though his wife keeps up local church connections. His brother Marc is of similar mind, still holding to the name and convictions of a Catholic, but hardly ever going to church and certainly not making his confession or abiding by other Catholic rules of personal discipline. His wife, English by birth, had come to Belgium after the war and is now so naturalised that it is easier for her to talk in French than to revert to her native tongue. She too is a lapsed Catholic and is now to meet Louis for the first time. She is looking forward to it very much.

Finally there is Bob (or Robi) who is the joker of the group. He and his wife arrive even later than Louis and are soundly ribbed by the others for being as 'late for class' as Robi usually was years ago. Yet here is a man, with a wife who is attractive and chic, who has never lost his boyishness though he has utterly lost whatever religious faith he once had. He is unashamedly the agnostic of the group. The fact that he is still the only one who works on the shop floor as a Porsche car spare-parts storeman underlines the fact that, as so often in the West, the church seems to be wedded largely to the middle and entrepreneurial classes. His wife would deny that, however, for she has remained a practising and devout communicant. She quietly expresses, her great regrets that Louis, who was such a great companion, as well as teacher, for her husband and his pals, should have taken the path he has. Like others in the party she was not condemning Louis for his actions. Yet she could not but feel sad that someone, with so much affection to give and so much influence to wield, should have surrendered all that made him so distinguished and now joins them simply as a layman and a husband. As a happily married woman herself she was clearly not running down the estate of matrimony. As a practicing Catholic, however, she obviously felt that something was wrong when a priest with Louis' gifts and qualities should finish his days in so ordinary a way. You could see that she was struggling hard to convey to a stranger something very difficult and yet something very near and dear to her heart. It certainly said something about her view of the priesthood.

By now Louis and his wife had arrived after having had some difficulty in parking their car. He is no longer the black-clothed, black-haired, smooth-cheeked priest in his middle forties that appears in one of his 1950 books. Here is a man in his late sixties, with grey or whitening hair, his brow carrying the marks of not a few of life's harder experiences, his cheeks a little less plump and his clothes those of any other Belgian who earns enough but not that much. Yet, despite the changes, there are still the clear, searching and affectionate eyes, the mind sharp and alive, a smile and a warm, firm handgrip for grown men whom he knew first as adolescents, and a flow of natural, understanding talk. Above all you soon realise the facet of Louis Evely's character that specially endears him to so many who know him. He has the ability to listen to what others are saying, to weigh their words and to respond when it is timely to do so — and only then. This gives his own words a weight and an acceptance that makes possible easy conversation and yet brings its own flavour and contribution to it. The result of listening to others, he shows you instinctively, is that they then listen to you when it is your turn to speak. As you listen to Louis Evely you recognise a man who knows the true value of words, who thinks about what he says and yet is never pompous with it. As he spoke on this occasion you could almost feel yourself back in the grounds of the school where these men were first brought together. Lessons were over and there was time to talk freely together about anything and everything. You could see the 'master' in the midst of the 'Fifteen' (for that was the original number of the group, of whom three have already died) and you could pick out Robi telling them one of his jokes, Robert wanting to raise some matter of a more serious kind, Marc wanting to get a football team settled — the whole company engrossed in a 'family life' centering on this one man — Fr. Louis, Abbé Evely.

As at every such gathering there were reminiscences, not least for the benefit of the wives present. They dragged up all the nicknames they had for the 'Principal' and for other less amiable members of the staff. They recalled the practical jokes that they tried to play on Louis, and he on them. They started to recall members who were not there and asked each other where this man or that had finished up. Louis was able to let them have some information from letters he and Mary had received in the last few years and above all Louis was able to start telling them what had happened to himself and his wife since they were married. For it is not possible to meet the Louis Evely of today without meeting also the wife whom he loves so much and who so clearly loves him. To try and meet Louis without Mary is to meet only an incomplete person and he would be the first to underscore that fact. To see them sitting together in that hotel lounge, her eyes sparkling with pride for the man who was her husband, and he so very obviously aware of her presence and happy to find her well received by those old pupils, was to recognise that if the Abbé of earlier days was a man wrapped up in the persons of his pupils and proud of them, he was now no less a happily married man who was very much wrapped up in Mary and proud to belong to her. In a strange sort of way he was not the same man and yet he was exactly the same.

It was during a lull in the tale of his adventures since 1970 that one of the party, I think it was Marc or Jean, his brother, suggested that they continue the story over some proper food which had been arranged elsewhere. We bundled out into the square, each separating to get his car or give someone a lift to the chosen restaurant. Within ten minutes we were there, in the parish of St. John the Baptist and turning into the stable yard of an old and rather dilapidated town house almost underneath the church's walls. Through a rough and unpainted door, into a plain colour-washed vestibule, turning right down some stone steps with a cast-iron balustrade and into the vaulted cellars (une vraie cave). In this pleasantly-dimmed, warm and attractive series of alcoves there stood one table set for just our number. A check table-cover (what else?) and a knife, fork, spoon and two glasses to each place. It was time for lunch à la Bruxelloise and for the next two hours the food kept coming, the wine flowed, the tongues wagged, and human beings who had once been young friends restored that bond as adults and drew others of us into it.

'Do you remember', said Robi, 'that game you taught us to play at night? You would tell one or two of us at supper time that the game was on. At midnight we would wake up every one else in the dormitory, having first removed all the light bulbs and turned off the switches so that everyone had to move about in pitch darkness. The only words we were allowed to use were the waking-up ones, "It's time", and after that everyone had to remain completely silent whilst we left our rooms and did whatever we had been told to do in such a situation. Some had to scale a wall, some had to climb a tree, some get through the college gates without disturbing the night porter, though he was also in the game. His job was to catch us, I know, and if he did and asked us what was going on, we had to say nothing. He would then pretend to get angry at our silent insolence and if a boy tried to defend himself by arguing he was immediately told that he had failed in the game because he was talking! It took a lot of nerve not to say anything under those circumstances, but my! how we loved those night outings'. While he or one of the others was remembering things like this there would be a pause in the course of the meal and even the wives would be waiting upon every word.

The men were not unaware of what Louis had done as one of the resistance fighters in the war. The very reason that they had chosen these cellars for our lunch meeting was because this place was one of the hide-aways which the resistance fighters in Brussels had used during the latter part of the war and they wanted me to see them. It also fitted Louis into a setting which they knew that he deserved. They had known him first when the war was over but when his bravery with the Maquis was still not forgotten. They even asked him to tell them something about those days and he told them reluctantly, about one time when he met three teenage College boys on the outskirts of the school, with only a revolver, two grenades, and instructions to try and put a nearby radar station out of action! Yes, those were crazy days, he told us, but we were all aware that this was still the same patriot, the same enemy of evil who had flitted from one hide-out to another. It was one more aspect of a man whom we could only fully know as we looked back beyond the face and the clothes, the marriage and the teaching days that were so prominent at that moment. Here was a man who could enjoy a practical joke, discuss philosophy in Latin, feel a hurtful word, recite the liturgy and show deep and lasting affection for man and woman and child. As we ate and drank with him that day in the increasingly smoky cellar we knew how real a person he was for us. This was a man who had come to terms with real life. As he had once written:

'Every stage of life is both a dying and a being born . . . One is born into an unknown world in which one has to come to terms with new forces in solitude and at constant risk. Two attitudes are therefore possible and we have to choose constantly between them. It is the same choice that confronted Adam and Eve when they were driven from the Garden of Eden. They could either wander round the edge of the lost paradise, seeking to recapture the delight of it and looking for the chance moments of pleasure and delight. Or they could turn their backs on it, and set off to wrestle and work together to attempt to remake, by their will and effort, something of what wondrous childhood which they kept alive in their memory . . . Paradise is always ahead of us, not behind. We must neither forget it nor be content with simply recalling it, but believe that, with God's assistance, we can actually re-create it.'

That is what is at the heart of Louis Evely. As we emerged again into the street on that May afternoon, some to go back to their offices, some to a delayed holiday, some to their factory or shop, and others of us to our hotel, we realised afresh that today's meeting had not been a dream or make-believe. Into the last few hours of a Brussels day there had come afresh for old boys and new friends a sense of a vibrant and distinctive human being. For those who had never met him before it was clear that they were not likely to forget him. For some the image had been brought up to date. For the readers of this book it is only an introduction. In the pages that follow we shall seek to complete our acquaintance with one who is a MAN, but who also knows whose man he is.

2 *Willingly to School*

Louis was born in the residential district of Brussels known as Schaerbeek. It lies just to the north of that ring of boulevards that surround the inner part of the city, nestling behind the Botanical Gardens and straddling the upper end of the Rue Royale. It is a part of Brussels which has changed little in the last hundred years. The fact that the city was not too badly shelled or bombed in World War II means that the houses, churches and schools are largely the same as when Louis Evely's parents came to live there at the turn of the century. Though M. and Mme. Delhaye, Louis' maternal grandparents, were business people of Liège, Louis cannot recall them, since they died when he was still very young and he never thought to ask about their original home. His father's parents came from Brussels and were successful brokers, so that Louis' first recollections of his paternal grandfather were of a man who was very well off. This grandfather lived by the sea, but also travelled a great deal, and during the First World War had a villa in Spain. Though he provided for his wife and their only child, Louis' father, he had deceived her with another woman during their early years of marriage and they had agreed to separate. Louis' grandmother, however, remained in Brussels and it was here that she brought up her son.

In one of the now rare family photographs belonging to Louis' older sister Annie, their father appears in a young medical officer's uniform sitting on a studio garden bench. His turnout is immaculate, his dress sword lies across his knees, his right hand is clasping a pair of white leather gloves and his French-style officer's peaked cap lies on the seat by his side. Above the high, stiff neckpiece you are confronted with a handsome, intelligent face with eyes deep and well-set under strong eyebrows. The nose is firm and long, a neatly-trimmed and receding moustache just reveals the gentle and well-formed mouth, beneath which is a dimpled chin that is nonetheless strong and regular, whilst a clear, tall brow tops the whole with a rich head of hair, divided, of course, by an impeccable parting. He is a young man of obviously elegant ways who takes pride in his appearance and who knows that he has some ground for his pride. That he was a source of admiration to his mother is easily imagined, and doubtless there were a number of girls who must have thought him a most suitable match. He, too, was obviously not averse to the attractions of the opposite sex, though his mother may well have found it somewhat disturbing when this boy of hers, having matriculated from his college in Brussels to the University of Louvain, met Louis' mother, Emilie Delhaye, whilst he was still a student and married her before he took his final degree.

What is worth noting is that Louis' father was originally a classics scholar, as well as taking a first class degree in medicine. All through his childhood Louis never remembered his father being very far away from books or the very fine library which he had collected. He was, says Louis, always 'occupé', and this meant that his relationships with his children suffered because they could never get really close to him. He was also very much the martinet, as pictures of him also suggest. One's appearance was everything. People had to be on time for meals, had to do their duties, or be in bed, according to strict rules. His views on women were clear — their place was in the home. Louis' sister will still tell you that following in the distinguished footsteps of her two brothers, of whom Louis was the second, she too wanted to be a student of medicine like her father. He refused to consider it for a moment. Her job, he told her, was to emulate her mother, to marry, to settle down, and raise a family. In that sense he was a fair example of his day. He provided for his home, he expected to be respected, to be fed and looked after, to be obeyed and to be generally allowed to enjoy himself once the day's or the week's work was over. Holidays were always taken at the same time and by the sea, and there was always a time in the year when everyone's wardrobe was examined and the necessary arrangements made for its renewal.

Not that Louis was all that impressed with the holiday arrangements that his parents made. As he was to make very clear to other children's parents later: 'Holidays at the seaside are not recommended except for the very youngest children. For older children they become very monotonous and anything you do to provide amusement is very costly. The family usually finds itself split up; teenagers go off in groups looking for something to do, meet up with casual acquaintances and generally finish up idling away the time doing nothing in particular. The ideal holiday, on the other hand, is to rent a house in the Ardennes, a country villa, or camp in the grounds of a large house there. . .' Louis certainly knew, when he wrote those words, what camping in the Ardennes could be like.

Louis' father was, it would seem, largely a beloved figure-head, a rather remote, somewhat unapproachable and certainly semi-mysterious figure who never deserted his family but who also seemed separate from the deep experiences of their growing-up. It is interesting to discover that there are no pictures of the whole family together. The most common one is that of Madame Evely and her three children. The studio of the photographer is shown on the back as 'Polar Photographs, 48 Chaussée de Haecht' — just around the corner from their home.

The relationship with their mother was a very different matter.

Though M. Evely was not only faithful to but even very fond of his handsome wife throughout their long years together, and she even more fond of him, it was on her that there rested the main burden of bringing love and affection into the lives of their children. Though in herself far from cultured, not very well educated and in some respects very narrow in outlook, she was a traditional mother-figure. She was available, huggable, a willing listener, a shoulder to cry on after one of father's strictures, someone who showed obvious pride in her children's achievements and who was no less convinced than her husband that women were meant to be housewives. Though, as a born mother, she tried to avoid having favourites, Louis' sister will tell you that there was a remarkable bond between Louis and his mother. 'No woman ever seemed to match up to my mother for him', she said. 'If mother steadily began to put Louis on a pedestal for us to all to admire it was no less true that Louis seemed to act as if nothing but sunshine flowed out of Mama'. You can already see this happening in the family portrait. The older boy with his Eton collar, bow-tie and first well-cut jacket – and watch-chain! – stands a little aloof and a little querulous as if determined to be a 'little man', though still holding on to the pedestal in the foreground. Annie, the next in age, clutches her mother's left elbow as if determined not be left out of the circle. In the centre, with his hand held firmly by his mother's right, standing hard up against her shoulder and in the most immaculate of sailor suits, is Louis, with an open book in front of them both. Together, they seem to be saying, we have nothing to fear. Louis' childish five-year-old face is serene and chubby. He is safe and he knows it.

Their first home was 137, Rue Gaillait, and Louis lived here until he was 12. Shortly after the family portrait was taken he began to attend the local parish school of St. Servies, Rue Quineaux, where he soon learned how to use one of the most important arts of his life – the ability to read. Because of M. Evely's views about the place of women in the home there were few things that the boys were expected to do once they had changed out of their school clothes, taken their meals and, later, finished their homework. Annie recalls that though she loved playing with the boys a great deal and that Louis in particular was a rare one for practical jokes and for making fun of her, there were not many days when Louis was not found curled up somewhere with a new book. She even remembers how he read them all at a rapid rate. As time went on this love of books grew rather than diminished and in his teens Louis recalls that he must have been getting through as many as three books a day in the holidays. What an impression reading made on him is revealed in one of the letters which he wrote to parents when he was himself a teacher of young boys. Much of what he wrote then is a direct recall of his own youth. . .

' "Come on, Peter, shut that book and have your supper."

'Peter slowly gets up out of the armchair still reading the book, his face glued to it as if he is in a dream. He slowly makes his way across the room, still totally immersed in what he is reading, knocking into the furniture, until, very reluctantly, he comes to the edge of the sideboard, puts the book down, still open so that he can get back to it as soon as the interval for eating is over, and then sits down with the others. He is still looking rather vacant, unable to take in the immensity of the delight of what he has just been doing and still caught up in the imaginary world into which he has been transported and the vistas which have opened up for him. He sits there for a moment or two absolutely still and then as he comes to and sees the other faces around him, he smiles with an inner delight as if to find that there are still some things which are the same, he says an inner 'adieu' (just for the present) to his dreams and begins to join in the family conversation. . .

'Just what do you do with this youngster who is, as it were, hypnotised by his story of 'Tintin', or some other adventure story or thriller? Do you just let him read what he wants or are you able to help him? Reading for more than 80% of those boys who are attracted to it is not an art, an exercise or an essay into culture – it is the brooding desire to be on one's own, the headlong and pleasurable plunge into forgetfulness, a kind of mad delight at being able to avoid reality. . .

Does that disturb you? Do you want to say that reading only encourages a false view of life and confuses our children with too many imaginary ideas and situations? I want to encourage you to believe that it is quite the reverse. What is unreal, what is so often an attempt to avoid and run from reality, is life as it is very often lived, that mean, niggardly life into which too many grown-ups want to push children too soon under the pretext that that is what life is really about. Children that have other insights, and an instinct fed on other material, will refuse to believe that. Because they cannot believe those who are their elders they turn to books; because grown-ups do not make any effort to understand them (did this reflect Louis' view of his own father?) they go where they can admire and learn from those who are really fully grown – the heroes and the great thinkers of literature. There is nothing in this world so precious for a child as his faith in the greatness of men, the beauty of life, its worthwhileness, its endless variety and scope, its tragic nature and the mystery of our end. If that is the kind of 'real life view' that we want to help our children to have then there are never enough books – of adventure, of travel, and conflict, whether they be novels or biographies or anthologies of poetry or even books on 'How this or that began' . . .

'Reading for a child is the best means there is to help him explore the whole wide world in all its true dimensions of space and time, whilst at the same time helping him to see what kind of a person he can become within himself, whether it is by comparing himself with the subject of the story or the author who wrote it. . . What is more, the great delight of reading is that you do it on your own, with only yourself for company, that solitariness which is so feared by modern man and from which so many try to run away. As Mounier puts it: "the very core of being a truly human being is to know how to help men to accept and live with themselves when they are on their own."

'So what are we going to do about it? Let me make a few suggestions. First of all I want you to read to even your youngest children from well-tried works, good verse, and to read it as if you too loved it. Tell them fairy stories and adventure yarns and don't be afraid of telling them over and over again. Tell them things that will awaken, in turn, both dreams and reality, thoughts and action, poetry and prayer, scenes and ideas. There will soon come a day when your child will want to go exploring this world all for himself. You still have a job to do, guiding their steps, showing them new avenues, listening sometimes to the results of their travels into their new world. If we don't help our children in this part of their education then we should not be surprised if we fail in helping them in other parts. In fact their whole education will be less complete than it ought. . .

'So if we are to be really careful about what we choose let's start with the Gospels or selected parts of them, the tales of Grimm and Perrault, the poems of Victor Hugo and Rostand, the fables of La Fontaine, the Odyssey and the Iliad, and the story of Roland. Then when you have got to the point where they stop playing games in the garden based on the events of the Swiss Family Robinson or Robinson Crusoe perhaps you can start them off with their own reading. . .

'Here I would choose two great sections — the imaginative stories of knighthood, the story of William of Orange, the Four sons of Aymon, Fenimoore Cooper and Kipling's jungle books or Puck of Pooks Hill; and then the great stories of air and sea adventure, the famour Polar expeditions of Byrd, Scott, Amundsen, Charcot, mountaineers, cave and underwater explorers (Casteret and Engel), and then the great pioneers of sanctity, (Joan of Arc, Don Bosco, St. Francis, the Curé d'Ars, Père de Foucauld) and the lives of Jesus by Dickens and Mauriac.

The other great section would be the writers who look at the actual world that is all around us, the books on bees and birds and the plants of the earth . . . Jules Verne is quite indispensable: a child who has not read Jules Verne is probably ignorant about the principles which govern every kind of modern gadget. Such a child will never be able to make sense of our contemporary civilisation. How else can he understand the principle of what is lighter than air unless he reads "Five weeks in a Balloon"; or what is heavier than air without "Robur the Conqueror"; or what is under the oceans without reading "5000 Leagues under the Sea". . . and for that matter what can he know about the world of tomorrow unless he reads "War of the Worlds" by H. G. Wells, "The

Master of the World" by Benson, or "The Fantastic Future" by Devaux?

'From there we can pass on to the humourists, Mark Twain, Dickens, Daudet, Jerome K. Jerome, and "The Little Prince" by Saint-Exupéry. . .'

There is surely no need for anyone who reads these words to doubt that here was the child become a man — a child that had read all these books and was now able to commend them as worthy of other children because they had helped to form his own life. This was not a catalogue — this was a record of experience, and it all began in that house in the Rue Gaillait where a little boy was allowed to touch and take down his father's books and eventually rifle the library at school. To this day Louis Evely will tell you that Jules Verne is essential reading for any child.

School therefore provided for Louis the very framework for his reading that he needed. As he also wrote later, 'Don't just read whatever happens to come to hand. You only retain things worthwhile from books when they are related to your current occupation or if they are linked with some idea or subject which you want to pursue. You always ought to have some line of study, some piece of research in hand and about four or five books connected with that which are still waiting to be read. Only so will you be able to counteract the temptation to just read idly or those transient, superficial items which the modern news and publishing media will flood you with.' That was another lesson he obviously learnt at his primary school, and the fruits of this omnivorous and seemingly endless reading were soon to show themselves.

At the age of 12 the family moved house to the Rue Royale, No. 239, and Louis only had a short walk into the Chausée de Haecht to reach the Institut Ste Marie where his secondary education could begin. He was by now a somewhat serious and meditative child and another photograph of the period shows him sitting back to front on a garden bench, not elegantly like his father but with his chin resting on a hand and arm which are in their turn resting on his knee, an adolescent version of the statue by the French sculptor, Rodin. There is the same broad brow and the neatly combed hair of his father, however, whilst the same deep-set eyes, the same firm nose and the long fingers all tell you that he is the son of Dr. Evely. Beside him sits a girl who appears in several of the pictures of this period, a girl who aroused new feelings of affection and who, had things turned out differently, might have been more to him than simply a teenage sweetheart. As it was they played tennis together, they went on family picnics, they even went for walks and visits to the Zoo together, but always with another friend or friends in attendance. That was, as some of us find it hard to recall now, the custom of those days. Louis admits that he was fond of her and she was obviously glad to be seen out with this growing, well-mannered and not unhandsome scholar who had an interest in so many things and was such an entertaining companion.

At school he began to shine. Within the first year he was fourth in Latin class and first in Greek. He had already proved that he could write intelligently and he did his homework. At the age of 13 he was to come under the influence of the only man whom he regards as having had any real influence upon him other than his father. That man was Fr. Hemeleers. This man taught them History and Geography and though Louis streses that his teacher had no 'heart', he will also tell you that here was a born instructor, a man who only expected and hence got the best, a man who was clearly accompanied by the necessary information. It was Hemeleers who gave him insights into life and knowledge which no-one had ever offered him before and has never equalled since. It is worth noting that one of the pupils in the same school was the boy who is now Cardinal Suenens, the present Primate of Belgium. That Louis was always clearly treated as Hemeleers' favourite pupil may have been a factor that influenced their relationship later.

Certainly Fr. Hemeleers was fully alive to the kind of scholars that he had in his charge. Fr. Hemeleers could soon detect that Louis was in danger of becoming a lonely and reclusive child and that he needed to be brought out of himself before he was much older. Because Louis respected his teacher he was ready to listen when, one day after school, Hemeleers told him that he ought to join the Scout movement. The idea at first appalled Louis. The idea of wearing a bush hat at 14 years of age, of leaving home in order to go and camp in some wet and unpleasant field, of having to mix with all and every sort of strange boy and learn things which required the use of one's hands rather than one's head – the whole thing seemed preposterous. It was only as the challenge of the whole thing became clearer to him, the test it would be of his courage and determination, the opportunity to excel in competition and perhaps the sense of adventure which his wide reading had already stimulated that Louis began to accept, and then positively to welcome, this new kind of leisure activity.

He still recalls the first time he walked down the Rue Royale in his new Scout hat on the way to a meeting and heard three pretty girls tittering as they passed him by. That was when he was just 14 and by the time he was 16 he had learnt to swim fully-clothed, to play various sports and to want to be in the teams, to enjoy running and to fend for himself in first aid and simple cooking. He became a Patrol leader, and after another year had been appointed Leader of the whole troop. By the time he was within sight of going to College he was the Troop Scout Master and was guiding the lives and activities of over 100 boys. Through homesickness and the first dread of leaving the comforts of his home he had already graduated to being an eager hiker, someone who could carry his full pack for a fortnight's trekking, and who could even choose the most suitable kind of camp site.

Fifteen years later he wrote a long article on the benefits and the purpose of scouting when he himself had had the experience of being a soldier under rough country conditions. These are some of the things which he could then say about this formative period of his own adolescence.

'The patrol is a vital way of life and a perfect means of establishing a sense of purpose and order for boys. It puts boys into direct contact with someone who is their senior and yet whose influence is never questioned and who represents to them the law and spirit of the whole camp. Scout discipline is accepted because it turns obedience into a game: people do what they are told because there is fun in all the different ways of doing it – hoisting flags, giving special salutes, learning patrol cries, making reports around the camp-fire, and so on. Even the games are all organised and yet the boys hardly realise it. You don't tell boys to amuse themselves – you have a wide game. You even organise their singing. As for sweeping up a hut or removing litter round a tent – what they would turn up their noses at at home is now done with relish because it all reflects on their patrol inspection!' You can almost feel in those words the deep chords that were touched in the life of the growing student. What this scouting meant to Louis in the days of the ministry that lay ahead we shall see in chapter 5. What it had done for him in helping to widen his circle of friends and interests was to be reflected in the way that he tried in his turn to help boys like himself.

Louis was not unaware of the deep changes that were at work in him as a result of this new-found interest. He learnt for the first time what it was like outside the more charmed circles of the classroom and the fireside at home. He discovered that there were people whose opinions had to be listened to and whose feelings about certain matters were as strong, if not always as well expresed, as his own. He learnt to use a cycle as he had never done before and he can still recall vividly the tour of French cathedrals that was organised and the first visit he paid to England. The Anglican parson he then visited taught him to poach rather than to speak English. He learned above all to delve below the surface with the people he met, to avoid the barrier of class or dress or the level of education. He started, in fact, to live and he never ceases to be thankful that just when he needed it there was this organisation to which he could be directed. He may no longer be a scout but when he needed it the movement was there.

There was also another aspect of Louis' life which was now developing – his attitude to religion. His mother was a devout and regular communicant who not only attended church but felt that it was essential to appear religious. She went to church, says Louis, to satisfy her religious needs: she was, like many other such women, open to superstition and found in the church and its customs a real security. Though she attended Mass and confession and would keep all the usual festivals she was not more closely involved in it – either in seeking to deepen her understanding of the church's teaching or in any group or office. She lived her life, including church membership, to a set pattern and the benefit she derived from her religious observances satisfied her according to her needs. When she died in 1962 the obituary in the local newspaper spoke of her being 'fortified by the ministrations of Religion and consoled by apostolic Benediction "in articulo mortis".' That was how she would have wanted it to be and that is how it was. She was by far the most devout member of her whole family.

For Louis the church was a strange and separate institution. He could not be unaware of his mother's devotion and her attendance at the local parish church but he remarks that from the first time that he was aware of it, sitting by her side and doing what she did because she asked him to and he loved her, it 'seemed like a prison'. The vastness and the awesomeness of the church building, the air of mystery and the unreality of so much that was said there all seemed to suggest another world to which one had to belong but which was cut off from the fresh air and the adventure around it. Louis believed in God for he had never been led to imagine that it was possible not to and if, as he was growing up, there were times when he wanted to deepen his faith or try to meet God it was only in the church building that he expected to do so. The idea that God and the other centres of his life could somehow become intertwined never occurred to him at this stage and so the church was part of another life, a rather crabbed and confined part of life, a necessary but not altogether attractive kind of 'prison'.

Moreover Louis was not impressed with what he could only regard as the mediocrity of the clergy. The intellectual level of their sermons, the attitude they seemed to adopt towards quite petty moral issues, their general appearance and their absorption with the round of religious ceremonies — all these things failed to attract him as a boy and as a growing man. The lack of close involvement in the parish by his mother meant that it was some time before he was enrolled as an altar-boy or got involved in other parish activitis. Like many of his school friends he thought of the clergy in their sombre cassocks as 'corbeaux' (crows) and the idea of joining them was something that never occurred to him until the days of going to University drew nearer. His father, also no eager churchman and rather nominal in his observances compared with his wife, asked Louis, now the only boy in the family since his older brother had already died, which was to be his choice — Medicine or the Church.

How could Louis decide? There were only two men to use as his yardsticks, the one his teacher who was a priest and the other his father, a doctor. His facility with the ancient languages, his love of such philosophy as he had already studied, his growing desire to be of some use to the community and above all his deep admiration of Fr. Hemeleers — possibly all these swayed him though he still wonders why he chose as he did. Deep down he knows still that he would have liked equally to become a healer of peoples' bodies. Yet when he was asked to choose he did so. He told his parents that he wanted to become a priest. His father was agreeable and his mother overjoyed. Perhaps, for her, there was not a little sense of still being able to keep Louis for herself.

'Happy the parents', he reflected once, 'who have taught their children that the greatest religious truth, much more important than any dogma, any sacrament, rite or opinion, is that religion is always open to new revelation and that nobody has a monopoly of its truth. The children must learn not to judge it by what they have seen around them, or just by what they have seen of it in their own lives, but be ready to accept that it is always full of surprises, and always greater, more wonderful and more of a blessing than ever they have yet discovered it to be'. Those were brave words that may not seem to have reflected Louis' own experieence up to this point but which would be very much put to the test in the years that were to follow. What is certain is that Louis did not have the same start in his new pilgrimage towards ordination that he had in reading or scouting. He had real need of faith and hope as he stepped out into something that was both uncertain and unknown.

3 *Becoming a Priest*

The city of Louvain, or Leuven as the Flemish call it, lies to the north-east of Brussels in the province of Brabant and on the river Dyle. The University was founded in 1425 and was designated the principal Catholic University of the country in 1835. It history since then had been as stormy and disrupted as that of the city in which it stood. In the first World War Louvain formed the centre of the Belgians' principal line of defence against the German attack. When it was finally taken the church of St. Peter, the law courts, the theatre, the Academy of Fine Arts and other ancient buildings, including the University library, were razed to the ground by the Germans on the pretext that the civilian population had joined in an attack on the invading troops. This act of vandalism, however, provoked great Allied feeling and under the terms of the Versailles treaty Germany was ordered to deliver to the city and university Mss. and prints equivalent in value to those destroyed during the war. It was therefore to a city still recovering from the effects of that destruction, and in a new library only just rebuilt through the generosity of American donors, that Louis came to start his next period of work.

Having decided to take the path to ordination he was settling down to the nine years of study and preparation which would lead to that goal. Five of those years would be spent here in Louvain, the first two qualifying for a degree in 'Philosophie et Lettres' and the next three in obtaining a doctorate in Law. In terms of scholastic work they were to be hard years, especially those spent in grappling with the intricacies and complexities of Thomist philosophy. Louis now realizes, however, that the effect of such study on his whole way of thinking and the sharp disciplining of his mind furnished him then, and has provided him ever since, with an invaluable method of analysing and appreciating any subject. As he writes in his book, 'A Religion for our Time', (p.55): 'Taking reading, for example, the best moments of the book are those when I stop reading, and when, going my way on the impulse which the book has given me, I invent my own thought, thanks to the genius of the author'. There was plenty of opportunity for that kind of experience in those years and it could be that he made use of his opportunity not only well but even too well. That his clarity of thought and the ability to express it stem from these years there can be no doubt and the results, first class honours in both courses, soon proved that his long and lonely hours of reading and thinking in his 'cell' (as he called his allotted cubicle) were put to very good use. His parents were, of course, justly proud.

They were very good times in every sense. He now had a full opportunity to try out his new-found talents for making friends and within a short time he was part of a group of seven or eight fellow-students with some of whom he still maintains occasional links. One of their common interests was cycling and Louis can recall many of the fascinating trips which they took together, not only visiting places of interest but opening up all sorts of subjects for conversation as they rode along and sharing with each other the insights that their studies and general reading provided. What they did in the open air they continued to do, like students down the ages and in every university, around someone's gas fire until the early hours of the morning. They never became a closed group. They were ready to part for the vacations and enjoy the change of going to their own homes, but they returned each term ready for more exchanges and arguments, especially over matters which had arisen during the vacation.

It was with them too that Louis began to explore, in a way that he had not done so fully hitherto, the delights of the cinema and the theatre. He was still far enough away from the restraints of a seminary ordinand to be able to attend such places with a clear conscience and it was what he experienced during those years that explains why to this day he is a devotee of good cinema production, of a gripping TV serial, or of well-produced and worthwhile theatre drama. When, in the years that were to follow, he had the care of other young people, not all that much younger than himself, he could still vividly appreciate the effect on them of the new media which his generation saw being born. For him the miracle of the 'talkies', the new range of a radio set (the TSF, or telephone without wires, in his native French language) and the sudden burst of creative dramatic production which came with the inter-war years — of Shaw, Priestley, Eugene O'Neill and Ibsen from abroad and of Anouith, Dumas, Guitry and Claudel from France — all this came as a new release to the imaginative powers of this young student of letters. Such experiences taught him fresh truths about the kind of world in which he lived and to which as a priest he would one day have to minister.

One of the things which Louis and his friends did together was to pray. He had already begun to take a more personal interest in the church to which he was preparing to give his life and the less frequent mid-week attendances at Mass which had been usual until now were steadily replaced by a daily visit to the sacrament, until by the end of his first course Louis was making a daily communion. Yet the praying of Louis and his friends was not done only in church: they were members of the new Catholic Youth Movement which had just begun to spring into life in response to a call by the Pope. Pius XI had had the vision of an active missionary laity taking the good news of the Christian Gospel to their neighbours and fellow-workers in the newly-developing cities all over Europe. It was a Belgian seminarian, Joseph Cardijn, who had dedicated himself to providing the means by which young Christians could take part in this fresh 'crusade'. Standing by the death-bed of his father, a coal-merchant, who had worked himself into the grave in order to see his son through College, Joseph determined that when he was ordained he would devote himself to two objects: to devise some method by which the working class might hear afresh the truths of the faith which they so superficially accepted or else ignored, and to seek every proper means by which the lot of the lower classes might be improved. Knowing the cost of work and its toll on the health and spirit of those amongst whom he had grown up he was led to start one of the twentieth century's strongest Catholic movements – the J.O.C. (Jeunesse Ouvrière Chrétienne – Young Christian Workers). It was this movement to which Louis and his friends now became attached.

What particularly caught the imagination of these young men and women, for it was from the start something in which young people of both sexes could be and were involved, was the flexibility of the organisation. Whilst the first concern of Fr. Joseph, now Bishop and later Cardinal, Cardijn was with the needs and the opportunities amongst working class people he soon recognised that here was a tool that could be used amongst all kinds of workers – even those who worked in universities and schools. By 1929 and 1930, only a few years after the launching of the whole undertaking there were local gatherings of JUC (Jeunesse Universitaise Chrétienne) groups whose concern was to win over to the Church the students and their teachers. It was into this particular branch of the movement that Louis Evely thrust himself. Here was a chance to test his own convictions about the faith that he was preparing to propagate and to see in what ways the students around him would react to the customary, and also fresh, ways of presenting the facts of the Creed.

Since the heart of the Young Christian workers' operation was to form groups providing mutual support and guidance, especially for those newcomers drawn in by the approaches of JUC members, it was natural that Louis and his friends should find themselves at prayer. The JUC ethos taught Catholics a new sense of what it was to gather in God's presence outside the church premises and to do it together. The group members were encouraged to speak about the people they were currently trying to contact and the problems and successes which they also experienced. The prayer in which they engaged was thus a prayer that broke away from the formal patterns in which many of them had been brought up and encouraged them to express their thoughts and hopes in a language, and about issues, that could easily be overlooked in traditional church services. In France and at this very same period, the result of this new approach to prayer was forming the first stanzas of the 'Prayers' of Michel Quoist. It is therefore no surprise to find that Louis Evely not only refers to Quoist in his later books but also reflects the same understanding of what it is that creates real Christian fellowship and strategy: '. . . that "pooling" of the aspirations of each individual towards the Lord, the desire to help one another on the spiritual as well as the material plane, constitute the essentials of life of a local group and the material for its periodical meetings.' (The Faith of a Modern Man, p.84).

With his usual thoroughness and dedication Louis not only discharged the duties of his own part in the group but became so active and involved that by the time he had entered into the second of his degree courses he had been elected President of the whole JUC work in the University. When one realises that this in no way affected his studies, that he was enjoying a full social round with its parties and dances, that he had time for his friends and was also preparing a doctoral thesis one can appreciate the ability and the capacity of this tall and handsome young man. It is no surprise to know that he remembers his days at Louvain with great affection. He had the greatest blessing of any active and health man, many things to occupy him and a sense of achievement in all the things he undertook.

Yet underneath all this activity, below the facility with words and the bright, sharp intellect that was being formed and appreciated by an increasing circle of admirers there was, so Louis will tell you, a strange sense of sadness. It was strange because everything would seem to suggest that it was unfounded. Unlike many others who, even when they reach university level, are uncertain about their future he knew for sure where he was bound and what lay ahead of him. He knew what gifts he had to offer and the confident possibility that he would be able to attain all that he set himself or that others expected of him. Still, lightheartedness never seemed to be his. He knew that somehow or other there was an unfulfilled gap in his life, a feeling that something was not quite right which he could not quell. He was subconsciously troubled.

What may well have been wrong was that as he progressed in his academic studies he felt less and less sure that he was right to surrender himself to the kind of life which the priesthood might require of him. After all, he had come to a decision on this matter with very little in the way of sound guidance to help him. He had felt, as he later put it for others, that 'in the bosom of one's family and because of the family such a vocation would be one that was acceptable. Mum and Dad were so pleased at such a decision, so full of goodwill and delight at the news, and had themselves so obviously thought of it as one of the things that a son of theirs might do. They were so full of good deeds, helping others and making so many sacrifices for the family that it was surely right to copy their example in some way — to show one's own ability to love, to give oneself, to renounce something of the fulness of life. 'Yes', he wrote, 'it can happen that a boy becomes a priest because he feels that by doing so he will have been faithful to the best that he has received from his parents.'

If that was not the way of it then perhaps another alternative was this: 'A young man of sixteen or seventeen years of age suddenly becomes aware of the new life-force that is his. Nothing seems too difficult to undertake; he feels as if he could move mountains and that is not simply because he is inexperienced. Something in him tells him that "what you achieve as a mature person is only the result of your best amibitions as a young person". So he looks round for something costly to tackle, something that will leave him free to serve the great causes of the world without the encumbrance of a family or the demands of others in it and which will yet test to the full the whole of his personality. That young man becomes a priest because that is the biggest sacrifice that he can make and the best offering that he can render.'

Somewhere, beneath and behind these words which he uses to describe what is still the truth about many a vocation to the Christian priesthood lies the clue to the disturbance which Louis admits to having felt during these years of his early twenties. We know that he was a born academic. He enjoyed the life at Louvain and he clearly made a great deal of headway as he passed through it. He learnt to savour the rich human relationships of fellow students, both male and female, and the social life he led cannot have disguised from him the joys and the satisfactions of being a lover, a husband and a father if he so wished. He had already discovered gifts of leadership in more than one walk of life and there was, it might seem, no obstacle to his reaching the higher ranks of lecturer and Professor if he wished. Yet a word of promise given, a sense of the sacrifice that he ought to make, the awareness of what his loving and devout mother may feel, even the growing and sensitive awareness of God himself — all these had to be weighed on the other side. Was he sad because he was, for once, unsure in his inner being. It could have been some deep sense of foreboding.

Whatever it was the year of 1932 began to remove his uncertainty, at least for the time being. He finished his second course on the same high peak of achievement in the University as his father had done before him and at Graduation day he was awarded the Premier prize of the whole course. The Médaille d'Or was awarded for coming first in each of his six years at College. In 1932 he was also first in both the Law and Thomist Philosophy schools. He was the idol of his parents, of his classmates, of his tutors, of the whole assembly and before him there must have seemed to be a future of great distinction and even greater satisfaction. Because of his obvious ability, and the course he had just completed, he was excused any further preparation and was admitted at once to the Grande Séminaire at Malines.

He also began to feel so much more light-hearted and relaxed in spirit. People began to comment on the change in his attitude. 'You seem so much more content', they would say, 'and you look happier.' He was. The time for pondering was over and the way ahead had been chosen. His final work and its rewards at the University seemed to suggest that as a priest he would still have plenty of opportunity for using his gifts and playing some part in the academic life of his country and his Church. He now settled down to the business of learning to do the same. That it was a life of much greater discipline than he had been used to was no problem. He had been a scout, he had been a member of the JUC, and now he was bound by the rule of another institution. It was not for ever and if this is what had to be done then it was up to him to do it and to excel at it.

It was a time when Louis had his first introduction to the discipline of military service. As a student and also a prospective ordinand he had been exempt so far from any military conscription but during their four years at Grand Seminary the men were expected to undertake special service in the state Medical units. They did not stop their studying during their period of service and they were under the special care of unit chaplains but they were put into uniform and sent to join a normal military formation. Though not asked to carry arms they learnt what would be required of them in the event of active service, they became acquainted with military law and procedures, and they were provided with a certain amount of medical knowledge. Louis' past experience in the scouts again came to his assistance. What was even more interesting was that both Catholic and Protestant seminarians were billeted together during this time of service. Louis was able to exercise his great gift of listening to another point of view. Indeed, he exercised it so well that he was eventually criticised by his unit chaplain for fraternishing too closely with one of the Protestant pastors. Louis disagreed with what he regarded as a narrow-minded outlook. There was a sizeable row and he was reported to the seminary staff.

What was all too evident, and before very long, was the obvious gap between the ability of an Evely and the general run of the other seminarians. There were those amongst the seminarians who despised him and were quite prepared to tell him that he was 'bourgeois', 'too clever by far' and even 'stuck up'. Not that he was the only one to be so described. Amongst his contemporaries at the Seminary were Roget Aubert, who was the later biographer of Pope Pius IX, and Charles Moeller, who was to become the Rector of the great Jerusalem Bible School, both of them scholars of a very high order. They too were given nicknames that suggested the concealed jealousy or envy of the other students. These for the most part were boys who had come to the Lesser Seminary after a few years in secondary school or had started even earlier. They were mostly men from the countryside and Louis could only think of them as 'peasants'. It was certainly true that he did not find their company congenial since their topics of conversation were limited and their interest in the outside world very restricted indeed. The contrast with his circle at Louvain was too sudden and too sharp.

This was not the whole of the story. Because he could now devote his whole time to the study of religious subjects, liturgy, dogmatics, church history, church law and apologetics, moral theology and pastoralia, Louis began to examine them as he had never done before. He came to them with a background of critical and analytical thought, of wide reading and awareness of the world's problems that was lacking in the experience of most of his fellows.

In addition to this penetrating kind of approach he also had two other fatal gifts. Not only would Louis penetrate to the heart of what he was taught and then proceed to dissect it into logical and illogical parts, to separate what was consonant with rational thought and what was unproven, but he could suggest better ways of stating the matter so that all that was true was more clearly seen. Moreover he could express what he so clearly saw and wished to express in a prose style that left no-one in any doubt as to the thesis which he was submitting for acceptance. It was never the case with Louis that he could plead confusion in the ideas he expressed or imprecision in the way he put them. For good or ill, and it was soon seen to be the latter, Louis' past training was beginning to show. He had come from a world in which imagination, originality, comprehension, and above all lucidity were the hallmarks of excellence. In the Grand Seminary it was soon evident that what was required was exactly the opposite of all these.

In one of the first books which Louis Evely wrote in the 1950s, a book entitled 'L'Église et les Sacrements' (Church and Sacraments) there occur these telling words in the chapter headed, 'Juridiction' (Authority). 'The Lord has only caused us to be obedient to men so that we may submit ourselves the more certainly to God. To desire to obey a God who is invisible in heaven is not enough. . . Christ has given us this sure guarantee of how we may prove our obedience — he tells us to obey God as we find him manifested on earth, the God incarnate in history, the God who is real and alive and with us all our days even unto the end of time.

'That is why we are not called to obey either our own caprices or those of our superiors. The faithful, in rendering their obedience to the Church, continue the obedience of Christ to the Father, And the hierarchy, when it issues commands, is continuing that same mission which the Father confided to the Son: 'As the Father has sent me, so I now send you'.

'However, this power that the Church holds from Christ must be exercised as He would have exercised it: as the Good Shepherd who does not govern with a rod or iron; who comes not as one to be served but to serve others. The Church's head is gentle and humble of heart. He does not seek his own glory. The Church has to take immense pains to ensure that she is holy enough to weild this tremendous authority of command and to see that it is not vitiated by hardness of heart, false pride or naked self-seeking.

'Christ has called us to be obedient to fallible men. It does us no good if we try to pretend that we do not have to obey or that they are infallible. . . But it is up to these superiors to see to it that when they ask us to obey they awaken in us the desire to obey the Christ who is evident in what they require.'

That is heady stuff. It was teaching that received an official imprimatur and which sails near to, but does not transgress, the boundaries of traditional instruction about ecclesial authority. What it says is all based on the teaching of the Bible and that was why, coming from the hand of a respected and acknowledged teacher, it was not only printed and circulated for use in seminaries in Belgium but in training centres all over the French-speaking world. What was so written and printed then, even before Vatican II, was one thing — but similar fresh and precise thinking about an accepted theme in the course of a man's first year at the Seminary was quite another. It is not at all surprising that within 3 months of his entry the staff member teaching dogmatics was reprimanding Louis for the content of his essays and some of his addresses. What was wrong, of course, was that this student wasn't reproducing the accustomed 'line' which had been given in the course. This student was actually daring to present the subjects for consideration, not only in his own terms but with a freshness and an insight that was almost, if not actually, beyond the apprehension of his teacher. It was interesting to learn that what this priest actually said to Louis was, 'I do not like what you write — it frightens me!'

That was only one of several such interviews that were to follow in the days ahead. It disturbed Louis then, as it has disturbed him frequently since, that the Church seems fearful of losing her authority and her preeminence as soon as someone appears who is given a new insight into the ancient truths of the faith and who has the ability and the strength of mind to express what he sees. To quote him again, 'Too many of the faithful are like shareholders in a great commercial enterprise: they receive their dividends but that is the sole interest they take in the whole organisation. The worst service anyone can render to any authority is the servility which encourages authoritarianism. The clericalism with which many accuse the priesthood is often simply the natural result of passivity among the laity . . . Our job is to think, search out, and collaborate constantly with those in authority, to let them know our views, to keep them informed and submit our own suggestions. Obedience in the Church is a matter of conscience — not an invitation to lack of interest.' Louis simply practiced what he was to preach.

The four years passed and the time for ordination drew near. It was to take place on April 4th 1937 in the Cathedral of Malines and Cardinal van Roey was to be the principal celebrant. Prior to the ordination everyone was expected to attend an eight day retreat which on this occasion was to be held in the Lesser Seminary of St. Joseph which happened to be free. What pleased Louis was that one of his best friends, who is now Under-Secretary of the Council for the Defence of the Faith, was also to be ordained. He was delighted that they would be able to share these days together. Louis recalls that he was very contented during this week of quiet. He prayed a good deal and he was at last ready for the step of being ordained that was now so close. Perhaps there came into his mind at that point such an awareness of what it is to be a priest, as he was to describe in a school letter of 1956: 'The priest is a man who adores God, rendering him the homage not merely of a servant but also of a son. He is one who should be able to spend his life reflecting on both how fearful and awesome God is and yet also how gentle and understanding a father we have. The priest is a man who is always seeking for God, pouring out his love to him, giving him the glory that is his due. The great moments of a priest's life are those that he spends in prayer and at Mass, in the presence of this adorable Majesty, realising not only that he is our Judge in the future but our father and our friend from now until eternity.'

His prayers took him on through the retreat addresses, which he hardly heard because he was so caught up in the enormity of what he was about to do with his life, or rather what he believed God was asking of him in his life. Louis even describes his state as 'walking on air'. Indeed so absorbed was he in his spiritual preparation that it was only on the last day of the retreat that Louis' friend, Charles, asked him if he was not going to visit the Jesuit Retreat Conductor. At first Louis said that he had not thought of doing so because he could not think what more the priest could do for him at this stage. The friend advised him otherwise, saying that it would be better if Louis did put in an appearance as otherwise it might create a bad impression and would be noted against him. He said that there was no need to go for more than five minutes or so but it would allay any suggestion of superiority on Louis' part. Louis reluctantly agreed, and eventually, full of goodwill, he went to the Jesuit in his room.

He talked with the Conductor about this and that for most of the five minutes and then, just as Louis thought that the conversation was about to end, the Conductor asked Louis if he was the young man who was a Doctor of Law and Philosophy from Louvain. Louis said that indeed he was, to which the priest immediately retorted that in that case he would be most interested to hear what Louis thought of the Seminary life that he had just experienced. The Conductor made out that he was currently interested in finding out how things were and if improvements could be made.

Louis says that he was reluctant to respond at first and tried to put off the enquiry by saying this his life at the Seminary was at an end and that he was now prepared for the important work that lay ahead of him. The priest insisted, again emphasising that what such an experienced scholar thought about training for the priesthood would help him when conducting further retreats for ordination. Louis then felt that he had to comply and responded in the only way he knew, which was to tell the truth as he saw it, and of course he did so with an incisiveness and clarity that left his hearer in no doubt as to his opinions.

He said that he had been very happy in the Seminary because he was able to do his own studying and reading, thinking and discussing with friends. He admitted that it had been a good discipline for him to undergo this very different mental, social and intellectual experience but when one considered the poor chaps who had only had seminary training as their preparation for the priesthood he thought it was disgraceful. What they underwent were barrack room procedures with a kind of classroom indoctrination which quite prevented their individual development and rendered them utterly unproductive save as cyphers of an institution. They would spend all their time forbidding things about which they had neither fully thought nor even had experience, and they would no doubt be exemplary in impressing on their flocks every negative kind of feeling that they could recall. He was distressed at how shallow was the whole approach and he would not be at all surprised if most of the men never opened another book during the rest of their lives whilst yet imagining that they had a monopoly of the whole truth. They were conditioned and manipulated until all they had become was a set of robots, machines for reproducing certain words and gestures to order.

What concerned Louis most of all was that this was the only kind of formative process to which they would ever be exposed. They were and would always be individualists — men who were conditioned to live alone, not just because they would be unmarried but because they were cut off from every kind of awareness of the world in which they were now going to minister. They were devoid of all the arts which would allow them to communicate or to associate with others. As for the doctrine they were taught, it was mainly instruction in how to prevent heresy. It seemed to concentrate more on keeping them 'unspotted from the world' rather than helping them to spread the good news in it. Louis, whilst following the course, had tried continually to ask himself, what out of all this will I want to pass on to the people of today? What is the message of joy of the love of God, in what I am being taught? Frankly, there had been nothing: he had had to discover it all for himself. It was all very sad. There was nothing more to say.

The conductor, who had, of course, assured Louis at the outset that what was said in his room was confidential and between them alone, wanted Louis to say more, assuring him that what had already been said so forcefully and with feeling was most interesting. Louis repeated that there was nothing more to be added. It was not a subject on which he wanted to dwell further as it gave him too much pain to recall it. Moreover he did want to leave the retreat at the time stated as he was due to meet his father. They parted and Louis thought no more about what had just happened.

When the family visit was over Louis returned to the Seminary to prepare for his ordination the next day. As he entered the building he was taken to one side by a very good friend of his who told him that Canon Gillet, Louis' confessor and spiritual director, wanted to see him urgently. As Louis sat down in the latter's room the priest asked him what it was that he had done during his ordination retreat. Louis then replied, 'I said that I had done a lot of praying and had been very calm and happy. That did not satisfy my confessor and he pressed me to think what else I had been up to. I could not think of anything else because the spiritual side of the retreat was uppermost in my memory. Then suddenly I realised. He was asking me about something that no-one except the Retreat Conductor and I had known about. I told him something of what I had given as my impressions of the seminary. It was then that he utterly shocked me.

'He told me that he had gone into the Refectory that same evening with the Rector and other staff of the Seminary, and the priest who had taken the retreat repeated most of what Louis had said to him in total confidence. "You've got some strange people among these seminarians", he had said, "some really independent spirits — and proud. I have just had this Louis Evely to see me". Most of my own comments were then relayed to everyone. Of course it had caused a terrible commotion and the effect was not one that I would be very pleased to hear. It appeared that until that moment I had been selected all along for the staff of the Institut de Philosophie et Lettres, a Faculty of the University of Louvain, and that on my being ordained I was to have taken up my place there at once. Now it was not at all certain that I would even be ordained.'

Louis was overcome. He at once went to see the Rector to explain how it had all happened and stress that a confidence had been breached. When at last Louis was admitted to the Rector's room he was received with every appearance of courtesy and kindness and told not to worry. Louis continues: 'I now realise that all his assurances were just hypocrisy — he kept calling me "son" — and he obviously never heard me when I explained the circumstances of the whole affair. He simply went on saying that it was not a serious business — that it would remain between ourselves (though it seemed a bit late for that) — that I was not to worry

— that he quite understood the situation — that I must not excite myself about this, especially on the eve of my ordination, and I must stay calm. I agreed to all this but I cannot deny that I was very apprehensive and I knew that something dreadful could happen'.

He had not long to wait. Three or four days later Louis was sent for by the Director of a boys' college in the diocese in order to be told what was to be his assignment. The Director welcomed him very warmly as one who was highly qualified but he also pointed out that the assignment at the College was a punishment for what he had said at the Ordination retreat. Louis was to teach religion to boys of 6-7 years of age and to be a deputy master looking after the most difficult of the school boarders. It was a long way from the Senior Common Room of the country's leading centre of learning. Yet the Church had commanded and Louis was one of her priests. In a very real sense, it was his first Waterloo.

4 *Learning to Teach*

The Cardinal Mercier College to which Louis was now appointed stands on the very outskirts of the town of Waterloo just south of Brussels. It was still comparatively new, having been founded in 1924 to commemorate the golden jubilee of the ordination of the famous Belgian Primate whose name it bears. It was purposely built in what was then completely open country so that the pupils could enjoy fresh air, extensive views and that freedom from the pressures of urban life which most of their fee-paying parents had to bear. To this day, though the school has now more than twenty times as many pupils, there is a sense of airiness and space around the various buildings and from the upper floors of several houses you can see the Forest of Soignes which was in 1937 one of the first noticeable landmarks on the horizon. It was initially a school for 75 boarders only but at the time Louis Evely joined the staff the number of buildings had increased from one to three and the 600 boys included day students and even preparatory scholars. In addition to the original house with its steeep gabled roofs, its mock half-timbered frontage and circular French-style turrets there was now a huge classroom complex and a still newer house specially put up for the permanent boarders. The houses that now so closely flank the school had not then appeared and in the gardens that greeted the latest member of staff on his arival there had recently been unveiled a new statue of the Cardinal on a vast stone-blocked plinth. It tells you something of the school's reputation and status that this ceremony had been performed by Leopold III, King of the Belgians, accompanied by his ill-fated consort, Queen Astrid. That was on June 30th, 1935.

There were three departments in the school — one for the preparatory pupils, from six to twelve years of age; one for those studying the 'humanities' (Latin, Greek, basic philosophy and the natural sciences, along with mathematics); and another for 'Commerce' (dealing with economics, administration, the social sciences and training in technical skills). The staff included laymen though the Director of the School and the heads of each department and of each house were priests. That was how it was to continue for the next twenty years after Louis' arrival, though it is no longer the case and the change was in no small part due to the influence exercised by Louis after he himself became Principal in 1948. At the time of Louis' arrival the Principal was Abbé Hanon.

It being only April there still remained three months of the school course to complete and Louis was asked to start by teaching religion, spefically the Catholic Faith, to children of six, seven and eight years of age. Louis tackled it with what can only be described as the Waterloo spirit. Just as that town witnessed a possible defeat changed into a notable victory, so Louis made a resolve that what some, and certainly his family, might have regarded as his apparent dêbacle, should be turned into something really worthwhile. He might not be one of the youngest professors of Louvain University, but he could become one of the best teachers in this new school. Indeed, he now recognises that it was the need to so understand the faith of the Catholic Church that he could clearly present it to small boys which further sharpened his ability to write for other audiences later. It was soon apparent to the Director and the whole staff that here was a teacher of great ability and promise. Within a matter of weeks Louis was asked to supervise the older boarders as well.

It was in this area of personal, teacher-pupil relations that Louis began to do his own learning and to make some of his most perceptive contributions in the educational field. Here again he admits that within the confines of a University nothing of this would have been possible though he might equally have been spared the self-questioning that was bound to follow about how the Church generally manages her own personal, and personnel, relationship problems.

He soon discovered that the older boarders were both ill-disciplined and badly brought up. The Principal at that time wanted his college to be built on a foundation of trust and in this he was copying what he had seen and learnt from some of the best public schools in England. The result was that parents with difficult children were often advised by frustrated headmasters of preparatory schools to send their boys to Cardinal Mercier College. You only had to be with the boys a short while, says Louis, to realise that you were likely to have a problem in dealing with them. For instance, the school rules required that boys should do one hour of sport a day. None of the pupils seemed to want to do it but preferred to saunter about the grounds, go for an illicit smoke, chat in odd corners and generally waste the time for recreation. As long as they did not work or make themselves a nuisance there was no member of the staff to learn just what they did and certainly no one in authority to see that they did actually get some exercise.

The Principal also made it clear that if they owned up to anything they did wrong he would never punish them. If therefore one of the teachers took them out for a walk or on an expedition and they misbehaved by disobeying his instructions, trying to make dates with the passing girls, dodging into shops to buy sweets or cigarettes, or even disappearing for most of the time they were out, they only had to run up to the Principal's room on their return, confess all that they had done wrong and nothing more happened. When their master went to report them he would be told that as the boys had already confessed the Principal had forgiven them and that was the end of the matter. The staff's authority was completely undermined, and the boys knew it.

One of the first things that Louis had to impress on the boys whom he was now asked to supervise was that he would never ask them to do anything which he himself was not willing to do. In that way, he stresses, he was first able to make the point that as he would have to do whatever he asked of them the boys realised that he meant what he said. When, therefore, it was time for sport the first person out on the sports field was Louis himself. The pictures of this tall young priest with his soutane tucked up around his waist as he joins in a game of football or handball are almost as surprising today as they most certainly were when they were first taken. The idea of a priest actually getting in there with the boys was unheard of and yet from being mere spectators of the 'kids' who played with 'Father' the older boys were drawn into games of their own and soon there had to be an agreement as to how long Louis played with one group or another. It did not happen in a few moments, it took time, but it did happen and it happened without endless remonstrations by the teacher on the one hand and constant negative reactions from the scholars. When someone came amongst these adolesccents who was prepared to share life with them they began to take him and what he had to say seriously.

The same thing began to happen in the classroom. After a year Louis was asked to teach Latin to the 14 year-olds. They were known to smoke and chatter through most of the lessons which they attended. When Louis began it was no different but rather than spend time arguing and playing the game of confession to the Principal Louis simply got down to making his Latin lessons as interestingly serious as he could. He gave time to those who wanted to learn and allowed the others to come round in their own good time. Because the boys knew what the priest was like out of the classroom as well as in it they steadily changed. They all began to pay attention and at last the results of their work began to show.

It was in caring for them as real persons out of the classroom that Louis constantly made his mark. When he came to the college he also found that the boys were obsessed with their sexual sins. This was because they each had a Director of Confidences who would see them individually in his room where they would confess to him their peccadilloes. The effect of this, as Louis soon saw, was that many boys were more concerned about what they were going to say in confession and whether they had actually sinned rather than with living wholesome and normal lives. Louis called this method of dealing with the boys 'angling' and he thoroughly disagreed with it. It still seems to him that this encourages a wrong relationship between the boy and the member of staff, even if the latter is a priest, and also makes the whole matter of sex one that grows out of all proportion to other adolescent concerns. It seemd to him that what should be happening was to give these 'poor fish' a much happier and fresh pool in which to swim. Instead of all the time trying to save them from a stagnant sinfulness they should be given a chance to express their natural sexuality in other ways. It was to this matter that Louis gave a great deal of thought because he could see that it affected more than just the private life of each boy: it was doing harm to the whole fabric of school relations.

Part of the answer came in his new method of organising the life of the school boarders. Though he began to devise his new system before the war interrupted his teaching career it was after the war that it was put into full operation and was also explained to the parents in one of his first letters to them as the new Principal. He wrote this:—

'There are many wise parents who take great care over their children, who see their real needs and adjust their actions to deal with them. They will alter the family pattern, change their rules and even their own demands according to the growing characters of their offspring. We should like to copy their example and so we want to tell you this: we shall do as you do. We shall care for and watch over your children. For us too there are no boys who are just the same. And we shall be ready to alter our methods, our attitudes and our discipline if we see that that is what will really serve the best interests of your children. That is what we like to think is our better method!'

He then continued to outline what this would mean in practice. It meant that in addition to the usual 'horizontal' arrangement of pupils as juniors, middle school and seniors according to age there would be a new 'vertical' arrangement which would affect boys from 14 to 18 years of age. 'It has seemed to us', he continued, 'that the educational atmosphere would be improved if boys with different characteristics could begin to share more as a family. The "seriousness" and the "experience" of the more senior might help to moderate some of the boisterousness and lack of thought of the younger ones. On the other hand the freshness, the enthusiasm and the respect which the latter might possess would sometimes affect the staidness and re-awaken the fondness of the older boys. It is easy for the older boys sometimes to think that they are "the tops" and to forget their responsibilities for those who follow them up the school. By this method of association they can each begin to realise that they have duties, not to the school or to the staff but to one another. To help others to keep the rules almost always mean that you keep them yourself. The aim of our School, which is to engage in helping boys to grow up and become men and to help others to do the same can only be enhanced when we have boys who do not only keep rules but encourage others to do the same.'

It was obvious but because it was so it worked. Some of the long-standing staff regarded it as a stroke of brilliance and it began to show its effects in many directions. After the different age groups were combined there was much less difficulty with sexual matters.

It was not that they could be kept from carnal knowledge, but because they now played together, worked together, and were responsible for each other in a new way there was a more natural respect for each other's bodies as well as for each other's minds and talents. As they were given a measure of self-government there was no need for the staff to puzzle out new ways of punishing them or seeking to avoid punishment as Abbé Hanon tried to do. It was the elected members of the 'vertical' teams who had the responsibility for general good behaviour or the correcting of misdemeanours. The pupils were more fearful of their peers than ever they were of public or staff opinion. It was made clear that if anyone was afraid of the discipline exercised by the elected group they could always choose to remain under Louis' personal supervision. There were no takers.

One example of how this 'rule by one's peers' became accepted in the college is shown by an incident which Louis recalls during one of his return visits after having left the staff. Invited by the new teacher to look in on one of his old classrooms he found the boys quietly working away. Suddenly one of the boys got up, took his book and knelt on the floor in front of his desk and then started writing in his exercise book. The reason for this apparently inexplicable behaviour was, Louis discovered, that the pupils had all decided that if anyone disturbed the rest of the class for any reason, the punishment was that they had to spend ten minutes on their knees doing their work. Louis thought this rather excessive, but it was one more pointer to the fact that when pupils are self-governing they can be more strict that the teachers themselves.

The encouragement of self-help and self-government, by having team leaders who were chosen every term, did not mean that Louis was released from all responsibility as a leader and teacher himself. On the contrary it meant that Louis could now devote himself to giving counsel and advice to the boys who became the elected leaders and also to devising more and more ways in which the school life could become interesting and worthwhile. Louis describes one such experiment. 'We decided to have an Initiative Day. The boys were told that they could do whatever they liked. They were free to go anywhere and to undertake any activity that appealed to them. The only requirement was that everyone was to be back in the main hall by suppertime and after our meal we would expect everyone to say briefly what he had done with the day. They were especially taken with the idea that we would postpone lights out so as to allow everyone to report on his day's outing. When supper was over we all sat around in a huge circle, as if at a scout camp fire, and listened to everyone's report. There were some who had gone off on their own, some in twos and threes, some on bicycles, and some who had gone to catch a train. There were some who had just gone home to see mum. With all that opportunity for freedom to explore the world a little more they had just wanted to return to mother's skirts. Everyone laughed at this. Especially as they also heard how others had gone to see a sick friend, some had really explored the countryside, some had visited a museum, some had even drawn a picture or written a poem about the place they had seen. The time for reports just flew by and most of them went to bed eager to have a second chance to "take the initiative" and use a day as best they could'.

There were other experiments too. There was the day for bravery, and in order to get into the finals for that day you had to pass one or two tests. One of them that Louis recalls was that the boys had to picck up a live wasp with two fingers, hold it so that it did not sting, and bring it alive to him. It may sound a petty thing to do but for the boys concerned it was a real test of courage both to attempt it and to succeed in completing it.

One of the teachers who served for many years with Louis, Raymond Gillet-Nitens, was only too glad to share with me something of the impression that Louis made on the boys whom they both taught. He was, says Raymond, a very great teacher and there was no question that the children loved him as well as respected him. They called him 'Dr. Philosopher' and from the time that he became Principal in 1948 there was hardly a member of staff who did not admire him and find him a leader worth following. What Louis brought to his teaching, and it was still so unusual in his day, was a natural grasp of psychology. To put it in Christian terms, says Raymond, he 'knew what was in man'. Because he could see so deeply he could also understand how and why people would react as they did. Moreover his natural sociability, his warm cordiality, a deep streak of care for others as human beings and his desire that people should be encouraged to develop their abilities to the utmost – all these meant that whilst he demanded high standards from all his pupils, he also managed to guide them wisely because he could uncover their faults without destroying them in the process. It was this that endeared him to so many.

Raymond's son, Fernand, now a teacher at the College in the Commerce section, was one of those whom Louis had on one occasion to reprimand because the boy had been found stealing wine after he had served at the altar in the school chapel. Just because Louis was so friendly, says Fernand, and knew everyone by name, it made my going to his study on this occasion all the more difficult. I was only eight years old remember, and here I was going to see a priest, a tall, strong and respected priest, about something wrong which affected the most sacred area of our Catholic life. I paused on the threshold of his room. What would he say – or do? My parents were so ashamed and had told me so. Fernand entered the room, and there was Louis sitting in an easy chair.

Louis beckoned him to another chair so that they could look at each other. '*You* know why we are here', he said, 'and so do I. It's because you and I serve at the altar together. What interests me is that you are not only fond of wine, but you know which is the best to sample. I like a server who values good wine and I would not want one who didn't. The only thing is, do think more carefully about what is the best time to sample it, and make sure that it's yours to sample. Is there anything more to be said?' Fernand sat there amazed. There was no scolding, no dwelling on what was perfectly well known to them both, and yet the Principal had made his point very clearly – you like the wine we use but there is a time and place for taking it. The incident has already remained with Fernand for half a lifetime and he will never forget it – or the way in which it was handled.

On another occasion, Fernand added, a very serious situation arose which was called the 'Battle of the Chestnuts'. In one of those fits of defiance that can sometimes seize young boys, especially when they are united in some cause, there was a threatened mutiny of 400 of the boys when the Abbé Hanon had said that because of the danger caused by throwing chestnuts at each other the boys were forbidden to gather them, string them or play with them on any part of the school premises or on the way to or from school. One morning the teachers found this vast crowd of boys, all holding their stringed conkers in their hands and refusing to come into the classrooms until the Principal had changed the rules. The mood of the boys was as surly and ominous as could be. The teachers were uncertain what to do, and then Louis appeared. He had quietly left the scene, found himself the largest conker he could reach and put it on a string. He now came from amongst the teachers and asked whoever thought he was the best conker-striker to come and take him on. If he won then Louis promised to speak to the Principal, but if he lost then the rest of the boys must disperse and throw their conkers away. The tension broke, the teachers and the boys formed a rough arena and the contest took place. Whether it was Louis' stronger arm or just good luck it will never be known but the splitting of the pupil's conker brought an end to a very ugly scene.

In another of his memorable addresses to parents in the School magazine Louis had a telling passage about this matter of dealing with adolescents. 'This headstrong and wild young person as he appears to you is, if only you are aware of it, someone who has not yet discovered in whom he can finally put his trust. What he denies to your face he will as likely defend behind your back. If only you could realise how very sensitive he is, how near to tears though he puts on an angry face, how full of regard for you when you are not there, how changeable in his moods, and how much he wants support when he is all too aware that he has done wrong. Just a word of kindness, a word of renewed confidence on your part, can penetrate that tough exterior which he thinks he has to put on in order to defend himself from your wrath. If only you knew how he hurts himself, despises himself, and is so near to giving up all hope, and how much he relies on how he feels, what his pals think, what public opinion thinks, then you would not think he was beyond the pale! You would see, as we do, in each of his acts of revolt a strangled cry of deep distress and an appeal for help and you would drop everything in order to aid his all too weak independence, and whilst you would offer him protection, at the same time taking him seriously as the man that he is striving to become, you would gently and discreetly provide him with some of the means whereby he could both claim and achieve that very manhood.'

What also struck Raymond and his son so forcibly was the power and clarity of Louis' preaching. Fernand can recall to this day many of the sermans which Louis preached when Fernand was a young teenager in the college. He recalls one occasion that particularly struck him. Louis spent the whole sermon as if he were on the phone to one of the great prophets of the Bible and by this method he not only captured the attention of the boys but also managed to convey what might otherwise have been very difficult teaching for schoolchildren. Indeed what was as remarkable as the style of Louis' preaching was the emphasis which he obviously laid on preaching as part of Christian worship. Raymond described him as 'évangélique', or as a man who turned constantly to the Bible for the source of so much that he taught in his lessons and in his chapel addresses. In the days before Vatican II such an emphasis was not at all common and Louis' practice was therefore all the more noticeable.

It was not only in his preaching, however, that there were marks of pre-Vatican II attitudes with Louis. It was during his time as Principal that there arose the need for a new recreation hall in which they could play basketball and badminton and also have a much larger and better equipped programme of gym periods. At the same time the chapel for the school was beginning to prove too small for the weekly school Mass to which all scholars were expected to come and it occurred to Louis that if a balcony was included in the new building it would be possible to use the new hall for both kinds of re-creation. Indeed it would underline the very thing which he had wanted for some time to point out to the school — the close relationship which ought to exist between the work and worship which we render to God every day. It would also allow the celebration of the Mass to be conducted in a more family setting with the altar in the centre of the school assembly rather than in the traditional East-end setting then customary. What Louis planned for came to pass and ten years before the present westward-facing position of the priest at the Catholic Mass had been encouraged by Vatican II, the boys at Cardinal Mercier college were becoming accustomed to it.

There was one other facet of Louis' teaching career which cannot be overlooked. We have seen in an earlier chapter how Louis began to be involved in the Scout movement, and what it did for him as an adolescent. Something of that experience was now brought to bear on the developing life of the College. Scouting, with its emphasis on self-discipline and the importance of being a useful member of a patrol was the perfect organisation to complement the 'vertical' arrangement in his school system. As there were some old farm buildings on the edge of the school property it seemed only right to use these as the Scout headquarters, and into the development of the school troop this energetic and ubiquitous priest could naturally throw himself. It was by design that he did not take the leadership of the troop into his own hands, but his was the spark that got it going and every mention of it that he could make was used to the full. Nor was it by accident that when there was the chance to develop the spare rooms under the boarders' lounge and dormitories for leisure activities some of the space was given over to activities that would enable those who were scouts to gain more badges. It stressed the outdoor activity which Louis wanted to encourage, and it played no small part in developing those very pursuits which came to be noted in the curriculum — obstacle chases, swimming, life-saving, sailing, camping and hiking. It was a pursuit that was to serve Louis well in part of his wartime years.

It was the dedication of the man, his willingness to undertake whatever was put before him that slowly marked him out as a prospective Principal of the whole College. When, even before his wartime service, he was appointed the head of the Commercial department of the school, there were many who thought that this was one more case of Louis' abilities being undervalued, if not misused, by his superiors. Though there may well have been good reason to regard this as a further rebuff, Louis looked at it quite differently. By then he had realised that his ability to teach and control difficult situations was recognised by his colleagues. The Commercial department of the school was the most indisciplined and least prestigious section of the whole school. At the time, classics was the chic thing to do — the intelligent pupils took Greek and Latin, and those who were not good enough did commerce, accounting or allied subjects. The result was those in the commercial section of the commercial section of the college were thought of as the failures. Louis' appointment as the head of this section, therefore, could be seen as a mark of rebuke, but it was also a sign of appreciation. If anyone could manage these boys and this work it was Evely. It was in that spirit that he tackled what was a quite novel and strange area of study for him. The proof of what he accomplished is that to this day the commercial section of the school has been able to hold its own against the other departments, and as we saw at the outset of this story, some of the closest friends that Louis still has amongst old boys are from the classes that he taught at that time.

At this point we might hear a word from Louis himself when he took over the post of Director. 'At the beginning of each year, when the pupils returned from their holidays, there was always a retreat – three days of prayers and sermons. Immediately after my appointment I said that all the pupils and teachers were invited. The boys were not only less academic, they were also tough. However, all came to make their confession and communion except three, and after the mass was over, we had lunch, and I made a point of lunching with those three, so that they did not feel "excommunicated". The result was that these commercial kids apparently began to like me – "the most brilliant professor of humanities who came to us and liked us", is what they began to say. We had a sort of "union of the poor" and I was their leader. I wanted to form a boarders group, so that there would be in each class a group of pupils who would know me as their Director, and also to support each other. Like that, we got on very well, and the other teachers were also happy, because they felt that someone was at last doing something for these poor pupils. The commercial teachers, you see, had always felt inferior – the great professors were the teachers of the classics.'

In 1948 Cardinal van Roey, the Primate of Belgium, approved a new appointment at the school. Abbé Evely, Doctor of Law and Doctor in Thomist Philosophy, was to be the new Principal of the College. The school magazine on that occasion commented as follows: –

'He has for more than ten years rendered this school valuable service. In this community of our boys, his astounding capacity for work, his natural ability as a teacher, and his priestly bearing, have been the admiration of us all. The boys all respect him as their teacher, a fine educationalist, and a Maquis chaplain of distinction. We thank our revered Primate for having chosen him as our fourth Principal and may M. Evely share with us many years as our guide and father in this college!'

That appointment was the culmination of many happy days of teaching. Louis loved his work and especially his boys, even though he like teaching anyone. On one occasion he ws visiting the home of a boy when the boy's mother asked if he would possibly help her thirteen-year old daughter who was having difficulty in learning the names of the capitals of African countries. In half an hour's tuition, Louis was able to show the girl how to learn and retain those names. From that day to the present that girl says that she could never possibly forget the names of those capitals. Such was Louis' ability as an instructor.

As you walk around the school buildings, which have hardly changed since Louis was in charge, even though their capacity was doubled during his time as Principal, you can see that something of the spirit of relevant and real religion which his imprint left on the place. In some of the boarders' houses there are a series of posters in the hall and on the stairs. Their messages have a very Evely ring — 'Be an engine, not a brake: don't drag, get going!' 'To father a son is fine: to behave like a man is even better'; 'Do I realise how privileged I am compared to so many others?' and 'There is always something to do'. You find the same sort of poster 'decoration' on the dormitory stairs in other houses: 'Man finds himself when he measures up to obstacles' (a quote from Antoine de Saint-Exupéry) and another with the words 'walk in the faith' beneath a picture of a typically straight French road with poplars and setts. You feel that the whole campus is shot through with a religion that links every part, buildings, boys, and staff. The creation of that link has owed a great deal to Louis Evely, and his own remaining affection for the place, despite all that has happened to him since he left over a decade ago, is revealed as one walks around the college with him today. His eyes linger on the original house for boarders, and his hands stretch to touch a noticeboard or a desk in one of the classrooms, he walks proudly past the football field, and stands gazing into the past as he comes to the swimming pool. Here, in this school complex, was the whole central core of his life's work, unsought, unexpected, unforgettable, and unique. Fernand Gillet summed it up with the words, 'When things get to an awkward stage these days, we always say, "these are no longer Evely times" '.

That learning and teaching experience was not uninterrupted, however, for the uncertainties of wartime came to disturb the family spirit which Louis and his boys had begun to establish. On November 9, 1939, there was a general alert of an all-out offensive by the Germans following their surprisingly short and decisive campaign against the Poles. Every reservist in Belgium was told to report, and Louis at once put on his uniform, got out his bicycle, and was one of the first to arrive at the enlistment centre to which he was directed. He was detailed to join a medical unit and reported to the officer in charge. He found the spirit of most of the men around him to be one of apathy or depression, and he was not surprised at the collapse of his country's forces when they were under pressure in the following year. Yet the test was not to come for some time, since the Germans found themselves caught up in a battle with Norway, after overrunning Denmark, and this drew away a good deal of their attention during the winter months. Louis was in fact stood down and was told that he could return to his school, but must report at once if the threatened invasion did in fact materialise.

It was in early May, 1940, that Louis and his boarders were woken at 4 o'clock one morning by the sound of heavy bombs falling not far away. As the daylight broke, and the bombing continued, the staff held a hurried meeting and decided that they should arrange for the dispersal of the boarders to their homes. Most of the morning was spent in contacting parents, guardians or friends of the boys, as well as getting them to buses, trains and such cars as could come for them. By midday, Louis was free to put on his reserve officer's uniform, get out his bicycle again and see what he could do to help by reporting to the chosen assembly point. He was in fact the first person to show up there, though when the others began to arrive, they were again looking reluctant and demoralised. The first arrivals asked him if he thought that they were really at war.

They were soon put in charge of the 'trains sanitaires', that is, the trains for transporting the wounded from the front to the rear hospitals. As the Germans advanced, Louis' unit took the patients first to Bruges, and latterly to Ostend. The trains were bombed, the stations were bombed, and Louis and his companions had all sorts of adventures. They were even presented with one passenger who was a certified lunatic, whom the authorities in Bruges said should be locked up. 'Fine', said Louis, 'but where?' He was told to take the patients to an air raid shelter, but he imagined the station being bombed, and the only person that might then be found would be this dangerous lunatic. So Louis said that it was not possible to find a really secure place, and the best that could be done was to lock him in a couchette. In fact the patient was not really dangerous, but just someone who became very excitable.

In this reserve unit, stationed on the outskirts of Brussels, all Louis' earlier fears about the morale of the troops were to be confirmed. The commander under whom he served as chaplain was a professional soldier, and had all the faults of one. He was a pleasure-seeker, out for an easy life, a heavy drinker and smoker, a man who swore, was scruffy and unbelievably lazy. Louis recalls one occasion when all the officers had been summoned to the commander's comfortable quarters, and those who wished to had been suitably supplied with a drink. Whilst they were discussing the present situation, a newly-wounded soldier was reported as being at the door and needing attention. Louis could not believe his ears as they all began to argue about whose turn it was to go out and deal with the case. Someone said that the commander should go, as he had done nothing so far. The commander retorted by saying 'No, you should go, because you are the youngest'. The fact was, as Louis now realises, that the commander was not simply lazy, but like many other professional soldiers, also very frightened. He had a revolver – as had all the officers, including Louis, – and at the slightest cause the revolver would come out of its holster, and he would wave it around, whether there was any danger or not. It was all a sign of his nervousness and uncertainty.

Another day, news came in that there were two suspected parachutists near the station which they were supposed to be guarding. The commander said to Louis, 'You go, chaplain, and find out just what is happening. After all, these men have come down from the sky!'

Unarmed though Louis happened to be at that moment, he at once obeyed and made enquiries of the terrified sentries. It turned out to be a false alarm, but it also confirmed Louis in the sense of disgust with his country's so-called defenses. It also showed him how much organisation was going to be left in his hands.

For example, it being May the weather was very good. The German High Command had sensibly chosen such weather for their offensive. Yet, though the weather during the daytime was magnificent, the nights were very cold and the wounded soldiers in the hospital trains were almost frozen. The carriages stood abandoned in the station, and the locomotives that had once pulled them were all now parked in a shed. Louis therefore went to find the station-master and some of the drivers, and eventually persuaded them to attach the locomotives to the carriages and provide some heat.

It was, however, the extent of cowardice among the military personnel which disturbed Louis most. When there was a bombing, he was astounded to discover that if the commander and other officers were in the train, they would hide under the bunks on which the wounded soldiers were resting. If it was a really bad bombing raid, they would even hide underneath the wagons themselves, and make their way towards the air raid shelters in the station. It never seemed to occur to these soldiers that their responsibility lay with the sick and wounded who were in their charge.

There was also an astonishing level of disorganisation in the Army, and no-one seemed to know anything of what was happening. One day, in September 1940, at the hospital, Louis saw 45 soldiers in German uniform riding past on bicycles without even looking at the Belgian soldiers. It was in fact the German vanguard. There was such disorganisation that they had simply slipped in like butter. the Germans were well-organised, moving forward in small groups and, as Louis remarks, acting like well-trained Scouts. They always showed plenty of initiative and each group advanced as far as it could, testing the route, and cutting the lines behind them. The effect of this sort of penetration was that some of the local people wept whilst others of them said, 'Good, it's going to mean the end of the war'. It was that kind of apathy that troubled Louis most. And so, on one of the journeys to Ostend, he began to look for a boat to take him to England. He soon learnt, however, that all the fishing boats had left for England months ago. As Belgium was then technically at war, the fishermen discovered that they could make a better living in England, since the English fishermen had been mobilised, and there was no-one to do their job. So, says Louis, 'there I was, at the port, with my revolver in my hand, saying, 'You must take me to England', and they refused, saying that the commander of the port had instructed that no boats should leave as they would be bombed. As it was clearly impossible to leave the country, Louis returned to his men, and they were all duly interned in a camp in Holland.

He was there for two months, and he describes that period for himself and his country as 'la grande humiliation'. 'We would see German aircraft going overhead on their way to bomb Britain, and we would say, "they won't attack us any more, they will see that we get food", and so we became inured to what was happening.' It went on like that for two months, but eventually Louis and his fellow-prisoners began to organise themselves better for the sake of their morale, until one day they were informed that they were going to be freed. Though they did not know this, King Leopold had surrendered to the enemy so as to avoid further destruction in the south of Belgium, and the population were told to get back to their normal occupations so far as circumstances would allow. Louis, as a priest, was released from prison, and given the task of looking after sick people in a local hospital, but the opportunity came to secure his 'papiers de libération', he managed to find a bicycle, and to rearch Brussels. He at once visited his family and then returned to the college. The principal there had responded to the government's call and had started up the school again for any pupils who could attend.

Louis tried to pick up where he had left off months before. Though the country was now occupied by the enemy, he felt that it was going to serve the boys best if they were at least given some education which they could use in the future. He was happy to think that those who returned to the school had not forgotten many of the methods which he had taught them. He would, for instance, stay at his desk during a lesson and, having set the class to work, he was then available for any boy to come up to him for special help if he needed it.

One day, when they had just begun to put up the blackout panels against the windows because of the increasingly frequent British air-raids, a German soldier noticed that one of the sections was faulty and came to check it. Louis suddenly heard his heavy boots coming along the corridor, the classroom door stood open, and the soldier stood at the doorway with his rifle at the carry. Not one of the pupils' heads was raised or turned — they all just went on with what they were doing. The German was dumbstruck at his apparent failure to impress the class, and after a moment of embarrased silence, he about-turned and went away. That was a typical example of how engrossed boys could get in something which they found interesting.

Louis also noticed, however, that the boys were very impressed by the dedication, the discipline and the toughness of the young German soldiers who were now billeted on the school premises. The well-turned out appearance, the ability, the healthiness and the apparent initiative shown by these young men were in so many ways the very qualities which Louis' boys were themselves being encouraged to develop. The contact between the two groups was only too obvious when the boys would be playing their school games alongside a squad of drilling men. It sometimes became very real contact indeed, when a badly-steered football landed in the midst of the men who might be dressing their ranks. What certainly affected the boys was to see a 50 year-old soldier being punished by having to crawl endlessly up and down the school slopes until he almost collapsed with exhaustion – yet never complaining.

This wartime teaching life was to be interrupted once more before the fighting in Europe was over, but that is the next part of our story. For Louis, the whole experience of Cardinal Mercier college was one which he can never forget. What he learned there has been committed to writing in a book not so far translated into English and entitled 'Eduquer en s'éduquant'. (U.S. title: "Training Children to Maturity"). It does not contain anything which might be considered fresh or original today, but there is still a lot of difference between the newer and more liberal theories of education, including child participation, and their actual implementation. Louis wrote out of his experience, and with the practical evidence of what could be achieved, as a daily reminder before his eyes. For him, the whole of school life was meant to be, like the whole of life, a worthwhile and wholesome experience. He was eager that as he and his pupils looked back to those days at College, they would have something more than sentimental memories to treasure. As he himself put it, 'a measure of authority and a measure of freedom, a mixture of initiative and discipline, these are the things which are really important in my understanding of education. If these were there, suiting each boy with his special needs, then that was good education'.

5 *Wartime Interlude:*

The valley of the river Semois is an enchanting spot but it has never been one of the most popular areas to be visited by tourists in Belgium. The rich and dense forest-land that runs steeply down to meet the fast-flowing water creates its own sense of remoteness and secrecy. The roads are few and narrow, curving and twisting between great banks of grass and shrubbery and so overarched by pine trees and mountain ash that not only are they almost hidden from the sky but camouflaged from observation at ground level. The villages, Bohan, Membre, Laforêt, Mouzaive and Alle are all no more than large hamlets, clinging to the side of the river banks. Their houses are the product of the local earth, sturdy and substantial blocks of brown and gray stone with tall, well-set windows, many of them framed with white headpieces and thick sills, and some even carrying shutters. The buildings, mills and stables and storerooms, as well as the dwelling quarters all seem to have sprouted, like the surrounding trees, from roots well-bedded in the tough, hilly soil. There is a sense of timelessness and perpetuity. Gone are the traces of the big cities which are but two or three hours of driving away. You are almost on the frontier with northern France but you are in the very heart of the Belgian Ardennes.

It is a perfect terrain for guerrilla fighting. Though the term 'Maquis' first referred to a much more scrubby kind of woodland in the island of Corsica it was here, as in so many other parts of the whole Ardennes range, that in 1944 there had been established a highly effective section of the Belgian army of resistance. Its full title was 'Armée Secrète, Group d'Orchimont, Zone 5, Secteur V, Group D'. It is a description which reveals the increasing coordination that had grown up in the years following the traumatic experience of Belgian defeat in May 1940. From all over the country men of all ages had begun to leave their homes and their jobs so as to enlist in one or other of the resistance operations. The number was never massive but it was formed froma steady stream of recruits – not least made up of those whose families had been destroyed along with their homes, whose whereabouts could no longer be traced, even by efficient German records, whose jobs and workplaces were no longer available and who had a very personal reason for wanting to square an acccount with the invader. There were, also, a great many volunteers from those who lived in these remote and untouched valleys.

For Louis contact with this group was simply the result of a long series of events connected with the search for a friend. In June 1944 Louis found himself looking at a school that was empty of pupils and beginning to be occupied by wounded and even younger reserve soldiers of the German army. The attacks by the Allied airforces were becoming so effective around Brussels that it was reluctantly decided that the College staff could no longer be responsible for the boys, and especially for the boarders. A bomb had already killed over 200 young people locally and the decision was therefore taken to close the College until the war might be over. Even with an Allied invasion already launched there could be no telling when that might be. Louis, at any rate, was free to do as he pleased.

One of his special friends was an old classmate and fellow Scout leader called Abbé Stevens. Louis decided to try and find out what had happened to him for the last news from his family was that, after leaving for the Ardennes, he had managed to join the Maquis fighters but had then been wounded in an encounter with the Germans and taken prisoner. Louis was so fond of him that he assured the family that he would keep on looking until he knew what had taken place and would then let them know. He took a cycle and set off on the road south. It was a road that he was to take again for my benefit, through Gembloux, Namur, Dinant and then briefly across the present French border to Givet, and back again into Belgium to reach the northern slopes of the Ardennes and the villages of Nafraiture and Orchimont. In that area the people were at that time very frightened because the Germans had brought a whole division to comb the entire area in an effort to catch members of the guerilla forces. The local people were mostly unwilling to talk to Louis about the movements of Abbé Stephens since they could not know who was to be trusted, and already several of the men from every surrounding village had been shot in order to frighten the rest. Most doors either remained closed or were closed sharply when an enquiry was made, but at last Louis discovered some braver folk who confided the news that Abbé Stevens had been shot in the arm and taken prisoner to Charleville, on the French side of the frontier. Louis was then told that to try and cross at that point was impossible because it was closely guarded. Some lads volunteered to show him a little known path through the woods, and even agreed to go with him as far as the outskirts of Charleville if he was willing to take the risk. Since Louis had promised the Abbé family that he would go as far as he could to find news he accpeted the offer and following the 8 and 9 year-old boys he at last crossed again into France and struck the main road to Charleville. The boys now left him and he mounted his cycle and rode straight to the prison, only to find there that nothing at all was known about his friend.

Louis now searched the town cemetery in case Abbé Stevens had been buried, but there was no new grave bearing that name. He was as equally unsuccessful at the newspaper offices in Charleville, and even though he visited all the spots in the town where the Germans executed people he could find no news at all. At last he met a journalist who told him that the only way to find out what he wanted to know was to make contact with a certain prostitute who was very well known to the German troops. Wondering what might happen next Louis followed the reporter to the woman's house and waited while the man went inside and explained what information was needed. So far as she was concerned there was only one thing to be done. Louis should return to the prison with her since she knew the men there and was sure that she could look at the registers. Within half an hour the registers had been examined and the name of the woman's 'old friend' had been found, permitting Louis meanwhile to note the entry against Abbé Steven's name, 'Returned to Namur', just two days previously. Outside the gaol Louis remembers thanking this 'brave Frenchwoman' for her help before mounting his cycle to make the return journey. Back in Namur the prison authorities reported that the Abbé had again been moved on to Brussels. The trail was not yet over.

Whilst Louis had been making his first enquiries in the Semois valley district, and especially when he asked in Vresse, he was strongly advised to ask among the local Maquis. Louis had therefore decided at that point to make contact. Taking a certain wooded path he had found himself suddenly challenged by a sentry who appeared, it seemed, from nowhere. Having learnt his business, the sentry passed the visitor on to another point at which a second sentry 'emerged', then to a third and eventually to a clearing in which were assembled some 50 men. Having to live in constant hiding they were all pale and rather drawn, their clothes were constantly damp and the most that they could do to protect themselves from the weather was to huddle in confined wooden huts with great clods of earth as roofing and camouflage.

They could not cook very much because their fires would have been seen and since in any case fires need dry wood the regular rainfall in this countryside did not leave much fuel for use. To have made fires with damp wood and bracken would have been to give a clear signal to the constant spotter planes which came over the area. They looked, and as he was soon to discover for himself, were, pretty miserable. If their objectives were hazardous and their sacrifice seems today romantic and heroic the reality was much less dramatic. When Louis had been taken to their Commandant, Lt. Ryelandt, and had explained what he wanted to know about his friend, the lieutenant asked Louis is he would be willing to stay with them and to be their chaplain as the men were becoming low-spirited and very much in need of spiritual support and guidance especially as several of their comrades andd friends had been amongst the men recently shot by the Germans. Louis had then said that he would certainly be willing to consider it but first he would have to search out his friend. After that he would try to return.

Louis now had to cycle all the way back to Brussels, some 60 miles. Though he had been told that Abbé Stevens had been sent to the Military Hospital there the German hospital chaplain revealed why it was that the authorities continued to say that they knew nothing of him. It appears that the Abbé was kept hidden away and that is why it was no use any search being made in the normal wards. The chaplain confirmed the news that the Abbé had been wounded, but a German surgeon had cleaned the hole made by the bullet and drawn the skin together. He was not well enough at present to be moved but as soon as he was well enough he would be sent to Germany. The surgeon cooperated to the extent of deliberately trying to prolong the Abbé's stay in hospital by not giving the patient all the treatment he might require and thus delaying his recovery to the point when he would be well enough to travel. For this news the Abbé's family were certainly grateful.

After a few days Louis asked if there was something which he could send to the patient and the doctor and chaplain agreed. Louis sent a photograph of himself at his ordination. No writing was allowed by the chaplain who agreed to deliver it in person to the Abbé. The next day, during a most violent storm, Louis managed to enter the hospital whilst the guard at the gate was sheltering in the guardroom, but free to wander though he was he could not find his friend. He walked up and down amongst the German soldiers in their beds but there was not the least sign of his fellow-priest. In fact, as he learnt later, the Abbé had been in a basement section immediately beneath where Louis was searching for him.

Knowing that there was now little more that could be done for the Abbé Louis offered his services to the Resistance fighters in Brussels itself. One of their assignments was to see to it that patients like the Abbé were not in fact deported to Germany and if an attempt was made to remove them then the resistance plan was to attack and destroy the vehicle being used. As the days passed Louis began to think more and more of those men huddling in the rough forest dwellings of the Semois and since it seemed clear to him that the end of the war might come to the capital before such wounded men could be sent back to Germany he at last decided to leave Brussels and join the section around Orchimont. He was joined by another priest and between them they served all the groups on both sides of the valley of the Semois — Louis on the north bank and the other priest on the south. For the next five months Louis was to share the life of the Maquis.

Most of the men amongst whom Louis was now to live and work were local peasants who wanted to avoid being sent to forced labour camps in Germany. The Germans had soon started to select able-bodied farm workers for such treatment and many of these local boys would rather live the life of the Maquis than endure what was often a one-way trip.

These men were not brilliant fighters but they were brave, very well acquainted with the local countryside, solid and composed in temperament, and they were able to get provisions from their friends and neighbours in the nearby villages. In addition to them were others who might be thought to fit awkwardly into this rural setting – intellectuals, town-dwellers, professional men and orthodox soldiers. Their contribution, however, was that they were determined to fight the enemy and restore the freedom of their country. That they assumed leadership of the local resistance groups was natural, yet without the woodcraft of the men locals, the native doggedness and willingness of the countrymen, even the most inspired leadership would have achieved little.

If it was generally agreed that resistance in the towns took the form of espionage whilst that in the countryside was more likely to be sabotage, ambush and even direct attack, Louis discovered that in June, 1944, any military action against the Germans was forbidden since the reprisals taken against the local villagers could be very savage. Already the Germans were unable to patrol certain sections of the Semois countryside for fear of being picked off by the excellent shots among the Maquis and if they discovered that one or more of their men suddenly disappeared they would round up a dozen or more of the nearest villagers and shoot them on the spot. What was permitted was the assisting of parachute landings of ammunition containers and the occasional agent so that, through regular and close contact with London, General Piron could there inform the advancing Allied troops that on a given signal much more active disruption could begin behind the retreating German front lines.

Though it is now as difficult to find where the Maquis camps once were as it must have been for the occasional raiding parties of German companies it was possible for us to find one of the landing sites for the parachute operations. Very protected and impressive it still is some thirty-five years later. As you emerge from dense bracken and woodland, where sentries once positioned themselves to stop the approach of any unwanted stranger, you find yourself on a long, open and slightly inclined meadowland, entirely surrounded by trees but wide open to the sky and a clear landmark, because of the fires that must once have ringed it, to anyone flying over it at night. Standing on that natural dropping strip you could imagine the tense and eager men who once waited there for an expected aircraft engine and who ran out of the trees for the briefest of moments to pick up the 'gifts' which the fly-by-night caller had just left behind. You are also aware, even on a summer evening, of the perpetual sense of dampness all around, the sound of a snapping twig, the smell of pines, the desire for cover, the openness of the sky. When the planes had gone the fires were extinguished, the parachutes were buried in holes already prepared, the containers manhandled back to the camps and their contents shared out or stored away. Tommy-guns, chocolate, radio parts, cigarettes – it was all there, and week after week the hoard grew, the sense of being better and better prepared spread and the desire to attack the invader became more and more evident.

Meanwhile Louis began to exercise his priestly ministry amongst these fighters of the woods. He was chaplain to six of the camps and he would spend one or two days in each, learning how to move quietly and swiftly from one to the other. Indeed, finding the camps was itself an art for they were extremely well hidden and sometimes they were moved without warning so as to avoid being located by some chance discovery of the enemy. All the local men were Catholics, of course, and beside celebrating mass Louis would preach a sermon every day. Some of the outsiders who might be unbelievers would also attend the service if only because it relieved the boredom of their life in the wild, and it was partly from the reactions of these 'parishioners' that Louis was to appreciate some of the issues which any Christian apologist needs to reckon with today. He also learnt afresh, as he had in his teaching career, the importance of listening to others and relating the Catholic faith to the hard realities of everyday living.

Life in the camp could be uneventful and listless. When at last the orders came for more activity against the enemy it could only be undertaken at night and the hours of daylight during that summer seemed extraordinarily long. The Commandant and Louis would therefore try to organise pastimes for the men – gymnastics, trampoline sessions, books for them to read, talks and discussions on current affairs, whilst the men always listened to the English radio news programmes and then had them translated again for those whose knowledge of English if any was not as good as the others. Before night excursions many men would come to Louis for confession, whilst for injuries suffered in action as well as for treatment against colds, rashes, tummy upsets and all the other ailments of outdoor living their was a Jewish doctor and a nurse with the section, and a daily clinic was possible. After June 6th there were even German prisoners to look after. They were made to peel potatoes, to wash up and do some odd jobs, but they never made any attempt to escape. On the whole, however, the daylight hours did tend to drag and it was only as the sun began to go down that the atmosphere of excitement and purpose began to develop amongst the men. It was then, they knew, that the real work of their war was to be done.

One of their activities by night was to visit those Belgians who were known to have collaborated with the enemy. There were usually one or two of these in each village and it was the job of the Maquis to deal with such collaborationists by taking them prisoner, giving them a form of trial and dealing with them as then seemed right. One of Louis' early experiences was to see one of these 'traitors' brought back to camp and the commandant sitting in judgement, hearing the list of denunciations which the man had made to the Germans, as a result of which several local men had been caught by the Germans, sewn up in sacks and used for bayonet practice! This man was taken out and shot. It was the only such occasion at which Louis was actually present but he knew that other 'night tribunals' took place quite regularly.

Another activity was to assist Allied airmen who had been brought down in Belgium by leading them some 20 to 30 miles until they could meet up with other resistance fighters on the route down to France and Spain. Since the guides had to confine their movements to the hours of darkness it often meant a night of almost continual walking for the Maquis so that the men from the group could get back to their own sector before daylight returned.

It was not long after Louis' arrival in the area that the Maquis were allowed to begin more active operations against the enemy. Though, as a chaplain, there was no compulsion on him to join these sorties Louis felt that he must occasionally share in the full range of these men's lives and the following extracts from a description of one such attack were written by him shortly after it had happened. He called it, "My First Act of Sabotage".

"In a dark, dank strip of forest on one of the slopes of the Semois valley a group of men, bundled in the oddest assortment of clothes, are huddled round a tiny smokeless fire. You might at first take them for a bunch of local woodcutters or even tramps but if your eye followed the trees around them you would soon see a rough wooden rack with blackened metal objects hanging from it – their machine-guns. These tough maquisards, because that is who they are, are mostly pale, one of them is shivering with a fever, another has a thumb covered with a large bloody bandage and all of them have run out of words and crouch or stand round the pitiful fire, some of them smoking. . .

Suddenly they hear the sound of hastening steps and a tall, well-built figure emerges from the trees. The men spring to attention for it is the commandant coming to tell them what he and the adjutant have just heard on their radio in the tent a few metres away. 'It's good news', he says, 'We are to cut the telephone wires near the station at Bièvre. Sgt. Léopold will choose the 15 men who are needed. We shall need wire-cutters and a woodcutter's saw. There will be no explosives but you take your weapons and there will be three magazines to each man.'

The group comes to life. This promise of a new kind of 'recreation' produces an almost childlike sense of anticipation. The youngest members of the group unhook their guns, while others crowd round the huge, red-cheeked sergeant from the Ardennes who, in 1940, even though it was the first time he had seen the sea, set out for England from Dunkerque in a canoe. He was found by an English torpedo boat a few days later, straddling the wreckage of his craft. The jokers in the group will tell you that Léopold did not know how else to paddle it, even before it got damaged.

Those gathering round the sergeant are each pleading some reason why they should be chosen for this exercise.

'I've been too long around here without anything to do, so I ought to go', says one who seems to stress the point the more surely he feels that he will not be chosen.

'Don't come that', says a slender 17-year-old, 'you were part of the ambush for Cousot only yesterday: it's my turn'.

'Well, of all the luck', says a third quietly to Louis, 'They are going to sabotage part of my own village and I'm on guard duty!'

By eleven o'clock at night the camp is alive in a way that it never could be during the day. Men are checking their gear, downing their last mug of coffee and checking their arms again and again. Sgt. Léopold is going to lead the column because as an experienced poacher he knows the forest perhaps even better in the dark than in broad daylight. Sometimes during the journey, however, there will be a short discussion between him and Sgt. Dominique because the latter, as owner of part of the nearby forest and one who had hunted and poached there almost as much as Léopold, has a short cut to suggest, or even a wise detour.

I take the last place in the single file, (says Louis). Even during the trip it might be that one or other of the party would hang back a little to have a word with me, to confess something that was troubling them, and then after a word of pardon or encouragement take up their place in the file again. This was part of my special contribution to their work.

To reach the intended village we made a large detour so as to come close to the village on the opposite side to that which was occupied by the German troops. If by any chance we were seen the alarm for our capture would then be given the wrong way down the line, to Gedinne. As we came up to the outskirts the man in front of me moved off to one side, entered a potato field, dug up one of the plants, examined it and quickly got back into line. 'Padre', he said, 'those potatoes of mine are coming on well.' He said it with a simple kind of pride, smiling like an overgrown boy, as if he had been given a completely new lease of life by this brief return to his ancient occupation. Further on it gave others of us much delight to trample on the beetroots of a collaborationist even though we had to stifle our joy.

At last we were halted in a thick clump of trees so that we could receive our orders for the attack. The telegraph wires stretched alongside the railway line just below us, emerging from an underground channel, and then disappearing under the bridge which carried the main road across the track. The operation was to cut out a large section of the wires and to cut down the four pine trunks which formed the first pylon to carry the wires at this point. The problem was that only 400 feet away lay the large house that used to belong to Sgt. Dominique and which was now used as a barracks for over a hundred German soldiers. There were also constant guard patrols along the whole length of the track.

The commandant told everyone just what they had to do. As this was my first operation I felt nervous, a trifle cocksure, and then frightened to death—all in quick succession. I didn't want to move and yet I didn't want to stay where I was. I was full of admiration for the three men who were sent to take up their posts beyond the railway bridge so that they would take the first brunt of any attack if the Germans were alerted and came to see what was happening. They set off serious and yet proud to be chosen and with the cheery but whispered good wishes of their pals. Then others slipped away, some to the left and others to the right. The remainder were the key group with the tools. I joined them almost without thinking. . .

We made our way to the edge of the embankment. The slope was very steep and you could see the rails on the floor of the cutting. We made our way down to them through the brambles and thorn bushes which tore at our hands and clothes. Léopold had already got rid of his tool bag and his machine gun and having got his hands round the first pine trunk he had pulled himself off the ground, wrapped his legs also round the trunk and began to climb slowly but steadily to the top. Soon you could see his silhouette outlined against the night sky. I had visions of him being caught there in some sudden attack, having to come all the way down and being the last to try and escape into the protective shadows of the trees up above. He would never make it.

Instead you could see him stretch out his arm and the 'ping' of a severed wire seemed to penetrate one's stomach rather than one's ears. I clenched my arms as if to try and stifle the sound. Behind us there was suddenly a metallic sound and then what seemed like something being dragged over the cinders between the sleepers. Everyone turned with guns at the ready, only to realise that what had happened was that the severed wire had reached the ground and then writhed along the track until the tension ceased.

Léopold went steadily on with his cutting, letting the broken wires spring apart with a vibrant 'twang', and from time to time making a comment or letting out an oath as he missed a wire or his arms and legs began to ache. Encouraged by his calmness we would whisper to him pointing out the wires he might overlook. Whilst all this was going on Dominique would appear slowly over the parapet of the bridge, 20 feet above us and we knew that his unerring aim would certainly delay any sudden appearance of the 'Boches'.

At last Léopold slowly descended and the main job could get started. Whilst someone got to work with a metal saw on the main cable that held the four trunks together Léopold and another hefty local man picked up the large tree-saw, spat on their hands and got going on the thick wooden pillars of the pylon. The noise of the sawing sounded deafening in the otherwise silent darkness. We were all looking at each other with alarm. Surely we could not go on: surely the Germans must hear this? But Léopold, who had paused for a moment, shrugged his shoulders, signed to his partner, and the long, supple blade once more began to cut into the white heart of the tree.

About 20 yards down the track the upstairs window of a solitary house suddenly burst into light. The window was opened and a great white figure filled it and obviously began to lean out to discover what was going on. A man's shadow appeared on the wall beneath the light, a few words were obviously spoken and the upstairs figure, light and window were suddenly no more. The Commandant had also joined us to find out what was going on but he felt, around the saw, the same ring of confidence that we all experienced. It was as if the movement of the saw had the effect of giving us all new energy and strength. We became more and more confident. We chatted and joked and we pushed together against the half-sawn-through sections. It took many such efforts before the work was done. Meanwhile the others had loaded me with machine guns like a coat stand and as I lay on the nearby bank, and responded in my own body to their rhythmic heaving I could only think of what my school-pupils and scouts would think if they could see me at this moment. Nor could I help thinking that this was rather more serious than trying to climb street lamps when we were students in Louvain.

At last after much shoving and panting the pylon gave way, collapsing with a terrible crash and falling right across the railway track. I had leapt into the bushes with my machine guns clanking as soon as I knew that the pylon was going to fall and in three seconds flat there was not another man to be seen in the cutting. Those who had been acting as sentinels came loping in and when we had gained the clump of trees where we had paused earlier we stopped again to listen for any sounds of pursuit. There was nothing: at least nothing from the direction of the German camp. Either they had just not heard or they were afraid to venture out into the countryside in the dark. . .

From the other direction, however, there came the sound of a train, or rather a solitary locomotive. The sound grew, dull but steady, as the engine obviously proceeded up the track using its headlamp to scour the line. We heard it pull up as it came to the broken pylon. Well, we had at least escaped the repair gang but they would now give the alarm and that might make our return journey more difficult. The adjutant, who had been a Post Office engineer in civilian life, was pleased about one thing. 'They won't do it by telephone. At least we have seen to that for the time being.'

Despite that we got out of there as fast as we could. We fairly bounded across the main road, ignoring all the care which we had taken on the way out, and it was only an hour later, in the depths of an almost inaccessible wood that we sat down and enjoyed our sandwiches. People began to relax, to laugh, to tell jokes and to recall some of the little incidents of the night. But in everyone's heart there grew a new sense of pride, a feeling of something worthwhile achieved, and a new sense of comradeship and devotion to each other.

Two days later someone from the German post at Bièvre reported shamefacedly to the 'commandatur' at Dinant on the events of the night-attack and why the officer at Dinant had got no answers to his frantic phone calls since then. Yet, if the Commanding officer was surprised at what he heard it was to be as nothing to what he found when he went to his window after the man from Bièvre had been dismissed. Outside his office stretched 15 other men from other sections of his area all reporting that the same or similar things had been done by saboteurs all over the region. When the commandant of Orchimont Sector V, Group D received his instructions he was not to know that General Eisenhower had asked that all the Resistance troops should carry out the same kind of attack all throught the Ardennes. The defeat of the Germans was beginning. Our sector was ready for it.'

That was by no means the only operation in which Louis was engaged as his surviving friends from those days will gladly tell you. One of them, Van Cauwemberghe, showed me where an ambush had been planned for a convoy of German vehicles which had to turn sharply right into a small copse after driving down an open, straight road from the nearest village. The date was September 3rd and the plan was to allow two or three of the leading vehicles to cross the danger line before opening fire and launching their home-made bombs. In the event the driver of the leading truck sensed that something was wrong, pulled up short of the Bois de Lonet, and was of course attacked by the Maquis who thus gave away their surprise and their position. After firing on the second vehicle and its occupants the group decided to withdraw and as they did so a young German N.C.O. appeared with some of his clothes ablaze from the effects of a petrol bomb which had been lobbed into his vehicle. As he collapsed Louis ran over to him and tried to put out the flames around his burning body. Though the Germans were now coming from the rear trucks and the rest of the Maquis were retreating in stages under each other's covering fire Louis still continued to comfort the injured German and stayed with him until he died. Only then did he attempt to get out of his dangerous position and join his companions. Though unarmed he was of course fired on and yet managed to join the group with no serious injuries. It was this act which led to his second citation for distinguished conduct as reported in the official bulletins of the Resistance forces. The order of the Day for October 15th 1944, includes the details of both occasions and the first one reads as follows:—

'For the high sense of duty required of his office, which he has exercised despite great fatigue and danger and during incessant trips between the various sections of his group we honour Chaplain Evely (Brussels). With unceasing cheerfulness and good humour, being well-educated and of deep understanding, brave almost to a fault, always read to encourage the downhearted, sharing in the most uncongenial tasks and the most hazardous operations, he has played a decisive part in maintaining the morale of the group and thus played his part in the success of its activities.'

Van Cauwemberghe is only one of many who can testify to the justness of this citation. He himself, as a keen Scout, was not enthusiastic about living out of doors in five days of steady rain as he had to do when he at last joined up with the Maquis. Nor did he easily bear the full impact of a bout of dyssentery which affected the group after a S.S. security sweep of the area had caused the Maquis to live in the most primitive conditions. He knows what it means to have a bullet in your leg for days without any proper medical attention and to try and keep up your spirits when it is constantly snowing and you have no hot food to eat for a fortnight. All this and more is what Val and his fellow Maquis had suffered before Val saw the Abbé Stevens hit in an attack by the Germans and then hauled off as a prisoner. He was prepared to be critical of anyone who complained without good cause and who put his own comfort and wellbeing before the cause for which they had all come together. When, soon after Louis joined the group, Val was in charge of a party to protect the dropping zone and found the new 'chaplain' as one of his reserves he was disposed to be unfriendly. He had always questioned the point of those who go round in uniform, he questioned those in authority and the priestly caste was something he deeply disliked. The hours in the field under the stars changed all that. He started out by meeting another priest and discovered a friend and a man. When he was wounded again later he was to see what kind of a person this new chaplain was and his parents were no less impressed. To this day the impact of Louis Evely on Van's marriage, vocation and outlook on life is still very marked. A friendship forged under those conditions is not easily broken.

By October 1944 the effects of the invasion of Europe by the Allies were beginning to show. Though the Germans had made some last desperate attempts to stamp out local resistance by concentrated day sweeps of small areas which did mean the destruction of camp sites, tho' never camp personnel, there were also new arrivals in the area. These were French, English and American forward scouts who came to see if the Maquis were ready to receive and join up with the advancing units of the Allied armies. The Maquis were ready and when the first English tanks arrived the group made contact with them and were able to tell them where the nearest German armoured units were to be found. The

English were somewhat afraid that they might be out-gunned by the famous German Tiger-tanks but the Maquis were able to assure them that there were only the ordinary type of tanks in the vicinity and thus the English were able to surround the Germans, many of whom were forced to surrender. In only a few days time the tide of war had passed from their area and the way back to civilian life once more opened up.

It was on November 3rd, 1944, that the Commandant of Sector V, Group D, Lt. D. Ryelandt wrote these words to those whom he had led so successfully to a share in the victory to come. 'Our Group is dissolved as from this moment. But the spirit which has kept us going for many a long month will not cease. It will continue to live in us and to keep us united. It will affect whatever work each one of us now begins to resume. . . The marvellous adventure through which we have lived together will not leave us simply with moving and noble memories: it will continue to point us in a direction that we shall never again lose.'

What exactly that direction was and how it affected Louis in the days that followed is one of the threads that will affect this life-story. Where it led, and with whom it was not a little concerned, was revealed a little for me as I stood with Van and Louis in a little stone chapel, with its plain walls, stark altar, its memorial tablet to the dead who died in battle with a German armoured column on this spot and its simple belfry. Here in the heart of the Ardennes, amongst the forests that never change and the countryside of a devout people one knows instinctively that the way forward can only be with God.

6 *Echoes of Battle*

Louis' memories of the eventual liberation of Brussels are very vivid indeed. He can still recall the sense of joy and relief that came over everyone in the capital as the first British and American troops arrived. It was as if the whole city was invaded afresh by thousands of young men in every kind of uniform, speaking scores of different languages, of all shades of skin and all laughing and shouting and gesticulating to the Belgians about them. 'To someone as withdrawn and self-conscious as I still tended to be', says Louis, 'the openness of these strangers and the new sense of release and friendliness which they created amongst our people was something I can never forget. Whatever we had suffered, and though we still had to rebuild our country and our society, there was a wonderful sense of common purpose and shared eagerness that only the effects of war, and now its ending, could produce. After a remarkable week the festivities of the Liberation came to an end and people began to be grocers, or students, or bus-drivers and teachers again. Yet those days made me think very hard about what life together in society could be like.'

As he reflected on the events of the last six years, disrupted and largely unproductive as they might seem for his career, Louis began to analyse the lessons that might be learnt. There had been, for instance, the first serious recognition of the power of evil. He had always known that evil existed but now he had witnessed a new level, a new dimension, of evil, and in an organised form that deeply frightened him. He had read 'Mein Kampf' and appreciated the veiled wickedness of so much that Hitler had there threatened. Now he could measure his reading of it as a theory against the brutal reality of the occupation, the slave trains, the forced labour gangs, the system of informers, the torture chambers. It had not been a war like any other war, and the very success of so much that the enemy had undertaken led Louis to think, 'Is God so weak, and can evil be so strong?' The whole experience brought what had so often been academic exercises in theology and philosophy into the arena of human pain and personal tragedy. The problem of evil was no longer an idea — it was a fact of life that had to be wrestled with and resolved. Not to wrestle with it, not to be able to know how to face it and deal with it was to be less than a real person. For Louis it was an essential moment of growing up.

Part of this experience he describes as 'the throwing off of our masks'. In normal times most people go around wearing a mask which veils the

M. Evely, Louis' father, in dress uniform of a medical subaltern.

Mme Emilie Evely (née Delahaye) with her three children—(Louis is in the middle).

Louis (left) in his early teens with some of his friends.

Fr. Evely, the schoolmaster-priest, presents one of the boarders to Cardinal Roey for confirmation.

Abbé Evely on the day that he was appointed Principal of the Cardinal Mercier College, 1948.

The new house for the full-time boarders in the College, specially built under Louis Evely's direction.

Mass in the Recreation Hall. Even before Vatican II the new Principal was using French and facing the people across the altar. 'Mass in the round'.

Another surprise! The priests actually played in a football team against the boys. Louis introduced this idea also.

Using a folding and portable field **altar** *(above) Louis Evely, a chaplain to the Maquis, offers Mass in some remote camp in the Semois district.*

One of the groups at work in the grounds at Crest.

Louis Evely—now in his sixties.

Louis and Mary Evely.

kind of person that they really are but in wartime those masks either could not be or were not any longer worn. As Louis had seen during his military service the mask of his military superior had been removed and the true face of fear and cowardice had been revealed. A man who wore the insignia of leadership was recognised as having no courage. Instead, it would be someone who was supposedly his subordinate who took command, who maintained morale and who showed himself to be reliable, capable and responsible. During his time with the Maquis Louis recalled how some of them would be shot or wounded in action by the Germans and three or four days afterwards some fresh recruits would suddenly appear in the forest. These men were not exceptional in appearance but they would just say, 'That was my brother who was shot' or 'Since my nephew has been badly wounded you will be wanting a replacement so here I am.' There was even one small shopkeeper whom everyone locally despised and who was generally disagreeable by reputation. Yet when he joined the Maquis his mask fell off, he took every job that was thrown at him and he finished up be being one of the most respected men in the Section. It was amazing and unexpected but it happened.

Another lasting impression of the wartime days for Louis is therefore what he calls the 'sheer joy' of war. He admits that in the face of the evil that could not be denied it may seem dreadful to speak of delight. There was, however, this deep sense of solidarity and caring brotherhood which he had not met so strongly before. One could be a true Christian for the first time as one shared and served in wartime. You were able to give your life for others and to spend your days in the company of those who were full of the same spirit. 'It was quite overwhelming. There was an atmosphere of communion, of boundless generosity, of sheer self-offering which I have never experienced since. I know', adds Louis, 'that war is horrible. It multiplies orphans and widows but at the same time it does make men. Just as it must be that when a church is under persecution the finest qualities of people are likely to be revealed so it was with us. In spite of everything, there were, during the war and certainly in its last months in Belgium, some of the best and most beautiful moments of my life so far. I had never known such strong, honest friendship. We would share our last rations, our last piece of bread, our last blanket. People would risk their very lives for the wounded rather than leave them to the doubtful mercies of an enemy. We cared for each other, and all the time.'

All this has left an unmistakable impression on Louis' thinking ever since. What he has called 'the incredible capacity of man for sacrifice' is still evident as one of the marks of his thinking in recent days about death. Life, he would contend, as a biological or physical thing, is not all that important. We think it is and so we do a lot for that life. We care for our bodies, we feed them, we wash and carefully clothe them, but in a situation like war we realise that those are very secondary matters. Then we realise that such life is worth nothing. Its only value is the possibility of losing it for something much more worthwhile. It is when we begin to recognise that there is that dimension of life that we can grasp what life and death are all about.

These reflections, these echoes of conflict, were only part of the wartime effects on the Louis Evely who was now to resume his work at Cardinal Mercier college and soon to be its Principal. Pictures of him at this time show how the experiences of life have begun to leave their mark. His black cassock houses a tall, lithe frame topped with a head of short, neatly trimmed black hair with its slight curl, and beneath a now high and intelligent forehead the eyes, deep-set, are full of fun like the edges of his mouth. His fine nose and firm chin speak of one who is not afraid to make up his mind, choose a path and pursue it. He is already one who has had to guide men in the warfare of their own consciences as well as under the gunfire of an enemy attack and who yet knows that in his thirties and early forties he is blessed with good health and many talents. It can have come as no great surprise to him to discover that there was to be no shortage of applicants for his counsel.

Many of those who came to Louis for direction and advice are known only to God and to him. Their needs were private and personal and it is right that they should remain so. Whether these people came to this priest as formal penitents or as friends they would all be treated in the same way — as God's children requiring the best understanding and instruction that Louis could give them. From the number of those who came in this way, whether as boys who are now men, or adults who are that much older, there are two at least whose story may serve to show how Louis was involved with them at this time and who, of course, have agreed that their tale can be shared.

One of them is the Van Cauwemberghe who had first met Louis in the Ardennes when they were both serving with the resistance forces, though not always in the same section. Van, or 'Roland' as he was then known for security purposes, had been trained as a lawyer but, like several professional men, he had not been able to secure a place on transport to Britain after Dunkirk because only engineers and flyers were needed. He therefore turned his steps again to the city and joined the new born Maquis. For most of the war he had been used as a messenger across the southern half of the country, using his legal work as a cover for meeting other agents, whilst telling his family and friends that he was seeing clients. So carefully did he and other underground operators conceal what they did that throughout the war his parents had no idea that he was engaged in this kind of work, but neither did 'Roland' know that his own father was the co-ordinator of all the underground radio operators in the country. What is also interesting to realise is that though there has been so much play-acting and filming of underground activities, there are still alive men like 'Roland' who had to pass important 'documents' to a contact on a train whose only guide to a correct link-up was that his opposite number would have half the small finger of his right hand! It was, however, when another member of the Maquis was too quick on the draw to shoot a collaborator that Van was at last shot in the knee and his travelling job changed to one of more local activities in the sector where Louis was chaplain.

Following the end of the war Van became more and more dissatisfied with his work in the legal profession and at last he decided to attend the institute where Piaget was introducing young school teachers to his new ideas about pedagogy. It was there that Van met his future wife who was a Protestant and they began their teaching career together. It was their joint decision also to leave Belgium and go to the Congo, which was still a Belgian colony, to work as teachers there. During that time they decided to get married and Louis was asked to share in the ceremony. They spent four years in Africa and when, with a small baby and another expected, they began to think of returning to Europe it was to Louis that they turned for advice as to what they should do. With their special training and experience he persuaded them to start a school for difficult boys between the ages of 5 and 10. Louis, he admits, was the 'rock' on which both he and his wife depended and it was Louis' counsel which prevented their marriage from going on the rocks on more than one occasion. It was Louis moreover who drew Van's wife, who is still a Protestant, into a deeper and more appreciative understanding of Catholicism. Compared with the narrowness of French Protestantism, she appreciates the comprehensiveness of her husband's and Louis' religion. Despite all that has happened since those 'mad days' with their trying pupils she still regards Louis as one of their truest and closest friends. Without his wise counsel and support she knows that she and Van would not now enjoy the more mature family life that is theirs.

The other confident was Marie-Cécile van der Meersch. Marie, or Mary as she is now more usually known, had been engaged during the early part of the war to a man with whom she was deeply in love. She was prepared to wait for marriage until the fighting was over but sadly her fiancé, an heroic leader in the resistance forces, was killed. One of his last wishes was that she would still marry, and it was largely because of that request that Mary considered and accepted the possibility. One of her elder sister's close friends, Marc "X", proposed to her even though he knew that Mary regarded him only as a good friend and was well aware of Mary's real, if now lost, love. They married in 1947. It was because Marc and Mary began their marriage by living with Marc's parents that Mary and Louis first met. Louis had known Marc between 1942 and 1944 and after their wedding Louis continued to visit Marc's home. As he did so he could not help noticing the steady deterioration in Mary's general health and at last Mary felt that she could speak to him in confidence and reveal the difficulties between herself and her husband. Because the outcome of this particular confidence was to affect Louis so deeply it is only right that Mary should explain some of it in her own words.

'The death of my fiancé was obviously a terrible shock for me but I was so full of his enthusiasm, his spirit of generously doing what was right, that I wanted to bear his death without weakness. I did not cry. I just had one aim – to do what he had asked of me, to found a family and to live as he had lived. So about two years later I began to consider the request of Marc who said he was in love with me and who would respect me whilst enabling me to achieve my aim of having children. Of course it was a stupid thing to do but at that time life was much more idealistic, even dreamlike, and even my parents did not realise what a folly it was to commit myself to such a relationship. After all, his parents, with whom we lived for nine years because we could not afford a flat, were very influential. His father was a leading barrister, his mother was the daughter of a distinguished Belgian businessman. So it was a very powerful family, proud of its influence in the world, and one with which my parents were pleased to be connected.

'For me, however, with no money of my own and yet brought into this exalted world it was doubly embarrassing. Not only did my husband's parents regard me and treat me as a superior sort of servant but I discovered that they also regarded their son with contempt. That was how they had brought him up. I was therefore a despised daughter-in-law as well as a doubtful wife.

'I therefore felt that I had a duty to support him, and since he first presented himself as someone who understood fully how I was emotionally placed and who just wanted to help me I tried to play the part of a loving wife and a caring mother. The impression that everyone had for most of our first fifteen years together was of a very united and loving family. Indeed, I really wanted to love Marc, I needed to love him, but the truth came out between us all too easily and all too soon. It was not that we had scenes. We never did. What did emerge was the truth that he had revealed in one moment before our marriage. He admitted that he was not cut out to be a good husband or father, because he could not admit anyone into his innermost self, he was a loner. I therefore had to bring up the three children we had without him. Luc was born in 1948, Isabelle in 1951 and Claire in 1957. Yet what was worse was that he began to regard the children as a nuisance and to see them as the obstacle that prevented him from having me all to himself.

'The result was that I was trying to live two quite separate lives. When I was alone with the children I had one kind of life but when he was there it was like having another child to care for but one whose place had to be first, whose every wish and fantasy had to be satisfied. I soon began to show the effects. I had had a father who was frequently ill, pessimistic by nature and easily upset. Influenced by that sort of background you can appreciate that it did not help me to develop a strong, healthy nature myself. Though I was throughout faithful to my husband I could never enter into any deep discussion with him about our situation. He himself was unwilling to study anything deeply or to work really hard at anything. He would even be off work for weeks because of some imaginary illness or just to potter around. I could hardly make ends meet and began to be ill. It was to end in my being bedridden for eight months.'

In the midst of all those fifteen years Mary will tell you that her only support was Louis Evely. As a priest he could only encourage her to seek one goal — to work at her marriage and to do whatever was necessary to restore a loving home for her children. At the same time Louis was talking to Marc. Seeing the lack of interest that Marc took in his children Louis, the 'father' of a whole houseful of boarders, could only point out to Marc the duty he had to be a proper husband. The response was frequently the same, 'There is nothing to worry about. Everything's fine.' It was not. It was this kind of experience of a marriage in travail that was to find its expression in a book that was first published about 1960, 'Amour et Mariage' (Love and Marriage). In a chapter entitled 'Le dialogue conjugal' Louis wrote this:

'Bachelors put up protective screens. Yet there are enormous numbers of married men who are bachelors without knowing it, who are always making excuses for what happens, who march out when things don't go just right, who withdraw into themselves like the proverbial oyster. . .

'Disagreements between married couples at least show that there is still some sort of contact. When there are no disagreements it is because there is no longer any real contact. When there is no longer any chance to explain to each other what is happening, when you don't fight about things any more, that is the sign that you have both lost all hope of being heard. Silence kills love.'

We shall have to return to the sequel of this last relationship of Louis with Mary and Marc in another part of our story but what is increasingly plain is that it was through these experiences that Louis not only became more than a schoolboys' priest but also began to understand more fully the needs of men and women around him. It became increasingly clear to him that if the Catholic faith which he professed had any validity at all then its relevance had to be seen in all these facts of life which were now being unveiled to him. He saw more clearly the need that ordinary people have to grasp the implications of the faith which they are taught. It seemed to him that in too many instances religon and life were too sharply distinguished. He began to see it as his task to show how they interrelate. In 1953 he was already expressing this in a paper written for the magazine, 'Droit et Liberté' (Freedom and Law). The title of his paper was 'HOPE'.

Speaking of the attitude adopted by most Christians to the facts of the Advent (Christ's second coming, the Last Judgement) Louis wrote this: —

'It is not that people refuse to believe what the church teaches about this. They accept that teaching without demur, but also without the slightest interest, because it does not seem to be a matter that really concerns them. And yet when things get too bad, when the world scene begins to darken and family, social or international relations turn sour people will soon start shouting that the end of the world is at hand, and try to find in that cry some kind of ready-made solution to the issues that beset them. Moreover they reckon that by making that sort of response they are exempt from any efforts, prayers or new thinking which might bring about a fresh answer to their difficulties. All too easily they claim to have need of that forgotten quality — the simple faith of the early Christians.'

Louis would have none of this. 'A Christian's true faith in the 'Parousia' (the second appearing of the Lord) bears no relationship to this kind of pessimism and resignation. A real Christian awaits the return of his Lord with confidence and expectancy."

No-one more surely affected Louis' thinking at this time than Charles de Foucauld. As Louis began to recognise the gift which he had for interpreting the faith afresh for ordinary Catholics it was to this favourite 'saint' of his that he was particularly drawn. In one of the school magazines for the early 1950s there is an interesting item. It reads, 'On the evening of Holy Thursday: M. Duguet, the brother of one of our staff, will give a talk in our boarders' house on Charles de Foucauld. Some marvellous coloured slides will illustrate the life of this hermit saint of the Sahara.' If to this snippet one connects the inclusion of the life of de Foucauld amongst the essential reading which Louis earlier recommended for all boys we begin to sense the attachment which Louis felt with this martyr of the Church. But who was Charles de Foucauld?

That he is one of the world's most remarkable characters the many biographies already written about him readily testify. Born in 1858 he was still alive for the first sixteen years of Louis Evely's life and his assasination on the doorstep of his hermitage at Tamanrasset in the heart of the Sahara made front-line news even in the midst of a World War. Vicomte Charles de Foucauld, to give him his full title, was first of all a wealthy young cavalry officer whose exploits as a playboy and womaniser were the talk of French society. In 1883/4, however, he conceived the notion of exploring the hinterland of Morocco, disguised as a Jew, and not only visited places never before seen by any foreigner but so recorded and drew what he saw that it formed the first official survey of that area of North Africa. He was immediately acknowledged as a distinguished member of many French scholarly societies. He was then 25. Three years later he had a total conversion as he was making his confession to a lifelong friend and guide, Abbé Huvelin in Paris, and, to quote his own words, 'My religious vocation was born at the same moment as my faith.'

After three years of waiting to test his patience and his vocation Charles de Foucauld entered a Trappist monastery in the south of France but thinking that the life there was not hard enough he asked to be transferred to one of the order's most exacting houses in the north of Syria. Here the monks tilled the soil and slept in a rough shack above the cowshed. Still the life was not hard enough for de Foucauld and after 7 years with the order he asked to be released. He went to live as a kind of meditating caretaker, first alongside a convent of nuns in Nazareth, and then at another religious house in Jerusalem. During this time an idea was growing which had come to him in the house at Akbès in Syria. It was the notion of a congregation of his very own, 'The Little Brothers of Jesus'. Since it was an extension of this idea which was to influence Louis Evely it is worth our learning a little of what Bro. Albéric, as de Foucauld was then known, had in mind.

The brothers were to live in small communities and with accommodation that was of the humblest kind – three rooms at the most. A chapel, a dormitory-cum-workroom and a room for guests. They were to work nine hours a day, to go barefoot, to have only one tunic and to subsist on two meals of porridge a day. Their prayers were to be simple and in the language of the people amongst whom they lived 'so that the poor could feel at ease amongst them'. The day was to close with the adoration of the Blessed Sacrament. As René Voillaume has said 'This first rule of Father de Foucauld's was so strict as to be inapplicable.' That indeed explains why, in his lifetime, Bro. Charles never had any great rush of applicants as his companions. Only one ex-Foreign Legionnaire made the effort and he had to give up after a few months for the way of life expected was more than he could physically bear. Nevertheless, says Voillaume, this rule 'incarnates with great force the primary factor of Charles' ideal' (of) consecrating by the religious profession, out of love for Jesus the Worker, and in imitation of his life at Nazareth, the poverty, the daily toil and the social status of the poor amongst mankind.'

It was when he wrote a second version of his rule and stressed the need for his 'Little Brothers', and perhaps some 'Little Sisters', to go where the people were most abandoned that Fr. Charles, who had now become a priest, recognised his own final vocation. It was those people of the Sahara that he knew so well whom he recognised as being the ones whom God desired him to serve. There was then not a single Catholic priest in Morocco and it was there that he ought to go. In the event Fr.

Charles went to the country east of Morocco, a thousand miles inside the 'void' of the Sahara desert and as the sole member of his race. The Tuareg of the Hoggar built him a small mud construction roofed in with palm trunks just like their own dwellings and it was there that he served. Waiting upon God, acquiring the ancient Berber language of these powerful nomads (Tamashek), and penetrating the secrets and customs of his neighbours he prayed that he might in time be able to win them for Jesus. His converts were minimal. His reputation was immense. His death, sudden and dramatic.

'In his lifetime', writes his most eminent biographer, Jean-Francois Six, 'Charles de Foucauld had few followers, but so irresistibly did the force of his example and ideas draw men to himself that since his death many men and women in all parts of the world have responded to his call. His spiritual family includes not only the Little Brothers and the Little Sisters of Jesus, but also priests and lay people of all classes and occupations who carry out his imitation of Jesus at Nazareth in other secular institutes and free associations.' It was in 1908 that de Foucauld first conceived the idea of his 'lay missionaries'. On March 11th, 1909, he was writing to a French friend, 'I have long been tormented by the thought of the spiritual abandonment of so many unbelievers, and especially by that of the Moslems and unbelievers in our colonies. At the same time I have seen love of material things and vanity taking an ever growing hold on the Christian world.' He now outlined his idea of a lay Confraternity to work alongside priests and nuns. 'The duties towards unbelievers of those brothers and sisters who are not priests or religious would be all the more important because they can often do more for unbelievers than can priests, monks or nuns. It is easier for them to form relationships and friendships with them, to come into contact and mingle among them. . . Their occupations — administration, agriculture, commerce or whatever it may be — can, if they wish, bring them into touch with others continually. With the help of charity and the kindliness they themselves bring to these contacts, they can if they wish form true friendships that will open the most firmly closed of homes to them.'

It was a grand design even though Charles himself was not to live to see anything of it fulfilled. It was in the decades after the first World War that the idea matured but not until after 1950 that the secular fraternities of Charles de Foucauld began to flourish. It was a movement which had two attractions for Louis Evely. It was a movement inaugurated by someone for whom he had always entertained the greatest admiration. It was also the perfect vehicle for his work at this time — a means of helping Catholics to understand afresh the relevance of their faith in their life, and a method that touched the unused resources of that dimension of the church — the laity — about whom Yves Congar, de Lubac and Mersch were writing so effectively at this time. Into this movement Louis threw himself with all his vigour and concentration. His organising and teaching ability were as readily, and as effectively harnessed as they had been in the earlier days of his life with the JUC at Louvain. He was soon being considered as the senior chaplain not only to these lay fraternities in Brussels but for the whole country. His drive and enthusiasm rubbed off on to many of his school colleagues. In 1955, when preaching at the Requiem Mass for two of the College staff who had been tragically killed in a motor accident Louis commented, 'Abbé Boulanger was returning from a meeting of a lay Fraternity of de Foucauld which he seved as their chaplain and with whom he had spent an hour of adoring the Blessed Sacrament. After that period of contemplation he told those present that he had seen Christ with absolute clarity.' For Louis himself it was a time of new spiritual awakening and enrichment.

It was certainly a time of much preaching and teaching and writing. Having learnt, in a way that was totally unexpected, how to present the Catholic faith to some of the most unwilling of God's children in the College, Louis had to adjust his methods and style to reach the varied adult groups which he visited in Belgium and abroad. Anyone who picks up the paper-back, 'pro manu scripto' editions, of Louis Evely's talks to the de Foucauld Fraternities at this time will be struck at once by their layout and their conversational nature. Looking back I realise that it was this that first struck me when I picked up 'That Man is YOU' so many years ago. Now that I have had the chance to read that and the other works of the late 1950s in the original the effect is even more striking. The argument moves along — but very steadily. There is no attempt to bombard the reader, or the original listener, with a closely reasoned argument. The aim is to open up the mind and the awareneess of the other person by revealing one after another the slightly varied layers of meaning that in the end produce a more natural acceptance of what the teacher is trying to convey. The lay-out helps. The paragraphs are very short. Some of them made up of only one sentence, some of them two, and few of them more than five or six. The page itself seems to have places for a pause or reflection or even a chance to breathe. Two samples, first from a course on the Creed and then from one on 'How to pray', will provide just a glimpse of what Louis was providing at this time.

'Faith involves a stripping down, being made in the image of Him whose joy is to be poor and to give away everything he possesses. God can only get through to the poor because they alone share this common aim. Faith is first and foremost expressing our assent to the Beatitudes.

You cannot therefore possess faith. Rather faith dispossesses us. To attempt to use religion as a means of making ourselves more secure or to ensure that our voice is heard is to make a mockery of it. A religion that we just inherit, that comes all ready-packed and leaves nothing to be questioned, is not really a religion at all.

To believe in God, is to believe in Someone who is always just beyond our comprehension and who makes himself known to us all the time in one fresh revelation after another. Faith is not something that you acquire, it's a summons; it's not a guarantee of safety, but a life of risk; not a means of finding consolation, rather an adventure. You don't sit back in it, you are thrust out by it.

Just think what a test those contemporaries of Christ had to undergo: the Jews who, like us, really believed that they knew what to believe. They had faith in their religion, they believed in their priests, they believed in their parents and their religious instruction. . . yet God was in their very midst and they didn't believe in Him!

Surely you know people who have believed for so long that they don't believe any more. Who have expected something to happen for so long that they don't expect it any more. People who have replaced faith with dogmas, have started to prefer forms of words to real living, and rituals to truth. On what do you base *your* faith – on God Himself or on what someone has told you about God?

'Blessed are those who believe', recite so many good natured but quite unbelieving souls. Happy indeed, if you are poor!!!

To believe is to put yourself at the complete disposal of God. And no-one has heard the word of God who has not been called . . . to set out . 'Go . . .'.

We shall be the true sons of Abraham when we in our turn are prepared to leave our safe retreats, however religious they may seem (these too sublime acts of prayer, these half-digested sacramental rites, these ceremonies reassuring but empty) because otherwise we get so wrapped up in them that we imagine that there is no need for us to believe.'

The other passage may be shorter but it is just as indicative of Louis' approach at this time.

'Take grace before meals. It used to run 'Bless us, O Lord, and these your gifts. . .' Now we add, 'Bless those who have prepared our food' and having granted them a passing nod, we're content. Or perhaps we may add, '. . . and give bread to those who have none' after which we settle down to a hearty meal and let God worry about the rest of humanity. (Every man for himself, you know, and God for all. . .) That kind of prayer is the easy way out, shockingly cynical. Authentic prayer would have us insist, 'Make us find bread for those who don't have any,' because God has no-one but us to do the very things we ask him for.

There is something to meditate on: God has no-one but us to do the very things we ask him for. He established the Church – a living presence among men – to answer the same prayers it makes to God.

When we plead, 'Give us this day our daily bread', we needn't imagine he's going to bake little buns and send them down to us from heaven. We've lost touch with reality if we think he's going to turn stones into bagels, multiply loaves and make rolls rain down on the little Chinese children just because we mumble, 'Give us this day our daily bread'. Bluntly we are knee-deep in pious deception.

Any sincere prayer compels us to share what we have.'

If there is one thing which can be said immediately about these typical extracts it is that they are unmistakably clear in their meaning. It there was one characteristic to which many who knew and listened to Louis at this time have pointed me it has been the deceptive simplicity of almost all that he had to say. For those who knew him well it was evident that here at last was the distillation of years of careful thinking and watching by a man who cared greatly about people and about truth. These 'causeries' on Suffering and Family life, on the nature of the church and the meaning of the Gospels, were not the abstruse wrestlings of a wellread scholar but the sharp, perceptive insights of a trained priestly mind. All the reading and reflection which lay behind these words is gently and yet firmly concealed. What Louis was concerned about was the enrichment of the many and varied members of the Fraternities which he now served. As he encountered men and women from all professions and from none he had obviously reached one decision. The only way to be of greatest help to them all was to be so simple that everyone could grasp what it was that he was led to say.The groups of more professional people could then respond in their own special fashion.

One of those groups was centred on an old Belgian farm house at Ottignies. André and Cinette Ferrière, whose home it is, have been friends of Louis for a good deal of his life. André was in the scouts with Louis when they were both teenagers but it was the tremendous times during the later 50s and early 60s that they both recall when they had a band of doctors and their wives gathered for discussion, study, meditation and action in the kitchen and chapel of that home. André Ferrière is by any modern standards one of the most outstanding medical practitioners in Europe and the vast Clinic with its 400 beds and most uptodate equipment just a short distance away across the valley is living proof of what this doctor has achieved in one lifetime. His wife, too, is a woman of equal intellect and charm. A linguist and the holder of a theological doctorate she has sought like her husband to put her gifts at the service of the Catholic Church to which they both belong. The large, airy studio across the yard from their living quarters has been for years a place to which a string of lay people have come to be trained as catechists and teachers in a country where the drift from the Church has been as marked as anywhere else in Western Europe. To have the company and the care of such people as these provided for Louis areas of fulfilment and challenge that complemented his service as Principal of the College at Waterloo. What is strange and sad today is the awareness that all that promise and progress in lay growth and ministry had to stop. Why this had to happen is not as difficult to understand if the reader will again recall that we are thinking about the Catholic Church before the advent of John XXIII and the Council which he was to inaugurate. If it is puzzling to try and appreciate why fresh thinking and action around the liturgy, family life, the nature of the church, the scriptures and the sacraments should occasion such criticism and restriction that is at least some indication of the change in atmosphere now expected by the Catholic Church's friends.

A first clue to the conflict, an echo of battle if you like, appears in a letter written by René Voillaume, Prior General of the Little Brothers of Jesus in 1951. Writing from Rome on the 25th of June he said this:

'I have come to Rome this time, if anything, with an increased sense of the responsibilities weighing upon me in approaching, in all your names, the bearer of the authority of Peter. We have reached a point in our growth where, if our Fraternities are really to be the Lord's possession for Him to do with as He wills, we must be more immediately and more intimately conscious of belonging to the Church. . .

'The time would now seem to have come for us to place our faith face-to-face with the exigencies of a total obedience to Christ and, together, make a generous effort to put such total obedience into practice throughout the Fraternities.

'To begin with, let us say that to obey means to subject your will in all freedom to the will of another, and act in at least practical conformity with his judgement — unless infallible authority *per se* is involved — because that other is fully entitled to require such submission of your will. . .

'With our whole souls, we must believe in Rome's power to command us in the name of Christ; we must therefore believe as well that no harm can ultimately result from loyal submission, whether for the progress of good on earth or — and this more especially still — for that of the Kingdom of the Gospel. We must not hesitate for a single instant, even if these decisions seem to us to offer obstacles to some immediate good or if they appear contrary to the Church's progress in some particular part of the world. . .'

The reader will only need to set this statement over against what Louis would write in his book, 'The Church and the Sacraments' from which we have already quoted to see a growing division between himself and the leader of the Charles de Foucauld companies. It was not a total separation but it was a significant difference of emphasis and what is true about Obedience was to reveal itself also in the whole subject of 'Love' and 'Relationships'. Here you can detect the restriction self-imposed by Voillaume in talking about 'Love' from a celibate or community—life point of view, whilst for Louis Evely the very forum which he was called to serve was that of the average secular home. The subjects of Père Voillaume's letters in 'Seeds of the Desert' are almost identical with the titles of Louis' books throughout the 50s. The variance comes in the kind of 'kingdom' about which they were ultimately speaking.

In one of the last manuscript publications which Louis produced for the Secular Institutes of de Foucauld, a paper entitled 'Liberté' (Freedom) he wrote this:

'If the Church is today seeing a dropping away of great sections of our population and if she seems so trad and ill-equipped to deal with this phenomenon, it is because there has been no demonstration by deeds to our contemporaries of just what it means to be able to enjoy the life of the Church and to live it out simply and collectively as the Body of Christ in the world today.

'A religion that does that is both manly and free. It is a religion that has grasped what Christ has already promised in St. John: chapter 8, verse 31:

"If you obey my word you will be truly my disciples".

'That is it: you have to commit yourself. You cannot remain passive, silent, submissive. You have to care, to seek and to experiment. For Jesus compels us to a faith that acts.'

Those were fighting words. They were echoes of a conflict to come.

7 *Trying to Communicate*

Throughout the 1950s and 60s Louis' outside engagements steadily grew. He was widely acclaimed in Catholic circles as a speaker and teacher, especially where the French language was understood, and the number of his published works mounted. By 1966 he was figuring amongst the twenty most translated of all French-speaking authors, closely following Camus and Teilhard de Chardin and having overtaken so well-known a figure as André Maurois. Anyone familiar with his writing can easily understand his attraction, as a speaker as well as an author. One critic spoke of him as a 'tireless preacher, using natural, straightforward language that was full of evangelical freshness and which dealt with both the major concerns of the Faith and the world around us.' In 1969, Cardinal Luciani, known more recently as the short-lived Pope John Paul I, declared to a friend that 'The central religious problem is the gap between a purely formal and nominal Christianity, based merely on ideas, and an existential Christianity that finds expression in life.' (The Year of Three Popes: Peter Hebblethwaite. Collins, 1978, p.93) It was to this very problem that Louis addressed himself in everything that he wrote. The very titles of the books and papers that he produced in a steady stream convey his concern. 'Love Your Neighbour', 'A Religion for our Time', 'Prayer for Modern Man' and 'Lay Spirituality' are but a few of the works that enshrine his down-to-earth comments on a vital Christianity relevant for 20th century man.

Those who first encountered this increasingly popular teacher were impressed and enthusiastic. 'These meditations (on the Lord's Prayer) are unusually fresh and apt', wrote someone in the Times Literary Supplement, 'Much that is encouraging in the recent evolution of French Catholicism is reflected here . . . spirituality that is biblical and robust (with) avoidance of sentimentality, and the bloated language of traditional piety . . .'. Apart from the fact that Louis Evely was Belgian and not French that comment does fairly represent the tenor of Louis' impact and show the difference in approach that marked out his work. Another critic of this book, 'Religion for our Time' wrote, 'No spiritual writer of recent years has made an impact equal to that of Louis Evely. This compassionate, realistic, loving Belgian priest has almost singlehandedly rescued spiritual writing from the state of pious mediocrity and made it again a source of living, converting grace.' Anthony Faulkner, a contributor to the English Catholic paper, 'The

Tablet', made an even briefer but telling comment — 'Be prepared for delightful shocks when you read him. . .'

The characteristics that began to mark Louis were the same few but distinctive ones — freshness of insight, use of common, everyday prose, a natural acquaintance with the Bible and the personal implications of whatever truth was disclosed. Only those who pick up his books, which are now being reprinted, and read them at length can fully appreciate the effect of these combined features but the following brief extracts may give some indication of what it was that attracted a large and growing international readership up to 1970.

'Have you ever noticed', he wrote, 'that Christ never called on his disciples to pray until they approached him about it? They had no prayer meetings, no processions, nothing . . . and then they said, 'We would like to learn to pray like him'. What a good method of education for fathers to note. He never forced his children to pray but he prayed so well. . .'. Or this passage — 'An enormous amount of common sense is needed to do good. What is unfortunate is that, generally, as soon as people become good they automatically become so stupid!. . . (Jesus) warned us that in order to do good you had to be 'as wise as serpents and as harmless as doves', which some Christians realise by becoming as ugly as dragons and as silly as geese!' (Religion for our Time, pp. 72, 74)

Later on in that same book (p.95) Louis was to touch on something about which he felt extremely deeply — the corporate nature of a truly religious life. He writes, 'But if the sacraments were again to become communal, things would be quite different; we would enlighten one another! From time to time married people come to confess together. I can assure you that the examinations of conscience are well done. A collective preparation is indispensable in order to make a true judgement of one's own life.'

'Secondly, the average believer is unable to repent by himself. Passages of the Gospel ought to be read to him; the word of God ought to be proclaimed to him; what he has lost should be revealed to him, and he should be given the desire to come back.

'And finally, he is unable to make preparation all by himself. All this ought to become communal again, except that avowal, though it is not as sensational as you imagine. The avowal of sins is secondary, though in our times it has been made the essential part. The very name of the sacrament shows this distortion: 'Confession'. But the true name of the sacrament is the Forgiveness of Sins.

'We have forgotten that the sacrament is above all an act of God, a gesture of love and compassion by God. We have emphasized the (painful) gestures of man instead. Confession is what *you* do: '*I* confess'.

'There ought to be such a celebration of the forgiveness of sins that it would make the love of God *sensible*. It would wake us up, resurrect us to the love which God has for us.'

The ground of all Louis' thinking on this point was strictly theological. 'Why is our religion essentially a religion of community?', he asks his reader, 'Because God is community! And because we must become like him, "perfect, as the Father is perfect".'

"God had to be more than one to be God. If God were solitary, he would not be God, He is God only because he is Father. He is God only because he is Son. He is God only because he is love exchanged, and this is the Holy Spirit.'

It is within this context of necessary community that Louis reinterprets the hard saying of 'extra ecclesiam, nulla salus'. 'To me', he says, 'this means: outside of a church, of a communion, of a community, there is no salvation Outside of charity, no salvation. That is why our Lord gave us a sacrament without substitute . . .' Yet Louis is not able to accept a false sacramentality, and that is what he had experienced too often.

'In the Mass we say, "It is truly right and just, proper and fitting for salvation, that we always and everywhere give thanks to You. . ." and then you go back sadly to your stupid life, to your stupid cooking, to your stupid laundry, to your stupid factory, to your stupid office, where you are going to live your stupid life saying "Oh, it is terrible to fall back into other things" . . . That is why the sacraments are so ineffective. They no longer have any human context. . .

'It is useless to distribute sacraments to people who do not pray, who do to want to pray, who do not want to die, who want only one thing: to remain as they are, in spite of everything.

'The sacraments ought to be celebrated in such an authentic, expressive, and living way that it would be impossible to participate in them without feeling this obligation to die, and this call to be resurrected.' (pp.98 - 105)

We have seen already how during his teaching career Louis sought to recover for his pupils a fresh sense of the wonder and power of the Eucharist. His steps to create a sense of participation, to involve the boys in the action of the Mass, to see the point of a sermon and to realise the meaning of communion — all these were new and questionable steps in those pre-Vatican II days. Even more upsetting to the authorities was Louis' desire to say the Mass in French. Indeed, he was so eager to start in this direction that he discussed the matter with the Papal Nuncio, the Vatican representative in Belgium. Louis had preached one Sunday at a parish church and was invited to lunch afterward by the Curé there. The Nuncio also happened to be present.

Realising that here was someone in direct touch with Rome Louis asked him why there was still no move to have the Mass in French. The answers that Louis got were all predictable — and to Louis' mind, idiotic. The Nuncio underlined the universality of the Latin which was so in accord with the world-wide nature of the Catholic Church and meant that wherever a Catholic might find himself he could have the same Mass in the same language. Foolish as he now realises his retort to have been, Louis could not help observing, 'I see; so in order to enable those who travel abroad to feel at home with the Mass I have to feel like a stranger as long as I stay at home. In my own country, and especially if I am one who does not understand Latin I am to be treated as a foreigner.' The Nuncio was furious.

What made things worse, however, was that during the following week, when writing his weekly article for 'Témoinage Chrétien' (Christian Witness) Louis reported this conversation though without mentioning who had been involved. He set out all the official arguments he had heard – the need people have for mystery in worship, the sense of the sacred, the universality of Latin, and so on. . . and then he countered them. He pointed out that there was surely only one mystery in the Church, the mystery of the Word of God, and that the whole work of the Church was to expose this mystery to the fullest light. 'Of course', Louis added, 'the more we try to explore the mystery the more mysterious and astonishing it becomes because we shall never understand how and why God can love us as he does. Yet if we try to hide the mystery under the veil of an unknown language we are suggesting that the mystery is so fragile that to talk about it in straightforward modern language may destroy it altogether. Pagan religions need incomprehensible rites and language because they went to impress and overawe people. The Christian mystery, that of the Incarnation, is so inexplicable, so astonishing and unbelievable, that nothing, least of all our efforts to try and grasp something of it, will ever affect its truth.'

Before we consider further the effects of this kind of comment we need to pause for a little and recognise Louis' constant and growing emphasis on understanding the Bible as the source of truth about God's Word for men. He has written about it in several books but there is one passage in particular which focuses what Louis was feeling. It comes in his book, 'Love your Neighbour';

'Of all the books in my library,' says Louis, 'There is one which I am perfectly certain will never be borrowed. I have no fear that I shall lose it. My visitors are interested in all my books except that one. No-one has any desire to read it, no curiosity towards it; each one is sure that there is nothing in it for him. That book is, of course, the Bible.

'All this indifference is going to cause us some embarrassment when we get to heaven . . . You believe that you know Christ, but you can know him only insofar as you know the Gospel. That, too, you believe you know because you have heard over and over again certain passages, like the wise and foolish virgins, the talents, the salt of the earth, the treasure hidden in the field. But let anyone question a Christian on some point of Scripture and he shows at once his lack of knowledge. He does not know the text, nor its meaning, he has never reflected upon it, he has never taken the trouble to inquire about it!

'Furthermore, and you know how true this is, he never speaks of it spontaneously. He has nothing to say about it. He has no desire to speak of it. The mouth speaks from the abundance of the heart. Our silence on any truly religious subject comes from our incompetence, from our lack of interest, from our coldness of heart.

'But you may say, I have tried, I began reading the Gospel but it said nothing to me. . . If the Gospel does not speak to you it is because you have not read it as you should. You have read it as though it were an ordinary book, looking for the subject, the plot of the story and the conclusion.

'But the Gospel is not an ordinary book. It is a sacred book, a book by which you communicate with God, as in the Eucharist. Suppose a little altar boy, wanting to know how a host tastes, should, by accident, pick up a consecrated host. It would not be a sacrilege because the child did not know that it was consecrated, but neither would he be receiving holy communion. He supposed it to be but ordinary bread and, for him, it was no more than that. He would not receive an atom of grace. In the same way the sacred Scripture, if it is read as though it were an ordinary book, will be for its reader an ordinary book, closed, sealed, profaned.

'The Bible should be read, so to speak, on one's knees, touched with the utmost respect, opened as though one would listen, as though one would consult him who speaks. . .

'The Gospel is actual. It would not be worth a second of attention if it spoke to us only of things that took place two thousand years ago. When you receive communion, you do not receive the Christ of two thousand years ago but the Christ who is living, and loving you, today. And when you read the Gospel it is he who is speaking to you.'

This was not simply the impression of a Vatican II style of thinking. In one of those regular letters to parents of his pupils to which frequent reference has been made in this story Louis writes on the same subject — fifteen years earlier.

'After you have tried to introduce your children to God by means of his spirit evoked in your family life', he wrote 'you ought, as parents, to help them to discover God also in His Book. . . You will need to introduce them successively to the unfolding revelatoin of God's love from the time of the Garden of Eden, when God spoke familiarly to Adam in an evening hour, encouraging man to speak freely, to trust himself and to rely utterly on the Lord. Then, carrying on the story you can show how God spoke through the prophets until that day when he spoke through his only Son, that Word made flesh and entrusted to us. . . Yes, it is your privilege to tell them the stories of all who suffered and were persecuted for their faith until at last they long to give themselves in love for what is right — like Abel, Joseph, Moses, Isaac, David. . .'

It was not only the stark, evangelical truth of the Bible which left its mark on Louis' thinking. It also affected his style. There is about everything that Louis has written in recent years a characteristic openness and sharpness, an unavoidable simplicity of expression which reflects the directness of scriptural writing. It was no coincidence that the lay reader in a Kent parish should mistake the style of this Roman Catholic priest for an Evangelical Protestant.

It was not only as a writer, however, that Louis was able to communicate. He was much in demand as a speaker and lecturer. His first visit to Canada was in 1963 when he was invited by the Principal of a French-Canadian college, and his programme included a conference for teachers and students, a retreat for priests and a course of addresses for members of the Fraternity of de Foucauld. In 1965 he returned at the invitation of the Canadian Broadcasting Company to preach at a series of televised masses throughout Lent. Each Sunday there was a Mass and during the rest of each week there was a programme of varied speaking engagements. There were radio broadcasts and towards the end of that visit there was even a feature on his life so far. It included his comments on many matters of current religious concern. What he had to say was heard by more than just his French-Canadian audiences.

There was also a trip to the Cameroons. He was invited there for some five weeks and was asked by Mons. Zoa, the Archbishop, to participate in conferences so as to explain to his clergy what had been discussed at that time in the Vatican II sessions. On his arrival, however, Louis discovered that the local Jesuits and Dominicans were very angry about his invitation since they regarded the African clergy as their 'property, their own personal domain'. The result was that Louis was limited to just one group of African teachers at one mission station. They were very poorly educated, many of them not having even a primary education diploma and all of them extremely poor. Yet as Louis spoke to them he was amazed to discover how similarly they had developed in their ways of thinking to teachers in other parts of the world that he knew. They asked the same questions, had the same needs and the same expectations as their counterparts in France, Canada, Belgium or Italy. They were just as critical of the clericalism in the Church and they had a thirst for the teaching of the Gospel which was open, direct and alive. Louis found that he could talk to them with a joy and an ease which he rarely found elsewhere. What might so easily have proved to be an entirely wasted journey turned out to be a real opportunity for communication. To make the findings of Vatican II availble and understandable to that audience meant that Louis' own understanding of it had to be clear and simple.

He was also invited to the Catalan area of Spain by a number of religious organisations. In Barcelona University, where the first conference was to be held, some very conservative Catholics, members of the Order of Christ the King, created a disturbance by invading the conference hall with swords, sticks, knives and revolvers, and attacked the Jesuit priests and students' chaplain who had invited him. The intruders tore Louis' papers out of his hand and put an end to the proceedings for a time. Even though the police were phoned they took two and a half hours to arrive so that those who had caused the disturbance had largely left and the police never arrested anyone. Louis was asked if he would continue, which he did, though without any notes, and in a room that had been devastated.

The third conference was to be on prayer and the room was crowded. This time they were meeting in a large building full of offices but it did not deter the arrival of those determined to break up the meeting. They slowly invaded the whole block, started throwing things out of the office windows, broke window panes, squatted on the floor of the room in which Louis was speaking and eventually threatened to set fire to the place unless he stopped. Again the police were sent for and this time it took them an hour and a half to arrive. Though Louis was then able to continue his address it was not before the police commandant had expresed his bewilderment as to why anyone would want to cause a riot over the subject of 'Prayer'. The next session had to be abandoned since some of the students who turned up arrived with truncheons in their satchels and Louis felt that if he gave his talk it might result in acts of bloodshed.

Later on Louis discovered that the reason for the protests during his visit was that two older Jesuits were angry with the young priests, and particularly the chaplain, who had invited him to speak. There was even a public argument between the two sides and Louis was asked to make some kind of condemnation of the rioters. This he wisely refused to do. The disagreement, however, began to get so heated that Louis was taken with some friends to see the provincial Governor of Catalonia who listened to the story but who obviously did not want to get involved. As far as he was concerned it was the role of the police to prevent disturbances and he declined to interfere. The homes of all Louis' friends were put under surveillance and there were even pickets outside wherever he was staying, though he moved from one house to another almost every night.

At last it was decided by Louis' friends that he should return to Belgium and since it was not safe to travel by train, which was the way he had come, he was taken by car along quiet country roads to the frontier. There he shared a last cup of coffee with his friends before taking leave of them. It was whilst he was doing so that another traveller, recognising Louis, came over and shook hands with him, thanking him for some of the things that Louis had been able to say in the meetings. 'Don't confuse the Catalans with the "occupiers" ', he said, referring to the Spaniards, 'It wasn't what you were saying that caused the riots: it was all a matter of politics and the question of free speech.'

Whether that was so or not it did not help Louis. On his return to Brussels his Bishop sent for him and told him that everywhere he went he discovered that Louis caused the same impression. He provoked disorder. Louis tried to defend himself by saying that if the Bishop were going on what he read in the papers he would know that there was always someone ready to create more upset by talking about communists or heretics or progressives. He hoped the Bishop would believe that he was none of these things. The Bishop did not on this occasion suggest any discipline but Louis could begin to feel that he was not getting through to his superiors. He was soon to learn how right that was.

Louis had already begun to disagree over certain things with Léon Suenens. Writing his regular, one-column articles for 'Témoignage Chrêtian' Louis had begun to build up a large circle of appreciative readers. One day, however, Suenens, who was then Vicar General, came to the College and said, 'Evely, I want to speak to you.' He told Louis that the Cardinal (Van Roey) was very displeased with the articles and when Louis asked why, the answer was that they were not written in the right kind of tone. It seemed to the Cardinal that Louis was treating sacred things too lightly and was adopting a too frivolous and critical an approach. Suenens thereofore advised Louis to stop writing for this paper though he was not to say that he had been forbidden to do so. He should pretend that he did not have enough time to write any more. What hurt Louis most of all was not that he gave up doing something he enjoyed but the deceit involved in explaining it. The message that came through to him on this matter was that such a church was sick.

It was over the publishing of one of Louis' books, however, that he and Léon Suenens, the latter now a Cardinal, were to disagree even more sharply. This time it concerned an Imprimatur for 'That Man is You'.

When the book was completed the Editor asked Louis if he knew anyone well-known in French-speaking churches who might write the Preface. As Louis had never had time to cultivate the 'famous' his Editor came up with the suggestion of Père Yves Congar. Though Louis had never met Congar he had, like many of his contemporaries, read all that Congar had written and found himself in sympathy with his ideas. Louis particularly approved of Congar's views on the 'Place of the Laity in the Church', a view to be widely endorsed by the later findings of Vatican II. The only problem that seemed to occur to Louis was whether so recognised a scholar could possibly be interested in writing a Preface for the work of an insignificant and humble schoolteacher. The Editor told Louis that Congar had read all that Louis had written and was delighted to be asked.

There was a problem, however. Yves Congar was himself in some disgrace with Rome, having written a book with the title, 'Chrétiens Désunis' (Disunited Christians). His views on ecumenism in days before the term 'Separated Brethren' was approved and accepted had led to his being sent to England 'as a penance' since he spoke little English and therefore could not communicate with others. He had already been forbidden to teach Dominican students. He was even compelled to seek *two* imprimaturs himself before any further work of his could be published — one from Rome and the other from his Dominican superior. It was from the latter that he obtained permission to write the preface for 'That Man is You'.

As the book was to be published by a French firm it would have been quite in order for Louis to obtain an imprimatur from a sympathetic Bishop in that country. In order to try and restore some lost confidence, however, Louis sought out Cardinal Suenens. 'I have written a book and seek your approval of it', he said. Suenens not only agreed, says Louis, but even seemed quite proud to be asked and three weeks later Suenens sent the book to the publisher saying that he was quite happy with it. The book appeared and was a great success.

Two months later Louis was summoned by the Cardinal. He told Louis that he had caused a great many problems. The book had been denounced in Rome, and a number of French bishops had writen to Suenens saying that they found the work intolerable. Louis asked what had been said in his defence as the Cardinal had approved it. Suenens said that he had said nothing, and he would like to know who had given the book its imprimatur.

'You did', said Louis.

'No', replied the Cardinal, 'I never gave any such thing.'

'But I gave you the book myself so that you could approve it.'

'I thought you were simply giving it to me to read', said the Cardinal, 'I thought you already had an imprimatur.'

The Cardinal had apparently seen the imprimatur granted to Yves Congar for his preface to the book and had imagined that this covered the whole work. Louis was sure that this was only an excuse, but it did not change the next remark of the Cardinal

'You will have to do something about it and quickly', he said, 'or you will be summoned to appear in court at Rome.'

Louis was taken aback. What could he do? The Cardinal said that he would have to make some changes in the text but Louis here stuck in his toes. He was not prepared to change what he had written, particularly as the Cardinal had previously read it and like it.

Suenens then suggested that they should nominate a panel of three theologians, chosen by Louis, who could read the book and indicate anything that was ambiguous or open to misunderstanding. While Louis agreed to any changes that would clarify the book's contents he remained adamant about not altering the opinions expressed. Accordingly Canon Gillet, Pierre de Locht and one other were invited to meet and comment. They did so. They could find nothing to disagree with, and they even told Louis that it was a very good book. For the sake of appearances they changed a few phrases in the last chapter about Heaven, as that was the subject on which Rome had commented, and also in the section on Mary. Then the Cardinal wrote to Rome saying that a commission had met and certain changes had taken place. As the book was already being sold in bookshops, and was in many libraries it hardly seemed to matter. What struck home with Louis was not so much the procedure through which he had passed as the attitude of the Church which had required it. In another book which Louis Evely now regards as the one in which he has so far best expressed his deepest thoughts about the whole nature of religion and life ('Our Prayer') he wrote these words:

'James and John desired to bring down fire from heaven upon that village in Samaria. That is a typically ecclesiastical way of doing things. But Christ was angry with *them*: "You do not know of what spirit you are," he said, "The Son of Man has come not to destroy men's lives but to save them".'

These words written in 1968 were but a sharper, more biblical expression of a similar opinion which Louis had expressed in his first book twelve years earlier. He had written then, 'The Church has to take the very greatest care to see that she is holy enough to exercise this awful power of giving orders, and does not allow herself to be corrupted by formality, pride or self-interest.' It is a message that Louis has gone on trying to communicate, as in his book, 'If the Church is not to die . . .' (1971) –

'Catholics have still not freed themselves from childish and guilt-laden interpretations of authority: "The Church is our Mother, and one does not criticise one's Mother. The Pope is the Holy Father, and one would surely not wound his heart . . . The bishops have a right to our filial trust. . ." (when all the time you know that for "filial" you should read "infantile"). But surely the Church is US; she gives birth to us and we then give new birth to her; she is as much our daughter as she is our mother; and there is just no way in which she can avoid self-criticism.' (p.59. My translation).

Nor were these kinds of thoughts peculiar to Louis. As Peter Hebblethwaite has so graphically reminded us the whole nature of the church its discusions in Vatican II. One view that was now in the open 'gave the primacy to the whole People of God as a priestly people. Within this people there is a diversity of ministries. Here one can see that the transition from "ministerial priesthood" to "priestly ministry" was not just a semantic quibble, for to speak of the "priestly ministry" was to suppose that there were many ministries in the Church, ministries of healing, teaching, exhortation, consolation, and even administration; and among them was the priestly ministry. Those who took this starting-point emphasized that the priestly ministry was a service or a function in the Church, and not so much a stage. They were therefore prepared to look at the multiple needs of the Church, and open to experiment and inventiveness. . .' [op. cit. p. 62]

It was within this general climate of changing opinion and yet unchanging structure that Louis in his mid-fifties began to ask himself what should be his ministry in the years that might still lie ahead of him. He had been associated with Cardinal Mercier College for almost 20 years, the whole length of his priesthood, and every attempt that he had made to widen his influence or contribute to the thinking of the greater Church had resulted in some obstacle, some modification, some form of condemnation. It was time, he believed, to reconsider his ministry and to do it whilst he was still free to choose.

The way he took was hardly surprising — it was the first step of his lifetime exemplar, Charles de Foucauld. Louis decided to test his vocation in a Trappist monastery in the valley of the Drôme where the Abbot was a long-standing friend. Louis went there for a long period in 1959 and 1960 as an oblate and there is no doubt that in this troubled period of his life the established round of worship, especially the chanting of the psalms, created a rhythm, a silence and a sense of rest which was of great help to him. He had ample opportunity also to deepen and extend his awareness of the scriptures and to meditate on them. Yet despite the warmth and friendliness of his reception, despite Louis' continuing ability to listen, to pray and to think hard about the things of God, it was plain that he could not so cut himself off from the world as to find in the conventual life that ministry which was the best for him. His friend, the Abbot, was wise enough not only to see this but to help Louis to see it as well. Your task, the Abbot made clear to him, is to speak and write of the things of God. Go and do it!

If it thus became clear to Louis that he was not to be a monk it also became clear that he could not continue as a priest in the traditional sense. He might not be made for the enclosed order of the Carthusians but he equally felt that he could no longer bear the limitations of the 'priestly ministry'. In his book, 'In the Christian Spirit', he writes this:

'You have the same relationship with God as you have with your neighbour . . . We no longer have a religion of temples and priests, a hothouse religion, but a religion of the open air. . . The example of someone like Charles de Foucauld can help us to build this lay spirituality . . . Charles de Foucauld even renounced the Real Presence to serve the Touaregs! He realized that the presence of a man living in Christ was more urgent and efficacious than the presence of the Host.'

Whether Charles de Foucauld would have been all that happy about such a 'lay' interpretation of what he was compelled to accept, despite his unquestioned priestliness, is a matter that cannot be resolved. For Louis it was certainly a ground for consideration. What he had to say; what he could in fact do; what, above all, as a mature man he felt in his heart and spirit he could be, and become, could all be as adequately and perhaps more satisfyingly fulfilled as a layman than as a priest. In 1968 he again sought an interview with a member of his old school and the Cardinal of his country, Léon Suenens. What Louis was asking for was the Cardinal's imprimatur for the publication of Louis' works in French, especially as this was given so readily by church authorities for works published in other languages. Suenens was firm in his refusal. Louis asked if he could be granted a 'censor' with whom he could discuss the matter but the Cardinal made it clear that it was not so much the ideas expressed as the style in which they were presented. What disturbed him was the ingenuousness of Louis' manner, the lack of proper gravity in dealing with religious subjects. He mentioned a priests' retreat at which he had been present recently and during which, in the course of the silent meals, one of Louis' books had been read aloud. "Do you know", he said, "there was one moment when they all began to laugh. That isn't the way to respond to sacred matters. Your style is too human!"

That decided Louis. There was only one way left. He must give up his priestly orders and ask to be returned to the lay state. Only he would do it, not through Suenens, who might be unwilling to agree to such a step, but through Rome itself. That is how Louis came to be relieved of his priestly vocation and to be returned of his own free will to the status of a layman. He let it be clearly known that he was still a good Roman Catholic.

8 *A Layman Once More*

The first signs of the final crisis came in 1968, at a time when a survey of French Roman Catholic booksellers showed that Louis Evely's books were the most widely-read of all those by modern spiritual writers. Appropriately, the first sure evidence of a serious rift in Louis' continuing priesthood was contained in a letter to his ever-widening circle of friends and admirers in several continents. Always mindful of what friends mean and how much they welcome being told from the heart he wrote to them as follows:

'Dear Friends,

For some time now you have been aware of what I have been preaching and studying and you know that I have given myself heart and soul in seeking to effect that renewal in our church to which the Vatican Council has called us. Today, however, I have decided, after a great deal of thought and after consulting many others, to give up my programme of retreats and conferences, and to undertake a long period of meditation and reflection.

This step has not been imposed on me. I am taking the initiative myself because I think it more honest to stop speaking in the name of those who have doubts about my opinions and who would more and more often disapprove of what I was teaching if they heard me.

My differences of opinion with the hierarchy are, to my mind, of secondary and temporary importance, though I fear that as they at present see them they would regard my views as touching matters of real substance. Further, I no longer regard myself as having the right to claim their authority for what I say.

Do not for one moment imagine that "I have lost my faith"! Quite the reverse. My faithfulness to Christ is stronger than ever and my one desire is to relate my thoughts more and more closely to what he has revealed. I even dare to hope that the Church will one day come to approve my way of thinking just as at Vatican II she was prepared to recognise things which she had previously rejected. You may recall similarly that what I wrote in my first books just over ten years ago upset some people when it first appeared and yet such thinking is now able to be accepted almost everywhere.

I believe in this development of the Church (to which the Council bears witness even though we have so far only taken the first very tentative steps) and I feel confident that future events will resolve the difficulties of those, like myself, who remain part of the Church but who do not feel able, at this moment, to collaborate any longer with its leaders.

Meanwhile, I shall content myself by publishing in my own name ideas which bind no-one but myself and which may yet help to hasten this renewal. My next book, 'La Prière d'un homme moderne' (Our Prayer) will help you to appreciate still more both the reasons behind my decision and my deep attachment to Christ and to faith in him.

I thought I ought to tell you all this because I greatly value your concern and because I would like to think that I have your understanding whatever else happens.

Louis EVELY.'

For Louis' most intimate friends this statement was simply a step that set the record straight and enabled them to share with others the long-concealed disharmony which had been developing between Louis and his ecclesiastical superiors. For others it must have come as a real shock. To learn that the teacher and guide whom they so much respected and whose thinking and writing was of such evident benefit to an increasing circle of readers was out of sorts with the Church's hierarchy, and so out of sorts that he was prepared to discontinue his many and growing engagements, could not but be a surprise. Of course they had recognised the originality of presentation that appeared in everything that Louis spoke or wrote but the fact that books and programmes and lectures had flowed almost without ceasing for a decade hardly suggested that either Louis or the authorities were at odds or that there was any significant error in what was produced. In a subtle sense it is true that there was no error. Yet it is also true that so fresh and so comprehensive, whilst at the same time so transparent, was the explanation of the faith as Louis saw it that to those who were the guardians of the Catholic Faith it could only be disturbing if there was someone who approached doctrine from so biblical and evangelical a standpoint and did it in so undisguised a fashion. Louis had told his friends that if they read his forthcoming book they might understand better why he was taking the step that he was. One or two extracts from it may help to show the truth of what he was suggesting.

There was, first of all his comment on the Mass. 'We have repaganized the Eucharist into a pagan sacrifice' he wrote (pp.25, 26), 'we have turned God's offering to man into man's offering to God. Who "sacrifices" himself in the Mass? Man to God or God to Man? Who offers himself to the other? Who nourishes the other?

'The Father gives us his Son so that we may let him give himself to others in us. And all we have found to do with him is to offer Him "in sacrifice" to the Father. "Return to sender" as they say in the post office. How happy this must make him!

'To celebrate the eucharist is to make present among us the gift of God, the humility of God, the love of God for us, and to have it penetrate us so completely that we may make Him present, living and visible to all others.

'The sacraments are made for the faithful and the faithful are the sacraments of the infidels, the revelation to all people of good tidings.'

For readers of these words today there must come echoes of several other Catholic authors and apologists in the intervening decade who have begun to air similar opinions, not least in dialogue with those who do not belong to the Holy Roman communion. In 1969 and in the context of a Belgian Church which knew nothing as yet of the charismatic influence that was to appear in it and where the resistance to neo-Vaticanism was bound to be strong vis-à vis the Reformed tradition of the Low Countries, such an expression of the Eucharistic dynamic (and in such terse and unmistakable terms) was bound to be suspect and unpalatable. Louis was now aware of that and that is why he could no longer claim to be speaking in the Church's name. Yet no-one can say that this is anything but incarnationally-centred. The same is true of this passage about 'Charity' (pp.70/71) –

'If so many of our young people grow up without any taste for the Church it is because they have never really seen it. It has never been revealed to them. . . They have seen people who do not even look at one another, who obviously do not love one another, who go through the motions of even the sacrament of unity – the Eucharist, firmly resolved to remain completely separate. . . Does sharing the Eucharist make us better or worse? Are there really no more divisions among us? There are so many that no-one notices them any more. There are nothing *but* divisions among us. And there is nothing harder to get rid of.'

It was a sure and wise instinct in Louis that led him at this stage of his life to pause and move once more into the desert experience of his great exemplar-de Foucauld. Before he could decide how and where to proceed he needed to get out of the stream of engagements and conferences which could so easily engulf him and seek that close contact with his God that would alone bring him to the light for his path which he so genuinely wanted to find. 'Be careful', he had written, 'for an "activist" who prays little is more formidable than a tank.' He knew the temptation of the crowded diary and the adulation of the crowd that would follow and drain him. So, like a true Little Brother in spirit if not in the habit, Louis made his way to the place where, again like de Foucauld, the Trappists of the Languedoc might offer him a chance to reflect and to see the path ahead. 'A contemplative' wrote de Foucauld 'is one who possesses in the depths of his soul this essential truth that everything comes from God.' It was because Louis also knew this, that he took the path to the Abbey of La Frappe at Aiguebelle to which his friend, the Abbot who had served at Ste Marie du Désert in Toulouse, had now been transferred.

This time the purpose of his journey was somewhat different from the previous ones. No longer was he seeking guidance about the possibility of another type of priestly ministry — within or outside a monastic order — but whether he could continue his ministry as a teacher and writer in the priesthood at all. It was the right milieu for such a decision because it was so truly a place of silence and yet also a place where men of so many different backgrounds mingled together and found their way as the dedicated servants of God. Familiar as Louis was with the spiritual letters of Charles de Foucauld he could well echo these words as he waited in that setting for the guidance that he sought —

'My life is unchanged: divided between work and prayer I do almost no reading: I spend almost all my free time in church . . . Since our Lord is there, what else should I do? My spiritual life has not changed: it is filled with the presence of our Lord, and of his beloved saints who were with him on earth, and is one with that of those I love so much in this world . . . God has continued to give me the grace he has shown me ever since my first days in the monastery . . . He is there, so what more do I need? And he is perfectly happy there, so should not I be happy? Yet — I am not. For those I love in this world are suffering, or are disturbed and unhappy. I pray to him for them, very unworthily, but with all that is in my heart. Praying to our Lord for those I love is the chief business of the hours I spend at his feet — when I do what I can both for him and for them — and that is all that needs to be done (Six, p.22)

For Charles de Foucauld that passage in 1892 was followed in due course by his removing himself even further from the normal life and activities of men. For Louis this period of meditation and wrestling in the quietness was to lead him more surely back to the life from which his ordination had taken him. For it was in the course of this stay at Toulouse that Louis came to the clear decision that his life as a priest was over and that he should apply to the Church authorities for permission to return to the lay state. By Easter, 1968, the necessary application, consideration and authorisation for his relinquishment from his priestly authority and status had been granted by Cardinal Suenens, as his Bishop and the Primate of the Belgian Church, and Louis was now able to resume his place as an ordinary Catholic individual in the secular world. What lay behind this step and how he had come to it is best described in his own words and the letter which he wrote to his American publisher on June 5th.

'Dear Sir,

I received your kind letter of May 22nd and I am most happy to try and reply to it.

'Yes, I did ask for and have now been granted my return to the lay state. It was a step that had to be taken for loyalty's sake: I have never been able to say anything other than what I think, and I was no longer able to contradict statements by the Pope and his Bishops and still continue to appear as if I were under their command. After "Humanae Vitae", the Pope's "Credo", the speech he made at Bogotá, his pilgrimage to Fatima, and especially the great disillusionment of seeing the Roman Curia once more assume control and close all the doors which the Council had so properly opened, I could not collaborate further with the Hierarchy.

'My difference of opinion with the Pope and the Bishops, though they seem to me of secondary and marginal importance, are, I fear, such as they consider in the present state of affairs to be matters of substance. The Church still exacts from her priests a military discipline and a total obedience even in those things which are not matters involving infalibility. She does not accept "difficulties of conscience" except for other armies and "authorities" than her own! "Yet I do believe that one day she will accept my ideas, just as at Vatican II she authorised what had long been forbidden and allowed those theologians to be heard whom she had held hitherto in disgrace. Just as my books caused a scandal when they first appeared, and were even denounced by several bishops but are now accepted almost everywhere.

'The Church evolves: even as we struggle with those who represent it today we are preparing the ground for what will be tomorrow's crop. I have every confidence that sooner or later the problems of those who, like myself, remain part of the church though we feel that we cannot work with its leaders will be resolved.

'Meanwhile, I have requested this return to lay status so that I may continue to serve the Church with a layman's freedom, always ready to take up my priestly office again when the hierarchy have reconsidered the situation and I am allowed to offer my loyal and respectful cooperation but with full freedom of conscience.

'There is however something else to be said. From the moment that the news broke of my once more becoming a layman all the Catholic "loyalists", my "pious" opponents have stated that I was a "married man", or that I have left the priesthood in order to be married. That is a frame of mind which completely baffles me! Whilst it would be my right and would even be a wonderful reason for becoming a layman, even if I had discovered a true and deep love for someone, what has that to do with the value of my opinions? Indeed it is almost a matter of regret for me to have to deny this allegation. Yet you ought to know that I am not married and if I should wish to marry I shall make it public and have no intention of hiding the fact. Why should I when I will then have received. . . yet another sacrament.

'You may use this letter or any part of it for publication, just as you please. I am attaching a letter which I sent to my friends before I took the recent further step of asking to be restored to the lay state.

'You also ought to know that I have published here and there a very brief notice as follows: 'For some years now people who have not liked

Fr. Evely's opinions have attacked him by spreading the notion that he had become a Protestant or that he was already married, was about to commit suicide, had been forbidden to act as a priest, was the secret father of a family, had been committed to a madhouse and goodness knows what else. I need hardly say that these are all lies and slander. The truth is that in July last Fr. Evely asked to be restored to the lay state. His differences of opinion with the Hierarchy prevented him from continuing to seem to represent those with whom he was not in agreement. . . Fr. Evely considered that it was his duty to prepare for Vatican III from the moment that the Curia began to close the windows that Pope John XXIII and the Council had opened. So, in order that he might continue to serve the Church he asked for and was granted the freedom of a layman.'

'Please make use of that also in whatever way you wish.

'My book, "Prière d'un homme moderne", which I sent you in MS could, I think, very usefully introduce a whole series of books which dealt with the matter of praying today. Rather than provide "made-up" prayers as you suggest I would like to undertake some commentaries on, and modern adaptations of the Gospel. . .' and the Letter continues with other details of a publishing programme.

I have quoted this letter at length in order to convey the extent of Louis' concerns as he now began to come to terms with the practicalities of his new situation. His relationship with the publisher of his books for the English-speaking audience was going to be of crucial importance. All that Louis had earned previously as a writer, a lecturer and teacher had been at once handed over to the church. He had been fed and housed without charge and in order to buy books and essential clothes he had received the normal wage of a priest in those days, some BF 3000 per quarter, about £300 sterling. When Louis once more became a layman all that came to an end, and since as a priest he had never been required to contribute to the State Insurance scheme he now had no entitlement to a pension or to State support. If he had perhaps expected that the Church would show compassion on one of its hitherto faithful sons and clergy whose writings had been of such service in the recent past Louis was soon to learn otherwise. As far as the Church was concerned he no longer existed, and since it was by his own request that he had surrendered his priestly role the Church considered that its responsibilities for his welfare were at an end and it was upon *his* shoulders that there lay the responsibility for providing for his future. Louis Evely's situation simply serves to underline the plight of the many other priests who, before and following his own decision, have been placed in a similar situation. On the one hand Louis understands why it is that many more priests feel quite unable to take that kind of plunge even though some of them wish to do so. On the other, he points out that with over 5,000 priests taking his step over a five-year period it highlights the seriousness of their intentions. He himself had had to think very hard before he could, on the verge of 60, put himself at risk in this way.

The letter also reveals the criticism which a man has to meet if he dares to endanger the prospects of the Catholic Church by suggesting that he cannot find fulfilment in the priesthood, or that the hierarchy might perhaps not be perfect. What disturbed Louis at that time was not that people should be disappointed at his leaving the priestly ministry but that they should immediately impute to anyone who did so the most malicious and unjustified reasons for such a course. As his letter states it was as if any stone would do to throw at someone who dares to think of exercising his right of conscience in this way. The fact that he was not 'de-frocked' or put under any kind of disciplinary prohibition as a priest, and that he took the kind of disciplinary prohibition as a priest, and that he took the step he did out of an active and sincere desire to be honest with himself and the leaders of the church he served, did not seem to have any effect on many of his critics. As far as they were concerned he had no right to 'rock the boat' and to do so must mean that he had an ulterior motive and an uneasy conscience. In Catholic terms and in that social context it was most likely that the problem was one of sex. Hence the attacks.

There are those, of course, who whilst not joining their voices or comments to the harsher critics would still feel, as Louis' friends, that he was in some respects his own worst enemy. One of his admirers, and they are still legion, a layman who now occupies a post at the Cardinal Mercier ccollege, could only say wistfully that Louis Evely was right in what he saw and taught — but was 20 years to early! This man admits that Louis had his court of followers who would have done almost anything that he asked of them and though they would not wound him for worlds they were distressed when, even despite the constraints that seemd to be put on Louis, he reacted by giving up the very work which he did so excellently and on which so many had come to rely. To such followers perhaps the truest thing that Louis wrote about this incident was:

'I have never been able to say anything other than what I think'. Such candour is a clue to the man's character. It is admirable but it is also naive. One begins to notice a recurring theme in this whole story. It is that Louis' strength of conviction and insight made it well-nigh impossible for him to present his case diplomatically. The result was that he constantly antagonised those who did not share his outlook. The immense gift which he possesses of being able to marshal and express his own ideas so congently and decisively was itself a means of inflicting injuries that rebounded to his own hurt.

'To face the truth', he once said to me, 'and to face the possible surrender of being right, especially in a position of superiority and leadership, is exceedingly difficult, and not least for clergy, or bishops. To maintain the accepted hierarchy is for many people all that they know or care about. To make any kind of attack on that position even by one's own seeking for truth is to threaten and disturb something both deep and sensitive.' It was that exercise that Louis Evely too often succeeded in mounting.

"One can appreciate the sense of triumph amongst Louis' critics when, three years after his return to the lay state, Louis announced his marriage to Mary van der Meersch who was now divorced. For such critics it supplied the very proof they needed that, as always, it was because of a woman that he had wanted to give up the priesthood.

Louis and Mary will tell you that they had known each other for 20 years and yet such an idea had never previously occurred to them. Louis was absorbed by his vocation and Mary never imagined that love for her would lead him to give it up. She realised that a marriage built on the sacrifice of his ministry and her marriage would be destined for disaster.

Louis sought his release from church office for the reasons that have been explained already and Mary after twenty years of struggle that severely tested her health. During a six-month period in a clinic her psychiatrist advised her that she would never recover unless she separated from a husband whom she had never really loved and with whom she was unable to form a close relationship.

It was only when they were both free that they considered joining together their separate and lonely futures. Together they thought that they might build something that might still last. They were married on 4 December 1971. It cannot be denied that such a step gave delight to their enemies and even made their friends wonder . . .

If the step that Louis took of returning to the lay state was itself regarded as an act of self-indulgence and disobedience, then his marriage, and that to a divorced woman, was the final act of treason and self-destruction. It is a matter of constant regret to the couple themselves to realise that despite their own deep happiness and love they are now prevented by their act from being of any further service to the vast majority of Catholics around the world. If Louis was first allowed at least to become an unmarried layman, albeit reduced in status, he was and is now regarded as being 'dead and forgotten' as far as his Church is officially concerned. He is debarred from the very sacrament which he understands and loves so well, the Eucharist, and even the married state which he purports to enjoy does not in the eyes of the church really exist.

It is therefore not surprising that the books which he wrote and which were circulated and translated in their hundreds of thousands amongst seminarians and laity in countless Catholic circles across the world are now banned and deprecated amongst many Catholic readers. They are considered, officially at least, to be harmful or misleading, and from a publishing point of view the author who was fast becoming one of the most popular and profitable fell in one season to a level that hardly seemed to justify an occasional reprint. Not that the contents had changed – only the author's circumstances, and this, after all, was just one more way in which the Church could punish those who were unwilling to be disciplined and made to toe the line. It not only meant a real decline in circulation, however. It actively started doubts in the minds of those who had read and enjoyed Louis' books so that people really wondered if they had been subtly deceived.

Ironically, it looks from this vantage point as if Louis were again to bear the brunt of being, if not twenty years, then at least a decade, too soon for his physical requirements to be met. As Fernand Gillet comments, there are now many ex-priests who marry and yet who are still kept on in their teaching jobs. There was one monk of the Maredsous order who recently forsook his vows, married and is still permitted to teach in a Catholic school. There are even teachers who are divorced or married to divorced women, and there are college teachers who are even agnostics but who are still accepted because they are competent in their fields. The situation is now so much more pluralist and open than when Louis took the step he did. Though even Fernand is prepared to surmise that what was really the problem in the case of Louis Evely was not any of the things that have just been mentioned – Louis' problem was that he was too powerful as a personality, too able as a communicator of his views, too obviously a purveyor of the truth.

As Louis now reflects on this whole matter of the married clergy he produces arguments that, bearing the same hallmark of perceptivity and logic that colours so much of his writing and teaching, help one to see that even if he had not withdrawn from the institutional priesthood when he did he might have had to undergo still further punishments and trials which even he would have found quite intolerable. 'The priest', he has said, 'is a man "sacré" because he does not have sexual experiences. We who have married, therefore, are "profanes" because we have undergone just that experience. To marry and be a priest is impossible – not just undesirable! In the Eastern Churches a priest celebrates once a week so that he is able to cohabit with his wife on 6 days and then obstain from such marital relations on the eve of the day he celebrates. In the West the custom of daily celebration would make that impossible. It is not a rule of the New Testament but it is a rule of the church and so that is that. The danger is that it suggests that none of the laity are really pure whilst the priest alone is. Even married laity who think like this take care not to copulate on the night before they make their communion. Hence the fall of a priest to the sad state of matrimony is not just a regret but a disaster – it is more, it is a "decease", a real dying of the person concerned. That is why I received several notes and telegrams which read, "Are you still alive? Why are you not dead?" ' What Louis takes comfort in is the genuine concern of those of his contemporaries whose spiritual compassion and innate honesty are still open to men like himself. When someone wrote to the Abbé Michonneau and asked if he had heard that Louis Evely had 'died' that great parish priest and servant of God's mission had only one reply, 'Well, if he did die, that's not the end, for he has risen again!'

L'Ordinaire de Malines-Bruxelles a exécuté, le 12 juillet 1968, le rescrit romain, datant du 14 juin 1968, en vertu duquel Louis EVELY, à sa demande, a été dispensé de ses obligations cléricales et réduit à l'état laïc.

De ce fait ledit Louis Evely devra s'abstenir de l'exercice du pouvoir d'ordre et de juridiction, ainsi que de tout ce qui relève du ministère spirituel (prédication, retraites, récollections, conférence religieuses, etc.).

Malines, le 12 juillet 1968

+ L.J.Card.Suenens, archevêque
de Malines-Bruxelles.

The text of the document allowing Louis Evely to return to the lay state.

9 *A New Life of Service*

The following postcard from Switzerland in 1974 reached Louis and Mary Evely: —

'Dear Friends,
It is with a heart full of gratitude and deep joy that I think of those days which we have just spent with you. Your warm welcome, the open way in which we could share and exchange views, and the moments of relaxation with their sense of complete freedom . . . all these stay graven on my mind. 'Is' and I often speak of what we have been able to experience and to discover at your place. We dream of coming back and meeting you again. On Sunday Jacqueline visited us . . . very strong links have certainly been created there.
I do hope that when you come to Geneva in February you will be able to visit us. Be sure of all our love for you.
Isobel and Charlotte.'

This card from Switzerland is only one from a large pile of correspondence that has grown steadily since Louis and Mary Evely began to make their house in the valley of the Drôme, a place where groups of Christian people could meet. That greeting was from two nurses, but their words are merely echoed by another letter from a Catholic priest;

'I want to thank you most warmly for these few days which I have spent with you. I shall keep the happiest memories of my stay at Les Combeaux, and I want to thank you for your welcome which was at once both simple and very warm. Thank you, too, for letting me have the opportunity for joining in those times of meeting which were of such high quality and dealt with such important things. I return home enriched and with great delight at having seen you again.
George.'

One visitor, the wife of a Protestant pastor in Switzerland, broke out into verse,

"There are folk that I love
to have close by,
Those who seem far away
from my daily round.

There are those who take me by surprise
and make my heart turn over
like a stroke of thunder
as I wait to see them again.

Then there are folk
who come into my life
so tenderly
and stay there for ever.

There are people who live within me
secretly
in my very being
and to whom I call.

When joy almost chokes me
and my eyes fill with tears
and I know that they are there
somewhere, hidden. . .

They are there within me like a promise
of a love that is shared;

The bright, shining light of an Other
living there in my heart
like a deep secret burning
which prevents me from dying.

And if I am in need, their names
burst up like new flames,
so many they are, fine,
varied but true
they give me new life
these people I love.'

If, as some think, un-solicited testimonials are the best sort, then letters like these certainly bring great joy and satisfaction to Mary and Louis Evely. For these were the first-fruits of an act of faith by Louis and Mary as they started a new life together following the years of crisis which had just passed. They both realised that to begin afresh was not going to be easy, and therefore they had to discover not only the right place in which to build a home, but be commonly agreed on its use.;

Louis, now 60, was eager to end what had become the life of a vagabond, albeit a sophisticated type of vagabond. The constant travelling to retreats, to meetings, to clergy sessions — the responding to others' calls, as well as the habit of making ones home wherever one happened to be; all these were now altered by Louis' action. Yet that was only part of the story. It was not simply because he was now married, nor that he needed to watch his health more carefully. The urge to settle down seemed attractive. It was also that he could imagine a new kind of ministry — the providing of a place where those who might know 'crisis' and doubts about their faith could come and share them. Louis wanted a spot where visitors could discover beauty and know peace: where folk could unwind (what he called 'un endroit harmonieux'). It was to be a place where people would find it easy to think, to relax, to talk, to make friends and to pray. A place for some twenty people at most, and with few outside attractions.

During his months in the Abbey of Aiguebelle he had come to know the valley of the Drôme — that valley down which Hannibal had marched with his famous elephants. Louis had noted its comparative remoteness and natural beauty, the simplicity of the life that was lived there and the vines that grew in profusion on the sheltered hillsides. He sampled the home cooking of the region and let his eyes drift across the slopes of gentle, rocky hills to the first mountain ranges of Provence southward, the mountains of the Vercors (those haunts of the French Maquis during the Second World War) to the North. He savoured the long, sunny days of summer whilst not forgetting the fewer snow-laden days of a briefer winter. All this began to meet the bill, to point to a location for their new home. He asked friends to keep their eyes and ears open; he and Mary toured the district; he contacted local Estate Agents, and in 1971 they found Les Combeaux.

When you first see the Evely's present home you can recognise it for the southern French farm that it was built to be. Both Louis and Mary were adamant that the farm must not lose any of its original character, however much they might improve it, so the outside has remained almost exactly as it was. Of course the roof has been completely repaired and the shutters hang properly; a mass of well-tended but demanding flower-beds greets you as you approach the house; a little further up the rise on which the house stands you wil see a swimming pool that they have installed, but apart from the general sense of caring and informal tidiness which one associates with Louis and Mary Evely, the external structure of the house remains unchanged, and only the interior fully reflects the hard and careful work which they both put in to create this house of love and this home of welcome.

Despite the dilapidated state of the outhouses, the haybarn, the gallery and the surrounding pathways, Mary agreed that this could become the place for which Louis was looking. The weeds could be pulled, the fabric made waterproof, the tracks levelled, the interior redesigned, and the barn re-fashioned. Nothing could rival the views, the air, the colours of the landscape, the peacefulness and the sunsets.

To Mary, as an artist, the setting had its own appeal: whilst for Louis, apart from the hard work which lay ahead of him, it seemed tailormade.

The farmer who lived there wanted to sell at a reasonable price. For three years the farmer had believed that he was called to preach the Gospel to those in caravan and camping sites across France, and as soon as the sale was completed he bought a truck with the registration letters LLL and set off on his journeys. Since he was a member of the 'Lutheran League of Laity', the truck was a constant advertisement of his purpose. It is an interesting thought that as one preacher of the Gospel left Les Combeaux and drove down the lane, another — a rather different kind of teacher of the same Gospel — was about to climb the lane and take his place.

Yet it was one thing to find such a property and quite another to buy it. Louis had not been able to save out of his meagre pay as a teacher and that had long since ceased. His royalties were suddenly reduced and he had in any case allocated most of these to needy causes which he supported. The problem therefore remained. How could Mary and he ever hope to purchase a home for themselves, let alone a complete farm with all the land attached to it?

Within five to six weeks, however, the whole sale had been completed. Whilst Louis was right when he said of that period, 'I was not in a position to buy anything!' yet he and Mary had one asset which was worth more than cash in the bank. They had true friends. It was an old lady whom Mary and Louis had met in previous years, a Mme X, who offered to purchase the farm for them and then leave it to them as a permanent gift. The farmer was glad to settle the matter as soon as possible, the papers were signed and the farm changed hands. By the winter of 1972, Louis and Mary Evely were living and working in their new home, and Mary's children and several of their friends were helping with the alterations which have now transformed 'Les Combeaux'. In the gallery lounge of their home you will find a well-thumbed copy of 'Savoir Tout Faire' — the modern Frenchman's encyclopaedia of Do-it-Yourself techniques in the home. Flick through its pages, then look at some of the family photographs of Louis, a workman in winter and summer, and you will soon realise what this step meant to one who had been trained as a scholar and thinker. It was certainly a case of necessity being a hard master but it was also a time which he and Mary remember as one of double excitement — re-fashioning the farm buildings for a new kind of use, and laying the foundations of their own fresh relationship. Like most newly-weds they grew together as their new home emerged.

It took them two days to complete the essential work. Mary the artist became Mary the draughtsman, and then her children and Louis began to turn the drawings into a reality. It was hard work. Louis' royalties were a mere trickle. The fees from a constant round of retreats and conferences were there no longer. There were no more radio and television appearances and since Louis was no longer away on trips he was another regular mouth to feed. Building materials were not only expensive but they had to be brought to the site and then used before they suffered any deterioration. It was a hand-to-mouth existence. Yet the photographs show you a man who smiles, young people helping to create a whole new world, a garden beginning to emerge from the weeds and the rocks, and Mary blossoming in the midst of her re-designed 'ménage'. Without any suggestion of false pride she and Louis could, and do, rightly claim that it was 'all their own work'.

In 1973 the house was ready to receive their first guests. Many people had called as the work of re-building and renovation was in progress so that when it was known that they had finished they were hardly ever without visitors from spring to autumn. Most of those who visited came for one or two days at the most, and they soon began to feel as if they were running a hotel! They were making their home available to people who wanted to meet them, but Louis was not achieving his goal of using Les Combeaux for its best purpose. People were being touched but not in depth and they would depart just when they were beginning to open up. Louis and Mary had to think out their role and the programme afresh.

They have always been letter writers. Whilst Louis is again away on his visits abroad he writes every day, as does Mary to him. Mary writes every week to each of her children, and there was one point at which she was writing thirty letters in forty-eight hours. She has often spent six hours a day at her desk. They now began to correspond with the people who had read Louis' books and who had from time to time asked him questions about what he had said, or who wish to meet him to discuss further the arguments of his work. These readers were told about Les Combeaux and invited to come during the following summer for the inside of a week. What they discussed would depend upon their needs — whether it was 'Prayer', 'Family life', 'The Sacraments', or how to live out a Christian life. All that Louis and Mary asked was that they should make a modest contribution to their keep, and come with a willingness to meet others and be ready to open up about their concerns.

There was an immediate response to this invitation. Within a few weeks all the available places were spoken for, and Louis and Mary had a new kind of planning to do. With four weeks of being an 'extended family' ahead of them in 1974, they began to review the scene.

There was room for three single people to sleep in the house itself, but the rest would have to sleep in trailers, tents or in the lofts of the outhouses. In a shallow and sheltered depression across the field in front of the house, and between the rocks and under the trees, the other couples and families could set up their temporary home. At the foot of the depression was a sturdily-built washhouse and drying room where the campers could share a few creature comforts. There was also a gas ring, so the preparing of simple food indoors was always possible. Since the guests were to come in the summer, however, and the days would be usually very warm and sunny, it was not expected that the guests would need to worry about that.

Where do they come from, these visitors to Les Combeaux? They come from every point of the compass – from Paris and Marseilles, from Germany and Switzerland, from England and Spain. They come from the suburbs of great cities and the presbytery of a country village, from a hospital ward or the lecture rooms of a foreign university. They come from the ranks of doctors and lawyers, businessmen and students, engineers and ordinary workmen, nuns and married couples. They come as a result of friendship with Louis or Mary in previous days, or on the recommendation of those who have known them. They come as readers of Louis' books and as those who want help, sometimes desperately, and who turn eagerly to anyone who might be able to meet their need. They come, on occasions, as those who are curious to see what an ex-priest and his new wife could be like and how they manage their life together. Some come because they had once 'dropped in' casually on their way somewhere else and were so intrigued by what they encountered that they had to come back.

From the start there was no shortage of people wanting to join in the four or five sessions each summer. Indeed there is now hardly any need for the Evelys to advertise their gatherings. The word is getting around and apart from the new contacts who want to join 'the family', there are many who come two or three years running so as to build on what they have already received. It is one of the Evelys' jobs to make sure that they don't get swamped by past visitors taking all the places and preventing the growth of their circle. What is certain is that if the Evelys were to extend the number of their sessions there would still be no problem about filling the vacancies.

Increasing the number of sessions is not likely to happen. For one thing it is all run by Louis and Mary alone, though, when present, their children will help as much as possible. This means that Mary is not only hostess to all her guest, the chef who prepares the menus, and oversees their variety, the cook who makes the food she chooses, the head waiter and waitress all rolled into one – but also the scullery maid and housewife who clears up the kitchen and then buys in for the next day. The fact that Mary is expert in French cuisine, a maitresse d'hôtel, with a sense of imagination, who can also drive the well-worn Simca to collect supplies, does not alter the fact that she gets very tired. When the last of their visitors have gone in early August the Evelys are, to use their words, 'flaked out'. To have more parties is just not possible.

It is for the same reason that each session does not last for more than five days. The Evelys find the break between each 'visit' quite essential. The physical labour involved in looking after 20 people, besides themselves, is hard enough. To tidy the roms, do running repairs, keep the local spring fresh and clean for use, look after the garden, clean out the swimming pool which is so much in use, plan the next week's progammes and make sure that the camp site is ready — all this is a job for a whole team. Yet Mary and Louis are often responsible for the whole of it themselves. What might easily be forgotten is that part of the entertaining, part of the 'experience' for those who come, is the constant conversation and sometimes intimate dialogue between guest and host — the kind of conversations that begin at breakfast-time and don't end until the last farewells are said late at night. Yet it is on this release in communication that the uniqueness and, if one likes so to describe it, the 'success' of these sessions depends. What is said and shared in the more formal periods together is valuable — what follows in between a dip, or a walk to fetch the milk, or in a quiet nook where two can quietly unburden themselves to each other — this is what make this place so different for the many who come. Perhaps few can realise what a drain it is on the loving couple who entertain them — though 'entertain' is not exactly the right word.

What happens in the sessions? It can be put quite simply — people discover and talk with each other. Louis Evely remembers that three days after the very first session they ever held, a letter arrived from a woman who had been their guest. She told Louis and Mary that for eighteen years she had been aware that though she moved amongst people she could not communicate with them, could not break out of herself and relate to others. 'Now', she wrote, 'after a few hours in your home I can speak freely — and all because someone was ready to listen to me. Others were ready to show themselves to me, and I was ready to let them into my little cell.' It was to be the first of many such letters.

On the first evening the visitors gather in the gallery room after their first sampling of Mary's table. They relax in easy chairs, on scattered cushions or with their backs against the wall, whilst Louis welcomes them to this quiet corner of God's world. He does not start them on some great issue which he has prepared but introduces himself and Mary as ordinary people like themselves and then allows them to get to know each other before they go to their beds. Often he will invite a couple who have been to their home before to say something about their background, their home, what coming to Les Combeaux meant on a previous occasion, what is happening now in the place where they are, their hopes, their worries, anything. . . So conversation begins and slowly but surely everyone is drawn into the circle of encounter which has been begun. People begin to say things about their background and their work or homes which they rarely share with another. As Louis says, 'They want to talk, they need to talk, they have been afraid of talking . .

. now they discover that they can communicate, and someone is listening.'

At the start of each succeeding day the pattern begins to become clear. After breakfast they gather as a group and Louis introduces the subject which the group has chosen for this session. It may be 'Our Image of God' or 'Marriage', 'Death' or 'The Charismatic movement' — the subjects seem endless and are as varied as the lives of the visitors. This introduction is by way of a 'reflection'. It is not easy to describe the style of this particular man. It is never assertive, never dogmatic. 'My job', he would claim, 'is not to tell them what to believe. The very reason that many of our guestss are here is because they are already wrestling with the formal teaching which they have been given. My job is to reflect some of their anxieties, to show that I, too, have shared them: to let them see what my reflection on those difficulties has shown me and then let them loose to share their own reflections on the same subject.'

The session lasts for two hours. At the outset the anxiety is all too clear. There is the desire to attack in others the things which one most fears, the tendency to quote from a book which one has read and think that it solves the problem, the unwillingness to listen to another point of view or to fear that someone else will not hear you out. Louis and Mary see it as their job to try and unravel all this, to show that what have been problems for their visitors are or have been problems for them. Above all it is an opportunity for all present to start testing their thoughts by their lives, to start analysing their experience and thus to add to their understanding — even perhaps to be able to 'see' someone else's problem more clearly and be able to work it through with them. No-one ever objects once the sessions get under way, and by the second or third day there really is a change in the way people are responding, in themselves and to each other.

At around 11.45 it is time for a break, and a dip in the pool. The session ends but the talking goes on. Mary will tell you that some of her most taxing and yet rewarding moments have been in a bathing costume beside the pool. For some it is as if a dam had burst and they begin to realise that all their isolation and separation is being washed away. They realise that what they say is now heard, they are being understood and that they may have something to offer in unravelling the great mysteries of life. They discover that their humanity, far from making them unimportant, is the very thing which makes them unique and special. Yet, even as they discover their uniqueness they also rediscover their common bond with others — that others share their same questions, their fears, their hopes, their answers. Talk begins in earnest.

At 1 p.m. they are enjoying the food at the Evely's table. The talk continues amongst the trailing vines, with the mountains in the distance and the flower beds scenting the nearby paths. It is at moments like these that the full impact of Les Combeaux begins to be felt. Many write to say that what spoke to them was the combination of food and welcome, the scenery and the folk you meet. It is in the pouring of the wine and the peeling of fruit, the munching on home-baked bread and the supping of farmhouse broth, the warmth of a French summer day and the fact that you are yourself with others who are to show you themselves — it is all this that makes lunch-time not just an episode in the day but another moment of real life. One only has to read the letters to discover that this is what it is. 'We are not here', say Louis and Mary, 'to sell our summer parties or to make people 'our' clients. We are here to make the dumb speak, the ones who want to speak more at ease, and the ones who are confused at peace so that they can find their own way, hopefully God's way.'

The afternoon is for everybody to use as they wish; to walk, to sleep, to swim some more, to read, to think, to write, for lovers to hold hands. For Mary it is time to catch up with the household chores with Louis to help. For at 4.30 there will be tea and the talk will begin all over again. Another session will assemble and Louis will exercise that great gift of his — the gift of interpretation, the ability to sum up and express so clearly many of the thoughts and stivings that have been thrown up earlier in the day or the week. Those who have experienced this gift of his have devised a name for it. They call him an 'accoucheur', a midwife: one who has the ability to enable others' offspring to come to birth. In the realm of ideas that is indeed the function that Louis Evely now performs. He listens intently to what others say, he ponders on the content of their laboured efforts and then he brings to birth the best human embodiment possible of what it was that another was struggling to express. It is a gift that many priests and pastors would do well to develop.

By 6.30 Mary takes over with a relaxation period. Those who wish to do so are invited to leave the gallery room and climb the outside rear stairs to what was once a hay-loft over the present guest bedrooms. It is a simple but ample room, gently lit by the floor-level windows, shielded by their wooden shutters from the sun's full evening glare. In one corner stands part of Louis' library, a tall rough wooden bookccase bulging with the paper-backed editions so familiar to readers of French literature. On the other walls are some of Mary's own paintings, startling reds and contrasting blues, some of the canvases turned into her own version of a Turner landscape, and others portraits, still-life studies and abstracts of fascinating design. There are canvases too that rest against the floor and wall, their faces turned away, or not complete, telling us that the artist's work goes on and is never done. For the rest there are a few mats, some simple wicker chairs and lots of large soft cushions. It is a room for rest.

'To stop the motor racing you have to deal with the mechanism inside.' That, says Louis, is why they have developed this hour of exercise as part of the programme. It all started when Mary was herself in a state of mental and psychological disturbance prior to her divorce. She had started to learn certain breathing and relaxing techniques, a form of Yoga, when she was in the clinic for treatment and they had helped her so much that she continued them after her health had improved and she had remarried. When she told some of the first guests what she did each evening they asked if they could join her and from them on the invitation has been a continuing one. As part of the whole process behind the sessions this time each day is seen to be more and more important. To be free and to talk is one thing — to be free and to be able to be quiet is the other side of the coin. Here comes the chance to be reconciledd with oneself, one's body, thoughts and feelings — and to do it with others.

The object of these 'rest' periods is not simply to temper aggression and to calm the desire to be always 'doing'. Nor is it only to help the participant to reunite the physical and the more inward parts of one's nature, and to help someone to come to terms with themself as he or she really is — to be aware of oneself. It is true that part of the technique employed is to take in turn each part of one's body, the toes, the feet, the ankle, the legs and so on and to recognise and accept each part for what it is. The aim beyond this is to be open to God from whom no curtain separates us and who equally observes us in every detail for what we are. The aim, in fact, is to lead people to prayer. It is the means by which we so relax, so recollect who we are, so re-discover peace in ourselves, that God can make himself known to us, as he longs to. As we put aside our own aggression, the barrier of frustration that absorbs us, the fear that 'petrifies' us, and begin to be at rest with the person and the body we are, so God is able to reveal himself all over again. 'For that', says Louis, 'is what prayer is. To know God and to know myself'. Both are essential if prayer is to be real. Mary's exercises have this as their object.

It is more and more clear to Mary and Louis that whereas many people find it hard and unpleasing to face this contact with themselves, the people who come to them are only too ready to respond to this kind of help. The 'rest and relaxation' period is atended by most of the guests and as the days pass the time extends and after the hour set aside for this there will be some who want to go on for a much longer period, to doze, to sit or recline silently, to write something, or to meditate on a text. There are some too who find the whole experience much improved by having gentle music played or by playing a small instrument themselves. There are even some visitors who have asked Mary to make a record which would help people when they go home. Mary agrees that it would be a help from many of their visitors to be able to continue these 'rest and relaxation' periods when they got home. That there is ample need for such sessions in the rush of modern life seems obvious. There is only one snag. She cannot imagine when she would have time to make such a record.

By eight o'clock the tables have again been laid for dinner and the same pattern of ready conversation and tasteful food re-asserts itself. Evenings in this part of France can be especially beautiful and the sunsets painted by Mary reveal one of the great attractions of the Drôme. Relaxed in mind, heady with the fine air, amongst those who are becoming in a richer sense 'new friends' and without any of the burden of putting food on the table it is not surprising that supper, and the hours that follow it, are some of the most memorable in any year. The talk never stops, even though some make music. Everyone sings — or tries to. There are occasional mimes, dancing and sometimes a late-night stroll along the rough paths. It is always the end of a day to remember, as the letters make plain. As the time for bed approaches, Mary and Louis, though worn out, can be sure that people around them will sleep sounder and rest more peaceably than they have done for a long time.

Robert and Claudine are two of those people. Talk with them and you soon discover what coming to Les Combeaux has meant for them. 1976 was the second year that they came and the repeat visit was no less appreciated by them than their first. Their story is not particularly unusual and yet it is for that reason that it can stand as a fair example of what Mary and Louis are doing with the home they have made — and made available for others.

Robert is, like his wife, a born Catholic. He lives in a suburban parish of Paris with its 25,000 people and 2 or 3 priests. He was reared in all the formal methods of Catholic instruction and is currently a member of the Catholic Engineers Movement. He wants to practice and develop his faith and so has attended quite a few retreats and conferences. Yet something was missing, something he could not put his finger on. Claudine, menawhile, will tell you that seven years ago their marriage was in trouble. It was so clearly in a mess that a neighbour dared to interfere and offered Claudine a book to read — a book on Marriage, written by a man who then wasn't married, Louis Evely. The book amazed her.

'I liked the natural way in which he talked about marriage in this book', she says. 'He described the very things I had experienced. He used words that I would have used. He admits that Marriage *is* difficult! That was the first time I had heard anyone say this. I took note of what he also says, that marriage works in spite of the difficulties. One particular sentence which struck me was this, 'When you have the feeling that your marriage has taken out of you everything you can give, then you may be sure that it is a true one.' After reading that I had only one thought, to see this man, to see a priest who had not experienced the thing he wrote about and could yet write about it as if he had.'

Claudine persuaded her husband to read the book and as a result he too wanted to meet Louis. They were able to do this when Louis was conducting a retreat not far away, and then, five years ago, they came as one of the first couples to the sessions at Les Combeaux.

What struck Robert was that Louis the speaker is exactly the same man as Louis the writer. 'Moreover he makes contact with himself possible. I came to that session with some burning questions about the sacraments. He listened to my queries and then he answered what I had asked about. He speaks naturally and straightforwardly, with a turn of phrase and a set of words that I can understand.' Indeed, Louis can be so readily grasped that Claudine was afraid that her husband, with his knowledge of Teilhard de Chardin, would think Louis Evely too facile. It was not like that at all.

'What stands out as the fundamental difference between the normal kind of retreats and the sessions with Louis', says Robert, 'is that whereas the retreat conductors come prepared to trot out their own pet ideas, cooked up in their own little corner, Louis takes us just as we are and proceeds to illustrate the truth as he reflects on it from the incidents that have touched and affected us. Whereas other priests often make the events in our lives seem banal, Louis is prepared to treat us as if our insights could be important. Without speaking down to me I could see how someone who had his own technical jargon, as we engineers have ours, was helping me to understand the things about which I was puzzled. Do you wonder that I wanted to come back another year?'

If it were just that Robert and Claudine were intrigued with Louis' ability to answer their questions and talk to them about marriage in general then there would be nothing very special about that story. The fact is that in 1976 Robert and Claudine are more in love and more sure about their marriage than they have ever been. Talk has been turned into deeds — theory into life.

The same story, but with a slightly different emphasis, could be told over and over again in these last four years. As with Jacques and Louise, the introverted husband and the dominated wife. Jacques will tell you how the sessions at Les Combeaux last year altered the whole relationship between his wife and himself and affected their whole family structure. 'I was previously the boss; now we live as a couple who share things. Previously I used to become so nervously depressed that Louise would carry the whole burden of making the family work. Now she has shed all her resentment and I am released to do my part. Rediscovering the children together has been perhaps the most wonderful thing.' Claudine will tell you that Louise could be seen to change from session to session.

It is the effect of these changed family and home relationships which makes the greatest impact on the parish life from which these couples come. If you ask Louis what kind of effect these sessions have on the ordinary life of the churches he will admit that so far this is the hardest thing to describe and which it may yet be too early to expect. One thing which he hopes is that those who come with the temptation to leave the church will go back and start again, and those who find an answer to problems which have troubled them will be able to share their insights with their neighbours. What he is sure about is that they will not be able to go home with a new statement of the faith, but a fresh understanding of how they may be able to interpret anew the faith with which they came. Jacques will tell you that in a matter of weeks he was on new terms with his brothers, his parents and even some with whom he had broken off all contact whatsoever. He even took up 'boules' in order to meet some of their neighbours in the same block of flats.

It is because Louis and Mary have begun to see these results of their work that they can now think of their home as achieving the purpose for which it was planned. Louis will tell you that ever since he became a priest he has wanted to help the laity to realise their proper place, their true dignity, as members of the Christian community. All that he had learnt from de Foucauld helped to strengthen this resolve and that is why many of the steps proposed for the Church in the Second Vatican Council seemed to him so commendable. What hurts him is to discover that what was there proposed seems likely to be so little or so slowly realised. That is also why, in the way which now remains open to himself and his wife, he wants to do something to foster that purpose and realise his goal — for some. Here at least he can continue to serve the laity.

Compared with previous years it is a markedly restricted service but it is not confined simply to the summer weeks. There is still a stream of single visitors or family groups at other times of the year, some for a day and some for a weekend, and there are times when even the friendliness of the Evelys is strained and they find themselves having to write to someone and say, 'Not just at the moment'. For the year now involves Louis again in a number of journeys abroad, sometimes accompanied by Mary, and for each of these mini-conferences or training weekends there has to be special preparation which demands time and reflection. It is this for which Louis most often longs: time, amongst the many daily chores of the house, in which to lie or sit quietly and consider the issues which he knows are in the hearts of the men and women whom he meets. He may have articles to finish or a new manuscript to prepare, business letters to despatch and journeys to plan and organise, as well as parts of the property to decorate or repair. Both Mary's children and his own family and nephews and nieces may also come to see them. Time, therefore, even in the most quiet and slow-moving months of the winter, is never abundant and both Louis and Mary seek to make the most of it.

Though books have been only briefly mentioned here they still play a very great part in Louis' use of time. He reads a lot of novels of all kinds, from Mauriac and Graham Greene to James Bond and the most popular French detective yarns. He appreciates the questions raised by writers like Camus and Gide, St. Exupéry and Rostand. He enjoys Bernanos and even very modern authors like Robbe-Grillet, Marguerite Duras, Nathalie Sarraute and Christiane Rochefort. The influence on his thinking of Dostoevsky is something he freely admits, and Eugenia Guinzbourg and Solzhenitsyn have also made their mark. Amongst the poets he has most admired Claudel, Valéry and Péguy but Louis will tell you that he is not really a poet, though he once wrote a few poems that were included in a published collection.

Not surprisingly, being a communicator, he is an avid film-lover, but since coming into the country that has not been a pursuit easy to continue. Here at Les Combeaux, both he and Mary frequently watch television, and particularly historical series like Henry VIII, Elizabeth, or the great French epic by Druon on 'The Accursed Kings'. Documentaries, films on great artists or composers, and what is said and done in televised religious services also form his diet, though he also has a place for an easy chair and films which are pure distraction, a pleasure which he was not so easily able to enjoy in the days of his priesthood. Moreover, he can now give some time to listening to pop groups and ballad singers because they help him to understand the way younger people try to express themselves. 'They speak,' he once said, 'to my age'. Asked if he had ever tried to write a novel the reply was clear. He was not gifted with that kind of imagination. If he was anything, he was a thinker, not a painter with words. He hoped that he had a little poetry in his make-up but the gifts which a novelist needs were not his.

It is in the quieter moments of the year, however, that both Louis and Mary can be truly together. As the letters which have already been quoted make clear theirs is an apparent and deep harmony after the searing days through which they have passed. They find it easy to share their thoughts and their interests, their hopes and their fears. They complement each other, and Mary's children have long ago recognised this. Louis now has a critical listener to his papers and articles: Mary has an appreciative and thoughtful viewer of the new canvasses which she produces. Like two slender struts in the gables of their new home they secretly support each other in keeping Les Combeaux together and making it the place it is. It would now be hard to think of them apart and it is this, much more than any change of milieu, or even change from priesthood to lay status, which marks a new stage of Louis Evely's life. As surely married to his previous vocation as he was, he is no less linked indissolubly for the rest of his life to a wife whom he loves and who so manifestly loves and respects him. To see it is to know. To see it is for many who come to their home one of the healing events of their stay.

To such a couple it is therefore a constant regret to realise how completely their new-found relationship has prevented Louis from being of service, not only to many of the laity, but to priests as well.

As a writer Louis Evely will share with you his admiration for so much that Bishop John Robinson was saying at the same time as himself. In many ways the approach of the two thinkers has been very similar. Both have been trained to reflect deeply on Scripture and theology, and both have realised that it is time for some of the truths they have discovered and tested to be shared with a wider audience than students and professional churchmen. While Louis Evely never produced anything as 'popular' as 'Honest to God' the audience for whom Louis was writing in France and Belgium, or elsewhere through translations, was very similar. It was for single people and married couples, for secretaries and shopkeepers, nurses and clerks, teachers and foremen. Their common aim was to remove beams from the eyes of ordinary church members so that they could blossom as children of God, released from the misunderstandings and constraints that seemed to make the Christian life such a burden. It was interesting for Louis Evely to see the kind of treatment which his English contemporary received. Given the different circumstances of their respective churches, the results have been remarkably alike. At least, however, Bishop John Robinson is still allowed to write without any sort of Church censure.

Certainly there was a point at which, at the outset of the 70s, Louis might have looked about him as one who was no longer a priest, without any recognisable occupation, with no market for most of his books which were in print, and staring further rejection in the face. At that point he could well say, 'After thirty years — nothing!' It was a daunting prospect and many men who have surrendered their priesthood have been in that position. It tests a man, even if Louis would say that it tests most men unduly. They are asked to bear too much. For Louis only the deep affection of the right woman as his wife, a confidence in the power of the truth in which he still believes, and the clear and unshaken determination to devote himself to a continuing kind of ministry, have brought him through, a little older, much wiser and even more compassionate than he was before. When he and Mary tell you that their great concern is for the thousands of Christians, let alone others, who are lonely, frightened and uncertain about how to relate their faith to their life, they know what they are talking about. They have passed that way for a while. They have known the segregation that comes from being 'exiled' by close relatives and past friends. They know the uncertainty of a future for which to plan. They have even had to test their planning and hoping by the final touchstone of all — sheer faith. If they are beginning to find a new circle of love, an ever clearer purpose for which to labour and a base on which to build with confidence then it is because they have tested their work before God. For one thing that stands unquestioned in the household of Les Combeaux is that God, revealed in Jesus Chirst still works powerfully by his Spirit. The orthodox may question its operation but that faith is manifest.

In 1976 Louis and Mary visited a Swiss Protestant centre where individuals, groups and families in turn can meet and share their experience and problems. In the magazine 'Rencontre' (Meeting) the local pastor wrote after their visit:

'We found it rather embarrassing last Friday to have to explain to our children that the priest we were expecting to lead our weekend conference was coming with his wife! . . . but on Monday, as their car turned out of our drive, the children said, "those two are great. When can we go and stay with them?" During that weekend Louis and Mary Evely gave all the families who took part in the conference a little insight into the joy they share in having chosen the life together which they have — that of a priest reduced to the lay state, preferring adventure to institutionalism, the risk of confrontation rather than the ease of conformity. Their love is so real that everyone who took part in the conference not only could, but just had to, reassess their own . . . Louis Evely has a genius for being able to formulate ideas. Whilst obviously sensitive to the very spirit of the Gospel, he has such a profound understanding of people that he can express the essential truths about them in ways that are both sensitive and striking.'

A Catholic doctor and his wife from Clermont-Ferrand put it like this: 'Thank you for all that you are and have been for us. We hope that you are not too "drained", "worn out"! You have set out on a journey which has no way back and on which despair has no place. We would very much like to accompany you on that journey until it is over . . .'

So the letters continue to come and the postman, already a personal friend, walks through the ever un-latched door and greets the Evelys at their breakfast table. He rarely misses his daily call for he knows by now that this is no ordinary couple up the lane and around the hill from the village square where the post office stands. Here are two people whom many wanted to forget and who, in the eyes of their Church, might just as well not exist. Yet there they are, alive, eager, with their own special brand of inner beauty, a solace to many, a healing balm to an increasing circle, and an inspiration to their guests. If you watch the postman you will know that this is not just an official delivery — it is a service to friends. From that simple kitchen there run through his hands the messages that tell more and more of the world that Louis and Mary Evely — and their God — are alive and well.

10 *Still More to Say*

At the start of 1978 Louis and Mary began an entirely new method of keeping in touch with their friends. They launched a 16 to 20 page magazine called 'Échanges', which has appeared every other month until the present. Its home-made appearance, with photo-copied pages simply stapled together, and the light-hearted line drawings contributed by Mary, disguises the fact that here is a continuing medium for the flow of ideas and insights which Louis Evely produces. Just to run through the pages of the eight copies so far produced will assure any reader that the passage of years has in no way reduced either the range or the depth of his thinking. The meaning of happiness, the secret of a well-run home, the basics of prayer, the nature of baptism, the bringing-up of children, the essentials of Faith. . . these are but a few of the many topics that Louis and Mary have presented to their readers. Some of the letters they have received on these matters are also printed and so the 'Bulletin de liaison' (this link magazine) gets its name 'Exchanges'. Men and women who have met Louis and his wife continue to have a part in this process of sharing their thoughts. They may be separated by time and distance but they know very well that Louis Evely still has something to say.

As Louis approaches his 70th birthday it is hardly surprising that he should introduce a new topic in the most recent editions, 'Growing old gracefully'. Not that the emphasis is in any way one of resignation or exhaustion. On the contrary, Père Mounier, whose words are quoted, stresses that what we should still be seeking is quality of LIFE. 'Believe me', he writes, 'the one thing you have to do is to live, right up to the last minute, right up to the last second, LIVE! Don't worry, God will take such a life as if it were just what he willed . . . He won't ask you if you have been like me a Jesuit, or a Capuchin or a Franciscan; he won't ask you if you have been President of the Republic, Pope, Bishop, priest, or whatever. What he will ask you is if you have been the living person that he wanted you to be. . . So LIVE! Believe me! You sometimes hear that misleading remark: you have to succeed in life. We even go round praising people by saying that that is what they have done, they have succeeded. . .

'But at what? In making money? In having a top job? But that is not success. Just let anyone be without their money, their job, and in ten years they will almost certainly be totally forgotten. What we have to do is not to succeed in life, but to make our living a success. . . that's the message we have to get over to our children.'

There is nothing that Louis stresses more clearly than the importance of the quality of our living. In a book published in 1978, and only just translated into English, 'Questions de Vie et de Mort' (Seabury Press: Facing Death), Louis shows the connection between how we live and how we can approach death. 'There is only one true preparation for death, and that is to be so alive that nothing can ever extinguish the life you have . . . Be now what you would want to be for ever . . . Don't let us talk anymore about a 'future' life. All that concerns us is the life we now have, and, within that, the matter of what quality of life we enjoy. Future life is indeed the opium of the people; it is misleading folk to let them think that in the future there will be some change for which they have neither prepared nor striven in the life they have. True Christian faith is not directed to a 'future life' but to 'eternal life', and if it is truly 'eternal' then it only takes a moment's reflection to grasp that it has already begun. We are living it now, or else we are not living at all.'

It is because Louis has this deep awareness of the totality of our living and the eternal implications of what we do to ourselves and to each other on this side of the grave that he continues to feel so concerned about the way in which we present our religion to the modern world. It is not simply that Louis is passionately interested in the whole field of 'communication'. He is so concerned about that that this is a subject on which he believes that God has yet more to say through him and through a book that he has been preparing for some time. Yet 'communication' is not a technique or a theory, a mere matter for study. For Louis it is something that touches the whole fabric of relationships, the way we listen to others, discern their needs, express our compassion, share in their living, shoulder a cross. What he learnt about caring for his pupils in school is something that shapes and effects all his human contacts and the way he conceives the Church in her dealings with men. It is about this that he has still a very great deal to say.

In a pamphlet written by Cardinal Suenens shortly after Louis had returned to the lay state and was considering marriage the writer says, 'Sad to say, there are Christians who have left the Church because they are too bruised by its structures. The Church seemed to them too human to be a sacrament of God. But has not the Church fromt the very beginnings of its history been made of men of flesh and blood, beset with weakness and mystery just like the rest of us?' It would be interesting to know if Cardinal Suenens had certain recent experiences in mind. Certainly Louis Evely, who was not compelled to give up the priesthood, and who has never intended to leave the Catholic Church, would want to amend such words in two directions. He would want first of all to suggest that rather than being 'too human to be a sacrament of God' the Catholic Church has very often 'not been human enough to be such a sacrament'. No-one was more sure than Louis as a teacher that discipline is important but he knew also that the wielding of that discipline required human understanding and much sympathy. Christ called, yes, but he even more suffered for, his disciples. It is the element of caring for and supporting her children which he would find so often lacking in the Church whose faith he also shares.

The second modification, so far as he himself is concerned, is that very often the separation between Mother Church and her children has been due to the former's attitude of exclusion more than the latter's desire to withdraw. Louis appreciates that the Catholic knows the rules and if she or he breaks them then the consequences must be accepted. The truth for him and Mary is that whilst they in one sense regret a broken marriage, the seriousness of divorce, the shock of re-marriage between an ex-priest and a divorcee, they are both devout Christians, they love and follow Christ every day, they both miss their attendance at Mass, they both share in the commission of helping others to become members of the Christian family. Is it not, we might ask, a matter for some reflection when the rules of organisation so obviously do not fit the realities of the human situation? Of course it is a dilemma. It is also a matter on which there is still more to be said.

Louis would also feel that he has a great deal more to say about the nature of the priesthood. In 1971 Louis wrote a book which developed many of the ideas that had first appeared in 'The Church and the Sacraments' (1956) but were now developed in the post-Vatican II era. In a chapter entitled 'A non-religious Christianity' he expressed himself with his usual clarity.

'Vatican II started a reaction. One cannot appreciate the importance of the revolution it has begun unless it is recognised that by defining the Church as the People of God, the Church was secularised. It once more became primarily the laity, and all the rest (forms of worship, declarations of faith, hierarchy) were merely the means which it employed.

'The Council has thus begun to re-orientate the Church towards its proper Christian conception by restoring to its proper place the common priesthood of all the faithful and the spiritual worship which each is called upon to perform in his daily life: 'All their activities, prayers and apostolic engagements, their married and family life, their daily work, their spiritual and physical leisure pursuits, if these are all lived in the Holy Spirit, become — like even the difficulties of life, provided that they are borne patiently — 'spiritual offerings, agreeable to God through Jesus Christ' (1 Peter 2/5).' (From Lumen Gentium. 34)

'Such a statement removes all division between the sacred and the profane: everything which is shot through with love is sacred.

'We should not therefore be surprised by the present crisis emerging among the clergy. If all the laity are priests and are such in every part of their life and if the priesthood is thus laicised, or if the laity are thus considered sacred, what place is there for a priest who is not a layman. The traditional priest, the dispenser of sacred things, the mediator between the world of God and that of Man, no longer has any place in the post-conciliar Church.'

That a change was in prospect when Louis wrote those words no-one will deny. Seven years later the summing-up of the present position by Peter Hebblethwaite would also reflect Louis Evely's opinion. 'What is certain is that the old moulds of priestly spirituality were cracked by the Council, and that the task of devising a new pattern for the ministry is as yet unfinished.' ('The Runaway Church'. p.70) For Louis the term that best sums up the role of the new kind of Catholic priest is that already mentioned of 'accoucheur'. The nearest English equivalent, outside the maternity ward in which the term most naturally arises, would probably be 'enabler'. Louis sees the the priest in the old sense transformed into a person who assists the rest of the People of God to become the daily priests that the Gospel expects them to be. That means that the 'professional, full-time priest', if he is to continue as such will have to become much more a member of the public than hitherto. Louis once spoke with sadness of how, in 1977, he had stayed with a Catholic parish priest who had been so busy that he had never once eaten a meal with any of his parishioners during the last twelve months.

Of course Louis realises what a revolution that still requires in the attitudes and life-style of the clergy. It is not easy to shed in one generation the sense of superiority and pre-eminence that has been accorded to them. Having been set on a sort of pedestal as a priest, even though he voluntarily relinquished it, he knows what kind of a change that can mean. He knows too that there are still many older priests who are still very confusd. They were at ease as a 'magician', a sacrificer at the altar, but now that they have to share the Mass, preach from amongst the people, face the people over the altar, speak in a language that all can follow — and even be criticized — they do not now where they are and what to do. In the Latin they learnt, the Gregorian chant they acquired, the florid liturgy they had mastered, they had invested all their religious feeling and now — they have a streamlined rite, a text of much less poetic worth and music that has not yet found its fresh genius. The ironic thing, however, is that all this has come to pass because for all the superficial changes that have occurred the fundamental nature of the Church has not really altered at all.

In the introduction to his book 'If the Church is not to die. . .' Louis refers to a short passage in the Decree on Ecumenism no.6. It reads: 'The Church is called by Christ, and in the course of her pilgrimage, to this *permanent reform* of which she has constant need just because she is a human and earthly institution.' (My italics) It is because Louis cannot even yet see this principle being applied at the very heart of the Church's life that he both doubts the ultimate succcess of the Council and questions the value of what is happening in the interim. In an article which he contributed to a Protestant news-sheet in June 1977 he wrote this:

'The Catholic Church finds herself in a trap; she is the prisoner of her past, of her claims, of her "human traditions" which she prefers to any new initiatives of the Spirit. She is locked up in herself, having failed to draw the world under her control or protection. . . By definition, she is unable to move: she believes in her divine authority and she may not deny her pretended infallibility; she dictates how the faithful shall conduct themselves and what they may believe as if she were the sole interpreter of God in the world.

'Her politics may change, no doubt, as her standing in the world is reduced, but her basic principles remain and soon re-appear wherever the church may dare to apply them. . . For if the Catholic Church admits conscientious objections in the case of Lay States, she certainly refuses such a right to her ministers and the faithful: a Christian who doubts a single dogma is declared a heretic; a priest who cannot accept the ruling of "Humanae Vitae" in his instruction or in his penitential guidance has to go.

'This over-rigid system crushes men or expels them. Yet for several years now another solution has been emerging. It is that of the "Third Man" who without anger or fear, acts only according to his conscience, does not think that he has to leave the Church in order to follow the Gospel, does not excommunicate the Hierarchy but awaits the dawning of that day when it may be seen that it has nothing more to do! It is with that sort of man that ecclesiastical authority will henceforth have to reckon.'

Peter Hebblethwaite, who also left the priesthood and married, shares that kind of thinking although he has added another dimension and called such people 'Fourth Men'. He adds,'They are more inclined to find the true life of the Church in the local community and in the tasks which await him there than in messages emanating from Rome . .

Hans Küng, in his remarkable synthesis, "On being a Christian" (Collins, 1977), has provided them with a theology and a spirituality which do justice to their demand for rigour and sincerity. . . They find that a pilgrim faith which still asks questions is appropriate to a pilgrim Church.' ('The Runaway Church', p.263)

Louis would closely align himself with that kind of thinking. For him the 15 years that preceded the Council were a time of working towards so many of the things which the Council endorsed. For so thinking and speaking and writing he was, as we have seen, reprimanded, criticized, stopped from writing, refused permission to speak in certain circles. Then, after 1966, so much that he had striven for was approved by Vatican II, and he felt that just as he had foreseen where the spirit of

God might lead the Church so he should now continue his thinking and writing because Vatican II was by no means the end of the road. It was at that point that he realised what was still missing. He recognised that the Church could not readily adapt itself to persuasion instead of command. As soon as the faithful were given freedom to share and to comment, to exercise, that is, the responsibility of the People of God, it could not handle the situation. No longer were the faithful the lump to which the leaven of Church authority needed to be added. The people were now becoming the very leaven which the Bible commanded them to be. Of course the Church allows certain things to happen but that is only where it cannot prevent them happening. If it is thought that the ability, or the credit, of the Church to oppose certain things will not stand then it does not suffer the indignity of contending such matters. Yet the basic anxiety persists. Louis himself looks at the cases of Hans Küng, Ivan Illich, Franzoni, Fr. Lemercier and many others whom it has consistently disciplined, excommunicated and interrogated privately, and all since the 'liberalisation' of Vatican II. Married priests, above all, have suffered very severely and have even been described as 'Judases'. The principle remains the same, says Louis, even if it is not enforced so strictly.

It is still the case that those who are at the bottom have very little or no chance of being heard at the top. The dictatorship of those who govern only works because of the silent rebellion of those who are governed. There are increasingly fewer Catholics who believe in the natural means of contraception, fewer priests who unswervingly obey their Bishops, few bishops who do not allow some accommodation by their clergy and people in applying the Encyclicals or the decrees of the Roman congregations. What is still needing to be said is that the Church must significantly change her conception of Authority. There is less and less room for a Church which thinks it has the right to impose on the faithful their ways of thinking, their modes of conduct, even their political allegiances. What is now needed is a Church which exercises an influence towards rich spiritual nourishment, and applies the Gospel precept of Jesus, 'If you would be my disciples, if you would be perfect, then do the things I command you and you will be blessed.'

When I asked Louis Evely what was his favourite book he said that it was very difficult for an author to choose amongst his literary 'children' but whilst he thought that so far he had most fully expressed his thinking in 'The Prayer of a Modern Man' (in America known as 'Our Prayer') it was 'L'Évangile sans mythes' of which he was most proud. It speaks of the gospel in terms that take account of the outlook of modern men, for if Christ were to return today he would not use outmoded language or illustrations but would speak in terms that modern man could grasp and appreciate — even if he did not agree with them. It was this return to the biblical sources which Louis regards as one of the most important developments of modern Roman Catholicism. Such a return has begun to raise real questions about so many traditional interpretations of doctrine and faith. What Louis still wants to say is that the process has only just begun.

What, for example, is the significance of the *bodily* Assumption of the Virgin Mary, when many theologians of the Catholic Church already admit that their faith would not be altered if the body of Jesus Christ himself were found to have remained in the tomb? What indeed is the relevance of our physical body? The dogma of the Immaculate Conception no longer has any real meaning since it has been recognised that no-one any longer knows what is meant when we speak of Original Sin. As for Papal Infallibility, how could a man not be fallible? How can the Holy Spirit prevent the Pope from uttering something which affects with error even the most carefully-weighed and formally-stated truth? What it comes down to, Louis says, is that the Church has still not responded to the fact of the 20th century, the emergence of modern life. It has ferociously rejected it, sometimes, and even recently, with police-type methods, and still it is not prepared to grapple with what are the fundamental and inescapable questions that modern man has to answer if he is to retain his faith. What, for example, is revelation? What do we mean when we speak of 'The Word of God'? How are we to distinguish between what God has inspired and what comes through the interpretation and activity of men? For centuries we have said that Christ is man and God, but what does this mean for human beings today? If in Catholic interpretation such a man/God is a man without personal freedom or his own unique personality apart from that of God, then in what sense is such a being truly Man? And what of the Resurrection of Jesus? How are we to speak or conceive of that? If it is not to be the traditional idea of a re-animated corpse then what are we to believe?

These and so many more questions are matters of unfinished business with which the Second Vatican Council was not able to come to grips. Yet Louis would see them as quite germane to any Council of the Church that regards itself as a 'Pastoral' Church — the name it was given. As one who had travelled over much of the world Louis could hardly fail to see the pastoral implications of that further unasked and unanswered question — Is Christianity an absolute among all other religions and if it is then what does this mean for the Church's presence among men and women of other world-wide faiths? Surely a primary pastoral duty is to provide the faithful with nourishing and meaningful doctrine which can guide their daily living. For Louis it seems that the Church is still far from that and there is much more that remains to be said.

Despite the restriction which Louis has had to bear on his contribution towards worthwhile instruction in the Catholic faith it is quite clear that the last ten years have begun to show that there are audiences to whom his words do appeal. In 1978 a French publisher issued a new list of all Louis' work, with many new editions of previous publications, and the list numbered 20 titles. In addition to these Louis is wroking on further volumes and he hopes to have completed books on Communication and the Holy Spirit by the early 1980s. In every edition of the house magazine, 'Échanges', there are reviews of the books which Louis continues to read and reflect on and there can be little doubt that he is keeping abreast of much modern theological and philosophical thought. As a foretaste of what he thinks about the contemporary interest in Charismatic ministry the reader may care to hear these words written in 1977:—

'At a certain level of spiritual intensity, or even simply religious motivation, human nature breaks down and unfamiliar forces appear, having a surprising potential. The most spectacular are usually the least worthwhile. When a pipe is subjected to too great a pressure within it it is at the weakest points that an escape takes place. The move naïve seek to catch these 'outbursts' whereas the wise perfer to direct this tension to the point where it can be most usefully applied — in transforming human relationships.

'Incomprehensible outpourings of word-forms is one example of such less worthy manifestations, the escape cracks of nature in an emotion too strong and under the impact of holy things. Jesus, 'when filled with the Holy Spirit', was however too balanced a person to suffer such accidents. . .

'The real miracle of Pentecost, on the other hand, is that everyone heard the Apostles talking in his or her own language. Just imagine a husband who speaks the language of his wife, or a wife that of her husband, parents speaking the language of their children, and vice versa. Think of pastors who speak the language of their parishioners, or the other way round; or an intellectual who can express himself simply and a simple person who speaks without either uncertainty or bluster! Such miracles of communication, of love, respect and attention to each other are almost the exact opposite of that 'speaking in tongues' of which we so often hear.'

Does the reader still perceive, as I do, the clear, penetrating human and biblical quality that still characterises all that Louis Evely has to say. If so, that is something that others recognise and yet is, or has been, missed by many of Louis' Catholic contemporaries. Louis himself expressed this in a moving passage some seven years ago:

'What has surprised me most about my critics is how many bishops, priests, and devout laity have read my work without apparently recognising the apostolic longing, the lively faith, the spiritual experiences which others have found there. All they have seemed eager to do is to find out where what I say diverges from what they have come to believe, and especially from the 'set tribal formularies'. Any attempt to see whether we do in fact share a common faith seems inadmissible.

'I have often been accused of destroying the Faith and of trying to force doors open. My aim has simply been to draw on the treasures of Scripture and to discover 'things new and old'. If all I am to do is to repeat what has been said before what is the point of writing at all. If my ideas are only mine then why should anyone bother in any case? If, however, it may be that I am able to bring the reader to a fresh and vital re-reading of our church situation in the light of the Gospel then surely I shall indeed have rendered the kind of service which I am seeking to achieve.'

It is by such a continuing openness to the truth that Louis Evely is likely to see in the years that remain to him, (and he is a fit and active man for his age,) further recognition of the insights which he is so fitted to express. It is no coincidence that as the Roman Catholic Church is drawn into closer relationship with other Christians the work of this unauthorised child of hers is recovering more and more reputation, especially as his work is translated or republished in English and publishers recognise the quality of his thought. This is a style of Catholicism which can only commend itself to those who are free to test the truth of what they read and are not shackled by preconditioned arguments or fixed formularies. It is a style of Catholicism which many will recognise as the real thing . . . for this age. It might even be that it is the suffering and the one-time rejection of so gifted a son as Louis Evely could have been that is the seed from which a whole new stage of the Church's life could now spring. Certainly that is something of the confidence which Mary possesses as she sums up her own feelings about her husband: 'His faith is, of course, so very simple and natural. He has stood so much spite because he has followed what he believes to be the truth. Truth will in the end prevail.'

That is why I am sure that the Evely story has not yet come to an end. There is still more to be said and it will be people like Louis Evely who will help us to express it. If they do it will be because they were not afraid to face the stern realities of life when they had to be faced. That incidentally is just the conclusion reached by Peter Hebblethwaite who has walked some of Louis' way, though 20 years younger. In the close of 'The Runaway Church' he says this:

'The next twenty-five years will see the emergence of a new principle of relative equilibrium in the Church as the seeds planted by the Council bear fruit. The new model of the Church as a pilgrim and fraternal community serving the world will become dominant. It is not a matter of re-inventing the Church as though it had no history, but of recognising that the tradition is much wider and richer than we had supposed. The Pilgrim Church has an unfinished quality, it knows that it is still in the making, and that the possibilities are more open-ended than most people thought ten years ago. But if they are to be realised, crippling timidity must be abandoned. As the psychiatrist Dr. Jack Dominian has written: "If I were asked to point to one psychological reason why the hopes of Vatican II are so slow to develop, I would suggest that the retardation occurs at all levels when authority has been challenged legitimately and validly but has not had the psychological resources or insight to cope, and has retreated either in evasion, postponement or repression". . . One inevitably thinks, in contrast, of Pope John XXIII, who used to find sleep at night with the thought, "Relax, Angelo, it's not you who runs the Church, but the Holy Spirit".' (p.240) It is because Louis Evely has the strength to love that he has overcome the bitterness that could so easily have sapped his faith, dried up his powers of 'revelation', and turned him into a harsh critic of the Church which he still deeply loves. Writing most recently about 'Incarnation' he commented thus:—

'It is true that one only finds God in one's relation to others, but the real question is, what is the depth of that relationship. St. Paul says, 'As you are filled, so you will enter into the fulness of God' (Eph. 3.19)

'We shall never know God unless we go on loving; we shall only know the God whom we have become.'

It is a continuing story.

As I close this book I want to leave the reader with the Louis Evely that I have come to know over the last few years. Whether it has been talking with him in a Belgian hotel room, by the swimming pool at Crest, in the forests of the Ardennes, or in the corridors of the College he served, some things have still to be said about him. What they say about him the reader must assess for himself but for me they are the marks of a very wholesome and significant human being —

He offers you
- warmth of greeting but not sentimentality;
- his interest but not inquisitiveness;
- openness but not bonhommie;
- willingness to help but within reason;
- generosity but in simple things;
- a comfortable but far from luxurious home;
- talkativeness but not chatter;
- liveliness but an awareness of his limits;
- wisdom but never a sense of 'knowing it all';
- thanks for praise but never a sense of craving it;
- fondness for others but recognition of human faults;
- enjoyment of success but readiness to work for it;
- real faith but not cheap piety.

If there is more to be said others will have to say it.